Essential C++ for Engineers and Scientists

Second Edition

Jeri R. Hanly

University of Wyoming

Addison
Wesley

Boston San Francisco New York
London Toronto Sydney Tokyo Singapore Madrid
Mexico City Munich Paris Cape Town Hong Kong Montreal

Executive Editor: Susan Hartman Sullivan
Editorial Assistant: Galia Shokry
Senior Production Supervisor: Pat Mahtani/Juliet Silveri
Production Services: Brooke Albright, Trillium Project Management
Interior Design: Sandra Rigney
Cover Design Supervisor: Regina Hagen
Cover Designer: Susan Raymond
Executive Marketing Manager: Michael Hirsch
Print Buyer: Caroline Fell
Cover photo copyright © 2001 PhotoDisc, Inc.

Figure 1.1 Computer-Aided Design of an Automobile copyright 2001 General Motors Corporation. Used with permission of GM Media Archive. Figure 1.2 Using Robots in Automobile Manufacturing reproduced courtesy of Ford Motor Company. Figures 1.6, 1.7, 1.9, 1.10 are from Hanly, Jeri R., and Koffman, Elliot B., *C Program Design for Engineers*, figures on pp. 10, 11, 13, 17, copyright © 2001. Reprinted by permission of Pearson Education, Inc. Figures 5.3, 8.1, 10.10, 10.13 are from Hanly, Jeri R., Koffman, Elliot B., with J. Horvath, *C Program Design for Engineers*, figures and art on pp. 373, 589, 611, 642, copyright © 1995. Reprinted by permission of Pearson Education, Inc. Figure 7.5 Tracking Station in Canberra, Australia (courtesy of the Jet Propulsion Laboratory, California Institute of Technology, Pasadena, California.) Chapter 4 art in Programming Projects (footnoted in text) is from S. Kalpakjian, *Manufacturing Engineering and Technology*, copyright © 1995, Figure 31.4 from p. 962. Reprinted by permission of Pearson Education Inc., Upper Saddle River, New Jersey. Appendix B table has been adapted from Chapter 3 of the Borland C++ *Language Reference Version 5.0* Volume 4. Copyright © 1996. All Borland product names are trademarks or registered trademarks of Borland International, Inc. Corporate Headquarters: 100 Borland Way, Scotts Valley, CA 95066-3249, 408-431-1000.

The programs and applications presented in this book have been included for their instructional value. They have been tested with care but are not guaranteed for any particular purpose. The publisher does not offer any warranties or representations, nor does it accept any liabilities with respect to the programs or applications.

Library of Congress Cataloging-in-Publication Data

Hanly, Jeri R.
   Essential C++ for engineers and scientists / Jeri R. Hanly.—2nd ed.
      p. cm.
   Includes index.
   ISBN 0-201-74125-3 (pbk.)
   1. C++ (Computer program language)   I. Title.
QA76.73.C153 H36 2002
005.13'3—dc21   2001046140

For information on obtaining permission for the use of material from this work, please submit a written request to Pearson Education, Inc., Rights and Contracts Department, 75 Arlington St., Suite 300, Boston MA 02116 or fax your request to 617-848-7047.

   2 3 4 5 6 7 8 9 10—MA—04 03 02

This book is dedicated to my family:

Elizabeth and Keith
Brian, Kevin, and Trinity
Eric, Jennifer, and Mical

Contents

Preface

Essential C++ for Engineers and Scientists, Second edition, teaches the essentials of problem solving and programming using a subset of C++ as the implementation language. It includes many practical examples from a wide range of scientific and engineering disciplines. The text can be used for a first course in programming: It assumes no prior knowledge of computers or programming.

Although somewhat abbreviated, the C++ coverage in this book includes the features useful in typical engineering and scientific programs, and it demonstrates these features as they are actually used, not in isolation. Language topics are presented in an order common in teaching other languages: first the basic control structures (sequence, selection, and repetition), input/output operations, expression evaluation, and library functions, and then defining and calling the user's own functions. Next, the fundamental construct of an object-oriented C++ program, the class, is presented. After the chapter on classes, the text builds on the notion of object orientation while continuing the standard subject matter of an introductory programming course for engineers and scientists: arrays and strings, multidimensional arrays, a review of file manipulation, and an introduction to selected numerical methods.

When C++ offers multiple ways of accomplishing the same goal, the text usually selects just one and uses it consistently. For example, it teaches the use of references for output parameters and limits coverage of pointers to array parameters and to dynamically allocated arrays.

Changes in the New Edition

Throughout the text, all programming examples have been updated to conform to standard C++ use of namespaces. We have improved the book in many other ways as well:

- Integrated introduction to input/output file use with loop coverage
- Added presentation of structs
- Added smaller scale first example of classes
- Added member operators while retaining friend operators
- Expanded coverage of dynamically allocated arrays, both one- and two-dimensional
- Integrated standard string class into data type coverage beginning in Chapter 2 (retained Cstring basics in array chapter)
- Expanded numerical methods coverage by adding a case study on the use of augmented matrices to solve systems of linear equations
- Added case studies using decision structures for finch classification and file use for database representation
- Included more examples of reference parameters
- Expanded input error recovery coverage
- Added 50% more programming projects
- Created new appendices in response to reviewer requests:
  - Introduction to C programming language
  - Laboratory-style introductions to two C++ integrated development environments—Microsoft Visual C++ and Borland C++ Builder

Flexible Ordering of Topics

Professors who prefer to present topics in an order different from the one in the textbook should check the dependencies shown in Table P.1. Several sec-

TABLE P.1 Chapter and Section Dependencies

Chapter / Section	Assumes Prior Coverage of
Chapter 4	Chapters 2 and 3
Sections 5.1 through 5.2, Figure 5.8	Chapters 2 and 3
Chapter 5 (all)	Chapters 2 through 4
Sections 6.1–6.2	Chapters 2 and 3 and Section 5.1
Chapter 6 (all)	Chapters 2 through 5
Sections 7.1 through 7.4 (omitting last subsection of 7.3)	Chapters 2 through 5
Chapter 7 (all)	Chapters 2 through 6
Sections 8.1 through 8.3	Chapters 2 through 5, Sections 6.2 through 6.4, Sections 7.1 through 7.5
Sections 9.1 through 9.3	Chapters 2 through 5
Chapter 9 (all)	Chapters 2 through 5, Sections 6.1 and 7.4
Sections 10.1 and 10.5	Chapters 2 through 5
Sections 10.2 through 10.4	Chapters 2 through 5, Sections 7.1 through 7.3*

*(omitting last subsection of 7.3)

FIGURE P.1   Possible Orderings of Topics

Standard Order	Chapter
Basic computer terminology	1
C++ basics: statements, operators	2
Control structures—focus on if, switch	3
Control structures—focus on while, for, do-while	4
Input/output file basics	4
User-defined functions (single-result, void, using value and reference parameters)	5
Structs and Objects	6
Basic arrays	7
Objects for one-dimensional arrays	7
Objects for two-dimensional arrays and solving systems of linear equations	8
Input/output file use, error recovery, and file as database	9
Numerical methods for root finding, statistics, numerical differentiation and integration, first order ordinary differential equations	10

Numerical Methods as Early and as Extensively as Possible	Chapter
See standard order	1–5
Root finding—bisection method	5
Newton's method	10.1
First order ordinary differential equations	10.5
Basic one-dimensional arrays	7.1–7.4*
Statistics	10.2
Numerical differentiation	10.3
Numerical integration	10.4

(cont.)	Chapter
Objects introduction	6.2–6.4
Arrays	7.1–7.5
Multidimensional arrays and solving linear systems	8.1–8.5
Rest as time allows . . .	

Objects Earlier	Chapter
C++ basics and selection structures	1–3
Single-result functions	5.1
Simple structures and objects	6.1-6.2
Loops	4
Functions	5
Objects	6
Rest as desired	

Functions Earlier	Chapter
C++ basics and selection structures	1-3
Introduction to functions	5.1-5.2 (Fig. 5.8)
Loops	4
Functions	5
Rest as desired	

Objects Later	Chapter
See standard order	1-5
Basic arrays	7.1-7.4*
Input/output files	9.1-9.3
Numerical methods	10
Objects	6, rest of 7, 8
Rest as desired	

*(omitting last subsection of 7.3)

tions of the text are completely optional, with no subsequent dependencies: Recursive Functions (5.6), Class Reuse (6.7), and Heap-Dynamic Array Allocation (7.6, 8.4). Figure P.1 lists several different possible orderings of topics.

What About NO Objects?

A careful study of Fig. P.1 shows that if you prefer not to cover objects at all, you can still present all other language topics except multidimensional arrays and dynamic array allocation. We have chosen to show function parameters that are multidimensional arrays only in the context of an object representation. This choice stems from our conviction that such a representation is simpler, since students can pass matrices as input and output parameters in exactly the same way as they pass simpler objects.

Software Engineering Concepts

This text presents many aspects of software engineering. Early chapters on control structures take a process-oriented approach to analysis and design and demonstrate algorithm development through stepwise refinement of pseudo-code. These chapters also include sections on tracing and debugging code. Chapter 5 introduces procedural abstraction through user-defined functions, and Chapter 6's introduction of classes is interwoven with examples of the object-oriented design process first described in Chapter 1.

The book emphasizes early on the need for a consistent, readable coding style, and its examples demonstrate such a style throughout. The inside back cover of the text shows examples of most C++ constructs. In addition to serving as a quick reference to where these constructs are discussed in the book, this table can be used as a standard for style of indentation, bracket use, and naming conventions.

Pedagogical Features

This textbook uses a rich array of pedagogical features with which to engage the student.

Definitions of Important Terms.   Important terms are defined in the margins of the text.

End-of-Section Review Questions.   Most sections are followed by a set of questions that check the student's understanding of the material covered. Some questions call for the analysis and tracing of program fragments; others ask the student to write or to modify some code. Answers to the odd-numbered questions are in the Answers section; answers to the even-numbered questions are included in the on-line Instructor's Manual.

Programming Projects. Each chapter concludes with a set of programming projects. Answers to selected projects appear in the on-line Instructor's Manual, so instructors also have the option of distributing all or part of a solution and asking the students to complete, extend, or improve the solution.

Examples and Case Studies. The book contains a wide variety of examples and case studies specially selected to give the student glimpses of important science and engineering applications of computing. They are usually complete programs, functions, or class definitions rather than incomplete fragments. The following list presents by discipline the relevant examples, review questions, and programming projects:

Aeronautical Engineering

Catapult-launched jet acceleration, PP2-1, p. 68
Aircraft type determination, Sec. 3.4, RQ2, p. 92
Projectile flight, PP4-3, p. 151
Drag calculation, PP5-6, p. 216
Projectile launch angle, PP5-8, p. 217
Airborne location modeling, PP6-2, p. 269
Spacecraft tracking station, Ex. 7.4, p. 285
Aircraft database, PP9-2, p. 401

Atmospheric Science

Wind-speed classification, Sec. 3.4, RQ1, p. 92
Doppler weather radar, PP4-7, p. 153
Rainfall statistics, Ex. 7.3, p. 279
Meteorological database, PP9-3, p. 402

Biology

Finch classification, Sec. 3.6, p. 95
Bacteria culture growth, Fig. 4.10, p. 131
Tree classification hierarchies, Fig. 6.15, p. 253
Most probable number bacteria estimate, PP7-3, p. 325
Blood-sugar concentrations, PP10-10, p. 438

Biotechnology

Antibiotic testing, PP3-3, p. 106
Intravenous rate assistant, PP5-2, p. 210

Chemical Engineering

pH of a solution, Ex. 3.2, p. 88
Substance boiling points, PP3-2, p. 106
Compressed-gas cylinder identification, PP3-5, p. 107
Liquid acidity, PP3-9, p. 108

Mechanical Engineering

Internal combustion engine efficiency, Sec. 2.6, RQ2, p. 60
Freezer temperature estimate, PP2-3, p. 68
Speed of sound calculation, PP2-4, p. 69
Oil furnace efficiency, PP2-8, p. 69
Gearbox speed ratios, PP2-10, p. 70
Gas pressure calculation, Sec. 3.1, RQ2c, p. 74
Refrigerator performance, Sec. 3.2, RQ1, pp. 80–81; Sec. 5.1, RQ2, p. 165
Isothermal expansion of a gas, Sec. 4.1, RQ1, p. 115
Gas pressure variation, PP4-8, p. 154
Vehicle fuel efficiency, Ex. 5.1, p. 158
Solar heating, Sec. 5.7, p. 199
Heat transfer functions, PP5-7, p. 216
Metal database record, Ex. 6.1, p. 220; database search, Sec. 9.4, p. 391
Automobile simulation, PP6-6, p. 272
Boat engine failure analysis, PP10-7, p. 436
Force on car brakes, PP10-9, p. 437
Ship deceleration, PP10-14, p. 439

Numerical Methods

Bisection method, Fig. 5.29, p. 198
Linear systems solution, Sec. 8.3, p. 350
Newton-Raphson method, Sec. 10.1, p. 406
Secant method, Fig. 10.4, p. 412; PP10-1, p. 434
Numerical differentiation, Sec. 10.3, RQ1, p. 425
Trapezoidal rule, Fig. 10.14, p. 427
Simpson's rule, Sec. 10.4, RQ1, p. 428
Euler method, Ex. 10.2, p. 431
Runge-Kutta method, Table 10.8, p. 432
Observed function object with numerical method members, PP10-8, p. 437;
  PP10-12, p. 439

Petroleum Engineering

Tank monitoring, PP4-6, p. 153

Physics

Weight and mass of object on Earth, Sec. 3.1, RQ2b, p. 74
Wavelengths of visible light, PP3-1, p. 105
Metal expansion, PP4-2, p. 150
Center of gravity, PP8-2, p. 368
General measurement conversion, PP9-6, p. 404

Statistics

Age of population, Sec. 4.1, RQ4, p. 116
Arithmetic mean, Fig. 10.5, p. 414
Standard deviation, Fig. 10.7, p. 416

Linear regression, Table 10.3, p. 418
Correlation coefficient, Table 10.4, p. 420
Data set object, PP10-6, p. 436

Code and Input Highlighting. Many programming examples use shading to draw the student's eye to sections of the code that demonstrate the current topic of interest. Additionally, all examples of program runs shade user-entered input to distinguish it from computer-generated output.

Pitfalls and Chapter Reviews. Each chapter concludes with a discussion of common programming errors, followed by a summary of important points in the chapter, and a table of new C++ constructs.

Comprehensive Index. Every textbook has an index, but this book's index is truly a pedagogical feature. Constructed by hand, the index includes terms, concepts, and examples from all chapters and appendixes.

Appendixes and Supplements

Reference tables of C++ operator precedence and C++ constructs appear on the inside covers of the book. Appendix A compares C++ to its parent language, C; Appendix B gives selected run-time functions available in standard libraries; and Appendix C summarizes selected I/O facilities. Appendix D is a reference for the standard string class; Appendix E is a reference of C++ operators; and Appendix F is a list of ANSI C++ keywords. Appendixes G and H introduce popular C++ integrated development environments and Appendix I lists the ASCII and EBCDIC character sets.

The Instructor's Manual includes suggestions for teaching each chapter, two quizzes for each chapter, a bank of exam questions, solutions to even-numbered review questions, and solutions to selected programming projects. It is accessible by qualified instructors only. Please contact your sales representative through the World Wide Web.

The example program code is available online at http://www.aw.com/cssupport (follow the links from there). Within the text, the programs that can be downloaded from this website are marked with the following icon:

Acknowledgments

Many people assisted in the development of this book. I am very grateful for the numerous examples and programming exercises contributed by Joan C. Horvath of Takeoff Technologies. I especially thank my University of Wyoming colleagues who have so graciously answered my questions. From

Computer Science, they include Allyson J. Anderson (who prepared much of the answer key and the Instructor's Manual), John F. Ellis (who suggested the finch classification case study), Michael J. Magee, and John H. Rowland; from Geography, Lawrence M. Ostresh; from Mathematics, G. Eric Moorhouse; and from Mechanical Engineering, Dennis N. Coon and Donald A. Smith.

The reviewers of this manuscript were enormously helpful in suggesting improvements and in finding errors. They include:

Hyder A. Ali, California State University at Northridge
Christopher T. Alvin, University of Wisconsin at Madison
Todd Arbogast, University of Texas at Austin
Tom Bullock, University of Florida
Stephen B. Dobrow, Farleigh Dickinson University
Martin Granier, Western Washington University
Tom Hill, University at Buffalo
Jacob Y. Kazakia, Lehigh University
Andrew Kinley, Rose-Hulman Institute of Technology
Dr. JoAnn B. Koskol, Widener University
Donna L. Occhifinto, County College of Morris
S. D. Rajan, Arizona State University
Robert A. Rouse, Washington University St. Louis
Chi N. Thai, University of Georgia
Anthony Trippe, Rochester Institute of Technology
Tom Walker, Virginia Tech
Dr. David T. Young, Louisiana State University

I am grateful for the ongoing support of the Addison-Wesley team in this endeavor: Computer Science Executive Editor Susan Hartman Sullivan was responsible for initiating the new edition, Galia Shokry was the editorial assistant, Patty Mahtani supervised the design and production of the book, and Michael Hirsch developed the marketing campaign. Trillium Project Management and Publishers' Design and Production Services, Inc. coordinated the conversion of the manuscript to a finished book.

J.R.H.

Computers: Revolutionary Machines with a Simple Design

1

In developed countries, life in the twenty-first century functions in a veritable sea of computers. From the coffeepot that turns itself on to brew your morning coffee, to the microwave that cooks your breakfast, to the automobile that you drive to work, to the automated teller machine you stop by for cash, virtually every aspect of your life depends on **computers**. These machines receive, store, process, and output information and can deal with data of all kinds: numbers, text, images, graphics, and sound, to name a few.

The work environment of engineers and scientists has not escaped the impact of computer technology:

computer
a machine that can receive, store, transform, and output data of all kinds

- An engineer in Detroit uses a computer-aided design (CAD) package to create alternative designs for a new automobile (see Fig. 1.1). The computer tests each design for structural strength and expected behavior under a variety of road conditions. After the engineer chooses the optimal design, the computer generates instructions to control the car's manufacture by robots and programmable machine tools (see Fig. 1.2).
- A scientist in New Jersey moves to Australia but continues joint research with colleagues in New Jersey. The collaborators conduct ongoing discussions of ideas by exchanging e-mail messages several times a day over the Internet.
- When a supertanker is damaged off the California coast, engineers of a spill-response team use a notebook computer to predict where the spill will come ashore based on input of up-to-date wind and water current information.
- A chemist in Wyoming uses the graphic output from the mass spectrometer, a computerized tool for determining the chemical structure of molecules, to identify the products of a chemical reaction.

FIGURE 1.1 Computer-Aided Design of an Automobile

FIGURE 1.2 Using Robots in Automobile Manufacturing

This chapter presents the rather simple design of the machine that has revolutionized twenty-first-century civilization. You will study the kinds of software available to harness the computer's power and the types of languages used to direct a computer's behavior. We will also introduce you to the process of designing robust new applications and discuss why it is important for you to learn how to write your own applications.

1.1 Computer Components

From the tiny computer that runs your calculator to the supercomputer used by the National Weather Service for weather prediction, computers of all sizes have the same basic components. Figure 1.3 shows these essential elements: the CPU, memory, secondary storage, and input and output devices.

FIGURE 1.3 Essential Components of a Computer

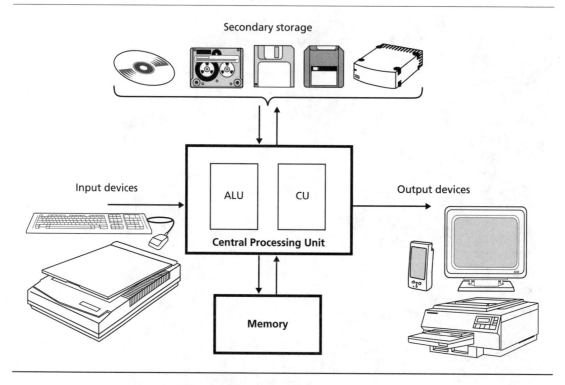

Central Processing Unit

The **central processing unit (CPU)** is the computer component that transforms data from one form to another. It consists of two sections: the arithmetic/logic unit (ALU), which contains circuitry to perform arithmetic operations such as addition and subtraction of numbers and to make logical comparisons such as "greater than" and "equal to," and the control unit (CU), which decodes each machine instruction and sends signals to the other components telling them what operations to perform in order to carry out the instruction.

The circuitry of a modern CPU is housed in a single **integrated circuit (IC)** or chip, millions of miniature circuits manufactured in a sliver of silicon. An integrated circuit that is a full central processing unit is called a **microprocessor**. A CPU's current instruction and data values are stored temporarily inside the CPU in special high-speed memory locations called **registers**.

Memory

Computer memory is comparable to a collection of numbered mailboxes. Figure 1.4 illustrates the two essential attributes of a memory cell: its address

FIGURE 1.4 Computer Memory

0	LDA 14
1	ADD 15
2	STA 14
3	HLT
4	153
5	'A'
6	6.5
7	0.00014
8	gray pixel
9	'!'
10	0
11	0
12	0
13	0
14	10
15	7
...	

(the numbers 0 to 15 in Fig. 1.4) and its contents, or value. A memory cell always has exactly one value—it is never empty, and when a new value is stored in a cell, the old value is lost. Computer memory is also referred to as **random-access memory (RAM)** because the cells can be accessed randomly, in any order desired, simply by providing a correct address.

Like the central processing unit, memory is housed in integrated circuits. RAM is volatile: It requires continuous power to retain its values, so a power outage would cause loss of all stored data.

All data stored in memory (indeed, all data manipulated by a computer) are represented **digitally**, that is, as binary (base 2) numbers composed of strings of the digits 0 and 1. Thus Fig. 1.4 is not really a precise model of memory, since it does not show addresses and contents as binary numbers, but rather, as the meanings represented by the binary numbers. A more accurate model of memory cell 5 would be:

Address   *Contents*

00000101   0000000001000001

Like base 10, base 2 is a positional number system, so our *address* means

random-access memory (RAM) integrated circuits representing a collection of numbered cells for storage of instructions and data of all kinds; cells can be accessed in any order

digital representation binary numbers made up of the digits 0 and 1

Base 2	0	0	0	0	0	1	0	1	Total
Conversion	0×2^7	0×2^6	0×2^5	0×2^4	0×2^3	1×2^2	0×2^1	1×2^0	
Base 10	0	0	0	0	0	4	0	1	5

Similarly, we could convert the *contents* of memory cell 5 as $1 \times 2^6 + 1 \times 2^0 = 65_{10}$, which is the code commonly used for the character A. However, this memory cell's contents would be no different if it represented the integer 65. The meaning of a memory cell's value is determined entirely by how the computer uses it. A memory cell can store a numeric value, a character, a picture element of an image, or a machine instruction, since the computer represents all of these in digital form.

bit
one binary digit

byte
amount of memory needed to represent one character (8 bits)

word
amount of memory that a computer views as a single unit of information

The smallest unit of data is a single *bi*nary digi*t*, or **bit**. A **byte** of data, typically 8 bits, is the amount of memory required to represent a single character. Memory cell 5, pictured earlier, consists of two bytes, but the first byte is actually unnecessary. You will note that the value of the first byte is zero. A memory **word** is the number of bits viewed as a single unit of information by a particular computer system. The word size of the memory from which we extracted cell 5 is 16 bits, which was at one time a common word size for personal computers. However, newer personal computers use 32-bit or even 64-bit words.

CPU–Memory Interaction

program
list of instructions that direct the work of a computer

A computer's work of transforming information from one form to another is directed by a list of instructions called a **program**. The memory pictured in Fig. 1.4 contains a tiny program fragment in words 0..3. If variable a is being stored in location 14, and variable b in location 15, the little program is equivalent to the statement

a = a + b;

which means "add the values of **a** and **b** and store the result in **a**."

Before
a | 10
b | 7

Statement   a = a + b;

After
a | 17
b | 7

In order to do what this statement instructs, the CPU and memory interact as follows:

1. The control unit signals memory that it needs the value of word 0.
2. When memory responds, the control unit places the value of the memory word (a binary number that means LDA 14) in the CPU's instruction register. The control unit decodes the instruction, which means "Load the accumulator with the value in memory word 14," and signals memory to provide the value of word 14.
3. When memory responds, the control unit signals the ALU to copy the incoming value into the accumulator, another CPU register.

Steps 1–3 have executed the instruction in word 0. Steps 4–6 will execute the instruction in word 1.

4. The control unit signals memory that it needs the value of word 1.
5. When memory responds, the control unit places the value of the memory word (a binary number that means ADD 15) in the CPU's instruction register. The control unit decodes the instruction, which means "Add to the accumulator the value in memory word 15," then signals memory to provide the value of word 15.
6. When memory responds, the control unit signals the ALU to add the incoming value to the accumulator.

Similarly, steps 7–9 will execute the instruction in word 2, storing the accumulator's value (17) into word 14 and erasing 14's previous value. This repetitive sequence of bringing in, decoding, and executing instructions is called the **fetch–execute cycle**.

fetch–execute cycle
CPU's repeatedly bringing in instructions from memory, decoding, and executing them

Input/Output Devices

Input and output devices perform the transformations that allow nondigital creatures such as humans to communicate with digital computers. The most common input device is the keyboard, which converts the typist's keystrokes into the digital representation of the same information. For example, when the typist holds down the Shift key and strikes the A key, the keyboard transmits 65 (01000001_2), the digital code for capital A. There are digital codes associated with the keyboard's control keys in addition to those that represent letters, digits, and punctuation. These codes represent Backspace, Enter, Escape, Space, and Tab, to name a few (see Appendix I).

Not long ago, most human interaction with computers was accomplished by typing lines of text. Today's computers, however, usually use a **graphical user interface (GUI)**, which allows the user to issue commands by pointing to icons (small pictures) or special text on the screen and making a selection. A variety of pointing devices are available for input of position/selection data. In addition to the mouse shown in Fig. 1.3, there are track balls and touch pads. A scanner (see lower left corner of Fig. 1.3) converts an image to a grid of numbers in which each number represents the color of one picture element (pixel). Touch screens, such as those used in fast-food restaurants,

graphical user interface (GUI)
pictures and menus displayed to allow user to select commands and data

sense where finger pressure is applied and convert this positional information to the command or data represented by the image displayed at this position. A growing number of computers are equipped with speech recognition programs that permit the user to issue commands by speaking into a microphone.

Common output devices include monitors and printers. Most computers also have speakers for audio output.

Secondary Storage

Computer systems provide storage in addition to main memory for two reasons. First, computers need storage that is permanent or semipermanent so that information can be retained during a power loss or when the computer is turned off. Second, systems typically store more information than will fit in memory.

Figure 1.5 shows some of the most frequently encountered **secondary storage** devices and storage media. Most personal computers use two types of disk drives as their secondary storage devices: *Hard disks* are usually attached to their disk drives, whereas *floppy disks* and *zip disks* are removable. The **disk** itself is a thin platter of metal or plastic coated with a magnetic material. Each data bit is a magnetized spot on the disk, and the spots are arranged in concentric circles called *tracks*. The disk drive read/write head accesses data by moving across the spinning disk to the correct track and then sensing the spots as they move by. A typical high-density floppy disk can store 1.44 MB (megabytes—see Table 1.1) of data, a zip disk can store 100 MB or 250 MB, and some hard disks provide many gigabytes (GB) of storage.

Most of today's personal computers are equipped with **CD drives** for reading data stored on compact disks. Some of these drives can also write data to CDs. A CD is a silvery plastic platter on which a laser records data as a sequence of tiny pits in a spiral track on one side of the disk. One CD can hold 680 MB of data. An increasingly common secondary storage device that uses similar technology is the **Digital Video Disk (DVD)** drive. By using smaller pits packed in a tighter spiral, a DVD stores 4.7 GB of data on one layer. Some DVDs can hold four layers of data—two on each side—for a total

secondary storage
units such as disks or tapes that retain data even when the power to the disk drive or tape drive is off

disk
thin platter of metal or plastic on which data are represented by magnetized spots arranged in tracks

CD drive
device that uses a laser to access or store data on a compact disk

digital video disk (DVD)
silvery plastic platter with up to 17 GB of data storage

FIGURE 1.5 Secondary Storage Media

| CD | Magnetic tape | Floppy disk | Hard disk | Zip disk |

TABLE 1.1 Terms Used to Quantify Storage Capacities

Term	Abbreviation	Equivalent to	Comparison to Power of 10
Byte	B	8 bits	
Kilobyte	KB	1,024 (2^{10}) bytes	$> 10^3$
Megabyte	MB	1,048,576 (2^{20}) bytes	$> 10^6$
Gigabyte	GB	1,073,741,824 (2^{30}) bytes	$> 10^9$
Terabyte	TB	1,099,511,627,776 (2^{40}) bytes	$> 10^{12}$

capacity of 17 gigabytes, sufficient storage for as much as nine hours of studio-quality video and multi-channel audio.

Magnetic tape drives serve as secondary storage devices for backup of data. It is unwise to rely on a single disk copy of an important document, so copies of all important data should be written to tape at regular intervals. The disadvantage of a tape drive is that it is a sequential-access device: It must move past data in the order in which it was stored on the tape. In contrast, disk drives are essentially random-access devices: They can move the read/write head directly to the desired track, and disks spin so rapidly that once the head is positioned on the right track the wait for the desired data to spin past the head is minimal.

Information kept in secondary storage is stored in named units called **files**. The device directory of these files is usually divided into categories called subdirectories or folders, which in turn can be divided into further subcategories. The complete pathname of a single file contains a representation of the path to the file through this directory structure and includes the name associated with the disk drive and the names of all the subdirectories, in addition to the name of the file. The rules for constructing a pathname vary from system to system, so you will need to find out the conventions used by your system. Here is a possible pathname for a file on an IBM-compatible PC:

file
named collection of data stored on a disk

```
c:\compons\ics\cpus\pent.txt
```

This pathname states that file pent.txt is found on disk drive c in the cpus subdirectory of the ics subdirectory of directory compons.

Connecting Computers

The explosion we are experiencing in worldwide information access is primarily due to the fact that computers are now linked together in networks so they can communicate with one another. A **local area network (LAN)** connects computers and other devices in a building by cables, allowing them to share information and resources such as printers, scanners, and secondary storage devices (see Fig. 1.6). Local area networks can be connected to other

local area network (LAN)
computers, printers, scanners, and storage devices connected by cables for intercommunication

FIGURE 1.6 Local Area Network

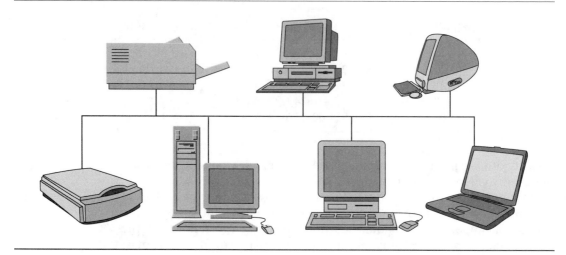

LANs using the same technology as telephone networks. Communications over intermediate distances use phone lines, and long-range communications use either phone lines or microwave signals that can be relayed by satellite (see Fig. 1.7).

FIGURE 1.7 A Wide Area Network with Satellite Relays of Microwave Signals

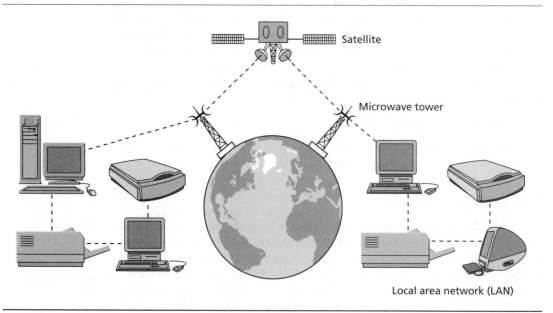

A network that links many individual computers and local area networks over a large geographic area is called a **wide area network (WAN)**. The most well known WAN, the Internet, connects university, corporate, government, and public-access networks. The Internet is a descendant of the computer network designed by the U.S. Defense Department's 1969 ARPAnet project. The goal of the project was to create a computer network that could continue to operate even if partially destroyed.

The most widely used aspect of the Internet is the **World Wide Web (WWW)**, the universe of Internet-accessible resources that are navigable through the use of a graphical user interface.

wide area network (WAN)

a network such as the Internet that connects computers and LANs over a large geographic area

World Wide Web (WWW)

a part of the Internet whose graphical user interfaces make associated network resources easily navigable

Section 1.1 Review Questions

1. Order these secondary storage media from smallest capacity to largest capacity:
   a. compact disk   b. digital video disk   c. floppy disk   d. zip disk
2. What is the name of the cycle in which the CPU repeatedly brings in instructions from memory, decodes, and executes them?

1.2 Computer Software

In the previous section we surveyed the components of a computer system, components referred to collectively as **hardware**. We studied the fundamental operations that allow a computer to accomplish tasks: repeated fetching and execution of instructions. In this section we focus on these all-important lists of instructions called computer programs or computer **software**. We will consider first the software that makes the hardware user-friendly. Then we will look at the various levels of computer languages in which software is written and at the process of creating and running a new program.

hardware

physical components of a computer system

software

computer programs

Operating System

The collection of computer programs that control the interaction of the user and the computer hardware is called the **operating system (OS)**. The operating system of a computer is often compared to the conductor of an orchestra, for it is the software responsible for directing all computer operations and managing all computer resources. Usually part of the operating system is stored permanently in a **read-only memory (ROM)** chip so that it is available as soon as the computer is turned on. A computer can look at the values in read-only memory but cannot write new values to the chip. The ROM-based portion of the OS contains the instructions necessary for loading into mem-

operating system (OS)

software that controls interaction of user and computer hardware and that manages allocation of computer resources

read-only memory (ROM) chip

integrated circuit containing information that can be accessed, but not changed

booting a computer
loading the operating system from disk into memory

ory the rest of the operating system code, which typically resides on a disk. Executing this load of the operating system is called **booting the computer**.

Here is a list of some of the operating system's many responsibilities:

1. Communicating with the computer user: receiving commands and carrying them out or rejecting them with an error message
2. Managing allocation of memory, of processor time, and of other resources for various tasks
3. Collecting input from the keyboard, mouse, and other input devices, and providing this information to the currently running program
4. Conveying program output to the screen, printer, or other output device
5. Accessing data from secondary storage
6. Writing data to secondary storage

In addition to these responsibilities, the operating system of a computer with multiple users must verify each individual's right to use the computer and must ensure that each user can access only data for which he or she has proper authorization.

Table 1.2 lists some widely used operating systems. An OS that uses a command-line interface displays a brief message called a *prompt* that indicates the OS's readiness to receive input, and the user then types a command at the keyboard. Figure 1.8 shows entry of UNIX commands requesting a list of the names of all the files in subdirectory `misc` of directory `temp` of the floppy disk drive. In this case, the prompt is >. (In this figure, and in all subsequent figures showing program runs, input typed by the user is shown in

TABLE 1.2 Widely Used Operating Systems Categorized by Original User Interface Type

Command-Line Interface	Graphical User Interface
UNIX	Macintosh OS
MS-DOS®	Windows
OS/2	X Windows
VMS	

FIGURE 1.8 Entering a Directory-Display Command into UNIX Command-Line Interface

```
> cd /mnt/floppy
> cd /temp/misc
> ls
gridvar.cpp     gridvar.exe     griddata.txt
```

FIGURE 1.9 Accessing Disk Drives through Windows

shaded rectangles to distinguish it from computer-generated text.) In contrast, operating systems that use a graphical user interface provide the user with a system of icons and menus. To issue commands, the user uses the mouse, track ball, or touch pad to point to the appropriate icon or menu selection, then pushes a button once or twice. Figure 1.9 shows the window that pops up when you double-click on the "My Computer" icon in the top-left corner of the desktop of a Windows GUI. You can view the directories of the floppy disk (A:), hard drive (C:), or CD (D:) by double-clicking the appropriate icon. Today's operating systems typically allow the user to choose whether to use a GUI or a command-line interface.

Application Software

Application programs are developed to assist a computer user in accomplishing specific tasks. For example, a word processing application such as MS-Word or WordPerfect helps to create a document, a spreadsheet application such as Lotus 1-2-3 or Excel helps to automate tedious numerical calculations and to generate charts that depict data, and a database management application such as Access or dBASE assists in data storage and quick keyword-based access to large collections of records.

Computer users typically purchase application software on CDs and **install** the software by copying the programs from the CD to the hard disk. One can also download a wide variety of software from the World Wide Web. Some applications are free, but for many the user must pay a license fee. When buying software, always check that the program you are purchasing is compatible with both the operating system and the computer hardware you plan to use. We have already discussed some of the differences among oper-

application
software used for a specific task such as word processing, accounting, or database management

install
make an application available on a computer by copying it from CD to the computer's hard drive

ating systems; now we will investigate the different languages understood by different processors.

Computer Languages

machine language
binary number codes understood by a specific CPU

assembly language
mnemonic codes that correspond to machine-language instructions

Developing new software requires writing lists of instructions for a computer to execute. However, software developers rarely write in the language directly understood by a computer, since this **machine language** is a collection of binary numbers. Another drawback of machine language is that it is not standardized: There is a different machine language for every type of CPU. This disadvantage also applies to the somewhat more readable **assembly language**, a language in which computer operations are represented by mnemonics rather than binary numbers and variables can be given names rather than binary memory addresses. Table 1.3 shows a tiny machine-language program fragment that adds two numbers along with an equivalent fragment in assembly language. Notice that each assembly-language instruction corresponds to exactly one machine instruction: The assembly-language memory cells labeled A and B are space for variables; they are not instructions.

To write programs that are independent of the CPU on which they will be executed, software designers use high-level languages, which combine algebraic expressions and symbols taken from English. For example, the machine/assembly-language program fragment shown in Table 1.3 would be a single statement in a high-level language:

```
a = a + b;
```

This statement means "Add the values of variables a and b and store the result in variable a (replacing a's previous value)."

Many high-level languages are available today. Table 1.4 lists some of the most widely used along with the origin of their names and the application

TABLE 1.3   A Machine-Language Program Fragment and Its Assembly-Language Equivalent

Memory Addresses	Machine-Language Instructions	Assembly-Language Instructions	
00000000	00000000	CLA	
00000001	00010101	ADD	A
00000010	00010110	ADD	B
00000011	00110101	STA	A
00000100	01110111	HLT	
00000101	?	A	?
00000110	?	B	?

TABLE 1.4 High-Level Languages

Language	Application Area	Origin of Name
FORTRAN	Scientific programming	*Formula translation*
COBOL	Business data processing	*Common Business-Oriented Language*
Lisp	Artificial intelligence (AI)	*List processing*
C	Systems programming	Predecessor language was named B
Prolog	Artificial intelligence	*Logic programming*
Ada	Real-time distributed systems	*Ada* Augusta Byron collaborated with nineteenth-century computer pioneer Charles Babbage
Smalltalk	Graphical user interfaces; object-oriented programming	Objects "talk" to one another via messages.
C++	Supports objects and object-oriented programming	Incremental modification of C (++ is the C increment operator)
Java	Supports Web programming	Originally named "Oak"

areas that first popularized them. Although programmers find it far easier to express problem solutions in high-level languages, the problem remains that computers *do not* understand these languages. Thus, before a high-level language program can be executed, it must first be translated into the target computer's machine language. The program that does this translation is called a **compiler**. Figure 1.10 illustrates the role of the compiler in the process of developing and testing a high-level language program. Both the input to and the output from the compiler (when it is successful) are programs. The input to the compiler is a **source file** containing the text of a high-level language program. The software developer creates this file by using a word processor or editor. The format of the source file is text, which means that it is a collection of character codes. For example, you might type a program into a file called myprog.cpp. The compiler will scan this source file, checking the program to see if it follows the high-level language's **syntax** (grammar) rules. If the program is syntactically correct, the compiler saves in an **object file** the machine-language instructions that carry out the program's purpose. For our program myprog.cpp, the object file created might be named myprog.obj. Notice that this file's format is binary. This means that you should not send it to a printer, display it on your monitor, or try to work with it in a word processor, because it will appear to be meaningless garbage to a word processor, printer, or monitor. If the source program contains syntax errors, the compiler lists these errors but does not create an ob-

compiler
software that translates a high-level language program into machine language

source file
file containing a program written in a high-level language; the input for a compiler

syntax
grammar rules of a programming language

object file
file of machine-language instructions that is the output of a compiler

FIGURE 1.10   Entering, Translating, and Running a High-Level Language Program

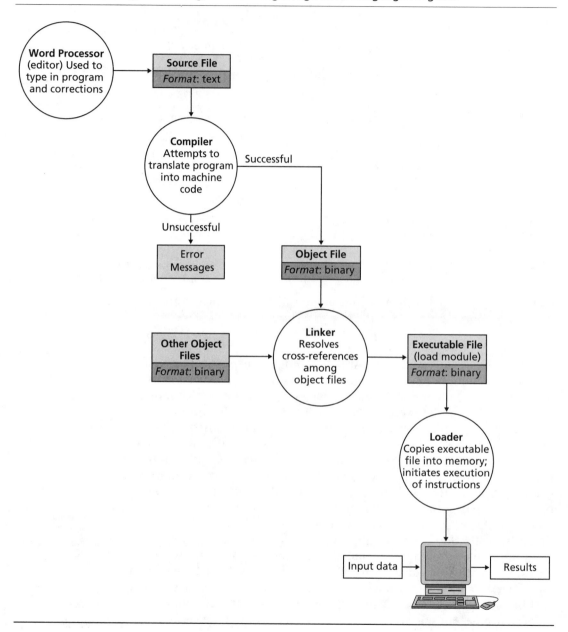

ject file. The developer must return to the word processor, correct the errors, and recompile the program.

Although an object file contains machine instructions, not all of the instructions are complete. High-level languages provide the software developer with many named chunks of code for operations that the developer will likely need. Almost all high-level language programs use at least one of these chunks of code, called *functions* and residing in other object files available to the system. The **linker** program combines these prefabricated functions with your object file, creating a complete machine-language program that is ready to run. For your sample program, the linker might name the executable file that it creates myprog.exe.

linker
software that combines object files to create an executable machine-language program

As long as myprog.exe is just stored on your disk, it does nothing. To run it, the loader must copy all its instructions into memory and direct the CPU to begin execution with the first instruction. As the program executes, it takes input data from one or more sources and sends results to output and/or secondary storage devices.

Some computer systems require the user to ask the OS to carry out separately each step illustrated in Fig. 1.10. Today, however, many high-level language compilers are sold as part of an **integrated development environment (IDE)**, a package that combines a simple word processor with a compiler, linker, and loader. Such environments give the developer menus from which to select the next step and simply fills in the missing steps automatically should the developer try a step that is out of sequence. Appendixes G and H are brief introductions to two popular IDEs—Microsoft Visual C++ and Borland C++ Builder.

integrated development environment (IDE)
software package combining a word processor, compiler, linker, loader, and tools for finding errors

The user of an integrated development environment should be aware that the environment may not automatically save to disk the source, object, and executable files. Rather, it may simply leave these versions of the program in memory. Such an approach eliminates the expenditure of time and disk space needed to make copies, and it keeps the code readily available in memory for application of the next step in the translation/execution process. However, the developer does risk losing the only copy of the source file in the event of a power outage or serious program error. To prevent such a loss when you use an IDE, be sure to save the source file to disk after every modification, before attempting to run the program.

C++

This textbook introduces you to C++, a high-level language developed at AT&T Bell Laboratories by Bjarne Stroustrup in the early 1980s. C++ extends the systems programming language C, which originated in the early 1970s and is the language in which the UNIX operating system is written. C++ and C share the same basic control structures and data types, and we compare their similarities in Appendix A. The power and flexibility of C++ and its ability to represent and manipulate objects have made it a popular language in industry for a wide variety of applications. The International Standards Organization adopted the standard for C++ in 1997.

Section 1.2 Review Questions

1. When you boot a computer, what is being loaded from disk into memory?
2. What do you call the system of binary codes understood by a specific CPU?

1.3   Object-Oriented Programming

object-oriented programming (OOP)
methodology that creates programs composed of semi-autonomous agents called objects

Table 1.4 indicates that C++ differs from its predecessor language C in its support for **object-oriented programming (OOP)**. Traditional procedural programming views data as static collections of values to be manipulated and transformed. In contrast, object-oriented programming views software as simulation of a world populated not with static data, but with objects—semi-autonomous agents having prescribed responsibilities. OOP defines an object by encapsulating what it is (its data components) with what it does (its responsibilities). The rising popularity of object-oriented programming stems in part from the fact that the OOP view of the world more closely models reality than does the procedural programming view. Also, classes of OOP objects can often be reused in other projects, thus shortening development time.

OOP organizes objects in classes that have the same components and behavior. The classes, in turn, are arranged in a superclass–subclass hierarchy, and objects in the subclasses *inherit* data and behaviors from their superclasses.

In addition to the use of classes and inheritance, object-oriented programming is characterized by the use of *polymorphism*—giving a single name to behaviors that are operationally different but conceptually the same. Polymorphism is common in natural languages such as English. For example, when you are offered a piece of steak to "eat," you automatically reach for a knife and fork and embark on several minutes of concentrated chewing and swallowing. When you set out to "eat" a bowl of vanilla ice cream, however, you equip yourself with a spoon and tend to skip the chewing altogether. So, what is the operational definition of "to eat"? Clearly, it varies depending on what you are eating. In a similar fashion, an object-oriented language lets software developers create operations or functions with one name but with multiple behaviors depending on the data to which they are applied.

Software Engineering

Software engineering is the development of new computer applications through an orderly problem-solving process incorporating analysis, design, implementation, testing, and maintenance. At all stages of system development, the software engineer is concerned not only with writing a program that functionally solves the problem that it should solve, but also with creating a system that is well documented and that incorporates computer code that is easy to read and to modify to accommodate changing circumstances. Additionally, the object-oriented software engineer is always alert for situations in which classes of objects developed previously can be reused, and such a developer routinely concludes a new project by evaluating which of its classes should be saved and generalized for likely reuse in future projects.

There are many models of the software design process. Most follow the same steps but divide them into different numbers of basic stages. Our model divides the elements of the object-oriented software development process into six stages.

Stage 1: Requirements Specification

This stage includes activities designed to answer the question, "What should this application do?" A complete answer will list the sources and format of expected data, the kind of output to be produced, and the nature of the program's interaction with the user.

Stage 2: Analysis

Next, object-oriented program developers read the specifications document with the goal of identifying the kinds of objects whose behavior will be modeled. This identification process involves listing for each candidate object the following properties:

1. Its attributes or data components (What knowledge does it possess?)
2. Its behavior (What questions should it be able to answer? What services does it provide?)
3. Its relationships to other objects (a *kind-of* relationship: Is it just a specialized version of another type of object? a *part-of* relationship: Could such an object be one component of another class?)

The analysis phase is not complete until the population of candidate objects can account for every detail of the specifications.

Stage 3: Design

In the design stage, software developers review and refine the descriptive model produced during analysis. They weigh the pros and cons of various alternative ways of creating objects with the desired attributes and behaviors, then diagram the relationships among classes of objects. Developers review libraries of existing classes and identify candidates for reuse in this project, and they develop *algorithms* (step-by-step procedures) for the behaviors of objects that require newly defined classes. Finally, software developers specify all the possible interfaces among software objects and between the objects and the outside world.

Stage 4: Implementation

When the system design document is well written, implementation through writing C++ code is quite straightforward. At this stage, developers take great care to produce readable code. To this end, they meticulously follow the programming style that is conventional within their development team. Figure 1.11 shows two C++ programs that accomplish the same purpose. However, version B follows the style conventions illustrated on the inside covers of this

---

FIGURE 1.11 Two Programs That Accomplish the Same Purpose

Version A

```
#include <iostream>
using namespace std;
int  main()
{char  x;  double y, z;
cout << "C(ompact)  I(ntermediate)  S(tandard)  L(uxury)" << endl;
cout << "Enter vehicle class => ";  cin  >> x;
cout << "Enter amount of carbon monoxide emitted (grams) => ";
cin >> y;  cout << "Enter miles driven => ";  cin >> z;
double r = y / z;
cout << "Carbon monoxide emission of " << r << " g/mi ";
if (coRate <= 3.4)
cout << "meets ";
else cout << "exceeds ";
cout << "permitted emission of " << endl << "3.4 g/mi." << endl;
return  0;}
```

Version B

```
//
//    Determine if new vehicle meets carbon monoxide emissions standard.
//

#include  <iostream>
using namespace std;

const double MAXCO = 3.4; // maximum g/mi of carbon monoxide allowed
```

FIGURE 1.11 *(Continued)*

```
int  main()
{
   char   carClass;      // first letter of vehicle class: Compact,
                         //    Intermediate, Standard, Luxury
   double  coEmitted,    // grams of carbon monoxide emitted
           miles;        // miles driven during test

   cout << "C(ompact)  I(ntermediate)  S(tandard)  L(uxury)" << endl;
   cout << "Enter vehicle class => ";
   cin  >> carClass;

   cout << "Enter amount of carbon monoxide emitted (grams) => ";
   cin >> coEmitted;
   cout << "Enter miles driven => ";
   cin >> miles;

   double  coRate = coEmitted / miles; // g/mi of carbon monoxide emitted
   cout << "Carbon monoxide emission of " << coRate << " g/mi ";

   if (coRate <= MAXCO)
        cout << "meets ";
   else
        cout << "exceeds ";

   cout << "permitted emission of " << endl << MAXCO << " g/mi." <<
      endl;

   return 0;
}
```

textbook and version A does not. Even though you do not know C++, take a moment to evaluate for yourself which program you would prefer to try to understand and to modify. Table 1.5 summarizes some of the style rules followed in version B. There are many alternatives to the details of these particular rules. For example, some programmers prefer names that use underscores (co_rate, co_emitted) rather than interspersed capital letters (coRate, coEmitted). What is critical is not the details of a particular set of style rules but the fact that programmers working together establish a set of rules and follow them consistently.

TABLE 1.5 Sample Style Rules That Improve Code Readability

Names	All names are meaningful. In names that combine two or more words, all words after the first are capitalized.
Constants	Constant values that could change if the program were used in a different context are given meaningful names consisting of capital letters and underscores.
Documentation	All code is prefaced by comment lines (lines beginning //) summarizing the purpose and limitations of the code. Most variable names are explained in comments also.
Spacing	At most one statement is placed on a line. Blank lines are included between major sections of the program.
Indentation	The program's logic imposes a certain structure on the code. Lines are indented/unindented to reflect this structure.

The final aspect of implementation is testing the system to verify that it meets the specifications. Some test cases must be designed on the basis of the requirements document, whereas others should be defined while considering the logic of the code. These test cases should be saved as part of the system documentation.

After verifying that a new system meets its "specs" (requirements specifications), software engineers must discharge two types of follow-up responsibilities—reuse review and maintenance/upgrades.

Stage 5: Reuse Review

Developers in an object-oriented programming environment must review every project to identify classes of objects likely to be needed in subsequent projects. These classes should be generalized as much as possible and catalogued for future reuse.

Stage 6: Maintenance and Upgrades

maintenance
fixing software errors discovered after the software is deployed

upgrades
changes to software that provide new features or support new devices or operating systems

Software developers have continuing responsibility for an application after it is deployed. Inevitably there will be reports of errors that must be fixed, a process termed **maintenance**. After each "fix," the revised system must be run on the saved test cases to ensure that the fix did not cause a "break" elsewhere. Maintenance programmers also make **upgrades** to the software that are necessary to permit the system to work correctly with new input/output and storage devices and with new CPUs and new versions of the operating system.

1.4 Computing for Engineers and Scientists

You may wonder why university curricula for engineers and scientists include instruction in solving problems using a general-purpose programming language such as C++. After all, most of the computer-oriented work of engineers and scientists uses existing application programs. Report writing utilizes standard word processors, technical presentations can be prepared using presentation graphics software, much data analysis and production of explanatory graphs can be done with spreadsheets, and databases of background information can be stored and accessed using commercial database management software. In addition, specialized software packages are now available for every branch of science and engineering.

Nevertheless, engineers and scientists still benefit greatly from the ability to write their own programs. Despite the existence of much off-the-shelf software, problems inevitably arise that are outside the range of problems solvable by the application software to which an individual scientist or engineer has immediate access. Moreover, it is critical that those responsible for expanding society's technical knowledge and for applying the principles of science and mathematics to society's problems not come to view any software package as an infallible oracle, overlooking its possible limitations. Engineers and scientists who have designed, implemented, and tested software personally are simply better equipped to evaluate software created by others. Finally, advances in specialized software for science and engineering disciplines are usually initiated by professionals who combine knowledge of their specific discipline with an understanding of the inner workings of software. Only such individuals are in a position to obtain a clear view of both the problems the professional still needs help in solving efficiently and the means of providing this help through software.

Chapter Review

1. The basic components of a computer are main memory and secondary storage, the CPU, and input and output devices.
2. All data manipulated by a computer are represented digitally, as base 2 numbers composed of strings of the digits 0 and 1.
3. Main memory is organized into individual storage locations called memory cells.
   - Each memory cell has a unique address.
   - A memory cell is a collection of bytes; a byte is a collection of 8 bits.
   - A memory cell is never empty, but its initial contents may be meaningless to your program.
   - The current contents of a memory cell are destroyed whenever new information is stored in that cell.

- Programs *must* be loaded into the memory of the computer before they can be executed.
- Data cannot bé manipulated by the computer until they are first stored in memory.

4. Information in secondary storage is organized into files: text files and binary files. Secondary storage stores information in semipermanent form.

5. A CPU runs a computer program by repeatedly fetching and executing simple instructions.

6. Connecting computers in networks allows sharing of resources—local resources on LANs and worldwide resources on a WAN such as the Internet.

7. Programming languages range from machine language (meaningful to a computer) to high-level language (meaningful to a programmer).

8. Several system programs are used to prepare a high-level language program for execution. An editor enters a high-level language program into a file called the source file. A compiler translates the source program into machine language (the object program). The linker links this object program to other object files, creating an executable file, and the loader loads the executable file into memory. All of these programs are combined in an integrated development environment (IDE).

9. The user communicates with the computer by issuing commands to the operating system.

10. Use the first four stages of the object-oriented software development process to design and implement a program. Write programs in a consistent style that is easy to read, understand, and maintain.

Chapter 1 Review Questions

Fill in the blanks to complete the following statements.

1. The _____ _____ _____ is the component that serves as the "brain" of a computer.

2. A(n) _____ _____ , or "chip," is a sliver of silicon that contains a large number of miniaturized circuits.

3. A(n) _____ is an entire central processing unit on a single integrated circuit.

4. A(n) _____ is a high-speed memory location found inside the central processing unit.

5. Computer _____ is composed of integrated circuits with many numbered cells for data storage.

6. A character can be stored in one _____ of memory.

7. Common personal computer _____ sizes include 16, 32, and 64 bits.

8. A(n) _____ is a list of instructions that direct the work of a computer.

9. _____ _____ is composed of units such as disks or tapes that retain the data stored even when power is lost.

10. On a magnetic disk, data are represented as _____ _____ arranged in concentric tracks.

11. On a CD or DVD, data are represented as laser-written pits arranged in a _____ .

12. A(n) _____ _____ _____ such as the Internet connects computers over a large geographic area.

13. The physical components of a computer system are collectively called _____; the programs that run on a computer form a collective called _____ .

14. The software that allocates computer resources and controls the user's interaction with the hardware is the _____ _____ .

15. When you _____ a new application, you copy it from a CD to your computer's hard drive.

16. Compilers can find _____ errors (violations of the grammar rules of the high-level language) in source files.

17. _____ _____ is the development of new computer applications through an orderly problem-solving process incorporating analysis, design, implementation, testing, and maintenance.

18. _____ _____ is the stage of the software design process that answers the question "What should this application do?"

19. Object-oriented analysis identifies each object's _____ , _____ , and _____ to other objects.

20. After an application program is deployed, developers continue to be responsible for _____ of the system (fixing errors) and _____ to the system that permit it to work with changes in other hardware and software.

Basic Elements of a C++ Program

2

This chapter presents two very simple C++ programs as a means of introducing you to the most basic elements of C++. We begin with the fundamental executable unit of a C++ program, the statement. You will then learn how an interactive program gets data from the outside world and how it communicates the program results to the user.

You will study how C++ represents numeric, character, logical, and string data, and you will learn about the operators that the language provides for numeric calculations as well as the functions that C++ predefines to carry out calculations for which it has no operators. You will also learn about the concept of a namespace and how to gain access to names defined in a namespace. The chapter concludes with a discussion of the various kinds of program errors and how you detect and fix them.

2.1   Simple C++ Program

We begin the chapter with Fig. 2.1, a simple environmental engineering program that could be used at a coal-burning power plant. Do not worry if you do not immediately understand all the details of these programs. We will give you the big picture first and return to explain the details in subsequent sections.

"Clean Air" legislation restricts the sulfur dioxide emissions of coal-burning facilities to about one pound per million Btu's of energy generated. Factors affecting emissions rates include the energy content and sulfur content of the coal and the use of *scrubbing*, a reprocessing of the combustion gases to remove sulfur. The program in Fig. 2.1 calculates the number of pounds of sulfur dioxide emissions per million Btu's of energy for a given coal sample. The program reflects the fact that complete oxidation of *n* pounds of sulfur produces approximately 2*n* pounds of sulfur dioxide. The output indicates emissions levels both without and with scrubbing, assuming that scrubbing would remove 80% of the sulfur dioxide emissions.

FIGURE 2.1 Sulfur Dioxide Emissions Program

```
//
//   Calculate sulfur dioxide emission rate for a coal sample — without
//   scrubbing and with scrubbing that is 80% effective
//

#include <iostream>
using namespace std;

const double OXIDATION_FACTOR = 2.0;   // oxidizing n pounds of sulfur
                  // produces about 2n pounds of sulfur dioxide
const double SCRUB_EFFICIENCY = 0.8;   // scrubbing combustion gases
                  // reduces sulfur dioxide emissions by 80%

int    main()
{
    int     sampleId;                // input - sample identification number
    double  sulfurContent;           // input - % of sample that is sulfur
    double  energyContent;           // input - number of Btu per pound

    // Get data on coal sample
    cout << "Enter sample identification number => ";
    cin >> sampleId;
    cout << "What percent of the sample is sulfur? => ";
```

FIGURE 2.1 *(Continued)*

```
cin >> sulfurContent;
cout << "How many Btu's of energy from one pound of the sample? => ";
cin >> energyContent;

// Calculate emissions rate for burning this sample
double poundsDioxide = sulfurContent / 100.0 * OXIDATION_FACTOR;
double emissions = poundsDioxide * 1000000.0 / energyContent;

// Calculate emissions rate with scrubbing
double withScrubbing = emissions - emissions * SCRUB_EFFICIENCY;

// Display results
cout << "Sulfur dioxide emissions of coal sample " << sampleId <<
      " with sulfur content of " << endl;
cout << "    " << sulfurContent << " percent and energy content of "
      << energyContent << " Btu per pound:" << endl;
cout << "        Before scrubbing: " << emissions <<
      " pounds per million Btu" << endl;
cout << "         After scrubbing:  " << withScrubbing <<
      " pounds per million Btu" << endl;
return 0;
}

Enter sample identification number => 541
What percent of the sample is sulfur? => 3
How many Btu's of energy from one pound of the sample? => 12000
Sulfur dioxide emissions of coal sample 541 with sulfur content of
    3 percent and energy content of 12000 Btu per pound:
        Before scrubbing: 5 pounds per million Btu
        After scrubbing:  1 pounds per million Btu
```

The first four lines of Fig. 2.1 are a block comment describing the purpose of the program. A *comment*, which always begins with a double slash, is ignored by the compiler and is included only to assist the reader of a program. When the C++ compiler encounters a double slash (//) anywhere on a line, it makes no attempt to translate the rest of that line.

The lines

```
#include <iostream>
using namespace std;
```

make it possible for this program to use cout << to display messages and cin >> to get data from the user. The first of these lines is a **preprocessor**

preprocessor directive

a C++ program line beginning with # that provides an instruction to the processor

directive, a command that gives instructions to the C++ **preprocessor**, whose job it is to modify the text of a C++ program before the program is compiled. A preprocessor directive begins with a number symbol (#) as its first nonblank character.

Many actions that are necessary in a computer program are not defined directly by the C++ language. Instead, every C++ implementation includes collections of useful functions, operators, and symbols called **libraries**. Each standard library has a header file whose name is enclosed in angular brackets like <iostream>.

preprocessor

a system program that modifies a C++ program prior to its compilation

The #include directive gives a program access to a library by causing the preprocessor to insert definitions from a header file into a program before compilation. For example, the iostream library defines the names cin and cout and the operators >> and <<.

library

a collection of useful functions, operators, and symbols that may be accessed by a program

The lines beginning const give names to the values 2.0 and 0.8. They associate the name OXIDATION_FACTOR with the value 2.0, and the name SCRUB_EFFICIENCY with the value 0.8. Both OXIDATION_FACTOR and SCRUB_EFFICIENCY are constants, meaning that their values cannot be changed as the program runs.

Every C++ program must have a main function. In Fig. 2.1 this function begins with the line

```
int main()
```

statement

one or more lines of code ending in a semicolon

and consists of 17 statements enclosed in a set of curly braces ({}). A **statement**, the basic unit of a C++ program, is one or more lines of code and ends with a semicolon (;).

The first three statements tell the compiler to set aside space in memory for three variables that this program uses for data storage. The first variable, sampleId, is to hold a single integer, a type of data that C++ calls int. The other two variables, sulfurContent and energyContent, will hold numbers that may have a fractional part, a type of data that C++ calls double. Each of these three statements is followed by a comment specifying the purpose of the variable named on that line. The word *input* in these comments tells the reader that the values for the variables will come from the computer's standard input device—the keyboard in this case.

The section of the program that begins with the comment

```
//  Get data on coal sample
```

contains three statements of the form

```
cout << string of characters enclosed in quotes ;
```

Each of these statements displays on the screen a message telling the user what kind of information to enter as data. In the sample output shown after function main, the unshaded portions of the first three lines are the messages displayed.

Interspersed with these three statements beginning `cout <<` are three statements of the form

```
cin >> variable name;
```

These statements copy the values typed by the user (displayed in a shaded rectangle in the sample run) into the variables `sampleId`, `sulfurContent`, and `energyContent`.

In the program sections that calculate emissions rates, each statement has a dual purpose. First, it notifies the compiler to set aside space in memory for a variable:

```
double poundsDioxide ...
double emissions ...
double withScrubbing ...
```

Then it stores a value in the variable that is the result of a computation. The symbol / means "divided by" and the symbol * means "times," so the value stored in `poundsDioxide` is

$$\frac{sulfurContent}{100} \times OXIDATION\_FACTOR$$

The statement

```
double emissions = poundsDioxide * 1000000.0 / energyContent;
```

stores in `emissions` the value of the expression

$$\frac{poundsDioxide \times 1000000.0}{energyContent}$$

which is the number of pounds of sulfur dioxide emitted per million Btu's of energy produced. The statement

```
double withScrubbing = emissions - emissions * SCRUB_EFFICIENCY;
```

stores in `withScrubbing` the emissions rate after scrubbing has reduced the sulfur dioxide emissions by 80%.

The "Display results" section of the program contains four statements beginning `cout <<` that display the last four lines of the sample output. The quoted strings of characters are displayed without quotes, and variable names are replaced by their values in the output. Output of `endl` terminates a line of output and starts a new one: The cursor moves to the beginning of the next line. For example, this statement

```
cout << "This produces two" << endl << "lines of output." << endl;
```

would produce the output

```
This produces two
lines of output.
```

The final line of the program,

```
return 0;
```

is a statement that completes execution of function `main` by returning a value (0) that indicates that the function ran normally. This zero is the integer that `main` referred to in the header line **int** main().

Names and Keywords

All the names that the sample program uses for constants and variables are collections of upper- and lowercase letters and underscores.

```
OXIDATION_FACTOR      sulfurContent       emissions
SCRUB_EFFICIENCY      energyContent       withScrubbing
sampleId              poundsOxide
```

C++ allows such names to include digits as well as letters and underscores, but a name cannot begin with a digit. Thus these variable names are legitimate, too:

```
sample_id        K9          k9          _Begin
```

C++ would consider K9 and k9 to be two different names.

Notice that the data type names `int`, `double`, `char`, and `bool` and the operator `return` are also collections of letters. However, you cannot use these names for variables, because C++ reserves them as part of a list of **keywords** used for special purposes in the language. Take a moment to look at Appendix F, which is a list of all the names reserved for use as keywords.

keyword
a name given a special meaning by C++

Section 2.1 Review Questions

1. Read this C++ program. Then identify the line numbers of the statements that accomplish each of tasks (a)–(g). Some tasks are carried out by more than one line.

```
1    #include <iostream>
2    using namespace std;
3
4    int main()
5    {
6        double x;
7        int    q;
8
9        cout << "Enter a decimal fraction=> ";
10       cin >> x;
11       cout << "Enter an integer=> ";
12       cin >> q;
```

```
13
14          double sum = x + q;
15
16          cout << "Sum of " << x << endl << " and " << q
17                << " is " << sum << endl;
18          return 0;
19    }
```

    _____ a. Sets aside space in memory for a variable and stores a value in
              that variable.

    _____ b. Sets aside space in memory for a variable in which to store input
              data.

    _____ c. Displays a message telling the user what data to enter.

    _____ d. Displays program results.

    _____ e. Copies into a variable a value typed by the user.

    _____ f. Allows the program to use input and output operations.

    _____ g. Completes normal program execution.

  2. Show a sample run of the program in Question 1 in which the user enters 0.25
and –3 as the data.

2.2 Statement Execution

In the sample programs of Section 2.1, all the statements were executed once,
in order. In this section we look closely at what happens both on the surface
(the program output on the screen and input from the keyboard) and inside
the memory of the computer as each statement executes. We study a program that executes many statements in sequence but then selects one of two
statements to execute, skipping the other.

EXAMPLE 2.1 New vehicles must meet a carbon monoxide emissions standard of 3.4 grams/mile. The program in Fig. 2.2 uses data from a test drive to
determine whether a car meets this standard.

    Like the first program we studied, the program in Fig. 2.2 is interactive: It
takes input data entered by the user after displaying a message asking for the
data. This message is called a **prompt**. The program declares the variables
that are to hold numbers as type `double` and declares a variable named `car-`
`Class` to be of type `char`, indicating that `carClass` can hold a single character. Figure 2.3 traces the execution of function `main` showing both screen
output and memory from the start of the function up to the statement that
begins `if`. Up to the `if` all the statements are executed in sequence, but the
`if–else` contains two statements,

```
cout << "meets ";
```

prompt
a message that an
interactive program
displays indicating its
readiness to receive
input

FIGURE 2.2 Program That Skips a Statement

```
//
//  Determine if new vehicle meets carbon monoxide emissions standard.
//

#include <iostream>
using namespace std;

const double MAXCO = 3.4; // maximum g/mi of carbon monoxide allowed

int  main()
{
   char    carClass;  // first letter of vehicle class: Compact,
                      //    Intermediate, Standard, Luxury
   double coEmitted, // grams of carbon monoxide emitted
          miles;     // miles driven during test

   cout << "C(ompact)  I(ntermediate)  S(tandard)  L(uxury)" << endl;
   cout << "Enter vehicle class => ";
   cin  >> carClass;

   cout << "Enter amount of carbon monoxide emitted (grams) => ";
   cin >> coEmitted;
   cout << "Enter miles driven => ";
   cin >> miles;

   double coRate = coEmitted / miles; // g/mi of carbon monoxide emitted
   cout << "For class " << carClass <<
        " vehicle, carbon monoxide emission of " << coRate << " g/mi "
        << endl;

   if (coRate <= MAXCO)
       cout << "meets ";
   else
       cout << "exceeds ";

   cout << "permitted emission of " << MAXCO << " g/mi." << endl;
   return 0;
}
```

FIGURE 2.3 Trace of Carbon Monoxide Emissions Program in Fig. 2.2

Program

```
//
//   Determine if new vehicle meets carbon monoxide emissions standard.
//

#include <iostream>
using namespace std;

const double MAXCO = 3.4; // maximum g/mi of carbon monoxide allowed

int  main()
{
    char    carClass;  // first letter of vehicle class: Compact,
                       //    Intermediate, Standard, Luxury
    double coEmitted, // grams of carbon monoxide emitted
           miles;      // miles driven during test

→ cout << "C(ompact)  I(ntermediate)  S(tandard)  L(uxury)" << endl;
→ cout << "Enter vehicle class => ";
    cin  >> carClass;

    cout << "Enter amount of carbon monoxide emitted (grams) => ";
    cin >> coEmitted;
    cout << "Enter miles driven => ";
    cin >> miles;
                        . . .
```

Memory

3.4
MAXCO

?
carClass

?
coEmitted

?
miles

?
coRate

Input/Output

```
C(ompact)  I(ntermediate)  S(tandard)  L(uxury)
Enter vehicle class =>
```

FIGURE 2.3   *(Continued)*

Program

```
//
//  Determine if new vehicle meets carbon monoxide emissions standard.
//

#include <iostream>
using namespace std;

const double MAXCO = 3.4; // maximum g/mi of carbon monoxide allowed

int  main()
{
   char    carClass;  // first letter of vehicle class: Compact,
                      //    Intermediate, Standard, Luxury
   double coEmitted,  // grams of carbon monoxide emitted
          miles;      // miles driven during test

   cout << "C(ompact)  I(ntermediate)  S(tandard)  L(uxury)" << endl;
   cout << "Enter vehicle class => ";
→  cin  >> carClass;

   cout << "Enter amount of carbon monoxide emitted (grams) => ";
   cin >> coEmitted;
   cout << "Enter miles driven => ";
   cin >> miles;
                           . . .
```

Memory

```
  3.4
 MAXCO

   S
carClass

   ?
coEmitted

   ?
 miles

   ?
 coRate
```

Input/Output

```
C(ompact)  I(ntermediate)  S(tandard)  L(uxury)
Enter vehicle class => S
```

FIGURE 2.3   *(Continued)*

Program

```
int  main()
{
   char   carClass;  // first letter of vehicle class: Compact,
                     //    Intermediate, Standard, Luxury
   double coEmitted, // grams of carbon monoxide emitted
          miles;     // miles driven during test

   cout << "C(ompact)  I(ntermediate)  S(tandard)  L(uxury)" << endl;
   cout << "Enter vehicle class => ";
   cin  >> carClass;

→  cout << "Enter amount of carbon monoxide emitted (grams) => ";
→  cin >> coEmitted;
   cout << "Enter miles driven => ";
   cin >> miles;

   double coRate = coEmitted / miles; // g/mi of carbon monoxide emitted
   cout << "For class " << carClass <<
        " vehicle, carbon monoxide emission of " << coRate << " g/mi "
        << endl;

   if (coRate <= MAXCO)
       cout << "meets ";
   else
       cout << "exceeds ";

   cout << "permitted emission of " << MAXCO << " g/mi." << endl;
   return 0;
}
```

Memory

3.4
MAXCO

S
carClass

32.5
coEmitted

?
miles

?
coRate

Input/Output

```
C(ompact)  I(ntermediate)  S(tandard)  L(uxury)
Enter vehicle class => S
Enter amount of carbon monoxide emitted (grams) => 32.5
```

FIGURE 2.3 *(Continued)*

Program

```cpp
int  main()
{
   char   carClass;  // first letter of vehicle class: Compact,
                     //    Intermediate, Standard, Luxury
   double coEmitted, // grams of carbon monoxide emitted
          miles;     // miles driven during test

   cout << "C(ompact)  I(ntermediate)  S(tandard)  L(uxury)" << endl;
   cout << "Enter vehicle class => ";
   cin  >> carClass;

   cout << "Enter amount of carbon monoxide emitted (grams) => ";
   cin >> coEmitted;
→  cout << "Enter miles driven => ";
→  cin >> miles;

   double coRate = coEmitted / miles; // g/mi of carbon monoxide emitted
   cout << "For class " << carClass <<
        " vehicle, carbon monoxide emission of " << coRate << " g/mi "
        << endl;

   if (coRate <= MAXCO)
       cout << "meets ";
   else
       cout << "exceeds ";

   cout << "permitted emission of " << MAXCO << " g/mi." << endl;
   return 0;
}
```

Memory	
3.4	
MAXCO	
S	
carClass	
32.5	
coEmitted	
10.0	
miles	
?	
coRate	

Input/Output

```
C(ompact)  I(ntermediate)  S(tandard)  L(uxury)
Enter vehicle class => S
Enter amount of carbon monoxide emitted (grams) => 32.5
Enter miles driven => 10
```

FIGURE 2.3 *(Continued)*

Program

```cpp
int  main()
{
   char   carClass;  // first letter of vehicle class: Compact,
                     //    Intermediate, Standard, Luxury
   double coEmitted, // grams of carbon monoxide emitted
          miles;     // miles driven during test

   cout << "C(ompact)  I(ntermediate)  S(tandard)  L(uxury)" << endl;
   cout << "Enter vehicle class => ";
   cin  >> carClass;

   cout << "Enter amount of carbon monoxide emitted (grams) => ";
   cin >> coEmitted;
   cout << "Enter miles driven => ";
   cin >> miles;

   double coRate = coEmitted / miles; // g/mi of carbon monoxide emitted
   cout << "For class " << carClass <<
        " vehicle, carbon monoxide emission of " << coRate << " g/mi "
        << endl;

   if (coRate <= MAXCO)
       cout << "meets ";
   else
       cout << "exceeds ";

   cout << "permitted emission of " << MAXCO << " g/mi." << endl;
   return 0;
}
```

(arrow →) points to the line `double coRate = coEmitted / miles; // g/mi of carbon monoxide emitted`

Memory

3.4
MAXCO

S
carClass

32.5
coEmitted

10.0
miles

3.25
coRate

Input/Output

```
C(ompact)  I(ntermediate)  S(tandard)  L(uxury)
Enter vehicle class => S
Enter amount of carbon monoxide emitted (grams) => 32.5
Enter miles driven => 10
```

FIGURE 2.3   *(Continued)*

Program

```cpp
int  main()
{
   char    carClass;  // first letter of vehicle class: Compact,
                      //    Intermediate, Standard, Luxury
   double coEmitted,  // grams of carbon monoxide emitted
          miles;      // miles driven during test

   cout << "C(ompact)  I(ntermediate)  S(tandard)  L(uxury)" << endl;
   cout << "Enter vehicle class => ";
   cin  >> carClass;

   cout << "Enter amount of carbon monoxide emitted (grams) => ";
   cin >> coEmitted;
   cout << "Enter miles driven => ";
   cin >> miles;

   double coRate = coEmitted / miles; // g/mi of carbon monoxide emitted
   cout << "For class " << carClass <<
        " vehicle, carbon monoxide emission of " << coRate << " g/mi "
        << endl;

   if (coRate <= MAXCO)
       cout << "meets ";
   else
       cout << "exceeds ";

   cout << "permitted emission of " << MAXCO << " g/mi." << endl;
   return 0;
}
```

Memory

3.4
MAXCO

S
carClass

32.5
coEmitted

10.0
miles

3.25
coRate

Input/Output

```
C(ompact)  I(ntermediate)  S(tandard)  L(uxury)
Enter vehicle class => S
Enter amount of carbon monoxide emitted (grams) => 32.5
Enter miles driven => 10
For class 3 vehicle, carbon monoxide emission of 3.25 g/mi
```

and

```
cout << "exceeds ";
```

from which it selects one to execute. Consider the expression following the if keyword:

```
coRate <= MAXCO
```

This expression means that coRate is less than or equal to MAXCO. If this is true, the statement immediately following will be executed, and the statement following else will be skipped. If (coRate <= MAXCO) is not true, the statement following if will be skipped and the one following else will be executed. In the example traced in Fig. 2.3, the value of coRate is 3.25 and the constant MAXCO is 3.4. Since it is true that 3.25 is less than or equal to 3.4, the if selects for execution the statement

```
cout << "meets ";
```

Figure 2.4 shows the completed trace of the program.   ■

FIGURE 2.4 Trace of Selection Statement and Final Output of Carbon Monoxide Emissions Program

Program

```
int  main()
{
    char    carClass;    // first letter of vehicle class: Compact,
                         //    Intermediate, Standard, Luxury
    double coEmitted,    // grams of carbon monoxide emitted
           miles;        // miles driven during test

    cout << "C(ompact)  I(ntermediate)  S(tandard)  L(uxury)" << endl;
    cout << "Enter vehicle class => ";
    cin  >> carClass;

    cout << "Enter amount of carbon monoxide emitted (grams) => ";
    cin >> coEmitted;
    cout << "Enter miles driven => ";
    cin >> miles;

    double coRate = coEmitted / miles; // g/mi of carbon monoxide emitted
    cout << "For class " << carClass <<
            " vehicle, carbon monoxide emission of " << coRate << " g/mi "
            << endl;

 →  if (coRate <= MAXCO)
 →      cout << "meets ";
```

FIGURE 2.4 *(Continued)*

```
    else
        cout << "exceeds ";

    cout << "permitted emission of " << MAXCO << " g/mi." << endl;
    return 0;
}
```

Memory	Input/Output

Memory

3.4
MAXCO

S
carClass

32.5
coEmitted

10.0
miles

3.25
coRate

Input/Output

```
C(ompact)  I(ntermediate)  S(tandard)  L(uxury)
Enter vehicle class => S
Enter amount of carbon monoxide emitted (grams) => 32.5
Enter miles driven => 10
For class S vehicle, carbon monoxide emission of 3.25 g/mi
meets permitted emission of 3.4 g/mi.
```

Section 2.2 Review Questions

1. What do these statements display if the values input are 10 and 14?

```
cin >> num1;
cin >> num2;
if (num1 > num2)
    cout << "Sum of values = " << num1 + num2 << endl;
else
    cout << "Difference of values = " << num2 – num1 << endl;
```

2. What does this statement display if **a** is 8 and **b** is 4?

```
if (a < 3 * b)
    cout << a << " is less than " << 3 * b << endl;
else
    cout << a << " is greater than or equal to " << 3 * b << endl;
```

2.3 Input/Output Operations

In this section we examine the output operator << and the input operator >>. Here are two of the output statements we have seen so far:

```
cout << "C(ompact)  I(ntermediate)  S(tandard)  L(uxury)" << endl;
cout << "Enter vehicle class => ";
```

The name cout refers to the output stream associated with the program's standard output device, typically the screen. An **output stream** is a destination to which output is sent as a continuous stream of characters. The << operator inserts characters in an output stream, so it is called the **insertion operator**. The first output statement in the preceding display inserts 48 characters in the cout stream:

```
C(ompact)  I(ntermediate)  S(tandard)  L(uxury)<newline>
```

and then the next statement inserts an additional 24 characters in the stream, so the screen receives 72 characters. Notice that we have identified the character inserted by endl as **<newline>**. When this character is displayed on the screen, the cursor moves down to the beginning of a new line of output.

The second statement

```
cout << "Enter vehicle class => ";
```

does not insert endl in the output stream, so the cursor remains at the end of the output line, allowing the user to enter data on this same line. All characters entered by the user are automatically inserted in the cout output stream, and when the user types the Enter key, a newline character is inserted in the output stream.

Because the insertion of newline characters breaks the output stream into lines, several output statements can build a single line of output:

```
cout << "Carbon monoxide emission of " << coRate << " g/mi ";
cout << "meets ";
cout << "permitted emission standard." << endl;
```

Alternatively, one statement can build several lines of output:

```
cout << "One" << endl << "word" << endl << "per" << endl <<
   "line" << endl;
```

Just as C++ treats output as a continuous stream of characters, it also views the sequence of characters typed at the keyboard as a stream. Thus cin is the name of the input stream associated with the standard input device; typically the keyboard. The >> operator is called the **extraction operator** because it extracts one or more characters from the input stream for storage as

cout
name of the stream associated with the standard output device, usually the screen

output stream
an output destination for a continuous stream of characters

insertion operator (<<)
operator that inserts characters in an output stream

<newline>
a character whose insertion in an output stream causes the beginning of a new line of output

cin
name of the stream associated with the standard input device, usually the keyboard

extraction operator (>>)
operator that takes values from the input stream for storage in variables

a data value. The extraction operator expects that numeric values will be separated in the input stream by one or more blanks or newline characters. Single character values may or may not be separated by blanks. The extraction operator skips over blanks and newline characters when initially searching for a value. When the value needed is of type char, >> takes the first nonblank character encountered. If the value needed is a number, the extraction operator skips over any blanks and newline characters before taking the first group of nonblank characters encountered and trying to interpret this group as a number.

Consider these statements, which combine some code fragments used earlier:

```
cout << "Enter car class, amount of CO emitted, and miles driven => ";
cin >> carClass;
cin >> coEmitted;
cin >> miles;
```

The same values will be stored if the user enters the data in any of the following ways:

Three separate lines

```
S
32.5
10
```

All on one line

```
S 32.5 10
```

Spread over two lines

```
S       32.5
10
```

Each of these approaches to data entry results in a stream of input data in which the values S, 32.5, and 10 are separated by blanks, tabs, and/or newline characters.

We have seen output statements that make multiple insertions in the stream cout. Likewise, a single statement can extract multiple data values from an input stream. The single statement

```
cin >> carClass >> coEmitted >> miles;
```

has the same effect as the three-statement sequence

```
cin >> carClass;
cin >> coEmitted;
cin >> miles;
```

Section 2.3 Review Questions

1. Write a single statement that is equivalent to this sequence of statements. What is the output of these statements if `rate` is 50 and `time` is 2.5?

```
cout << "Distance = ";
cout << rate * time;
cout << " miles.";
cout << endl;
```

2. Write a sequence of statements that interact with the program user in this fashion:

```
Enter temperature (kelvin) => 302
Enter volume (liters) => 8.4
```

Your program fragment should store the first input value in variable `temp` and the second in variable `vol`.

2.4 Data Types

C++ programs manipulate data of many different types. The two most basic kinds of data are numbers and characters. In this section we examine how C++ represents characters and real numbers, and we study the arithmetic operators that C++ predefines.

Numbers

Like most programming languages, C++ defines two categories of numbers: integers and floating point numbers. **Floating point numbers** may have a fractional part and are represented in memory as two numbers, a binary fraction called the **mantissa** and an integer exponent.

The representation shown in Fig. 2.5 is comparable to scientific notation: For nonzero values, the mantissa and exponent are chosen so that the magnitude of the mantissa is between 0.5 and 1.0 and this formula is correct:

$$floating\ point\ number = mantissa \times 2^{exponent}$$

Because of the fixed size of the memory area reserved for a floating point value, not all real numbers can be precisely represented. For example, the base 10 fraction 0.1 is a repeating fraction in base 2 (just as 1/3 is 0.3333... in

floating point number
a number (that may have a fractional part) represented as a pair of numerals—a mantissa and an exponent

mantissa
the binary fraction that is part of a floating point number's representation

FIGURE 2.5 Internal Representation of a Floating Point Number

Mantissa	Exponent

base 10), so it cannot be represented exactly as a floating point number. The *representational error* depends on the number of bits (binary digits) used in the mantissa, but the value of the expression

```
0.1 + 0.1 + 0.1 + 0.1 + 0.1 + 0.1 + 0.1 + 0.1 + 0.1 + 0.1
```

will not equal exactly 1.0.

data type

a set of values and a set of operations defined on the values

A C++ **data type** is a set of values and a set of operations defined on those values. C++ provides three data types that represent floating point numbers: float, double, and long double. Floating point constants are written with decimal points, for example,

```
0.516
```

or with exponents, for example,

```
45e+2         or         15E-3
```

Reading the "e" or "E" as "times 10 to the power," we see that 45e+2 equals 45×10^2 (4500.0), and 15E-3 equals 15×10^{-3} (0.015). C++ defines the data type of these constants to be double, so we will use double as our basic type for floating point numbers. Table 2.1 shows the ranges for positive values of types float, double, and long double in a typical microprocessor-based C++ implementation. Positive values of type float range from 10^{-37} to 10^{37}. To understand how small 10^{-37} is, consider the fact that the mass of one electron is approximately 10^{-27} grams, and 10^{-37} is one ten-billionth of 10^{-27}. The enormity of 10^{37} may be clearer when you realize that if you multiply the diameter of the Milky Way galaxy in kilometers by a trillion, your numeric result is just 10^{34}.

C++ represents integers as binary numbers, so the range of values possible depends on the number of bits in the memory area. Table 2.2 shows the ranges of values represented by C++'s six integer data types: short, int, long, unsigned short, unsigned, and unsigned long. The data types that can represent negative numbers use the most significant bit (the leftmost bit) of the memory cell for the sign bit. This bit is used for magnitude in the unsigned types. Integer constants are written with no decimal point and no exponent:

```
100       -84       0       +25
```

TABLE 2.1 Floating Point Types in C++

Type	Approximate Range*	Significant Digits
float	$10^{-37} .. 10^{38}$	6
double	$10^{-307} .. 10^{308}$	15
long double	$10^{-4931} .. 10^{4932}$	19

*Range in a typical microprocessor implementation

TABLE 2.2 Integer Types in C++

Type	Range in Typical Microprocessor Implementation
short	−32,767 . . 32,767
unsigned short	0 . . 65,535
int	−2,147,483,647 . . 2,147,483,647
unsigned	0 . . 4,294,967,295
long	−2,147,483,647 . . 2,147,483,647
unsigned long	0 . . 4,294,967,295

C++ defines these constants to be of data type int, so we will use int as our basic integer type.

One fundamental advantage of using an integer data type is that any value within the type's range is always represented exactly; there is no representational error.

Numeric Error

Data type double is an abstraction for real numbers, and int is an abstraction for integers: They model these concepts, but in a simplified form. Just as the finite size of a type double mantissa limits the precision of the number, the finite size of the exponent limits the range of the number. Similarly, the finite size of an int limits the range of values representable. When an arithmetic operation yields a result too large or too small to be represented by the expression's data type, **arithmetic overflow** or **underflow** occurs. Typically this type of error is not detected at run-time and a program will consequently produce incorrect results. For example, overflow of an integer variable will frequently change the sign bit, so what should be a large positive result will be displayed as a negative number.

arithmetic overflow (underflow)
an attempt to represent a value too large (small) for the data type's range

Cancellation error occurs when addition of a tiny fraction (y) to a large number (x) yields a result equal to x because the finite precision of the representation does not accommodate all the significant digits of the result. For example, if the value of x is 5.21e+10 (52,100,000,000) both before *and after* the following statement stores the sum of x and 0.0025 in x,

cancellation error
addition of two values of greatly different magnitudes yielding a sum equal to the larger value

```
x = x + 0.0025;
```

then cancellation error has occurred.

Characters

C++ represents character values as numeric codes. A variable of data type char can store a single character. To represent a character constant in a program, we enclose the character in single quotes (apostrophes):

```
'A'      'b'      ' '      ';'
```

A few character constants are represented by an escape sequence enclosed in apostrophes. For example:

`'\n'`   newline character

`'\t'`   tab character

`'\f'`   formfeed character that means "finish this page and start a new one"

`'\r'`   return character that means "go back to column 1 of current output line"

`'\b'`   backspace character

`'\\'`   backslash character

`'\''`   single quote character

When you enter data to be scanned by a program, do not enclose characters in quotes.

character set

a set of binary numbers that encode the acceptable characters for a particular computer system

The numeric character codes used by a particular C++ implementation depend on the host computer. Appendix I shows two common **character sets**. The American Standard Code for Information Interchange (ASCII) uses consecutive codes from 65 through 90 for uppercase letters, codes from 97 through 122 for lowercase letters, and code values from 48 through 57 for the digit characters `'0'` to `'9'`. In both character sets the following relations are true, although in EBCDIC letters are not all consecutive codes.

```
'0' < '1' < '2' < '3' < ... < '9'
'A' < 'B' < 'C' < 'D' < ... < 'Z'
'a' < 'b' < 'c' < 'd' < ... < 'z'
```

ASCII characters fall into two categories: printable characters (codes 32–126) and control characters such as those that ring the bell, start a new page, move down to a new line, or move to the beginning of a line.

Since characters are represented by integer codes, C++ permits conversion of type char to type int and vice versa. For example, you could use the following fragment to find out the code your implementation uses for a question mark:

```
int qmarkCode = '?';
cout << "Code for ? = " << qmarkCode << endl;
```

Logical Values

C++ defines a data type named bool that has only two possible values—true and false. This is the type of the conditional expressions, such as x > 100 and y < = 0, that we will study in Chapter 3. Sometimes a program uses a variable of type bool to keep track of whether a certain event has occurred. The variable will be initialized to false, and after the event occurs the variable will be set to true.

FIGURE 2.6 Use of String Variables

```cpp
#include <iostream>
#include <string>
using namespace std;

const string LabelSentence = "Sentence Order";
const string LabelList = "\tList Order\n";
int main()
{
    string first, last, middle;
    cout << "Enter your full name with spaces between first and "
        << "middle\nand between middle and last => ";
    cin >> first >> middle >> last;
    cout << LabelSentence << '\t' << LabelList;
    cout << first << ' ' << middle << ' ' << last << "\t\t"
        << last << ", " << first << ' ' << middle << endl;
    return 0;
}
```

Sample Run

```
Enter your full name with spaces between first and middle
and between middle and last => Jeri Marie Ryan
Sentence Order         List Order
Jeri Marie Ryan        Ryan, Jeri Marie
```

Strings

One of the C++ standard libraries provides a data type string to represent a group of characters. Use of this data type requires inclusion of the preprocessor directive

```cpp
#include <string>
```

String variables and name constants are declared, initialized, input, and displayed in a manner comparable to numbers and characters, as demonstrated in Figure 2.6. Notice that you must use double quotes to enclose a string's value in a program, and you may include any of the special characters discussed earlier.

Section 2.4 Review Questions

Questions 1–3 are C++ program fragments along with the output they generate in one C++ implementation. Identify the error that has occurred in each.

Output

```
1. short n1 = 3000;
   short n2 = 30000;
   short sum = n1 + n2;
   cout << n1 << " + " << n2 <<            3000 + 30000 = -32536
      " = " << sum << endl;
2. float x1 = 35e+9;
   float x2 = 5e-6;
   float sum = x1 + x2;
   cout << x1 << " + " << x2 <<            3.5e+10 + 5e-06 = 3.5e+10
      " = " << sum << endl;
3. string message;
   if (0.2 + 0.2 + 0.2 + 0.1 + 0.05 == 0.75
                    // == means "is equal to"
      message = "Equal";
   else
      message = "Not equal";
   cout << message << endl;                Not equal
```

4. Which of the following values are legal **int**, **char**, **double**, or **bool** constants in C++? Indicate the type of each.

```
35    '-2'    '\n'    &    +13.2    9E-4    false    'Q'    .16    1456
```

2.5 Arithmetic Expressions

We have defined a data type as a set of values and a set of operations defined on these values. In Section 2.4 we considered the ranges of values that make up C++'s integer and floating point data types. Now we will study some of the operations defined for these data types.

In Figs. 2.1 and 2.2, we saw C++ programs that used the multiplication (*) and division (/) operators. In our section review questions we have used the C++ addition (+) and subtraction (–) operators. C++ also allows use of the minus sign as a negation operator. C++ defines these operators for all of its numeric types, but it defines the remainder operator (%) only for the integer types.

Multiple Operators

binary operator
operator that takes two operands

unary operator
operator that takes one operand

We evaluate C++ expressions that contain multiple operators in much the same way that we evaluate algebraic expressions. Table 2.3 defines the rules for evaluating expressions. **Binary operators** such as * take two operands: x * y; **unary operators**, such as negation, take one operand: –x.

Figure 2.7 illustrates these rules by evaluating step by step an expression containing several operators.

TABLE 2.3 Evaluation of Expressions

1. **Parentheses**	Evaluate parenthesized subexpressions first.
2. **Precedence**	Evaluate operators according to this precedence: (i) unary + unary − (ii) * / % (iii) binary + binary −
3. **Associativity**	If there is a sequence of two or more operators of the same precedence, evaluate unary operators right to left (right associativity) and binary operators left to right (left associativity).

As in algebraic expressions, it is legitimate to include in C++ expressions additional parentheses that do not affect the order of evaluation of the expression. For example, this expression is equivalent to the one evaluated in Fig. 2.7:

```
(p / (−q)) + ((r − s + t) * n)
```

Many software developers prefer to parenthesize subexpressions to improve the readability of complex subexpressions.

The value of a C++ arithmetic expression has a data type just as do variables and constants. If all of the operands of an expression are of the same data type, the expression's value is of that data type. Even the result of a division of two integers is an integer.

Operators / and %

When applied to integer operands, the operators / and % calculate the integer quotient and remainder, respectively. Figure 2.8 shows how 38 / 7 and 38 % 7 are calculated.

FIGURE 2.7 Step-by-Step Evaluation of p / −q + (r − s + t) * n

```
  n      p      q      r      s      t
10.0    4.8   −2.0    8.5   12.0    0.5
```

```
p / −q  +  (r − s + t) * n
              −3.5
                 −3.0
     2.0
     2.4
                    −30.0
        −27.6
```

Within parentheses, − and + are of the same precedence: apply left associativity.

Unary operators have highest precedence. / and * have same precedence: Apply left associativity.

+ has lowest precedence.

FIGURE 2.8 Integer Quotient and Remainder

$$
\begin{array}{r}
5 \leftarrow 38\ /\ 7 \\
7\overline{\smash{\big)}\,38} \\
35 \\
\hline
3 \leftarrow 38\ \%\ 7
\end{array}
$$

C++ requires that the value of n % m be nonnegative in all implementations if both n and m are nonnegative. If either n or m is negative, however, the sign of n % m varies depending on the implementation.

Mixed-Type Expressions

In an expression that has operands of both type `double` and type `int`, the expression result will be of type `double`. However, C++ still evaluates the expression operator by operator. For example, consider the expression

```
1.0 + 1 / 2
```

The first operator evaluated is /. Because its two operands are integers, integer division occurs, and the full step-by-step evaluation is

$$
\begin{array}{c}
1.0 + \dfrac{1\,/\,2}{} \\
\underline{0} \\
1.0
\end{array}
$$

The only mixed-type subexpression evaluated is 1.0 + 0, whose value is 1.0.

Some software developers prefer to avoid mixed-type expressions entirely. If your instructor asks you not to include mixed-type expressions in your programs, you will need to make frequent use of the explicit type conversion facility presented on the next page.

Assignment Statements

Like +, −, *, /, and %, the assignment operator (=) is a binary operator. It has lower precedence than any arithmetic operator, so in statements of the form

variable = expression;

the expression is fully evaluated first, and then the result is stored in *variable*. If the types of the expression value and *variable* are different, C++ converts the expression's value to *variable*'s data type before storing the value. For example,

```
int n = 35.5 − 0.6;
```

stores 34 in n, and

```
double q = 9 / 2;
```

stores 4.0 in q. The value of an assignment expression is the value assigned.

Automatic and Explicit Conversion of Data Types

We have encountered several cases in which data of one numeric type are automatically converted to another numeric type. Table 2.4 summarizes the automatic conversions we have seen. The variables in the table are declared and initialized as follows:

```
int k = 5, m = 4, n;
double x = 1.5, y = 2.1, z;
```

Avoiding Integer Division

In addition to automatic conversions, C++ also permits **explicit type conversions**. The program in Fig. 2.9 uses type conversions to prevent integer division. Because both totalScore and numStudents are of type int, evaluation of the expression

explicit type conversion
placing parentheses around the expression to convert and writing the desired type in front

```
totalScore / numStudents
```

would result in a loss of the fractional part of the average. Parenthesizing the value to be converted and placing the name of the desired type immediately in front causes the value to be changed to the desired data format before it is used in computation. Because this explicit conversion is a very high-precedence operation, it is performed before the division.

TABLE 2.4 Automatic Conversion of Numeric Data in C++

Context of Conversion	Example	Explanation
Expression with binary operator and operands of different numeric types	k + x value is 6.5	Value of int variable k is converted to type double format before operation is performed.
Assignment statement with type double target variable and type int expression	z = k / m; expression value is 1; value assigned to z is 1.0	Expression is evaluated first. Then the result is converted to type double format for assignment.
Assignment statement with type int target variable and type double expression	n = x * y; expression value is 3.15; value assigned to n is 3	Expression is evaluated first. Then the result is converted to type int format for assignment, and fractional part is lost.

FIGURE 2.9 Using Explicit Conversions to Prevent Integer Division

```
//
//   Computes a test average
//

#include <iostream>
using namespace std;

int  main()
{
     int totalScore;
     int numStudents;

     cout << "Enter sum of students' scores=> ";
     cin >> totalScore;
     cout << "Enter number of students=> ";
     cin >> numStudents;

     double average = double(totalScore) / double(numStudents);
     cout << "Average score is " << average << endl;
     return 0;
}
```

Although the program performs explicit conversions of both operands of the division operator in the expression in Fig. 2.9, explicitly converting only one would be sufficient because the rules for evaluation of mixed-type expressions would then cause the other to be converted as well. However, we could not achieve our goal by writing the expression as

```
double average = double(totalScore / numStudents);
```

In this case, the quotient totalScore / numStudents is computed first, resulting in the loss of the fractional part. The conversion to double simply changes this whole number quotient to type double format.

When an explicit conversion is applied to a variable, the operation carried out determines the value of the expression but does not change what is stored in the variable. For example, if x is a type double variable whose value is 5.4, the following statements will first display 5 and then display 5.4. The value of the expression

```
int(x)
```

is 5, but the value stored in x is still the floating point number 5.4.

Statements	*Output*
`cout << (int)x << endl;`	5
`cout << x << endl;`	5.4

Rounding

Converting a type `double` value to an `int` causes a loss of the value's fractional part. To round a positive value of type `double` to the nearest integer, add 0.5 before explicitly converting to an `int`:

$$
\begin{array}{r}
35.12 \\
+\ 0.5 \\
\hline
35.\cancel{62} \\
\end{array}
\qquad
\begin{array}{r}
35.51 \\
+\ 0.5 \\
\hline
36.\cancel{01} \\
\end{array}
$$

Section 2.5 Review Questions

1. Evaluate the following expressions step by step in the environment shown. Stop evaluation at any step where the result varies across implementations.

   ```
   double x = 14.5;
   double y = 11.0;
   double b, z;
   int  n = 9;
   int  m = 5;
   int  i, j, k;

   z = x - n / m;
   b = x * y + m / n * 2;
   i = int(x + 0.5);
   j = x * m - n % m;
   k = m / -n;
   ```

2. Repeat evaluation of the expressions in Question 1 given this environment.

   ```
   double x = 10.1;
   double y = 5.0;
   double b, z;
   int  n = 8;
   int  m = 2;
   int  i, j, k;
   ```

3. When used in this environment,

   ```
   double p, q, r;
   int    l, m;
   ```

each of the following statements contains at least one violation of the rules for writing arithmetic expressions. Correct these statements.

```
p = pqr;
q = 6(l - m);
```

4. Write the following formulas as C++ assignment statements using a minimum of parentheses:

$$\text{heat transfer: } q = \frac{kA(T_1 - T_2)}{L}$$

$$\text{cylinder volume: } V = \pi r^2 h$$

$$\text{relative error: } e = \frac{x - a}{x}$$

2.6 Additional Operators

C++ does not define operators for finding square roots, absolute values, or logarithms, or for raising numbers to a power. Instead, it provides predefined program units called **functions** that do these and other necessary calculations. The functions sqrt ($\sqrt{\ }$) and fabs (| |) are examples of predefined program units that carry out unary operations. To use such a function in an expression, write the function name followed by its single operand in parentheses. Figure 2.10 gives several examples.

function

a named unit of a program that performs a certain operation

A function can also implement a binary operator. For example, the C++ function pow implements exponentiation (raising a number to a power). The two operands are written in parentheses after the function name and are separated by a comma. Thus a C++ program represents x^y as

```
pow( x, y )
```

FIGURE 2.10 C++ Functions for Square Root and Absolute Value

To represent	Use this in C++
$\sqrt{x}$	sqrt(x)
$\sqrt{p-q}$	sqrt(p - q)
$\lvert y \rvert$	fabs(y)
$\lvert z \times r \rvert$	fabs(z * r)

FIGURE 2.11 Box Model of a Function

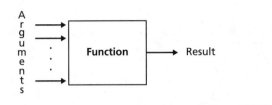

The operands of an operator implemented as a function are called the function **arguments**. These arguments can be any C++ expressions and they provide input to the function. Such a function can be modeled as in Fig. 2.11.

A function name followed by a parenthesized list of arguments is termed a **function call**. The **result** of the function is the value we substitute for the function call when evaluating a complex expression. Figure 2.12 shows a formula, its C++ representation, and a step-by-step evaluation for a given value of P.

A program that uses functions such as `sqrt`, `fabs`, and `pow` must have access to the C++ math library, a collection of predefined mathematical functions. The program includes the math library header file `<cmath>` as shown in the program in Fig. 2.13. The program rounds the flow estimate to the nearest cubic meter.

argument
a value or expression that provides input to a function

function call
a function name followed by a parenthesized list of arguments; can be used anywhere a value of the function's return type is legal

function result
value computed by a function

FIGURE 2.12 Writing and Evaluating a Formula in C++

Q = Business district firefighting flow rate estimate (m³/min)*
P = Population in 1000s

$$Q = 3.86 \sqrt{P} \left(1 - 0.01\sqrt{P}\right)$$

C++ Expression and Evaluation for $P = 100.0$

```
q  =  3.86  *  sqrt( p )  *  ( 1  -  0.01  *  sqrt( p ))
                                               ─────────────
                                                   10.0
                                         ──────────────────
                                              0.1
                                 ──────────────────────────
                                      0.9
              ─────────────
                  10.0
       ──────────────────
           38.6
              ──────────────────────────────────────────────
                         34.74
```

*George Tchobanoglous and Edward D. Schroeder, *Water Quality* (Reading, Mass.: Addison-Wesley, 1985), p. 14.

FIGURE 2.13 Firefighting Water Flow Rate Program

```
//
//  Estimate water flow rate needed for business district firefighting
//

#include <iostream>
#include <cmath>       // allows calls to sqrt
using namespace std;

int main()
{
   double population;  // city population
   double popThou;     // population in thousands
   int    flowEst;     // estimated water flow rate needed
                       //   (cubic meters per minute)

   cout << "What is your city's population?" << endl << "=> ";
   cin >> population;
   popThou = population / 1000;
   flowEst = int(0.5 +
           3.86 * sqrt( popThou ) * ( 1 - 0.01 * sqrt( popThou )));

   cout << "For business district firefighting, provide a water flow of"
        << endl << flowEst << " cubic meters per minute." << endl;
   return 0;
}

What is your city's population?
=> 130000
For business district firefighting, provide a water flow of
39 cubic meters per minute.
```

Predefined Functions and Code Reuse

code reuse

reusing units of code whose utility has already been thoroughly tested

Writing error-free code is a primary goal of software engineering. **Code reuse**—reusing, whenever possible, program fragments that have already been written and tested—is one way to accomplish this goal.

C++ promotes reuse by providing numerous library functions like sqrt that can be called to perform complicated mathematical computations. Table 2.5 lists the names and descriptions of some of the most commonly used

TABLE 2.5 Some Mathematical Library Functions

Function	Standard Header File	Purpose and Example	Argument(s)	Result
abs(x)	<cstdlib>	Returns the absolute value of its integer argument: if x is –12, abs(x) is 12	int	int
ceil(x)	<cmath>	Returns the smallest whole number that is not less than x: if x is 52.31, ceil(x) is 53.0	double	double
cos(x)	<cmath>	Returns the cosine of angle x: if x is 0.0, cos(x) is 1.0	double (radians)	double
exp(x)	<cmath>	Returns e^x where e = 2.71828...: if x is 1.0, exp(x) is 2.71828	double	double
fabs(x)	<cmath>	Returns the absolute value of its type double argument: if x is –5.732, fabs(x) is 5.732	double	double
floor(x)	<cmath>	Returns the largest whole number that is not greater than x: if x is 48.91, floor(x) is 48.0	double	double
log(x)	<cmath>	Returns the natural logarithm of x for x > 0.0: if x is 2.71828, log(x) is 1.0	double	double
log10(x)	<cmath>	Returns the base-10 logarithm of x for x > 0.0: if x is 100.0, log10(x) is 2.0	double	double
pow(x, y)	<cmath>	Returns x^y. If x is negative, y must be a whole number: if x is 0.25 and y is 0.5, pow(x, y) is 0.5	double, double	double
rand()	<cstdlib>	Returns a randomly chosen integer between 0 and the value of RAND_MAX, which is defined in <cstdlib>	no arguments	int
sin(x)	<cmath>	Returns the sine of angle x: if x is 1.5708, sin(x) is 1.0	double (radians)	double
sqrt(x)	<cmath>	Returns the nonnegative square root of x ($\sqrt{x}$) for x ≥ 0.0: if x is 6.25, sqrt(x) is 2.5	double	double
srand(x)	<cstdlib>	Initializes random number generator using x.	unsigned int	no result
tan(x)	<cmath>	Returns the tangent of angle x: if x is 0.0, tan(x) is 0.0	double (radians)	double

functions along with the name of the file to #include in order to gain access to each function. Most of the functions are in the cmath library, but those that handle integers are in the cstdlib library. A more extensive list of standard library functions appears in Appendix B.

If one of the functions in Table 2.5 is called with a numeric argument that is not of the argument type listed, C++ converts the value to the required type before using it. Conversions of integer types to floating point types cause no problems, but conversions of floating point types to integer types lead to the loss of any fractional part, just as in a mixed-type assignment. For example, if we call the abs function with the type double value −8.52, the result returned is the type int value 8. This result is the reason there is a separate absolute value function (fabs) for floating point arguments.

Most of the functions in Table 2.5 perform common mathematical computations. The arguments for log and log10 must be positive, and the arguments for sin, cos, and tan must be expressed in radians, not in degrees.

EXAMPLE 2.2   This formula is used to compute insulation resistance:

$$R = \frac{10^6 t}{C\left(\ln V_0 - \ln V\right)}$$

To write this formula in C++, we must use the log function from the math library.

```
#include <cmath>

    . . .

r = 1e+6 * t / (c * (log( v0 ) - log( v )));
```

Section 2.6 Review Questions

1. Consider an electric current i (amps) in a circuit containing a resistance R (ohms) and an inductance L (henrys). If $I = 0.5A$ is the current at $t = 0$, then under certain conditions, the time t (seconds) that it takes i to reach 0.05A can be calculated as

$$t = -\frac{L}{R} \ln \frac{i}{I}$$

Write this formula as a C++ assignment statement and evaluate it step by step for $R = 7.5\Omega$ and $L = 1.25H$.

2. Under certain conditions the efficiency (%) of an internal combustion engine can be computed from the compression ratio as

$$e = 100\left(1 - \frac{1}{R^{0.4}}\right)$$

Write this formula as a C++ assignment statement, and evaluate it step by step for $R = 6.55$.

2.7 Namespaces

A C++ **namespace** is a collection of identifiers such as names of functions, classes, and objects. In the simple programs we have seen so far, we have always followed our

```
#include <iostream>
```

directive by the directive

```
using namespace std;
```

The iostream library adds names such as `cout`, `cin`, and `endl` to the namespace called `std`. The directive

```
using namespace std;
```

allows our program to access all the names that are grouped as the collective named `std`.

An alternative to giving blanket access to all the names of a namespace is to specify only the names a program definitely intends to use. For example, the programs in this chapter refer only to these names from `std`: `cin`, `cout`, and `endl`. In each of the Chapter 2 programs, we could have replaced the general directive

```
using namespace std;
```

by three specific declarations:

```
using std::cin;
using std::cout;
using std::endl;
```

The larger the C++ program, the greater the likelihood that one may choose a name that conflicts with one of the names in `std`. For this reason, developers of large systems prefer the alternative of declaring from a namespace only the names that will actually by used.

This text consistently chooses the simpler

```
using namespace std;
```

However, be sure to check your professor's preference regarding which style you should use in programming assignments.

namespace
a collection of identifiers such as names of functions, classes, and objects

Section 2.7 Review Question

1. What is the minimal set of declarations of specific names from **std** with which you could replace the

   ```
   using namespace std;
   ```

directive in the brief program below?

```
// Create a title page

#include <iostream>
using namespace std;

int main()
{
    cout << "\n\n\n\n\n\n\n\n      Nesting Habits of Bats\n"
         << "                     by John Z. Doe\n"
         << "                     September 20, 2002\f";
    return 0;
}
```

2.8   Software Designer Beware

debugging

detecting, locating, and correcting errors in software

It is a fact of life in computer programming that much of a programmer's time is spent **debugging** the program—detecting and eliminating errors. Early programmers coined the term "debug" after they solved a malfunction of the ENIAC (the first large-scale digital computer) by removing an insect stuck in its circuitry! Some program errors are detected by the compiler, others show up as the program runs, and still others are detectable only through careful examination of program results.

Table 2.6 defines three major categories of errors and indicates which software can help find each error. Most C++ program development environments include **debugger software** that enables users to run a program one statement at a time (single-step execution), to run a program in segments by setting breakpoints where execution will pause, and to observe how the values of variables and expressions change during execution.

debugger software

program that allows a developer to execute a program one statement at a time or in segments up to selected breakpoints, and to observe the effect of each step/segment on program variables and output

Syntax Errors

Although a C++ compiler marks all violations of C++ syntax, the point at which an error is detected may not be precisely where the error occurred. For example, consider Table 2.7's list of errors you might make in typing the initial portion of the sulfur dioxide emissions program (see Fig. 2.14).

Sometimes a single syntax error can be responsible for several error messages. Always correct the first error marked by the compiler and then recompile the program before working on the second error.

Run-Time Errors

A run-time error occurs when a program asks the computer to carry out an illegal or undefined operation such as dividing by zero or taking the square

TABLE 2.6   Kinds of Errors

Error Category	Definition	Examples	Software to Use
Syntax	A violation of the grammar (syntax) rules of the programming language	Omitting a ; at the end of a statement Not declaring a variable Not closing braces {} or parentheses	C++ compiler: detects and marks all violations of C++ syntax
Run-time	An instruction that calls for the computer to perform an illegal operation	Dividing a number by zero Using up all available memory	Debugger software: single-step execution until error message appears
Logic	Program runs to completion but output contains an incorrect result	Algorithm is poorly designed Integer division is used unintentionally	Debugger software: watch evaluation of expressions that contribute to result

root of a negative number. A program might also request more memory than is actually available. Most such errors cause execution of the program to terminate immediately. To discover the statement that is calling for the illegal operation, use the debugger software to execute your program one step or one segment at a time until the error message appears. Then set up the debugger to display the values of all the variables used in the last statement executed, and rerun the program.

TABLE 2.7   Syntax Error Detection

	Error	Where Compiler Detects Error
❶	Omission of `using namespace std;`	First use of a symbol defined in namespace std—here it is the first use of `cout`.
❷	Neglecting to capitalize the i in the declaration of `sampleId:` `int sampleid;`	The line where `sampleId` is first used: `cin >> sampleId;`
❸	Omission of the ; at the end of the statement that displays the second prompting message	After scanning the first symbol of the following line (`cin`)

FIGURE 2.14 First Part of Sulfur Dioxide Emissions Program (circled numbers are keyed to Table 2.7)

```cpp
//
//  Calculate sulfur dioxide emission rate for a coal sample - without
//  scrubbing and with scrubbing that is 80% effective
//

#include <iostream>
using namespace std;        ❶

const double OXIDATION_FACTOR = 2.0;  // oxidizing n pounds of sulfur
                    // produces about 2n pounds of sulfur dioxide
const double SCRUB_EFFICIENCY = 0.8;  // scrubbing combustion gases
                    // reduces sulfur dioxide emissions by 80%

int  main()
{
    int     sampleId;  ❷       // sample identification number
    double sulfurContent,      // % of sample that is sulfur
           energyContent;      // number of Btu per pound

    // Get data on coal sample
    cout << "Enter sample identification number => ";    //  ❶  detected
    cin >> sampleId;                                     //  ❷  detected
    cout << "What percent of the sample is sulfur? => "; ❸
    cin >> sulfurContent;                                //  ❸  detected
    cout << "How many Btu's of energy from one pound of the sample? => ";
    cin >> energyContent;
. . .
```

Logic Errors

Some of the most difficult errors to find are those that allow a program to run to completion but cause it to produce incorrect results. To avoid missing these errors, a programmer must predict correct output for each set of test data. Figure 2.15 is an example of a program that runs to completion and displays incorrect results. By asking the debugger program to display all the program variables during execution, and by single-stepping through the program, you can quickly focus on the statement

```cpp
testFrac = testPct / 100;
```

FIGURE 2.15 Program That Produces Erroneous Results

```
//
// Calculate a student's grade based on weighted averages
//

#include <iostream>
using namespace std;

int main()
{
    int    testPct;
    int    hwPct;
    double testFrac;
    double hwFrac;
    double testAvg;
    double hwAvg;
    double overallAvg;

    cout << "Tests represent what percent of the grade? => ";
    cin >> testPct;
    testFrac = testPct / 100;
    cout << "What is your test average? => ";
    cin >> testAvg;
    cout << "Homework represents what percent of the grade? => ";
    cin >> hwPct;
    hwFrac = hwPct / 100;
    cout << "What is your homework average? => ";
    cin >> hwAvg;
    overallAvg = testAvg * testFrac + hwAvg * hwFrac;
    cout << "Overall course average = " << overallAvg << "%" << endl;
    return 0;
}

Tests represent what percent of the grade? => 60
What is your test average? => 91.5
Homework represents what percent of the grade? => 40
What is your homework average? => 95.2
Overall course average = 0%
```

which stores zero in `testFrac` rather than the desired `0.6`. The erroneous results are coming from the integer division of `testPct` by 100 and of `hwPct` by 100. Replacing both occurrences of 100 by `100.0` will quickly solve the problem.

Program Development to Simplify Debugging

You will find it easier to debug a program if you enter the implementation in stages. First, include in function `main` only the statements that prompt for and input the necessary data. Add statements that display these values and compile and run the code. Then, when this portion of the program runs correctly, add each step of the algorithm individually, including extra statements to display intermediate results, and rerun the code before adding the next step. Such step-by-step entry of the code and display of intermediate results are absolutely essential if you are working in an environment that does not provide debugger software.

Chapter Review

1. Every C++ program includes standard libraries and has a main function. The main function declares variables and executes statements to carry out an algorithm.

2. Variable names must begin with a letter or an underscore (the latter is not recommended) and consist of letters, digits, and underscore symbols. A keyword cannot be used as a variable name.

3. C++'s data types enable the compiler to determine how to store a particular value in memory and what operations can be performed on that value. Four of the C++ data types are `int`, `double`, `char`, and `bool`. The data type of each variable must be declared.

4. A C++ program that includes the preprocessor directive

   ```
   #include <string>
   ```

   can declare and use variables of type `string` to represent multiple-character values.

5. The executable statements encode a program's algorithm and are translated into machine language. Assignment statements are used to perform computations and store results in memory. The input extraction operator is used to get data, and the output insertion operator is used to display values.

6. Arithmetic expressions are composed of variables; constants; the arithmetic operators =, –, *, and /; explicit type conversions, and calls to mathematical functions such as `sqrt` and `abs` from libraries cmath and cstdlib.

7. An `if–else` statement chooses one of two alternative statements to execute.

▨ New C++ Constructs ▨

Construct	Effect
#include and using Directives	
`#include <iostream>` `using namespace std;`	Gives the program access to the header file for the standard I/O library. The header file includes information about the input extraction and output insertion operators and adds definitions of streams `cout` and `cin` to namespace `std`.
Constant Declaration	

`const double PI`
`  = 3.141592654;`
`const char STAR = '*';`
	Establishes 3.141592654 as the value of `PI` and `*` as the value of `STAR`. Executable statements cannot later change the values associated with these names.

Main Function Heading	
`int main ()`	Marks the start of the function where program execution begins, and states that `main` will return an `int` value.
Variable Declaration	

`double pct, wt;`
`char code;`
`int high = 5000,`
`  mid, low = 0;`
	Allocates memory cells named `pct` and `wt` for storage of double-precision real numbers, a cell named `code` for storage of a single character, and cells named `high`, `mid`, and `low` for storage of integers. Variable `high` is given an initial value of 5000 and `low` an initial value of 0. Other variables are left uninitialized.

Assignment Statement	
`distance =` `  velocity * time;`	Stores the product of `velocity` and `time` as the value of the variable `distance`.
Selection Statement	

`if (temperature <= 32)`
`  cout << "Roads icy\n";`
`else`
`  cout << "Roads wet\n";`
	Selects whether to output "Roads icy" or "Roads wet" based on the value of the variable `temperature`.

Input Extraction Operations	
`cin >> pct >> high;`	Copies input data from the keyboard into the variables `pct` and `high`.

Output Insertion Operations

`cout << "Percentage is "` `<< pct << endl;`	Displays a line with the string "Percentage is " followed by the value of `pct`.

Return Statement

`return 0;`	Final statement of function `main`—returns the integer value zero.

PROGRAMMING PROJECTS

1. Write a program that calculates the acceleration (m/s²) of a jet fighter launched from an aircraft-carrier-based catapult, given the jet's takeoff speed in km/hr and the distance (meters) over which the catapult accelerates the jet from rest to takeoff. Assume constant acceleration. Also calculate the time (seconds) for the fighter to be accelerated to takeoff speed. When you prompt the user, be sure to indicate the units for each input. For one run, use a takeoff speed of 278 km/hr and a distance of 94 meters.

   Relevant formulas (v = velocity, a = acceleration, t = time, s = distance)

   $$v = at$$
   $$s = \tfrac{1}{2} at^2$$

2. Write a program to assist in the design of a hydro-electric dam. Prompt the user for the height of the dam and for the number of cubic meters of water that are projected to flow from the top to the bottom of the dam each second. Predict how many megawatts (MW—1MW=10^6W) of power will be produced if 90% of the work done on the water by gravity is converted to electrical energy. Note that the mass of one cubic meter of water is 1000 kg. Use 9.80 meters/second² as the gravitational constant g. Be sure to use meaningful names for both the gravitational constant and the 90% efficiency constant. For one run, use a height of 170 m and flow of 1.30×10^3 m³/s. The relevant formula (w = work, m = mass, g = gravity, h = height) is $w = mgh$

3. Write a program that estimates the temperature in a freezer (in °C) given the elapsed time (hours) since a power failure. Assume this temperature (T) is given by

   $$T = \frac{4t^2}{t+2} - 20$$

   where t is the time since the power failure. Your program should prompt the user to enter how long it has been since the start of the power failure in whole hours and minutes. Note that you will need to convert the elapsed time into hours. For example, if the user entered 2 30 (2 hours 30 minutes), you would need to convert this to 2.5 hours.

4. Write a program that calculates the speed of sound (a) in air of a given temperature T (°F).

Use the formula: $a = 1086ft / s \sqrt{\dfrac{5T + 2297}{2457}}$

Be sure your program does not lose the fractional part of the quotient in the formula shown.

5. A manufacturer wishes to determine the cost of producing an open-top cylindrical container. The surface area of the container is the sum of the area of the circular base plus the area of the outside (the circumference of the base times the container height). Write a program to take the radius of the base, the height of the container, the cost per square centimeter of the material, and the number of containers to be produced. Calculate the cost of each container and the total cost of producing all the containers.

6. Write a program to take a depth (in kilometers) inside the earth as input data; compute and display the temperature at this depth in degrees Celsius and degrees Fahrenheit. The relevant formulas are:

$celsius = 10 \, (depth) + 20$ (Celsius temperature at depth in km)
$fahrenheit = 1.8 \, (celsius) + 32$

7. Write a program that predicts the score needed on a final exam to achieve a desired grade in a course. The program should interact with the user as follows:

```
Enter desired grade=> B
Enter minimum average required for a B=> 79.5
Enter your current average in the course=> 74.6
Enter how much the final counts as a percentage
of the course grade=> 25
```

You need a score of 94.20 on the final to get a B.

In this example, the final counts 25% of the course grade.

8. Write a program that calculates how many Btu's of heat are delivered to a house given the number of gallons of oil burned and the efficiency of the house's oil furnace. Assume that a barrel of oil (42 gallons) has an energy equivalent of 5,800,000 Btu. (*Note:* This number is too large to represent as an int on some personal computers.) For one test, use an efficiency of 65% and 100 gallons of oil.

9. Metro City Planners, Inc. proposes that a community conserve its water supply by replacing all the community's toilets by low-flush models that use only 2 liters per flush. Assume that there is about 1 toilet for every 3

persons, that existing toilets use an average of 15 liters per flush, that a toilet is flushed an average of 14 times per day, and that the cost to install each new toilet is $150. Write a program that would estimate the magnitude (liters/day) and cost of the water saved based on the community's population.

10. The ratio between successive speeds of a six-speed gearbox (assuming the gears are evenly spaced to allow for whole teeth) is

$$\sqrt[5]{M/m}$$

where M is the maximum speed in revolutions per minute and m is the minimum speed. Write a program that calculates this ratio for any maximum and minimum speeds.

Control Structures

3

C++ has a variety of control structures that allow programmers to selectively execute or to repeat sections of a program. This chapter presents these structures along with the operators needed to write expressions that describe the conditions for selecting or repeating a group of statements.

3.1 Three Essential Structures

Programming languages must provide three essential **control structures**, language constructs that determine which statements to execute and in what order to execute them. Table 3.1 summarizes the C++ structures in each category. **Sequential execution**, carrying out statements in the order in which they appear, is the default control structure; that is, statements execute sequentially unless one of the other control structures causes a change in the sequence. C++ programs begin with the first statement in main and execute succeeding statements sequentially unless another control structure is encountered. **Selection** structures choose one of several alternatives based on a condition. A selection structure executes the chosen alternative exactly once and skips the other alternatives. A **repetition** structure repeats a section of code as long as a certain condition is true.

So far we have seen programs using only two types of control structures: sequential control and selection. In the next section you will learn to write the conditions that are required in all selection and repetition control structures except the switch statement. Subsequent sections explore how to use each of the selection structures, both separately and in combination with other structures. Chapter 4 will focus on repetition structures.

TABLE 3.1 Summary of C++ Control Structures

Sequential

Statements are executed in the order in which they appear.	$statement_1$ $statement_2$ $statement_3$
A compound statement or block is a sequence of statements enclosed in braces.	{ $statement_1$ $statement_2$ . . . $statement_n$ }

Selection

One of several alternatives is selected based on a condition.

if statement: If *condition* is true, $statement_1$ is executed; otherwise $statement_1$ is skipped.	if (*condition*) $statement_1$

if–else statement: If *condition* is true, $statement_1$ is executed; otherwise $statement_1$ is skipped and $statement_2$ is executed.	if (*condition*)
	    $statement_1$
	else
	    $statement_2$

TABLE 3.1 *(Continued)*

switch statement: Value of *control* is compared to each label in turn; the statements following the matching label (up to `break;`) are executed and all others are skipped. The statements after `default:` are executed only if no label matches.	```switch (control) {``` `case label`$_{11}$`:` `case label`$_{12}$`:` . . . `case label`$_{1n}$`:` *statements*$_1$ `break;` `case label`$_{21}$`:` `case label`$_{22}$`:` . . . `case label`$_{2n}$`:` *statements*$_2$ `break;` . . . `case label`$_{n1}$`:` `case label`$_{n2}$`:` . . . `case label`$_{nn}$`:` *statements*$_n$ `break;` `default:` *statements*$_d$ `}`

Repetition

On the basis of the value of a condition, a statement or group of statements is executed one or more times or is skipped entirely.

while statement: As long as *condition* is true, *statement* is executed.	`while (condition)` *statement*
for statement: First, *init* is executed; then as long as *condition* is true, *statement* followed by *update* is repeatedly executed.	`for (init;` *condition*`;` *update*`)` *statement*
do-while statement: First, *statement* is executed once. Then, as long as *condition* is true, *statement* is repeatedly executed.	`do` *statement* `while (condition);`

Section 3.1 Review Questions

1. Classify each marked structure as sequential, selection, or repetition. The symbol == means "is equal to"; >= means "is greater than or equal to."

```
int main()
{
    int num, trial, div;

    cout << "Enter an integer=> ";
    cin >> num;

    if (num % 2 == 0)
        div = 2;
    else
        div = 0;
❶
    trial = 3;
    while (div == 0) {

        if (num % trial == 0)
            div = trial;
        else if (trial >= num / 2)
            div = num;
        else
❷          trial = trial + 2;
    }
❸   cout << "Result = " << div << endl;
    return 0;
}
❹
```

2. Consider the problem statements that follow. For each, indicate whether you would use sequential control only, or whether you would also need selection and/or repetition.

   a. Write a program that adds up a list of numbers entered by the user.

   b. Write a program that gets from the user the weight and mass of an object and displays a message stating whether or not the object is on earth.

   c. Write a program that prompts the user for a quantity (in moles) of oxygen along with its kelvin temperature and volume (in liters) and displays the pressure of the gas in atmospheres.

3.2 Conditions

The carbon monoxide emissions program of Chapter 2 uses the selection statement

```
if (coRate <= MAXCO)
    cout << "meets ";
else
    cout << "exceeds ";
```

to display either the word `meets` or the word `exceeds`. Which word is displayed depends on the value of the expression following the reserved word `if`:

`coRate <= MAXCO`

This is an example of a **condition**, an expression that is either true or false. Thus the value of a condition is of type `bool`. The condition

condition

expression that is true or false

`coRate <= MAXCO`

uses the relational operator `<=`, which means "less than or equal to." Table 3.2 shows `<=` and C++'s other relational operators along with the equality operators `==` (equals) and `!=` (does not equal).

The operators in Table 3.2 can compare both numeric and character values. We saw in Section 2.4 that each character is represented by an integer code, so a comparison of two characters is a comparison of their character codes. In a comparison of two capital letters, the letter nearer the beginning of the alphabet has the lower code; that is, the condition

`'A' < 'B'`

is true. Similarly, when comparing two lowercase letters, "less than" represents "earlier alphabetically." In a comparison of two digit characters, the lower digit has the lower character code, so the condition

`'0' < '1'`

is true. The relationships between the character codes for lowercase letters, uppercase letters, and digits depend on the character set used by a particular C++ implementation.

TABLE 3.2 C++ Relational and Equality Operators

kIce 273	kTemp 250	init 'J'	pressure 37.2	MAX_PRESSURE 38.5
Operator	Meaning		Example	Value
<	less than		pressure < MAX_PRESSURE	true
<=	less than or equal to		kTemp <= kIce	true
>	greater than		init > 'K'	false
>=	greater than or equal to		250 >= kTemp	true
==	equals		init == 'Q'	false
!=	does not equal		kIce != kTemp	true

TABLE 3.3 Multiple-Operator Conditions

Condition	Meaning
m * n > 0	The product of m and n is positive.
a + b <= c	The sum of a and b is less than or equal to c.
q % r == 0	r divides q evenly.

Table 3.3 shows some multiple-operator conditions along with their English meanings.

Logical Operators

Some conditions are too complicated to write with just arithmetic, relational, and equality operators. For example, you might need to check whether the value of n is between zero and 100. Mathematically, this expression would be

$$0 \leq n \leq 100$$

However, the symbol-by-symbol C++ translation,

```
0 <= n <= 100
```

does not have the same meaning. The C++ expression shown will likely trigger a warning from your compiler. If you ignore the warning (rarely advisable!) and execute the code, the expression will always have a value of true. The first part of the expression, 0 <= n, evaluates either to false or to true. Because of the C heritage of C++, type bool values can legally be converted to type int: false is converted to 0 and true to 1. Both values are less than 100. To correctly express the condition $0 \leq n \leq 100$ we need both the expressions 0 <= n and n <= 100 to be true simultaneously. C++ provides the logical operator && (pronounced "and") for this situation. Thus $0 \leq n \leq 100$ is correctly expressed in C++ as

```
0 <= n && n <= 100
```

To evaluate this expression, we must know the precedence of the relational and logical operators. Table 3.4 shows the precedence of these new operators along with the previously studied arithmetic and assignment operators. The table lists the operators from highest to lowest precedence.

Tables 3.5 to 3.7 show the values of expressions using && as well as the values of expressions using the other C++ logical operators: || ("or") and ! ("not"). The && and || operators require two operands. A condition using && is true only if both operands are true. A condition using || is false only if both operands are false. The negation operator ! takes one operand. If the operand is false, negating it gives a true result; if the operand is true, negating it gives a false result.

TABLE 3.4 Precedence of Operations

Operation	Precedence
function calls explicit type conversions	highest (evaluated first)
! unary + unary –	
binary * / %	
binary + binary –	
< > <= >=	
== !=	
&&	
||	
=	lowest (evaluated last)

TABLE 3.5 && Operator

operand1	operand2	operand1 && operand2 (read operand1 **and** operand2)
false	false	false
false	true	false
true	false	false
true	true	true

TABLE 3.6 \|\| Operator

operand1	operand2	operand1 || operand2 (read operand1 **or** operand2)
false	false	false
false	true	true
true	false	true
true	true	true

TABLE 3.7 ! Operator

operand1	!operand1 (read **not** operand1)
false	true
true	false

Variables of Type bool

Sometimes a program needs to keep track of whether a certain event has occurred or a certain condition has been met. We use variables of type bool for these situations. For example, if an employee is eligible for early retirement when the sum of his or her age and years of service is greater than 85, we could use the type `bool` variable `eligible` as shown in this program fragment:

```
bool eligible;
int  age, yearsService;
...
if ((age + yearsService) > 85)
     eligible = true;
else
     eligible = false;
```

Actually, we don't even need an `if` statement to assign the correct value to `eligible`. This assignment statement is equivalent to the `if–else`:

```
eligible = (age + yearsService) > 85;
```

Table 3.8 lists several examples of complicated conditions formed using logical and relational operators and numeric and boolean variables. Condition 1 of Table 3.8 might be used to determine whether a city would allow wood burning on a certain day. Figure 3.1 shows step-by-step evaluation of expression 1 when `pollutionIndex` is 3, `GOOD_CUTOFF` is 2, `windSpeed` is 10 and `LIGHT_BREEZE` is 5. Notice that not all the steps shown in Fig. 3.1 are actually necessary. The result of an `&&` operation is true only when both operands are true, so Step 2 was unnecessary. In fact, C++ would skip evaluation of `windSpeed > LIGHT_BREEZE`. Evaluating only as much of an expression as is necessary to know the result is called **short-circuit evaluation**.

short-circuit evaluation

evaluating only as much of a logical expression as is needed to determine its value

Expression [2] of Table 3.8 demonstrates the use of a type `bool` variable to represent the occurrence of an event or some other logical concept. Setting the variable `buildingCodeOK` to true indicates that building code provisions have been met; setting it to false means that some provisions have not been met. Expression [2] might be used to determine whether to call for an annual

TABLE 3.8 Complicated Logical Expressions

Condition	Possible English Paraphrase
[1] `pollutionIndex < GOOD_CUTOFF && windSpeed > LIGHT_BREEZE`	Pollution index is within "good" air quality range and there is some wind.
[2] `!buildingCodeOK || yearConstructed < 1980`	There are violations to the building code or construction predates 1980.
[3] `5.5 <= pH && pH <= 6.5`	pH is between 5.5 and 6.5 (inclusive): solution is mildly acidic.
[4] `!(temperature >= 68 && temperature <= 80)`	Temperature is outside tourist comfort range.

FIGURE 3.1 Step-by-Step Evaluation of Condition [1] from Table 3.8

```
       pollutionIndex < GOOD_CUTOFF  &&  windSpeed > LIGHT_BREEZE
             3               2              10             5
   ┌─────────────────────────────┐
1  │           false             │   ┌─────────────────────────────┐
2  │                             │   │           true              │
   └─────────────────────────────┘   └─────────────────────────────┘
3  ┌───────────────────────────────────────────────────────────────┐
   │                          false                                 │
   └───────────────────────────────────────────────────────────────┘
```

FIGURE 3.2 Step-by-Step Evaluation of Condition [2] from Table 3.8

```
       ! buildingCodeOK  ||  yearConstructed < 1980
              false
          ┌─────────────┐
1         │    true     │
2         │             │                short-circuited
          └─────────────┘
3  ┌───────────────────────────────────────────────┐
   │                    true                        │
   └───────────────────────────────────────────────┘
```

structural inspection of a public building. Figure 3.2 shows evaluation of Expression [2] when `buildingCodeOK` is false and `yearConstructed` is 1985.

Complementing a Condition

We have seen that the ! operator can be used to complement or negate a logical expression. We can also complement simple comparisons by using a different operator. For example, here are two expressions that are complements of the condition

```
data < CUTOFF
```

Complement 1

```
! (data < CUTOFF)
```

Complement 2

```
data >= CUTOFF
```

We form Complement 1 by applying the negation operator ! to the original condition. In Complement 2, we have replaced the < operator by its complement, >=.

To complement a more complicated expression, we can always use the ! operator in front of the parenthesized expression. However, DeMorgan's Theorem presents a way to complement any expression by replacing operators. DeMorgan's Theorem and its dual are

! (A && B) is equivalent to !A || !B
! (A || B) is equivalent to !A && !B

When applying this theorem, use the following steps to ensure the correct order of evaluation.

> ### *Applying DeMorgan's Theorem to Complement an Expression*
>
> 1. If the expression uses both the operator && and the operator ||, parenthesize the subexpressions that use &&.
> 2. Replace each && by ||, each || by &&, and negate each subexpression either by using or removing the ! operator or by replacing each relational or equality operator by its complement (e.g., > by <=, != by ==, etc.).

Let's complement this condition

```
veteran || age >= 60 && salary < 10000
```

in which `veteran` is a type `bool` variable indicating whether or not an individual is a veteran.

Step 1: Add parentheses.

```
veteran || (age >= 60 && salary < 10000)
```

Step 2: Negate subexpressions, replacing operators

```
!veteran && (age < 60 || salary >= 10000)
```

The original condition is true either for a veteran or for anyone aged 60 or more whose salary is under 10000. The complement is true for non-veterans who are under 60 years old or earn at least 10000.

Section 3.2 Review Questions

1. Using the variables/constants declared here, write C++ expressions for each condition.

```
int            heatRemoved, workDone;
const double   MIN_PERFORMANCE = 4.0
const double   MAX_PRICE = 450.0;
double         price;
const double   LOW_COEFF = 3.5;
const double   HIGH_COEFF = 5.5;
double         measDepth, degCelsius;
const double   MIN_DEPTH = 10.0;
const double   MIN_TEMP = 120.0;
bool           precip;
bool           windy;
```

a. Refrigerator performance coefficient (heat removed divided by work done) is at least 4 (`MIN_PERFORMANCE`), and price is no more than $450.

b. Refrigerator performance coefficient (calculated without loss of fractional part) is between 3.5 (`LOW_COEFF`) and 5.5 (`HIGH_COEFF`) (inclusive).

c. Measured depth is greater than 10 kilometers (`MIN_DEPTH`) or Celsius temperature is more than 120° (`MIN_TEMP`).

d. There is no precipitation and it's not windy.

2. Show step-by-step evaluation of the expressions you wrote for Question 1 using these variable values. Indicate where evaluation is short-circuited.

heatRemoved	workDone	price	measDepth	degCelsius	precip	windy
480	125	447.00	11.2	100.0	false	true

3. Complement each of these conditions in two ways.

a. x >= 0 && x <= 100

b. age >= 18 && age <= 26 && eligible

c. height < 60 && weight < 2.9 * height ||
   veteran && weight < 3.1 * height

d. attractive || salary > 150000.00 || assets > 1000000.00

3.3 Selection and Repetition

The coal-quantity-analysis program in Fig. 3.3 demonstrates the use of all three basic control structures: sequential execution, selection, and repetition. The purpose of the program is to add a list of numbers, each of which represents the number of tons of coal carried by one train scheduled for arrival at a power plant on a certain day. After entering the coal tonnage for all the trains for that day, the program user enters a zero. The program then compares the total coal to the minimum required for one day of power plant operation and displays an appropriate message. We have labeled with appropriate terminology the aspects of the program that we studied in Chapter 2.

The program in Fig. 3.3 is essentially a sequence of these operations:

1. Add up trainloads scheduled for the day.
2. Display the total amount of coal expected.
3. Display a message indicating whether the total is sufficient or whether it falls short.

In this sequence we have two steps that are too complex for straightforward implementation in C++. Step 1 requires repetition of some substeps:

Refinement of Step 1

1.1 Prompt user to enter amount of first trainload.
1.2 Copy from keyboard the number of tons in first trainload.

FIGURE 3.3 Program Demonstrating Three Basic Control Structures

```
//  Determine if scheduled coal arrivals are sufficient to fuel
//  electric power plant for one day

#include  <iostream>
using namespace std;
```
← *Standard Library & Namespace Inclusion*

```
const int MIN_COAL_REQUIRED = 10000; // minimum tons of coal
                                     // necessary for one day
```
← *Constant Declaration*

```
int main()
```
← *Main Function Heading*

← *Variable Declarations*
```
{
    int trainLoad,       // tons of coal in current trainload
        totalCoal = 0;   // tons of coal counted so far
```

← *Comment*
```
    // Add up trainloads scheduled for the day.
    cout << "Number of tons in first trainload (or zero to quit) => ";
    cin >> trainLoad;
    while (trainLoad > 0) {
        totalCoal = totalCoal + trainLoad;
        cout << "Tons in next trainload (zero to quit) => ";
        cin >> trainLoad;
    }
```
Input Extraction → (from `cin >> trainLoad;`)
Output Insertion → (from `cout << "Number of tons...`)
Assignment Statement → (from `totalCoal = totalCoal + trainLoad;`)

```
    // Display the total amount of coal expected.
    cout << "Scheduled coal arrival total of " << totalCoal <<
        " tons " << endl;

    // Display a message indicating if the total is sufficient or if
    // it falls short.
    if (totalCoal >= MIN_COAL_REQUIRED)
        cout << "is sufficient for daily operation." << endl;
    else
        cout << "falls " << MIN_COAL_REQUIRED – totalCoal <<
            " tons short of daily need." << endl;
    return 0;
}
```
← *Return Statement* (from `return 0;`)

FIGURE 3.3   *(Continued)*

Run 1

```
Number of tons in first trainload (or zero to quit) => 2000
Tons in next trainload (zero to quit) => 1200
Tons in next trainload (zero to quit) => 1500
Tons in next trainload (zero to quit) => 1000
Tons in next trainload (zero to quit) => 1400
Tons in next trainload (zero to quit) => 1800
Tons in next trainload (zero to quit) => 1300
Tons in next trainload (zero to quit) => 0
Scheduled coal arrival total of 10200 tons
is sufficient for daily operation.
```

Run 2

```
Number of tons in first trainload (or zero to quit) => 1000
Tons in next trainload (zero to quit) => 1200
Tons in next trainload (zero to quit) => 1500
Tons in next trainload (zero to quit) => 1000
Tons in next trainload (zero to quit) => 1400
Tons in next trainload (zero to quit) => 1800
Tons in next trainload (zero to quit) => 1300
Tons in next trainload (zero to quit) => 0
Scheduled coal arrival total of 9200 tons
falls 800 tons short of daily need.
```

1.3 Repeat as long as the number of tons is greater than zero:
  1.4 Add number of tons to total so far.
  1.5 Prompt user to enter amount of next trainload.
  1.6 Copy from keyboard the number of tons in this trainload.

Step 1.3 repeats the sequence of steps 1.4, 1.5, 1.6 as long as the values input are greater than zero. Step 2 can be represented as a single C++ statement that sends output to cout, but Step 3 requires a decision to select one of two alternatives:

3.1 If the total coal is at least 10,000 tons
  3.2 Indicate that scheduled coal arrivals are sufficient for power plant operation.
  Otherwise
  3.3 Indicate by how much the total falls short of what is needed.

By writing statements like our numbered statements 1, 2, 3, and their refinements 1.1, 1.2, . . . , we can identify which control structures are needed in

pseudocode

language of structured English statements used in designing a step-by-step approach to solving a problem

our algorithms while still thinking about the problem in English. Such structured English statements are called **pseudocode**.

A comparison of the pseudocode and C++ versions of our repetition and selection control structures is given in Table 3.9. Notice that both control structures have a parenthesized condition immediately following the initial reserved word `if` or `while`. The value of the condition in the `while` statement may cause the sequence of statements that depend on the condition to be skipped if the condition is false after the first input. On the other hand, the statements may be repeated once, twice, or many times. In contrast, the statements within the `if–else` are executed at most once. If the condition after `if` is true, the statement displaying the "sufficient" message is executed. Otherwise, the "falls short" message is displayed.

Look carefully at the statements following the `while` condition. A `while` statement allows for repetition of only one statement. Because we want to repeat three statements, we enclose these statements in braces, forming a single compound statement. If we need to execute multiple statements dependent on the value of the condition in an `if`, we also enclose those statements in braces, using this indentation format:

```
if (condition) {
    statement₁
    statement₂
    . . .
    statementₙ
} else {
    statement₁
    statement₂
    . . .
    statementₙ
}
```

The indentation helps the reader to understand the structure of the code. However, the compiler ignores the indentation.

Section 3.3 Review Questions

Which of the following steps would be implemented with a repetition structure, and which with a selection structure?

1. Form the product of a list of 20 numbers.
2. Label a number as negative or nonnegative.
3. Display a table of the Fahrenheit temperatures –5, 0, 5, 10, 15, . . . , 220 and their Celsius equivalents.
4. Process a list of numbers, labeling each as even or odd.

TABLE 3.9 Comparison of Pseudocode and C++ Structures

Pseudocode	C++
1.3 Repeat as long as the number of tons is greater than zero:	`while (trainLoad > 0) {`
1.4 Add number of tons to total so far.	`totalCoal = totalCoal + trainLoad;`
1.5 Prompt user to enter amount of next trainload.	`cout <<` `    "Tons in next trainload (zero to quit) => ";`
1.6 Copy from keyboard the number of tons in this trainload.	`cin >> trainLoad;` `}`
3.1 If the total coal is at least 10,000 tons	`if (totalCoal >= MIN_COAL_REQUIRED)`

3.2 Indicate that scheduled coal arrivals are sufficient for power plant operation.	`cout <<`
	`    "is sufficient for daily operation."`
	`    << endl;`

Otherwise	`else`

3.3 Indicate by how much the total falls short of what is needed.	`cout << "falls " <<`
	`    MIN_COAL_REQUIRED - totalCoal <<`
	`    " tons short of daily need." << endl;`

3.4 Nested and Multiple-Alternative Selection Structures

Nested Structures

The two examples of selection structures that we have studied thus far have used if–else statements to select which of two messages to display. Sometimes, however, as in Example 3.1, we must choose among three or more messages, so a simple two-way selection is inadequate. Because any selection structure is a single statement, we can use a second decision as either the true or the false task of another selection statement. Study the following comparison:

Simple Selection Structure Format	Nested Selection Structure Format

```
if (condition)                                if (condition₁)
    "true" task: statement executed when "true"    ⎡ if (condition₂)
        condition is true        task for      ⎢      statement₁
                                 condition₁ ⎨ else
                                            ⎢      statement₂
                                            ⎣
else                                          else
    "false" task: statement executed "false"   ⎡ if (condition₃)
        when condition is false   task for     ⎢      statement₃
                                  condition₁ ⎨ else
                                             ⎢      statement₄
                                             ⎣
```

EXAMPLE 3.1   Manufacturing engineers calculate the homologous temperature of a metal, the ratio of the absolute temperature at which the metal is to be shaped (T) and the melting point of the metal (T_m). They use the homologous temperature in classifying metal-shaping processes as "cold working" ($T/T_m < 0.3$), "warm working" (T/T_m in the range 0.3 to 0.5), or "hot working" (higher values of T/T_m). Using the if–else structure, we could express this classification in pseudocode as

1. If homologous temperature is less than 0.3
    2. cold working process
   else
    3. If homologous temperature is less than or equal to 0.5
        4. warm working process
       else
        5. hot working process

Figure 3.4 shows a C++ implementation of this decision process. Notice that checking the second condition (tHomologous <= MaxWarmWorking) within the else section of the first if–else has the effect of verifying that tHomologous is between 0.3 and 0.5, even though there is no reference to MinWarmWorking in this second condition. However, if tHomologous were not at least 0.3, this condition would not even be evaluated, since the condition in the first if would be true. A control structure placed inside another is a **nested** structure: Figure 3.4 uses a nested if statement.

nested
placement of a control structure inside another control structure

Multiple-Alternative Structures

We have noted that C++ uses spacing and indentation of statements to assist the reader of the code but that the compiler ignores such spacing. By re-

FIGURE 3.4 Classification of Metal-Working Processes

```
//
// Classification of metal shaping process based on homologous
// temperature (ratio of working temperature to melting point
// of metal, both on the kelvin scale)
//

#include <iostream>
using namespace std;

const double MIN_WARM_WORKING = 0.3,
             MAX_WARM_WORKING = 0.5;

int main()
{
    double tWorking, tMelting, tHomologous;

    cout << "Enter working temperature (kelvin) => ";
    cin >> tWorking;
    cout << "Enter melting point of metal to be shaped (kelvin) => ";
    cin >> tMelting;

    tHomologous = tWorking / tMelting;
    cout << "Homologous temperature of " << tHomologous << " indicates ";

    if (tHomologous < MIN_WARM_WORKING)
        cout << "cold working process." << endl;
    else
        if (tHomologous <= MAX_WARM_WORKING)
            cout << "warm working process." << endl;
        else
            cout << "hot working process." << endl;
    return 0;
}

Enter working temperature (kelvin) => 550
Enter melting point of metal to be shaped (kelvin) => 1355
Homologous temperature of 0.405904 indicates warm working process.
```

spacing the nested `if` of Fig. 3.4, we would create this multiple-alternative `if` statement:

```
if (tHomologous < MIN_WARM_WORKING)
    cout << "cold working process." << endl;
else if (tHomologous <= MAX_WARM_WORKING)
    cout << "warm working process." << endl;
else
    cout << "hot working process." << endl;
```

A nested `if` can be replaced by a multiple-alternative `if` when new decisions fall within false tasks (on `else` branches). A decision that falls within a true task must be written as a nested `if`. Example 3.2 uses a long multiple-alternative `if` statement.

EXAMPLE 3.2   The pH of a solution is a measure of its acidity. Table 3.10 shows pH values and their meanings.

The program in Fig. 3.5 displays the acidity level that corresponds to a solution's pH. In the sample run, the user enters a pH value of 9. Table 3.11 traces how this value causes display of `Solution is alkaline`.

TABLE 3.10   pH Values and Meanings

pH Range	Solution is
$pH < 3$	very acidic
$3 \leq pH < 7$	acidic
$pH = 7$	neutral
$7 < pH < 12$	alkaline
$pH \geq 12$	very alkaline

FIGURE 3.5   Program to Display Solution's Acidity

```
//
//  Characterize a solution's acidity given its pH
//
#include <iostream>
using namespace std;

int main()
{
   int pH;   // pH of solution
```

FIGURE 3.5 *(Continued)*

```
   cout << "Enter pH of solution => ";
   cin >> pH;

   cout << "Solution is ";
   if (pH < 3)
      cout << "very acidic." << endl;
   else if (pH < 7)
      cout << "acidic." << endl;
   else if (pH == 7)
      cout << "neutral." << endl;
   else if (pH < 12)
      cout << "alkaline." << endl;
   else
      cout << "very alkaline." << endl;
   return 0;
}

Enter pH of solution => 9
Solution is alkaline.
```

TABLE 3.11 Trace of pH Program if Input is 9

Statement	Memory	Effect
	pH ?	
cout << "Enter pH of solution => ";		Displays prompting message.
cin >> pH;	9	Copies value from keyboard into pH.
cout << "Solution is ";		Displays first part of results line: Solution is
if (pH < 3)		9 < 3 is false.
else if (pH < 7)		9 < 7 is false.
else if (pH == 7)		9 == 7 is false.
else if (pH < 12)		9 < 12 is true.
cout << "alkaline."		Completes results line: alkaline.

Resist the Parallel-if Temptation

When beginning programmers read the definitions of "cold working," "warm working," and "hot working" for Example 3.1 or the table of pH values and their meanings (Table 3.10), they frequently overlook the applicability of a multiple-alternative structure that uses if–else or else if–else if– ... else, and choose instead a sequence of single-alternative if statements, a structure we'll call the "parallel–if." Figure 3.6 compares our suggested multiple-alternative solution for the metal-working processes classification problem to such a sequence of single-alternative if statements.

Although the two code fragments generate identical output for all values of tHomologous, the parallel-if version is both less efficient and less clear to the reader than the multiple-alternative version. The parallel-if is less efficient because all three conditions (including one compound condition) are tested *every time* the code is run. In contrast, the multiple-alternative version tests, at most, two simple conditions and will test only one if the first condition happens to be true.

The reader of the multiple-alternative structure can see immediately that only one of the three output statements will be executed on any run. However, the reader of the parallel-if version will realize that exactly one line of output will be generated only after analyzing the three conditions and concluding that they are mutually exclusive and that they cover all possible values of tHomologous. Any time you find yourself writing code that is a sequence of unnested, single-alternative if statements, stop and analyze your conditions to see if a multiple-alternative structure would be suitable.

FIGURE 3.6 Comparison of Multiple-Alternative if and Parallel-if Structures

Multiple-Alternative if	Parallel-if

```if (tHomologous < MIN_WARM_WORKING)```
```   cout << "cold working process."```
```   << endl;```
```else if (tHomologous <= MAX_WARM_WORKING)```
```   cout << "warm working process."```
```   << endl;```
```else```
```   cout << "hot working process."```
```   << endl;```
	```if (tHomologous < MIN_WARM_WORKING)```
	``` cout << "cold working process."```
	``` << endl;```
	```if (tHomologous >= MIN_WARM_WORKING &&```
	``` tHomologous <= MAX_WARM_WORKING)```
	``` cout << "warm working process."```
	``` << endl;```
	```if (tHomologous > MAX_WARM_WORKING)```
	``` cout << "hot working process."```
	``` << endl;```

Braces In if Statements

In the `if` statements we have used so far, the task to be performed
been expressed as a single statement. Example 3.3 requires a sele
ment with a task that consists of a sequence of statements, a task
be represented as a brace-enclosed compound statement. Example
a second situation that requires the addition of braces.

EXAMPLE 3.3   We could make the coal trainload program of Fig
user-friendly by allowing the user to request instructions. The code ....
that follows uses a multiple-alternative `if` to display complete instructions,
brief instructions, or no instructions depending on the user's preference.

```
int instruct;

cout << "Would you like instructions? " << endl;
cout << "    (1) Complete instructions " << endl;
cout << "    (2) Brief instructions " << endl;
cout << "    (3) No instructions " << endl;
cout << "Type in a number followed by the <Enter> key => ";
cin >> instruct;
if (instruct == 1) {
    cout << "This program checks whether scheduled coal deliveries "
        << endl;
    cout << "will provide enough coal for one day of operation." <<
        endl;
    cout << "You will be prompted to enter the number of tons of "
        << endl;
    cout << "coal in each train load scheduled.  End the list of "
        << endl;
    cout << "train loads by typing a zero." << endl;
} else if (instruct == 2) {
    cout << "This program checks whether scheduled coal deliveries "
        << endl;
    cout << "will provide enough coal for one day of operation." <<
        endl;
}
```

EXAMPLE 3.4   Occasionally the compound-statement braces are needed even
when the dependent task is a single statement. Consider this structure:

```
if (!error) { // Version 1
    if (nextChar == 'Q')
        cout << "Quitting at user's request\n";
} else {
    cout << "Error in data\n";
}
```

If the braces were omitted, regardless of how the code was indented, the compiler would interpret it as

```
if (!error)
    if (nextChar == 'Q')
        cout << "Quitting at user's request\n";
    else
        cout << "Error in data\n";
```

because C++ syntax always associates an `else` with the most recent incomplete `if`. The first set of braces in Version 1 makes it clear that the `if` that compares `nextChar` to `'Q'` is a single-alternative `if`. Some software designers routinely include braces on all branches of `if–else` statements for clarity. ■

Section 3.4 Review Questions

1. Implement the following decision table using a multiple-alternative `if` statement. Assume that the wind speed is given as an integer.

Wind Speed	Category
Below 25	not a strong wind
25–38	strong wind
39–54	gale
55–72	whole gale
above 72	hurricane

2. Your nation's air force has asked you to write a program to label supersonic aircraft as military or civilian. Your program is to be given the plane's observed speed in km/h and its estimated length in meters. For planes traveling in excess of 1100 km/h, you will label those longer than 52 meters "civilian" and shorter aircraft as "military." For planes traveling at slower speeds, you will issue an "aircraft type unknown" message.

3.5 The switch Statement for Multiple Alternatives

controlling expression (of a switch)
expression whose value is matched to a case label to select the code fragment to execute

The `switch` statement may also be used in C++ to select one of several alternatives. The `switch` statement is especially useful when the selection is based on the value of a single variable or of a simple expression (the **controlling expression**). The value of this expression may be a character or of an integer type but not of a floating point type such as `float` or `double` or of type `string`.

EXAMPLE 3.5   Figure 3.7 shows a switch statement that implements the following decision table. The figure also includes an equivalent multiple-alternative if statement for comparison.

Class ID	Ship Class
B or b	Battleship
C or c	Cruiser
D or d	Destroyer
F or f	Frigate

The message displayed by the switch statement shown depends on the value of the controlling expression, that is, the value of the variable ship-Class (type char). First, this expression is evaluated; then, the list of case labels (case 'B':, case 'b':, case 'C':, etc.) is searched until one label that matches the value of the controlling expression is found.

FIGURE 3.7   Comparison of a switch Statement with type char Case Labels and an Equivalent Multiple-Alternative if

```
switch (shipClass) {
case 'B':                         if (shipClass == 'B'
case 'b':                             || shipClass == 'b')
    cout << "Battleship" << endl;     cout << "Battleship" << endl;
    break;

case 'C':                         else if (shipClass == 'C'
case 'c':                                  || shipClass == 'c')
    cout << "Cruiser" << endl;        cout << "Cruiser" << endl;
    break;

case 'D':                         else if (shipClass == 'D'
case 'd':                                  || shipClass == 'd')
    cout << "Destroyer" << endl;      cout << "Destroyer" << endl;
    break;

case 'F':                         else if (shipClass == 'F'
case 'f':                                  || shipClass == 'f')
    cout << "Frigate" << endl;        cout << "Frigate" << endl;
    break;

default:                          else
    cout << "Unknown ship class "     cout << "Unknown ship class "
       << shipClass << endl;             << shipClass << endl;
}
    .
```

Statements following the matching case label are executed until a `break` statement is encountered. The `break` causes an exit from the `switch` statement, and execution continues with the statement following the closing brace of the `switch` statement body. If no case label matches the value of the `switch` statement's controlling expression and if there is a default label, the statements following the default label are executed. If not, the entire `switch` statement body is skipped. ■

EXAMPLE 3.6 The `switch` statement that follows assigns to `int` variable days the number of days in a given month of a nonleap year. If the value of variable `month` is 1, it represents January, 2 means `February`, and so on.

```
// Determine the number of days in month
switch (month) {
case 2:
      days = 28;       // February
      break;

case 4:                // April
case 6:                // June
case 9:                // September
case 11:               // November
      days = 30;
      break;

default:
      days = 31;       // all the rest
}
```

```
cout << "Month " << month << " has " << days << " days." << endl;   ■
```

Using a string such as "Cruiser" or "Frigate" as a case label is a common error. It is important to remember that single character and integer values may be used as case labels, but strings and floating point values cannot be used. Another common error is the omission of the `break` statement at the end of one alternative. In such a situation, execution "falls through" into the next alternative. We use a blank line after each `break` statement to emphasize the fact that there is no "fall-through."

Forgetting the closing brace of the `switch` statement body is also easy to do. If the brace is missing and the `switch` has a default label, the statements following the `switch` statement become part of the default case.

Section 3.5 Review Questions

1. What will be displayed by this carelessly constructed `switch` statement if the value of `constructionType` is `'B'`?

```
switch (constructionType) { // break statements missing
case 'B':
case 'b':  cout << "brick" << endl;

case 'C':
case 'c':  cout << "concrete" << endl;

case 'F':
case 'f':  cout << "frame" << endl;
}
```

2. Write a **switch** statement that assigns to the variable **lumens** the expected brightness of a standard lightbulb whose wattage has been stored in **watts**. Use this table:

Watts	Brightness (in Lumens)
15	125
25	215
40	500
60	880
75	1000
100	1675

Assign −1 to **lumens** if the value of **watts** is not in the table.

3. Write a multiple-alternative **if** statement equivalent to the **switch** statement described in Question 2.

3.6 Problem Solving with Decisions

Each day new computer software is developed to meet the special needs of scientists in every imaginable field of study. Our next case study applies the decision-making power of C++ to a species classification problem.

BINDLOE ISLAND FINCH IDENTIFICATION[1]

CASE STUDY

Problem

Three species of ground finch (Geospiza) are found on Bindloe Island of the Galapagos chain. Each has a characteristic beak depth as indicated in Table 3.12.

Write a program to assist a group of ornithologists who are being sent to categorize all the finches on the island. The program should repeatedly

---

[1]Adapted from Robert E. Ricklefs, *Ecology*, 2nd ed. (New York: Chiron Press, 1979), pp. 241–2.

TABLE 3.12 Beak Depth of Ground Finches on Bindloe Island

Species	Beak Depth (mm)
G. fuliginosa	6.0—9.3
G. fortis	10.5—14.7
G. magnirostris	16.0—22.2

prompt the user to enter a beak depth or a zero to end the list of data. For each beak, display a category. Here is a short sample run demonstrating how the program should interact with the user.

```
Enter a beak depth(mm) or 0 to quit => 19.1
19.1 mm beak => species G. magnirostris
Enter a beak depth(mm) or 0 to quit => 5.8
5.8 mm beak is uncharacteristically small
Enter a beak depth(mm) or 0 to quit => 9.8
9.8 mm beak falls between characteristic depths of G. fuliginosa
   and G. fortis
Enter a beak depth(mm) or 0 to quit => 0
```

Understanding the Problem

Let's consider the table of beak depths and the sample run and identify all the messages that the program may need to display.

Situation	Message
1 Depth smaller than low end of G. fuliginosa range	`_ mm beak is uncharacteristically small`
2 Depth in G. fuliginosa range	`_ mm beak => species G. fuliginosa`
3 Depth between ranges for G. fulignosa and G. fortis	`_ mm beak falls between characteristic depths of G. fulignosa and G. fortis`
4 Depth in G. fortis range	`_ mm beak => species G. fortis`
5 Depth between ranges for G. fortis and G. magnirostris	`_ mm beak falls between characteristic depths of G. fortis and G. magnirostris`
6 Depth in G. magnirostris range	`_ mm beak => species G. magnirostris`
7 Depth larger than high end of G. magnirostris range.	`_ mm beak is uncharacteristically large`

Clarifying the Problem Statement

When we review Table 3.12 and our list of messages to see if we have covered the entire range of possible inputs, we note that Situation 1 needs more clarification. A beak depth smaller than 6.0 might include values such as zero or a negative number. Rereading the problem statement, we see that a zero value is to indicate the end of the data. However, there is no mention of how to process negative data. This oversight is typical of real-world problem specifications. Rarely does a client anticipate the software developer's every need! You must expect that you will need to ask your client (i.e., for this class, your instructor) some follow-up questions to obtain all the details of the problem that you need.

In this case, let's assume that your client answers, "It doesn't matter," when you inquire about how to deal with negative data. Such a reply is quite common in the "real" world! However, at this point your sense of professionalism should assure you that this issue does, in fact, matter. Keep in mind that the acronym **GIGO** (Garbage In, Garbage Out) is neither an unchangeable law of nature nor an appropriate motto for a programmer. Our motto is "Garbage In, Error Message Out," so we will need to include the display of an error message in the case of negative data input for beak depth.

GIGO
Garbage In, Garbage Out

Now we can identify the problem's constraints, inputs, and outputs, and sketch an initial approach.

Data Definition

Constants

```
LOW_FULIGINOSA        6.0 // mm
HIGH_FULIGINOSA       9.3 // mm
LOW_FORTIS           10.5 // mm
HIGH_FORTIS          14.7 // mm
LOW_MAGNIROSTRIS     16.0 // mm
HIGH_MAGNIROSTRIS    22.0 // mm
```

Inputs

```
depth  // bird beak depth (mm)
```

Outputs

One of eight messages:
```
_ mm beak is uncharacteristically small
_ mm beak => species G. fuliginosa
_ mm beak falls between characteristic depths of G. fuliginosa
    and G. fortis
_ mm beak => species G. fortis
```

```
_ mm beak falls between characteristic depths of G. fortis and G.
    magnirostris
_ mm beak => species G. magnirostris
_ mm beak is uncharacteristically large
Negative beak depth value is invalid
```

Algorithm Design

We will begin by designing an algorithm to process entry of one data value. We will investigate how to process a list of many data values later.

Initial Algorithm

1. Get a beak depth.
2. Display appropriate message for beak depth.

Selecting the appropriate message to display involves a decision process, so we refine Step 2.

Refinement of Step 2

2. Display appropriate message
    2.1   If `depth` is negative
             2.2   Display error message
        else if `depth < LOW_FULIGINOSA`
             2.3   Display "uncharacteristically small" message
        else if `depth <= HIGH_FULIGINOSA`
             2.4   Display "species G. fuliginosa" message
        else if `depth < LOW_FORTIS`
             2.5   Display "between G. fuliginosa and G. fortis" message
        else if `depth <= HIGH_FORTIS`
             2.6   Display "species G. fortis" message
        else if `depth < LOW_MAGNIROSTRIS`
             2.7   Display "between G. fortis and G. magnirostris" message
        else if `depth <= HIGH_MAGNIROSTRIS`
             2.8   Display "species G. magnirostris" message
        else
             2.9   Display "uncharacteristically large" message

Now that we have an algorithm to process one data value, we need to revise it to permit repeated data entry until a zero beak depth is entered. Although we have not yet studied all of C++'s repetition structures, we did see one structure in Fig. 3.3 and Table 3.9 that we can use as a model. The coal trainload program prompted the user for and copied into memory one data value before the beginning of a `while` statement. Then the first statements repeated processed the data, and the last of the repeated statements prompted for another data entry and copied the value into memory. Applying this model of repetition to the finch classification problem, we have our final algorithm.

Complete Algorithm

1. Get a beak depth.
2. Repeat as long as the beak depth isn't zero
    3. Display appropriate message:
        3.1 If depth is negative
              3.2 Display error message
        else if depth < LOW_FULIGINOSA
              3.3 Display "uncharacteristically small" message
        else if depth <= HIGH_FULIGINOSA
              3.4 Display "species G. fuliginosa" message
        else if depth < LOW_FORTIS
              3.5 Display "between G. fuliginosa and G. fortis" message
        else if depth <= HIGH_FORTIS
              3.6 Display "species G. fortis" message
        else if depth < LOW_MAGNIROSTRIS
              3.7 Display "between G. fortis and G. magnirostris"
                    message
        else if depth <= HIGH_MAGNIROSTRIS
              3.8 Display "species G. magnirostris" message
        else
              3.9 Display "uncharacteristically large" message
   4. Get next beak depth.

Figure 3.8 shows an implementation of this algorithm. At the end of the figure is a brief run of the program.

FIGURE 3.8 Program to Classify Bindloe Island Ground Finches

```
// Identify three Bindloe Island species of finches based on beak
// depth
// Species            Beak Depth
// G. fuliginosa       6.0 - 9.3
// G. fortis          10.5 - 14.7
// G. magnirostris    16.0 - 22.0

#include <iostream>
using namespace std;
```

FIGURE 3.8   *(Continued)*

```
//High and low cutoffs for each species' beak depth
const double LOW_FULIGINOSA = 6.0;        // mm
const double HIGH_FULIGINOSA = 9.3;       // mm
const double LOW_FORTIS = 10.5;           // mm
const double HIGH_FORTIS = 14.7;          // mm
const double LOW_MAGNIROSTRIS = 16.0;     // mm
const double HIGH_MAGNIROSTRIS = 22.0;    // mm

int main()
{
   double depth; // bird beak depth in mm

   cout << "This program identifies three Bindloe Island " <<
      "finch species/nbased on beak depth\n";

   // Get the first beak depth
   cout << "Enter a beak depth(mm) or 0 to quit => ";
   cin >> depth;

   // Continue identifying finches as long as the user doesn't enter a
   // zero beak length
   while (depth !=0) {
      if (depth < 0)
         cout << "Negative beak depth (" << depth << ") invalid\n";
      else if (depth < LOW_FULIGINOSA)
         cout << depth << " mm beak is uncharacteristically small\n"
      else if (depth <= HIGH_FULIGINOSA)
         cout << depth << " mm beak => species G. fuliginosa\n";
      else if (depth < LOW_FORTIS)
         cout << depth << " mm beak falls between characteristic " <<
            "depths of G. fuliginosa\n and G. fortis\n;
      else if (depth <= HIGH_FORTIS)
         cout << depth << " mm beak => species G. fortis\n;
      else if (depth < LOW_MAGNIROSTRIS)
         cout << depth << " mm beak falls between characteristic " <<
            "depths of G. fortis\n and G. magnirostris\n";
      else if (depth <= HIGH_MAGNIROSTRIS)
         cout << depth << " mm beak => species G. magnirostris\n";
      else
         cout << depth << " mm beak is uncharacteristically large\n";
```

FIGURE 3.8 *(Continued)*

```
        cout <<  "Enter a beak depth(mm) or )0 to quit => ";
        cin >> depth;
    }
    return 0;
}
```

```
This program identifies three Bindloe Island finch species
based on beak depth
Enter a beak depth(mm) or 0 to quit => 6
6 mm beak => species G. fuliginosa
Enter a beak depth(mm) or 0 to quit => 5.1
5.1 mm beak is uncharacteristically small
Enter a beak depth(mm) or 0 to quit => 6.2
6.2 mm beak => species G. fuliginosa
Enter a beak depth(mm) or 0 to quit => 7.3
7.3 mm beak => species G. fuliginosa
Enter a beak depth(mm) or 0 to quit => 8.4
8.4 mm beak => species G. fuliginosa
Enter a beak depth(mm) or 0 to quit => 9.5
9.5 mm beak falls between characteristic depths of G. fuliginosa
    and G. fortis
Enter a beak depth(mm) or 0 to quit => 10.6
10.6 mm beak => species G. fortis
Enter a beak depth(mm) or 0 to quit => 11.7
11.7 mm beak => species G. fortis
Enter a beak depth(mm) or 0 to quit => 12.8
12.8 mm beak => species G. fortis
Enter a beak depth(mm) or 0 to quit => 13.9
13.9 mm beak => species G. fortis
Enter a beak depth(mm) or 0 to quit => 15
15 mm beak falls between characteristic depths of G. fortis
    and G. magnirostris
Enter a beak depth(mm) or 0 to quit => 17.1
17.1 mm beak => species G. magnirostris
Enter a beak depth(mm) or 0 to quit => 19.2
19.2 mm beak => species G. magnirostris
Enter a beak depth(mm) or 0 to quit => 21.3
23.1 mm beak => species G. magnirostris
Enter a beak depth(mm) or 0 to quit => 22.4
22.4 mm beak is uncharacteristically large
Enter a beak depth(mm) or 0 to quit => 0
```

Section 3.6 Review Questions

1. Could a `switch` statement be used to implement the decision structure of the finch identification program? If so, write the `switch` statement. If not, explain why not.
2. The multiple-alternative decision structure of Fig. 3.8 checks for all possible values of **depth** except zero. If this is a flaw, write a multiple-alternative `if` that corrects the flaw. If not, explain why not.

3.7 Software Designer Beware

Remember that the C++ equality operator is ==. It is easy to slip and use =, the mathematical equal sign. The compiler will consider this a fatal error only if the first operand is not a variable. Otherwise, although your compiler may issue a warning, it will also generate code that produces incorrect results. For example, the code fragment that follows always displays x is 10, regardless of the value of x when the statement is encountered.

```
if (x = 10)  // misuse of = for ==
    cout << "x is 10" << endl;
```

The assignment operator stores the value 10 in x. The value of an assignment expression is the value assigned, so in this case the value of the `if` condition of the statement is 10. We have seen that C++ permits conversion of type `bool` values to type `int`. It also permits conversion of type `int` to type `bool`: The value 0 is converted to false; all other values are converted to true. Thus the 10 that is the value of x = 10 is converted to true, and C++ executes the true task.

Be careful when constructing complicated logical expressions using the operators && and ||. Remember that both operands must be complete logical expressions. For example, when verifying that x and y are both positive, we write

```
x > 0 && y > 0
```

not

```
x && y > 0
```

Similarly, when checking whether x falls in the range 5 to 10, we write

```
5 <= x  &&  x <= 10
```

not

```
5 <= x <= 10
```

Don't forget to parenthesize the condition of an `if` statement and to en-close in braces a single-alternative `if` used as a true task within a double-alternative `if`. The braces will force the `else` to be associated with the correct `if`. Also enclose in braces a compound statement used as a true task or false task. If the braces are missing, C++ will consider only the first statement to be part of the task. This can lead to a syntax error if the braces are omitted from the true task of a double-alternative `if`. Leaving out the braces on the false task of a double-alternative `if` or on the true task of a single-alternative `if` will not usually generate a syntax error; the omission will simply lead to incorrect results. In the example that follows, the braces around the true task are missing. The compiler assumes that the semicolon at the end of the assignment statement terminates the `if` statement.

```
if (x > 0)              // Error: braces missing
     sum = sum + x;
     cout << "Greater than zero" << endl;
else
     cout << "Less than zero" << endl;
```

An unexpected `symbol` syntax error may be generated when the compiler processes the keyword `else`.

When you write a nested `if` statement, try to select conditions that let you use the multiple-alternative format shown in Section 3.4. When possible, construct the logic so each intermediate condition falls on the false branch of the previous decision. If the conditions are not mutually exclusive (i.e., more than one condition may be true), test the most restrictive condition first.

When using a `switch` statement, make sure the controlling expression and case labels are of the same permitted type (`int` or `char` but not a floating point type and not type `string`). Remember that if the controlling expression evaluates to a value not listed in any of the case labels, C++ will skip the entire body of the `switch` statement unless there is a `default` label. Include such a default case whenever practical. Don't forget that the body of the `switch` statement is a single compound statement, enclosed in one set of braces. However, you do not enclose in braces the statements of each alternative within the `switch`; instead, end each alternative with a `break` statement.

Chapter Review

1. Use the three essential control structures—sequential execution, selection, and repetition—to control the flow of statement execution in a program. The compound statement is a control structure for sequential execution.
2. Use selection control structures to represent decisions in an algorithm. Choose either the `if` statement or `switch` statement to code decision steps in an algorithm.

3. Expressions whose values indicate whether certain conditions are true can be written

   - using the relational operators (**<, <=, >, >=**) and equality operators (**==, !=**) to compare values of expressions.
   - using the logical operators (**&&** (and), **| |** (or), **!** (not)) to form more complex conditions.

4. A hand trace of an algorithm verifies whether it is correct. You can discover errors in logic by carefully hand tracing an algorithm. Hand tracing an algorithm before coding it as a program will save you time in the long run.

5. Nested **if** statements are common in C++ and are used to represent decisions with multiple alternatives. Programmers use indentation and the multiple-alternative decision form when applicable to enhance readability of nested **if** statements.

6. The **switch** statement implements decisions with several alternatives, where the alternative selected depends on the value of a variable or expression. This controlling expression may be of type **int** or **char**, but not of type **float**, **double**, or **string**.

New C++ Constructs

Construct	Effect
if statement	
Single-Alternative	
`if (x != 0)` `    value = value / x;`	Divides `value` by x if x is nonzero.
Double-Alternative	

`if (temp >= 100.0)`
`    cout << "Steam\n";`
`else`
`    cout << "Water\n";`
	Temperatures 100.00 or higher are labeled as "Steam"; others are labeled "Water."

Multiple-Alternative	

`if (x > 0.0) {`
`    cout << "Positive\n";`
`    absX = x;`
`} else if (x < 0.0) {`
`    cout << "Negative\n";`
`    absX = -x;`
`} else {`
`    cout << "Zero\n";`
`    absX = x;`
	Assigns the correct absolute value of x to `absX` and displays one of three messages, depending on whether x is positive, negative, or zero.

switch statement

```
switch (size) {
case 'S':
case 's':
   cout << "Small\n";
   break;

case 'M':
case 'm':
   cout << "Medium\n";
   break;

case 'L':
case 'l':
   cout << "Large\n";
   break;

case 'X':
case 'x':
   cout << "Extra-Large\n";
   break;

default:
   cout << "Invalid size\n";
}
```

Displays one of five messages based on the value of size (type char). If size is not 'S', 's', 'M', 'm', 'L', 'l', 'X', or 'x', an error message is displayed.

PROGRAMMING PROJECTS

1. Wavelengths of visible light fall approximately into the range 0.4–0.7 microns. The table below shows the relationship between wavelength and color. Write a program that inputs a wavelength and then displays the associated light color. If the wavelength is shorter than 0.4 microns or longer than 0.7, display the message Wavelength outside visual range. Classify boundary wavelengths as the lower-wavelength color. For example, label a wavelength of 0.424 microns as violet.

Color	Approximate wavelength range (microns)
Violet	0.400–0.424
Blue	0.424–0.491
Green	0.491–0.575
Yellow	0.575–0.585
Orange	0.585–0.647
Red	0.647–0.700

2. The table below shows the normal boiling points of several substances. Write a program that prompts the user for the observed boiling point of a substance in °C and identifies the substance if the observed boiling point is within 5% of the expected boiling point. If the data input is more than 5% higher or lower than any of the boiling points in the table, the program should output the message Substance unknown.

Substance	Normal boiling point (°C)
Water	100
Mercury	357
Copper	1187
Silver	2193
Gold	2660

3. A pharmaceutical engineer is testing out new types of synthetic antibiotics that should kill either one or both of the common classes of bacteria, *gram-negative* and *gram-positive* bacteria. Write a program that takes as input a character indicating whether an antibiotic sample is effective against only gram-negative bacteria ('N'), only gram-positive bacteria ('P'), both classes ('B'), or neither class ('Z'). The program should allow the character input to be either upper- or lowercase. It should display different lists of instructions to a technician based on effectiveness against gram-positive and gram-negative bacteria.

```
Gram–positive:   Perform standard tests 1 and 5.
                 Record results in notebook #2.
Gram–negative:   Perform standard tests 2, 3, and 4.
                 Record results in notebook #3.
```

For samples effective on both classes, have the program display both sets of instructions. For samples effective on neither, display Throw away sample.

4. Write a program that takes the x-y coordinates of a point in the Cartesian plane and displays a message telling either an axis on which the point lies or the quadrant in which it is found.

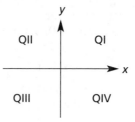

Sample lines of output:

```
(−1.0, −2.5) is in quadrant III
```

```
(0.0, 4.8) is on the y axis
```

5. Write a program that reports the contents of a compressed-gas cylinder based on the first letter of the cylinder's color. The program input is a character representing the observed color of the cylinder: `'Y'` or `'y'` for yellow, `'O'` or `'o'` for orange, and so on. Cylinder colors and associated contents are as follows:

orange	ammonia
brown	carbon monoxide
yellow	hydrogen
green	oxygen

Your program should respond to input of a letter other than the first letters of the given colors with the message, `Contents unknown`.

6. The National Earthquake Information Center has asked you to write a program implementing the following decision table to characterize an earthquake based on its Richter scale number.

Richter Scale Number (n)	Characterization
$n < 5.0$	Little or no damage
$5.0 \leq n < 5.5$	Some damage
$5.5 \leq n < 6.5$	Serious damage: walls may crack or fall
$6.5 \leq n < 7.5$	Disaster: houses and buildings may collapse
higher	Catastrophe: most buildings destroyed

Could you handle this problem with a `switch` statement? If so, use a `switch` statement; if not, explain why not.

7. Los Angeles sometimes has very smoggy conditions. These conditions are largely due to L.A.'s location between mountain ranges, coupled with prevailing winds off the ocean that tend to blow pollutants from the city's many automobiles up against the mountains. Three components of smog—ozone, nitrogen dioxide, and carbon monoxide—are a particular health concern. A pollutant hazard index has been developed for each of the three primary irritants. If any index rises above 100, the air is listed as "unhealthful" in forecasts to Los Angeles residents. If the index for any one of the three rises above 200, a "first-stage smog alert" is issued and certain activities are restricted in the affected part of the Los Angeles basin. If an index goes over 275, a "second-state alert" is called and more severe restrictions apply. Write a program that takes as input the daily hazard index for each of the three pollutants and identifies unhealthful or first- or second-stage alert situations.

8. Write a program that displays a message characterizing the level of force, in newtons, being applied by a robot hand attempting to turn a large threaded part into a machine. Force levels and associated messages are: 0, `Part not found`; 1–44, `Insecure grip`; 45–88, `Nominal grip`; 89–100,

Part may be misaligned; and above 100, DANGER—Part may be stuck. The program should also display a message if the force level input is bad data.

9. Write a program that displays a message reporting the acidity of a liquid flowing into a processing vat. The program input is a character representing the observed color of the liquid: `'R'` or `'r'` for red, `'B'` or `'b'` for blue, and `'P'` or `'p'` for purple. `'W'` or `'w'` (white) means that currently nothing is flowing into the vat. Messages to display include `No flow` and these messages keyed to color:

Color	Message
Red	Acidic material
Blue	Basic material
Purple	Neutral material

10. Write a program that interacts with the user like this:

```
(1) Carbon monoxide
(2) Hydrocarbons
(3) Nitrogen oxides
(4) Non-methane hydrocarbons
Enter pollutant number=> 2
Enter number of grams emitted per mile=> 0.35
Enter odometer reading=> 40112
Emissions exceed permitted level of 0.31 grams/mile.
```

Use this table[2] of emissions limits to determine the appropriate message.

	First 50,000 Miles	Second 50,000 Miles
carbon monoxide	3.4 grams/mile	4.2 grams/mile
hydrocarbons	0.31 grams/mile	0.39 grams/mile
nitrogen oxides	0.4 grams/mile	0.5 grams/mile
nonmethane hydrocarbons	0.25 grams/mile	0.31 grams/mile

---

[2] Adapted from Joseph Priest, *Energy: Principles, Problems, Alternatives* (Reading, Mass.: Addison-Wesley, 1991).

Repetition Structures

4

In this chapter you will study three C++ statements that allow you to specify a **loop**, the repetition of a sequence of program statements. The `while`, `for`, and `do—while` structures let you write C++ programs that rapidly repeat groups of actions on vast quantities of information. This chapter describes how to design algorithms containing loops and how to place one control structure inside another.

    Programs that repeat a group of statements can process large data sets, so this chapter also presents how to use data files to provide input to a program and how to send program results to output files. Loops that repeat a prescribed number of times are controlled by counter variables, and loops that accumulate a sum or product repeatedly add new values to an accumulator variable or multiply a variable by a new value. C++ defines two kinds of operators that are very useful in these contexts: Increment and decrement operators are used to update counters, and compound assignment operators are helpful in managing accumulator variables.

loop
control structure that conditionally repeats execution of a code fragment

Loop Form and the while Statement

op that we used in Chapter 3 in the power plant coal example is
the vast majority of loops—execution of the loop body is con-
hree basic components:

tion of the **loop control variable**
n of the **loop repetition condition**
the loop control variable

Figure 4.1 repeats the code fragment that adds up the quantity of coal scheduled for delivery. The essential loop components are labeled. A **loop control
variable** is a variable whose value controls whether the **loop body** is executed. In this example, trainLoad is the loop control variable. As long as
trainLoad is greater than zero, the loop body (enclosed in braces) is executed. In this example, the loop control variable is both initialized and updated by interactive input of values. Figure 4.1 shows the screen interaction
for input of 2000, 1800, 2400, 1500, and 0, and Table 4.1 shows a full trace
of the loop's execution on this input.

Consider what happens if the update of the loop control variable in Fig.
4.1 is omitted. As shown in Table 4.1, if the user enters a positive value in the
initialization step, the loop repetition condition is true and the loop body executes, adding trainLoad to totalCoal and displaying the prompt. However, with no statement to input a new value, trainLoad remains positive,
causing repeated (rapid) execution of the loop body with no end in sight.

...ition

expression involving the
loop control variable—if
the condition is true,
the loop body is
executed; otherwise the
loop exits

loop body

statement(s) forming
the code fragment to
be repeatedly executed

FIGURE 4.1 Loop from Power Plant Coal Program and Its Interaction with the Program User

```
        cout << "Number of tons in first trainload (or zero to quit) => ";
❶       cin >> trainLoad;
❷       while (trainLoad > 0) {
            totalCoal = totalCoal + trainLoad;
            cout << "Tons in next trainload (zero to quit) => ";
❸          cin >> trainLoad;
        }
        cout << "Scheduled coal arrival total of " << totalCoal <<
                " tons " << endl;
        Number of tons in first trainload (or zero to quit) => 2000
        Tons in next trainload (zero to quit) => 1800
        Tons in next trainload (zero to quit) => 2400
        Tons in next trainload (zero to quit) => 1500
        Tons in next trainload (zero to quit) => 0
        Scheduled coal arrival total of 7700 tons
```

TABLE 4.1 Trace of while Loop

Statement Executed	trainLoad ?	totalCoal 0	Effect
cout << "Number ... first train ... => "			Displays initial prompting message, and user types in 2000.
cin >> trainLoad;	2000		Copies keyboard input into trainLoad.
while (trainLoad > 0)			2000 > 0 is true.
totalCoal = totalCoal + trainLoad;		2000	Adds 2000 to value of totalCoal.
cout << "Tons in next ... => "			Asks user for size of next trainload, and user types in 1800.
cin >> trainLoad;	1800		Copies keyboard input into trainLoad.
while (trainLoad > 0)			1800 > 0 is true.
totalCoal = totalCoal + trainLoad;		3800	Adds 1800 to value of totalCoal.
cout << "Tons in next ... => "			Asks user for size of next train load, and user types in 2400.
cin >> trainLoad;	2400		Copies keyboard input into trainLoad.
while (trainLoad > 0)			2400 > 0 is true.
totalCoal = totalCoal + trainLoad;		6200	Adds 2400 to value of totalCoal.
cout << "Tons in next ... => "			Asks user for size of next trainload, and user types in 1500.
cin >> trainLoad;	1500		Copies keyboard input into trainLoad.
while (trainLoad > 0)			1500 > 0 is true.
totalCoal = totalCoal + trainLoad;		7700	Adds 1500 to value of totalCoal.
cout << "Tons in next ... => "			Asks user for size of next trainload, and user types in 0.
cin >> trainLoad;	0		Copies keyboard input into trainLoad.
while (trainLoad > 0)			0 > 0 is false, so loop exits.

FIGURE 4.2 Flow of Control In a while Statement

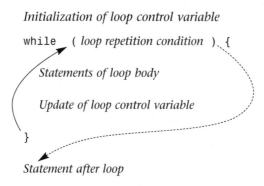

Initialization of loop control variable

while (*loop repetition condition*) {

  Statements of loop body

  Update of loop control variable

}

Statement after loop

infinite loop
loop whose repetition condition never becomes false, so its body executes repeatedly "infinitely" (that is, until the program is interrupted)

Such a loop is called an **infinite loop**. Before attempting to run your own C++ programs that include loops, be sure you know how your system lets you interrupt execution of a program containing an infinite loop.

Figure 4.2 summarizes the behavior of a while statement. It shows a generic while loop with arrows representing the control flow. The flow represented by the solid arrow is executed every time we reach the end of the loop body. The dashed arrow is followed only when the loop repetition condition is false. In all other cases, statements are executed sequentially.

Sentinel Loops

sentinel loop
data input loop that exits on entry of a predetermined value (the sentinel)

One loop commonly used for input of a list of data is a **sentinel loop**. This structure repeatedly inputs and processes values until input of a sentinel, a specific value that marks the end of the data. You must choose as the sentinel a value that is the same type as the data but could not be a valid data item. We frequently name the sentinel value as a constant. Here is a sentinel loop for interactive input of a list of integers. We assume here that –99 could not be a valid data item.

```
const int SENTINEL = -99;  // end-of-data marker
int      dataValue;

cout << "Enter data value (" << SENTINEL << " to quit) => ";
cin >> dataValue;
while (dataValue != SENTINEL) {
      // Code that processes this data value ...
    cout << "Enter data value (" << SENTINEL << " to quit) => ";
    cin >> dataValue;
}
```

Beginning programmers often fail to understand the need for one input before the loop and another at the end of the loop body. They might erroneously code a sentinel loop like this:

```
while (dataValue != SENTINEL) {
    cout << "Enter data value (" << SENTINEL << " to quit) => ";
    cin >> dataValue;

        // Code that processes this data value . . .
}
```

There are two problems with this approach.

1. dataValue (the loop control variable) is not initialized before the first test of the loop repetition condition.
2. The sentinel value is processed as a data value.

Counting Loops

We use sentinel-controlled loops for input of a list of data of any length. In such situations we do not know in advance how many times the loop body should be executed. Other times we do know that a loop should be repeated a certain number of times. In such cases we can use a **counting loop** —a loop controlled by an integer variable that keeps track of how many times the loop has been executed. The program in Fig. 4.3 applies our carbon monoxide emissions standard check to several vehicles in one run. Its repetition control structure (shaded) is an example of a typical counting loop that repeats its loop body *n* times:

counting loop repetition structure that executes a predetermined number of times and is controlled by a counter

1. Initialization of the loop control
   variable:
2. Test of loop repetition condition
3. Update of loop control variable

```
int ctrVariable = 0;
while (ctrVariable < n) {
    // Code to be repeated
    ctrVariable = ctrVariable + 1;
}
```

In Fig. 4.3, *n*, the number of times the loop repeats, is represented by the input variable vehicles. In other situations, *n* may be a constant. For example, a program that processes a year's data one month at a time might represent *n* as this constant NUM_MONTHS:

```
const int NUM_MONTHS = 12;
```

FIGURE 4.3 Counting Loop Example

```cpp
//
//   Determine if new vehicles meet carbon monoxide emissions standard.
//

#include <iostream>
using namespace std;

const double MAXCO = 3.4; // maximum g/mi of carbon monoxide allowed

int main()
{
    double coEmitted, // grams of carbon monoxide emitted
           miles,     // miles driven during test
           coRate;    // g/mi of carbon monoxide emitted
    int    vehicles;  // number of vehicles tested

    cout << "Number of vehicles tested => ";
    cin >> vehicles;

    int ct = 0;         // how many vehicles processed so far
    while (ct < vehicles) {
        cout << "Enter amount of carbon monoxide emitted (grams) => ";
        cin >> coEmitted;
        cout << "Enter miles driven => ";
        cin >> miles;

        coRate = coEmitted / miles;
        cout << "Carbon monoxide emission of " << coRate << " g/mi ";

        if (coRate <= MAXCO)
            cout << "meets ";
        else
            cout << "exceeds ";

        cout << "permitted emission of " << endl << MAXCO << " g/mi." << endl;
        ct = ct + 1;
    }
    return 0;
}


Number of vehicles tested => 4
Enter amount of carbon monoxide emitted (grams) => 38
```

FIGURE 4.3 *(Continued)*

```
Enter miles driven => 10
Carbon monoxide emission of 3.8 g/mi exceeds permitted emission of
3.4 g/mi.
Enter amount of carbon monoxide emitted (grams) => 34
Enter miles driven => 10
Carbon monoxide emission of 3.4 g/mi meets permitted emission of
3.4 g/mi.
Enter amount of carbon monoxide emitted (grams) => 50
Enter miles driven => 15
Carbon monoxide emission of 3.333333 g/mi meets permitted emission of
3.4 g/mi.
Enter amount of carbon monoxide emitted (grams) => 56
Enter miles driven => 15
Carbon monoxide emission of 3.733333 g/mi exceeds permitted emission of
3.4 g/mi.
```

Section 4.1 Review Questions

For each of the following situations, answer these questions:

    a. Do you know in advance how many times the loop must repeat?

    b. What is the loop control variable?

    c. What should be the loop repetition condition?

    d. What statements will initialize and update the loop control variable?

    1. Write a program to compute the final volume V_2 (in liters) to which one mole of an ideal gas at absolute temperature T and initial volume V_1 must be isothermally expanded in order to perform a given amount of work W (in joules). Your program should repeatedly prompt the user to enter W, V_1, and T until a W of zero is entered. The formula for V_2 is

$$V_2 = V_1 e^{\left(W/nRT\right)}$$

where R is the universal gas constant (8.31451 J/mol · K) and n is the number of moles.

                Variables: `vol1`, `vol2`, `work`, `kTemp`

                Constant: `R`

    2. This infinite series can be used to approximate π.

$$\frac{\pi^2}{6} = \frac{1}{1^2} + \frac{1}{2^2} + \frac{1}{3^2} + \frac{1}{4^2} + \cdots$$

Write a program that asks the user how many terms of the series to sum (`numTerms`) and then displays an approximation of π.

> Variables: `numTerms`, `ct`, `seriesSum`, `piApprox`

3. Using the infinite series described in Question 2, write a program that asks the user how close to π an approximation needs to be (`MaxError`). Then add up terms of the series and calculate the associated approximations until two successive approximations differ by less than `MaxError`.

> Variables: `ct`, `seriesSum`, `newApprox`, `prevApprox`,
> `diffApprox`, `MaxError`

4. The file `town.txt` contains one data line representing the age and gender (F = female, M = male) of each of the residents of a small town. Write a program that uses the data in this file to compute and display the percentage of the town's males who are 70 or older, the percentage of the females who are in this age group, and the percentage of the overall population who are 70 or older.

> Variables: `age`, `gender`, `inputStatus`, `totFemale`, `totMale`, `oldFemale`,
> `oldMale`, `fOldPct`, `mOldPct`, `totOldPct`

4.2   Interactive and Batch Processing

interactive mode
mode of software operation that directs the user to enter data at the keyboard or with a pointing device and processes the data immediately

batch mode
mode of software operation that processes data collected in advance and saved in files

Programs are often categorized as interactive or batch depending on their mode of receiving input. The programs we have studied so far were designed to run in **interactive mode**: Each program displayed prompting messages describing the data needed, and the user interacted with the program by entering the requested data at the keyboard. The programs displayed their results on the monitor. A program running in **batch mode**, in contrast, takes data from a file prepared and saved in advance. Such a program displays no prompting messages, but it may echo the data to the monitor or to an output file.

Program-Controlled Input and Output Files

C++ provides facilities for input and output file manipulation in the fstream library. Figure 4.4 shows a batch version of our power plant coal program from Fig. 3.3. This version takes all the input from the file `coaldata.txt`, echoes the data both to the monitor and to the output file `coal.out`, and sends the program results to both output destinations as well.

To use an input file, a program must first declare an input file variable and associate it with an open input file object. The statement

```
ifstream infile( "coaldata.txt", ios::in );
```

declares that the variable `infile` will refer to the input file `coaldata.txt`. This means that, like `cin`, `infile` can be used as the left operand of an input extraction operation. Similarly, use of an output file requires declaration of an output file variable and association of the variable with an open output file object. This is accomplished by the statement

```
ofstream outfile( "coal.out", ios::out );
```

Like cout, outfile can be used as the left operand of an output insertion operation.

The program in Fig. 4.4 takes a typical batch-processing approach: It extracts data from the input file using the >> operator, uses the << operator to echo these data with labels both to the output file and to the monitor, computes the program results, and displays these results on the monitor while also saving the results to the output file.

FIGURE 4.4 Batch Version of Power Plant Coal Program

```
//  Determine if scheduled coal arrivals are sufficient to fuel
//  electric power plant for one day
//      Input from file
//      Output to file and to screen

#include <iostream>
#include <fstream>  // needed for direct file manipulation
using namespace std;

const int MIN_COAL_REQUIRED = 10000; // minimum tons of coal
                                     // necessary for one day
const int SENTINEL = 0;

int main()
{
   ifstream infile("a:coaldata.txt", ios::in);
                // associate coaldata.txt with infile
   ofstream outfile("a:coal.out", ios::out);
                // associate coal.out with outfile
   int train_load,        // tons of coal in current train load
      total_coal = 0;    // tons of coal counted so far

   outfile << "Train Loads Processed" << endl;
   cout << "Train Loads Processed" << endl;

   // Add up trainloads scheduled for the day
   infile >> train_load;
   while (train_load != SENTINEL) {
```

FIGURE 4.4 *(Continued)*

```
        total_coal = total_coal + train_load;
        outfile << train_load << " tons" << endl;
        cout << train_load << " tons" << endl;
        infile >> train_load;
    }

    // Output the total amount of coal expected
    outfile << "Scheduled coal arrival total of " << total_coal <<
        " tons " << endl;
    cout << "Scheduled coal arrival total of " << total_coal <<
        " tons " << endl;

    // Output whether total is sufficient or falls short
    if (total_coal >= MIN_COAL_REQUIRED) {
        outfile << "is sufficient for daily operation." << endl;
        cout << "is sufficient for daily operation." << endl;
    } else {
        outfile << "falls " << MIN_COAL_REQUIRED - total_coal <<
            " tons short of daily need." << endl;
        cout << "falls " << MIN_COAL_REQUIRED - total_coal <<
            " tons short of daily need." << endl;
    }

    infile.close();
    outfile.close();

    return 0;
}
```

Contents of coaldata.txt:

2000
1200
1500
1000
1400
1800
1300
0

Contents of coal.out and output displayed on screen:

```
Train Loads Processed
2000 tons
1200 tons
1500 tons
1000 tons
1400 tons
1800 tons
1300 tons
Scheduled coal arrival total
of 10200 tons is sufficient
for daily operation.
```

When processing is complete, the program closes the input and output files using the statements

```
infile.close();
outfile.close();
```

Creating an Input File

You can use any editor or word processor to create a data file to provide input to your program. If you elect to use a full-service word processor such as Word or WordPerfect, be sure to save the file as "Text only." Alternatively, you could choose the editor that is part of your integrated development environment, which will likely save your file as plain text by default. When entering values into your file, just be sure to place them in the order in which the program plans to input the data.

Loops That Exit on Input Failure

When we write a batch program that processes a single collection of data taken from a file, we can take advantage of the fact that the C++ run-time support system can detect when a file extraction operation fails. If `infile` is the variable associated with our input file, immediately after execution of an extraction such as

```
infile >> data;
```

for which there is no valid data, the expression

```
infile.fail()
```

will evaluate to true. As long as extraction operations are finding values in the file that are the expected data type for the target variables, the value of this expression is false. Figure 4.5 shows a batch version of our power plant coal program that uses input-failure checking to control the input loop. At loop exit, the program checks the value of the expression

```
infile.eof()
```

to determine whether input failure occurred because the end of the data file was encountered or because invalid data were encountered. The letters `eof` stand for *end of file*. This program takes its data from the file `coaldata.txt` and sends results to the file `coal.out`. The figure shows the results of one run.

Notice that in C++ an input-failure-controlled loop is similar to a sentinel loop: It requires one extraction operation for input of the first data value before entering the loop, and another input operation at the end of the loop body. However, the input file contains no sentinel value at the end.

FIGURE 4.5 Input-Failure-Controlled Batch Version of Power Plant Coal Program

```cpp
//  Determine if scheduled coal arrivals are sufficient to fuel
//  electric power plant for one day
//      Input from file
//      Output to file and to screen

#include <iostream>
#include <fstream>  // needed for direct file manipulation
using namespace std;

const int MIN_COAL_REQUIRED = 10000; // minimum tons of coal
                                     // necessary for one day
int main()
{
    ifstream infile("a:coaldata.txt", ios::in);
                    // associate coaldata.txt with infile
    ofstream outfile("a:coal.out", ios::out);
                    // associate coal.out with outfile
    int train_load,        // tons of coal in current train load
        total_coal = 0;    // tons of coal counted so far

    outfile << "Train Loads Processed" << endl;
    cout << "Train Loads Processed" << endl;

    // Add up trainloads scheduled for the day
    infile >> train_load;
    while (!infile.fail()) {
        total_coal = total_coal + train_load;
        outfile << train_load << " tons" << endl;
        cout << train_load << " tons" << endl;
        infile >> train_load;
    }
```

FIGURE 4.5 *(Continued)*

```cpp
// Output the total amount of coal expected unless invalid
// data encountered
if (infile.eof()) {
    outfile << "Scheduled coal arrival total of " << total_coal <<
        " tons " << endl;
    cout << "Scheduled coal arrival total of " << total_coal <<
        " tons " << endl;

    // Output whether total is sufficient or falls short
    if (total_coal >= MIN_COAL_REQUIRED) {
        outfile << "is sufficient for daily operation." << endl;
        cout << "is sufficient for daily operation." << endl;
    } else {
        outfile << "falls " << MIN_COAL_REQUIRED - total_coal <<
            " tons short of daily need." << endl;
        cout << "falls " << MIN_COAL_REQUIRED - total_coal <<
            " tons short of daily need." << endl;
    }
} else {
    outfile << "Invalid data in file." << endl;
    cout << "Invalid data in file." << endl;
}

infile.close();
outfile.close();

return 0;
}
```

Loop-Priming and Loop-Control-Update Input Statements

loop-priming input statement
input of a value into the loop control variable immediately before a sentinel- or input-failure-controlled `while` loop

loop-control-update input statement
input of a value into the loop control variable as the last statement in the loop body of a sentinel- or input-failure-controlled `while` loop

We have seen that a requirement common to both the sentinel-controlled loop and the input-failure-controlled loop is the need for *two* input statements—one just before the `while` loop to give the loop control variable a value before the first test of the loop repetition condition (the **loop-priming input statement**), and a second input as the last statement of the loop body (the **loop-control-update input statement**) to keep the loop going or to cause it to exit. It is easy to slip and omit one of these inputs or to mistakenly place a single input statement at the beginning of the loop body as you would in a counting loop that inputs a list of data.

Section 4.2 Review Questions

1. Explain the difference in placement of statements that use << to display prompts and statements that echo data. Which placement do you find in interactive programs, and which do you use in batch programs?

2. Write a program fragment to implement this pseudocode.
   1) Open file **data.txt** and associate it with file variable **in**.
   2) Take the first value from **data.txt** and store it in **x**.
   3) Display the value of **x** with a label.
   4) Close the data file.

4.3   The for Statement

So far we have implemented all our loops using the `while` statement. C++ also provides the `for` statement, a repetition construct that has a designated place for each of the three common components of a loop: loop control variable initialization, test of the loop repetition condition, and loop control variable update. Figure 4.6 shows the form of the `for` statement along with a comparable `while` statement.

Execution of a `for` statement proceeds in this order (step numbers refer to the circled numbers in Fig. 4.6):

FIGURE 4.6   Comparison of for and while Statements

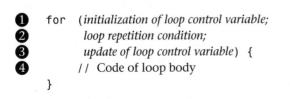

```
❶    for   (initialization of loop control variable;         initialization of loop control variable;
❷            loop repetition condition;                       while (loop repetition condition)  {
❸            update of loop control variable)  {                 // Code of loop body
❹            // Code of loop body                                 update of loop control variable;
     }                                                        }
```

Effect	Step
1	The loop control variable is initialized.
2	Loop repetition condition is tested.
	If it is false, execution continues with the first
	statement after the loop body of the for statement.
	If it is true,
4	the loop body is executed, and
3	the loop control variable is updated.
2	Loop repetition condition is tested.
	If it is false, execution continues with the first
	statement after the loop body of the for statement.
	If it is true,
4	the loop body is executed, and
3	the loop control variable is updated.
2	Loop repetition condition is tested.
	If it is false, execution continues with the first
	statement after the loop body of the for statement.
	If it is true,
4	the loop body is executed, and
3	the loop control variable is updated.
. . .	. . .

The {} around the loop body of the for statement are required only if the loop body contains more than one statement. Because it provides such a clear presentation of the standard loop control components, the for statement is a very popular control structure among C++ software developers. In Figs. 4.7 and 4.8 we show for loop versions of our recent counting loop and input-failure-controlled loop examples. If the loop control variable is declared where it is initialized, as is shown in Fig. 4.7, it can be used only through the end of the loop body.

FIGURE 4.7 Counting Loop Program That Uses a for Statement

```
//
//   Determine if new vehicles meet carbon monoxide emissions standard.
//

#include <iostream>
using namespace std;

const double MAXCO = 3.4; // maximum g/mi of carbon monoxide allowed

int main()
```

FIGURE 4.7 *(Continued)*

```cpp
{
    double coEmitted, // grams of carbon monoxide emitted
            miles,     // miles driven during test
            coRate;    // g/mi of carbon monoxide emitted
    int     vehicles; // number of vehicles tested

    cout << "Number of vehicles tested => ";
    cin >> vehicles;

    for  (int ct = 0;  ct < vehicles;  ct = ct + 1) {
        cout << "Enter amount of carbon monoxide emitted (grams) => ";
        cin >> coEmitted;
        cout << "Enter miles driven => ";
        cin >> miles;

        coRate = coEmitted / miles;
        cout << "Carbon monoxide emission of " << coRate << " g/mi ";

        if (coRate <= MAXCO)
            cout << "meets ";
        else
            cout << "exceeds ";

        cout << "permitted emission of " << endl << MAXCO << " g/mi." << endl;
    }
    return 0;
}
```

FIGURE 4.8 Input-Failure-Controlled Power Plant Coal Program with for Statement

```cpp
// Determine if scheduled coal arrivals are sufficient to fuel
// electric power plant for one day

#include <iostream>
#include <fstream>  // needed for direct file manipulation
using namespace std;

const int MIN_COAL_REQUIRED = 10000; // minimum tons of coal necessary for one day

int main()
{
```

FIGURE 4.8 *(Continued)*

```
ifstream infile("coaldata.txt", ios::in);    // associate coaldata.txt with infile
ofstream outfile("coal.out", ios::out);      // associate coal.out with outfile
int trainLoad,          // tons of coal in current trainload
    totalCoal = 0;      // tons of coal counted so far

outfile << "Trainloads Processed" << endl;
for  (infile >> trainLoad;
      !infile.fail();
      infile >> trainLoad) {
    totalCoal = totalCoal + trainLoad;
    outfile << trainLoad << " tons" << endl;
}
if (infile.eof()) {
    outfile << "Scheduled coal arrival total of " << totalCoal <<
            " tons " << endl;
    if (totalCoal >= MIN_COAL_REQUIRED)
        outfile << "is sufficient for daily operation." << endl;
    else
        outfile << "falls " << MIN_COAL_REQUIRED - totalCoal <<
            " tons short of daily need." << endl;
} else {
    outfile << "Invalid data in file." << endl;
}
infile.close();
outfile.close();

return 0;
}
```

Section 4.3 Review Questions

1.–4. Write code fragments for the loops needed in each of the situations described
in the Section 4.1 Review Questions. Write two versions for each: one using a
while loop and one using a **for** loop. (*Hint:* For Question 3, actually compute
the first two approximations *before* entering the loop.)

5. What output is produced by this program fragment?

```
for (int i = 0; i < 5; i = i + 1)
    for (int j = i; j > 0; j = j - 1)
        cout << i << " " << j << endl;
```

4.4 Operators That Change Their Operands

The only operator we have used that changes the value of one of its operands is the assignment operator (=). C++ defines other operators with this property: compound assignment operators and increment/decrement operators.

Compound Assignment Operators

We have seen several instances of assignment statements of the form

variable = variable op expression;

These statements include increments of loop counters

```
ct = ct + 1;
```

as well as statements accumulating a sum in a loop, such as

```
totalCoal = totalCoal + trainLoad;
```

C++ provides special assignment operators that make possible a more concise notation of statements of this type. For the operations +, –, *, /, and %, C++ defines the compound *op=* assignment operators +=, –=, *=, /=, and %=. A statement of the form

variable op= expression;

is an alternative way of writing the statement

variable = variable op (expression);

Notice that when you write

variable op= expression;

there is an implied set of parentheses around the expression, so the expression will be completely evaluated before calculation of

variable op expressionValue;

Therefore, there is no shorter way to write an assignment statement such as

```
t = t * x + 1;   // multiplication before addition
```

If we were to try to write this using *=, we would have

```
t *= x + 1;
```

which means

```
t = t * (x + 1);   // addition before multiplication
```

Table 4.2 lists the assignment statements just noted along with their equivalents using compound assignment operators. In addition, the table shows an assignment statement that decrements a counter, a statement that could be

TABLE 4.2 Using Compound Assignment Operators

Statement with Simple Assignment Operator	Equivalent Statement with Compound Assignment Operator
`ct = ct + 1;`	`ct += 1;`
`time = time - 1;`	`time -= 1;`
`totalCoal = totalCoal + trainLoad;`	`totalCoal += trainLoad;`
`product = product * data;`	`product *= data;`
`n = n * (x + 1);`	`n *= x + 1;`

used in a loop to compute the product of a list of numbers, and an assignment that demonstrates the relevance of the parentheses around *expression* in our preceding definition.

Compound assignment operators are especially useful when the target of the assignment is a single component of one of the composite data structures that we will study in Chapters 6, 7, and 8. In these cases, the use of a compound assignment operator is not only more concise, but also more efficient.

Increment and Decrement Operators

Each of the arithmetic operators that we have studied thus far has produced an expression value without changing the values of its operands. For example, after evaluating the expression x + y in the statement

```
if (x + y > Max)
     cout << "Sum larger" << endl;
```

the values of x and y are unchanged. C++ also provides operators that add 1 or subtract 1 from their operands, but these operators differ from other arithmetic operators in that

- their operands must be variables, and
- they *change* the values of their operands, a consequence called a **side effect**.

side effect
a change in a variable's value as a result of using the variable as an operand or argument

The increment operator is ++, and the decrement operator is --. Although these operators can be used within a complex arithmetic expression, they are used frequently just for their side effects, as in this loop in which the counter ct is to run from 0 up to limit:

```
for (ct = 0;  ct < limit;  ++ct)
 . . .
```

The value of the expression in which the ++ operator is used depends on the position of the operator. When the ++ is placed immediately in front of its operand (*prefix* increment), the value of the expression is the variable's value after incrementing. When the ++ comes immediately after the operand (*post-*

fix increment), the expression's value is the value of the variable before it is incremented. Compare the action of the two code segments in Fig. 4.9, given an initial value of 2 in i.

The decrement operator can also be used in either the prefix or postfix position. For example, if the initial value of n is 4, the code fragment on the left displays

```
3   3
```

and the one on the right displays

```
4   3
```

using these code fragments:

```
cout << --n;                cout << n--;
cout << n << endl;          cout << n << endl;
```

You should avoid using the increment and decrement operators in complex expressions in which the variables to which they are applied appear more than once. C++ compilers are expected to exploit the commutativity and associativity of various operators in order to produce efficient code. For example, the following code fragment may assign y the value 13 (2 * 5 + 3) in one implementation and the value 18 (3 * 5 + 3) in another:

```
x = 5;
i = 2;
y = i * x + ++i;
```

A programmer must not depend on side effects that will vary from one compiler to another.

FIGURE 4.9 Comparison of Prefix and Postfix Increments

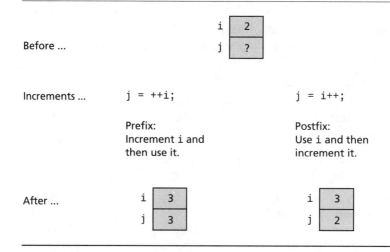

Displaying a Table

One common use of a loop is the display of a table of numbers. A program creates a table by first displaying column headings and then displaying the values of the table one line at a time. For example, consider the growth of a culture of bacteria. If the number of bacteria (N) in a certain culture at time *t* hours is modeled by the equation

$$N = 1000 \times 10^{0.0451t}$$

then if you were to display N at *t* = 0 hours, 5 hours, 10 hours, up to 50 hours, you would want a table like Table 4.3. This table displays integers with the ones digits of the numbers aligned. As a result, the number of spaces before the time value varies, as does the number of spaces between the *t* and *N* values. We cannot display such a table by repeatedly executing a statement such as

```
cout << '       ' << t << '                ' << nBacteria << endl;
```

This statement would misalign the values, as shown in Table 4.4.

C++ makes it possible to remedy this situation by providing a means of right-justifying values in a prescribed **field** of the output line. Here are the first and last lines of our desired table with spaces marked by ☐'s.

field
a fixed number of columns of an output line

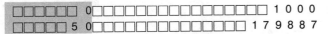

The *t* values are right-justified in a field composed of the first seven columns of the output line, the field displayed with shading. The N values are right-justified in a field of the next 20 columns. The C++ iomanip library provides a function setw that sets the width of a field in an output stream. You should insert a call to setw in the output stream immediately before inserting the ex-

TABLE 4.3 Growth of a Culture of Bacteria

Time (hours)	Number of Bacteria
0	1000
5	1680
10	2824
15	4747
20	7979
25	13412
30	22542
35	37887
40	63679
45	107028
50	179887

TABLE 4.4 Misaligned Table Values for Culture Growth

0	1000
5	1680
10	2824
15	4747
20	7979
25	13412
30	22542
35	37887
40	63679
45	107028
50	179887

pression whose value you wish to display. Function setw takes a single argument, the width of the field. The C++ program in Fig. 4.10 implements the display of our desired table of bacteria growth, and shows a sample run.

The statement that displays one line of the table for each iteration of the loop is

```
cout << setw(7) << t << setw(20) << int(nBacteria) << endl;
```

FIGURE 4.10 Program to Display a Bacterial Growth Table

```
//
// Display a table showing the number of bacteria present in a culture
// modeled by                   0.0451t
//                 N = (1000) 10
// Table displays number of bacteria at t = start,
// at t = start + incr, and so on until t > end

#include <iostream>
#include <cmath>
#include <iomanip>
using namespace std;

int main()
{
   int    start,    // starting time (hours)
          end,      // ending time (hours)
          incr;     // increment (hours)
   double nBacteria; // number of bacteria

   cout << "Enter start time, end time, and time increment => ";
```

FIGURE 4.10 *(Continued)*

```
   cin >> start >> end >> incr;

   cout << endl << "Time (hours)      Number of bacteria" << endl;
   for  (int t = start;  t <= end;  t += incr) {
       nBacteria = 1000 * pow(10, 0.0451 * t);
       cout << setw(7) << t << setw(20) << int(nBacteria) << endl;
   }
   return 0;
}
Enter start time, end time, and time increment => 0 50 5

Time (hours)      Number of Bacteria
     0                  1000
     5                  1680
    10                  2824
    15                  4747
    20                  7979
    25                 13412
    30                 22542
    35                 37887
    40                 63679
    45                107028
    50                179887
```

Displaying Octal and Hexadecimal Values

We have seen that C++ normally displays integers in base 10. To change the base for display to 8 or 16, insert in the output stream the manipulator oct for octal or hex for hexadecimal as demonstrated in Figure 4.11. To change back to base 10, insert dec in the output stream.

Aligning Floating Point Values

C++'s standard display format for floating point values does not create attractive tables. To create aligned output such as

```
      Fixed           Scientific
      19.80           1.980e+001
    4000.00           4.000e+003
17500000.00           1.750e+007
```

use the stream manipulators shown in Table 4.5.

Figure 4.12 demonstrates the use of the manipulators explained in Table 4.5, manipulators that are defined in the iomanip library.

FIGURE 4.11 Integers Displayed in Base 8, Base 10, and Base 16

Code Fragment

```
int n = 14, p = 45;
cout << "n = " << n << ", p = " << p << endl;
cout << "n(base 8) = " << oct << n << ", p(base 8) = " << p << endl;
cout << "n(base 16) = " << hex << n << ", p(base 16) = " << p << endl;
cout << "n(base 10) = " << dec << n << ", p(base 10) = " << p << endl;
```

Output

```
n = 14, p = 45
n(base 8) = 16, p(base 8) = 55
n(base 16) = e, p(base 16) = 2d
n(base 10) = 14, p(base 10) = 45
```

TABLE 4.5 Stream Manipulators from <iomanip> for Floating Point Output

Manipulator	Meaning
setiosflags(ios::fixed)	Use standard fixed-point (not scientific) notation: value set by setprecision determines number of digits displayed to right of decimal. Value is rounded or padded with zeros to fit.
resetiosflags(ios::fixed)	Turn off fixed-point notation.
setiosflags(ios::scientific)	Use scientific notation: value set by setprecision determines number of digits displayed to right of decimal. Value is rounded or padded with zeros to fit.
resetiosflags(ios::scientific)	Turn off scientific notation.
setprecision(n)	In either fixed-point or scientific notation, display n digits to the right of decimal. If neither fixed nor scientific flag is set, display a total of n significant digits.

FIGURE 4.12 Formatting Floating Point Values

Code fragment:

```
double x = 19.795, y = 4000.00, z = 1.75e7;

// Prepare stream to output floating-point values in fixed
// (non-scientific) notation with two digits to the right
// of the decimal point.
```

FIGURE 4.12 *(Continued)*

```
cout << setiosflags(ios::fixed) << setprecision(2);

// Output values on two lines in a field of 12 columns.
cout << "Fixed notation, 2 lines, field width 12, precision 2\n";
cout << setw(12) << x << endl << setw(12) << y << endl << endl;

// Change precision to display 3 decimal digits to the right
// of the decimal point.  Then display values in fields of
// 14 columns.
cout << setprecision(3);
cout << "Fixed notation, field width 14, precision 3\n";
cout << setw(14) << y << setw(14) << z << endl << endl;

// Turn off fixed notation and turn on scientific.  Then
// display two values.  Precision remains at 3.
cout << resetiosflags(ios::fixed);
cout << setiosflags(ios::scientific);
cout <<
    "Scientific notation, 2 lines, field width 14, precision 3\n";
cout << setw(14) << x << endl << setw(14) << y << endl << endl;

// Change precision to 4 digits after decimal point.
cout << setprecision(4);
cout << "Scientific notation, field width 14, precision 4\n";
cout << setw(14) << y << setw(14) << z << endl << endl;

// Turn off scientific notation.
cout << resetiosflags(ios::scientific);
```

Output:

```
Fixed notation, 2 lines, field width 12, precision 2
       19.80
     4000.00

Fixed notation, field width 14, precision 3
      4000.000   17500000.000

Scientific notation, 2 lines, field width 14, precision 3
     1.980e+001
     4.000e+003

Scientific notation, field width 14, precision 4
     4.0000e+003    1.7500e+007
```

Section 4.4 Review Questions

1. Trace the execution of the loop that follows for **n** = 8. Follow the format of Table 4.1 on p. 111.

```
sum = 0;
for  (odd = 1;  odd < n;  odd += 2)
    sum += odd;
cout << "Sum of positive odd numbers less than " << n <<
            " is " << sum << "." << endl;
```

2. What values are assigned to **n, m,** and **p** in this code fragment?

```
i = 3;
j = 9;
n = ++i * --j;
m = i + j--;
p = i + j;
```

3. Rewrite the code fragment of Question 2 without using increment or decrement operators. Do use compound assignment operators, and be sure the effect of the code is equivalent.

4. Trace the execution of the loop below for an input of 40.

```
1   num1 = 1;
2   cout << "Enter a number=> ";
3   cin >> num2;
4   while  ((num2 / num1) > 1) {
5           cout << num1 << "  " << num2 << endl;
6           num1 += 1;
7           num2 -= 3;
8   }
```

Follow the format of Table 4.1 on p. 111.

5. What output is displayed by this program fragment if the value of **x** is –28.749?

```
cout << setiosflags( ios::fixed ) << setprecision( 2 );
cout << setw( 10 ) << x << endl;
cout << setprecision( 4 ) << setw( 12 ) << x << endl;
cout << setprecision( 1 ) << setw( 12 ) << x << endl;
```

4.5 Input Errors

Extraction of numeric values from a data stream can proceed correctly only if the stream contains characters that represent numeric values. It is easy for a program user to accidentally enter an invalid character such as an uppercase letter O instead of a zero. The user might also enter a percent sign after a number when asked for a percent value. Here are the data input statements from the sulfur dioxide emission rate program of Fig. 2.1.

```
cout << "Enter sample identification number => ";
cin >> sampleId;
cout << "What percent of the sample is sulfur? => ";
cin >> sulfurContent;
cout << "How many Btu's of energy from one pound of the sample? => ";
cin >> energyContent;
```

Figure 4.13 shows two runs of the program with invalid input. In the first run, the user enters 501 where the middle character is not a zero, but an uppercase O. The first extraction operation stops at the O, and stores 5 in sampleId. The second and third extraction operations do not wait for the user to respond to the prompting messages because there is unprocessed data available: the O and 1 entered after the first prompt. However, since the next extraction is trying to find a numeric value to store in sulfurContent, it is unable to process the uppercase O. Once an input operation fails, subsequent inputs from the stream are not attempted unless the record of failure is acknowledged by the program. You see in the output that follows that the values displayed are garbage. In the second run, the sample id is entered

FIGURE 4.13   Giving Invalid Input to the Sulfur Dioxide Emissions Program

First Run

```
Enter sample identification number => 501
What percent of the sample is sulfur? => How many Btu's of energy from one
pound of the sample? => Sulfur dioxide emissions of coal sample 5 with sulfur
content of
     5.780406e-311 percent and energy content of 2.209912e-267 Btu per pound:
          Before scrubbing: 5.231345e-40 pounds per million Btu
          After scrubbing:  1.046269e-40 pounds per million Btu
```

Second Run

```
Enter sample identification number => 501
What percent of the sample is sulfur? => 10%
How many Btu's of energy from one pound of the sample? => Sulfur dioxide
emissions of coal sample 501 with sulfur content of
     10 percent and energy content of 2.209912e-267 Btu per pound:
          Before scrubbing: 9.050135e+271 pounds per million Btu
          After scrubbing:  1.810027e+271 pounds per million Btu
```

FIGURE 4.14 Improved Sulfur Dioxide Emission Program

```cpp
//
//  Calculate sulfur dioxide emission rate for a coal sample — without
//  scrubbing and with scrubbing that is 80% effective
//

#include <iostream>
using namespace std;

const double OXIDATION_FACTOR = 2.0;  // oxidizing n pounds of sulfur
                    // produces about 2n pounds of sulfur dioxide
const double SCRUB_EFFICIENCY = 0.8;  // scrubbing combustion gases
                    // reduces sulfur dioxide emissions by 80%

int main()
{
   int     sampleId;        // sample identification number
   double sulfurContent,    // % of sample that is sulfur
          energyContent;    // number of Btu per pound
   char    badChar;         // character causing error in data

   // Get data on coal sample
   cout << "Enter sample identification number => ";
   cin >> sampleId;
   cout << "What percent of the sample is sulfur?  => ";
   cin >> sulfurContent;
   cout << "How many Btu's of energy from one pound of the sample? => ";
   cin >> energyContent;

   if (cin.eof()) {
      cout << endl << "Unexpected end of file.  Program aborted" << endl;
   } else if (cin.fail()) {
      cin.clear();
      cin >> badChar;
      cout << endl << "Error in data.  First invalid character>> "
           << badChar << endl;
      cout << "Program aborted" << endl;
   } else {
      // Calculate emissions rate for burning this sample
      double poundsDioxide = sulfurContent / 100.0 * OXIDATION_FACTOR;
      double emissions = poundsDioxide * 1000000.0 / energyContent;

      // Calculate emissions rate with scrubbing
      double withScrubbing = emissions - emissions * SCRUB_EFFICIENCY;
```

FIGURE 4.14 *(Continued)*

```
      // Display results
      cout << "Sulfur dioxide emissions of coal sample " << sampleId <<
           " with sulfur content of " << endl;
      cout << "    " << sulfurContent << " percent and energy content of "
           << energyContent << " Btu per pound:" << endl;
      cout << "           Before scrubbing: " << emissions <<
           " pounds per million Btu" << endl;
      cout << "           After scrubbing:  " << withScrubbing <<
           " pounds per million Btu" << endl;
   }
   return 0;
}
```

First Run

```
Enter sample identification number => 501
What percent of the sample is sulfur?  => How many Btu's of energy from one pound
of the sample? =>
Error in data.  First invalid character>> O
Program aborted
```

Second Run

```
Enter sample identification number => 501
What percent of the sample is sulfur?  => 10%
How many Btu's of energy from one pound of the sample? =>
Error in data.  First invalid character>> %
Program aborted
```

correctly as 501. However, the value for sulfurContent is entered as 10%. The 10 is stored in sulfurContent, but the percent sign is left unprocessed until the extraction for energyContent. Since % cannot be validly processed when attempting to extract a number for energyContent, no new value is stored in energyContent, so again the program output is garbage.

The program in Fig. 4.14 is an improved version of the sulfur dioxide emissions program. Before attempting to process the data extracted, this program uses cin.fail() to check whether any input operations on the stream cin have failed. After detecting input failure, the improved program checks whether end-of-file caused the failure. If not, it makes it possible to resume input from cin by calling the function cin.clear. It then extracts the character that caused the input failure and displays it as part of an error message.

At the end of the figure are runs of the new program on the same faulty data shown in Fig. 4.13.

We could similarly improve the error message displayed by the coal arrivals program of Figs. 4.5 and 4.8 by clearing the input failure flag associated with `infile` and then extracting and displaying the invalid character.

Section 4.5 Review Questions

1. Revise the loops you wrote for Section 4.3 Review Question 1 so that your program would detect a user input error and display an error message that includes the first invalid character.

2. Revise the firefighting water flow rate program of Fig. 2.13 so that it would give a meaningful error message if a data stream error occurred on the input of population and would compute the necessary water flow only in the event of no data stream error.

3. Revise the coal arrivals program of Fig. 4.5 so that it displays an error message that includes the first invalid character if it encounters invalid data.

4.6   The do-while Loop

In the counting, sentinel-controlled, and input-failure-controlled loops that we have studied so far, we have always viewed the initialization and update of the loop control variable as two separate steps. This has been essential either because we used different code for the two steps (e.g., counter initialization: `ct = 1`; counter update: `++ct`) or because it was essential that we exit the loop immediately after execution of the last update (e.g., after the input-failure- or sentinel-encountering input).

In some cases, however, all values of the loop control variable receive the same processing, so there need be no distinction between initialization and update. The C++ do—while loop is an excellent control structure to use here. For example, if we want to give a program user multiple opportunities to enter a data value and exit only when the value is valid for use in our program, we need to repeat these steps:

1. Get a data value.
2. Check the data value.

until the data value we have is valid. A data value might be invalid either because of an error detected in the input stream or because the data item entered is outside the valid range. In case of error, the program must clear the input stream of the character causing the error. A data-validation input loop executes until a valid data value is entered.

The program fragment in Fig. 4.15 asks the user to provide the minimum and maximum values of the valid range and then repeatedly prompts the

FIGURE 4.15 Input Validation Loop Example

```
//
//  Gets an integer input value in the range from nMin to nMax
//  inclusive.  Displays an error message on input of an invalid
//  data type, and clears character causing error.
//

#include <iostream>
using namespace std;

int main()
{
    int nMin, nMax;    // input - minimum & maximum valid data values
    int inVal;         // input - data value to be validated
    char skipChar;     // input - character causing error on input stream
    bool error;        // error on input stream?

    cout << "Enter minimum and maximum valid values=> ";
    cin >> nMin >> nMax;

    do {
        cout << "Enter an integer in the range from " << nMin << " to "
            <<  nMax << " inclusive=> ";
        cin >> inVal;
        if (cin.fail()) {
            cin.clear();
            error = true;
            cin >> skipChar;
            cout << endl << "Skipping invalid character >> " << skipChar
                    << endl;
        } else {
            error = false;
        }
    } while (error || inVal < nMin || inVal > nMax);

        // rest of processing
}
```

```
Enter minimum and maximum valid values => 50 100
Enter an integer in the range from 50 to 100 inclusive => 60
Enter an integer in the range from 50 to 100 inclusive =>
Skipping invalid character >> 0
Enter an integer in the range from 50 to 100 inclusive => 100
```

FIGURE 4.15 *(Continued)*

```
Enter an integer in the range from 50 to 100 inclusive =>
Skipping invalid character >> O
Enter an integer in the range from 50 to 100 inclusive =>
Skipping invalid character >> O
Enter an integer in the range from 50 to 100 inclusive => 99
```

user for valid data until such a data item is entered. If the user enters non-numeric data, the program detects the error, extracts the invalid character from the stream and displays it, and resumes prompting for valid data. The loop repetition condition of the do–while, like those of the while and for loops, is a condition that is true when the loop body should be executed again: It is a "stay-in" condition, not an "exit" condition. Unlike the bodies of the for and while loops, which may not execute at all, the do–while's loop body is always executed at least once. The loop repetition condition is tested after the loop body executes.

Be careful when choosing a do–while loop. You must not use it when it is conceivable that the loop body should not execute at all. If you ever find yourself revising your code by inserting a decision statement that allows a do–while to be skipped completely, review carefully your choice of loop structure. Probably a for or while would be a better choice.

Section 4.6 Review Questions

1. Which of the following code segments is a better way to implement a sentinel-controlled loop? Why?

```
for  (cin >> num;              do {
       num != SENTINEL;             cin >> num;
       cin >> num) {               if (num != SENTINEL) {
     // Process num                     // Process num
}                              } while (num != SENTINEL);
```

2. Design an interactive loop that inputs pairs of integers until it reaches a pair in which the first integer evenly divides the second.

4.7 Problem Solving with Loops

Modems transmit computer data across phone lines. To do so, they convert sequences of zeros and ones, the binary numbers used for data representation in a digital computer, to analog signals of two frequencies. A modem transmits a data bit 1 as a high tone that is one time unit long; a sequence of 8 ones is sent as a high tone 8 time units long. The modem represents a data bit 0 as a lower tone. In the next case study we develop a program that demonstrates the behavior of a modem.

A CALLING MODEM

Problem

A calling modem transmits each data bit 1 as a 1270-hertz tone lasting one time unit, and each data bit 0 as a 1070-hertz tone. Write a program that displays messages indicating the tones that would be emitted for the data in the file `digital.txt`, a file of zeros and ones separated by spaces. The messages should take the form

```
Emit ____–hz tone for ____ time unit(s).
```

where the tone frequency changes in each message.

Understanding the Problem

Let's consider a brief data file that is correct for the problem stated and predict the messages to be displayed.

Sample Contents of `digital.txt`

1 0 0 0 0 1 1 0 1 0 1 1 1 1 0 0 0 1

Messages for Sample Data

```
Emit 1270–hz tone for 1 time unit(s).
Emit 1070–hz tone for 4 time unit(s).
Emit 1270–hz tone for 2 time unit(s).
Emit 1070–hz tone for 1 time unit(s).
Emit 1270–hz tone for 1 time unit(s).
Emit 1070–hz tone for 1 time unit(s).
Emit 1270–hz tone for 4 time unit(s).
Emit 1070–hz tone for 3 time unit(s).
Emit 1270–hz tone for 1 time unit(s).
```

Now we can identify the problem's constants, inputs, and outputs and sketch an initial approach.

Data Definition

Constants

```
HIGH_TONE  1270
LOW_TONE   1070
```

Inputs

```
digit      // current digit from file
```

Outputs

```
tone       // frequency of tone to emit
timeUnits // duration of tone
```

Algorithm Design

Initial Algorithm

With input-failure checking repeat

1. Get a digit.
2. Process a digit.

When we attempt to refine Step 2, we soon realize that processing the first digit differs from processing all the others. The first digit tells us the frequency and minimum duration of the first tone. The code to process all subsequent digits must be selected depending on whether the new digit continues a tone we have been building or signals the beginning of a new tone and therefore the end of the tone under construction. Before trying to refine our initial algorithm, let's revise it so it accounts for the first digit as a separate issue.

Revised Initial Algorithm

1. Get first digit.
2. Process first digit.
3. With input-failure checking repeat
   4. Get a digit.
   5. Process a digit.

Now we can refine Steps 2 and 5.

Refinement of Step 2

2. Process first digit.
   2.1 If digit is 1
         2.2 Store HIGH_TONE in tone.
      else
         2.3 Store LOW_TONE in tone.
   2.4 Set timeUnits to 1.

Refinement of Step 5

5. Process a digit

5.1 If `digit` is 0

    5.2 If existing tone is extended

        5.3 Add 1 to `timeUnits`.

   else

      5.4 Display message about completed tone.

      5.5 Start new tone (`LOW_TONE`) with minimal time.

5.6 If `digit` is 1

    5.7 If existing tone is extended

        5.8 Add 1 to `timeUnits`.

   else

      5.9 Display message about completed tone.

      5.10 Start new tone (`HIGH_TONE`) with minimal time.

Now if we test this algorithm, we discover that since times are displayed only after a digit change is encountered, the message describing the final tone is not displayed. This we correct by adding a step to the basic algorithm.

Corrected Algorithm

1. Get first digit.
2. Process first digit.
3. With input-failure checking repeat
   4. Get a digit.
   5. Process a digit.
   6. Display final tone.

Figure 4.16 shows an implementation of this algorithm that uses a `switch` statement for Step 5, since there are only two valid values for `digit`. This implementation also uses input validation loops for Steps 1 and 4. We store the digits not as integers but as characters, to reduce the need to check for input errors. Every digit is a valid character, but many characters cannot be converted to integers. At the end of the figure is a run on a brief correct data file.

FIGURE 4.16 Modem Demonstration Program

```
//
//  Demonstrate conversion of digital data (taken from file "digital.txt")
//  to analog tones. File must contain at least one valid digit.

#include <iostream>
#include <fstream>
using namespace std;
```

Comment

Standard Library & Namespace Inclusion

FIGURE 4.16 *(Continued)*

```
const int LOW_TONE  = 1070;  // calling modem low tone  (hertz)        Constant
const int HIGH_TONE = 1270;  // calling modem high tone (hertz)       Declarations

int main()                        Main Function Heading
{
    int  timeUnits;  // duration of one emitted tone          Variable Declarations
    int  tone;       // frequency of current tone (hertz)
    char digit;      // 0 or 1 scanned from file

    ifstream datafile( "digital.txt", ios::in );          File Variable
                                                          Declaration

    cout << "Demonstration of Digital to Analog Data Conversion" << endl
         << endl;

    //  Determine initial tone based on initial valid digit
    for  (datafile >> digit;
            digit != '0'  &&  digit != '1';                 File Input
            datafile >> digit)
       cout << "Ignoring faulty digit: " << digit << endl;
    cout << digit;
    switch (digit) {                    switch Statement
    case '0':
        tone = LOW_TONE;
        timeUnits = 1;
        break;

    case '1':
        tone = HIGH_TONE;
        timeUnits = 1;
    }

    // Convert digits remaining in file
    for  (datafile >> digit;              Input-Failure-Controlled for Loop
           !datafile.fail();
           datafile >> digit) {
       cout << digit;

       switch (digit) {
       case '0':
           if (tone == LOW_TONE) {  // tone continues
                ++timeUnits;
           } else {                 // tone changes
```

FIGURE 4.16   *(Continued)*

```
          cout << endl << "Emit " << tone << "-hz tone for " <<
              timeUnits << " time unit(s)." << endl;
          tone = LOW_TONE;
          timeUnits = 1;
      }
      break;

    case '1':
      if (tone == HIGH_TONE) { // tone continues
          ++timeUnits;
      } else {
          cout << endl << "Emit " << tone << "-hz tone for " <<
              timeUnits << " time unit(s)." << endl;
          tone = HIGH_TONE;
          timeUnits = 1;
      }
      break;

    default:
      cout << endl << "Ignoring faulty digit " << digit << endl;
    }
  }

  // Emit tone that was under construction when data ran out
  cout << endl << "Emit " << tone << "-hz tone for " << timeUnits <<
      " time unit(s)." << endl;

  datafile.close(); ◄──────    File Close

  return 0;
}
```

Contents of **digital.txt**

1 0 0 0 0 1 1 0 1 0 1 1 1 1 0 0 0 1

Output

Demonstration of Digital to Analog Data Conversion

10
Emit 1270-hz tone for 1 time unit(s).
0001

FIGURE 4.16 *(Continued)*

```
Emit 1070–hz tone for 4 time unit(s).
10
Emit 1270–hz tone for 2 time unit(s).
1
Emit 1070–hz tone for 1 time unit(s).
0
Emit 1270–hz tone for 1 time unit(s).
1
Emit 1070–hz tone for 1 time unit(s).
1110
Emit 1270–hz tone for 4 time unit(s).
001
Emit 1070–hz tone for 3 time unit(s).

Emit 1270–hz tone for 1 time unit(s).
```

Section 4.7 Review Questions

1. Rewrite the modem demonstration program in Fig. 4.16 using `while` statements for all loops and `if` statements for all decisions.

2. How will the modem demonstration program handle a nondigit character such as * in the middle of file `digital.txt`?

4.8 Software Designer Beware

Before running any programs that include loops, ask your instructor how to interrupt execution of a program that contains an infinite loop. Be sure to save your C++ source file to disk before compiling and running the program. Even if you are able to interrupt execution of a program containing an infinite loop, many systems will not return you gracefully to your program development environment, so unsaved files can be lost.

Here are two ways to double-check your program in order to prevent most infinite loops:

1. Verify that every iteration of a loop includes an update of the loop control variable. In `while` and `do–while` statements, the update is part of the loop body. In `for` statements, it is the third expression in the loop header.

2. Be sure that every loop repetition condition will eventually be false. If the condition uses the || operator, be sure that you want to exit the loop only if *both* operands of the || are false. If you want to exit if *either* operand is false, replace the || by &&. If the loop control variable is updated by data input, construct the loop repetition condition so it will be

false if a data stream error occurs. If the loop repetition condition becomes false only through input of a sentinel or by encountering end of file, a data stream error can cause the loop to "hang" indefinitely.

Chapter Review

1. Use a loop to repeat steps in a program. Two kinds of loops occur frequently in software: counting loops and sentinel-controlled loops. For a counting loop, the number of repetitions required can be determined before the loop is entered. For a sentinel-controlled loop, repetition continues until a special data value is input. Here is pseudocode for each loop form:

   Counter-Controlled Loop
   Set *loop control variable* to an initial value of 0.
   While *loop control variable < final value*
       Process current data set.
       Add 1 to *loop control variable.*

   Sentinel-Controlled Loop
   Get a *data value.*
   While the sentinel value has not been encountered
       Process the current data set.
       Get another *data value.*

2. We also introduced two other kinds of loops:

   Endfile/Input-Failure-Controlled Loop
   Get first *data value.*
   While there has not been an input stream failure
       Process the current data set.
       Get next *data value.*
   If not at end of file
       Display error message

   Input Validation Loop
   Get *data value.*
   If *data value* isn't in the acceptable range, go back to first step.

3. C++ provides three statements for implementing loops: `while`, `for`, and `do—while`. Use the `for` to implement counting loops and the `do—while` to implement loops that must execute at least once, such as data validation loops for interactive programs. Code other conditional loops using the `for` or `while`, choosing whichever implementation is clearer.

4. In designing a loop, focus on both loop control and loop processing. For loop processing, make sure that the loop body contains steps that perform the oper-

ations that must be repeated. For loop control, you must provide steps that initialize, test, and update the loop control variable. Make sure that the initialization step leads to correct program results when the loop body is not executed (zero-iteration loop).

5. Using input and output files requires several steps:

a. Include standard library `<fstream>`.

b. Associate a file variable of type `ifstream` (input file) or `ofstream` (output file) with the open file.

```
ifstream inf ("a:mydata.txt", ios::in);
ofstream outf("a:myout.txt", ios::out);
```

c. Use the input extraction operator (>>) and output insertion operator (<<) to read from and write to the files.

```
inf >> x >> y;
outf << "X = " << x << ", Y = " << y << endl;
```

d. When done with a file, close it.

```
inf.close();
outf.close();
```

6. To align numeric output in columns, use stream manipulators from <iomanip>: `setw` causes the next output (only) to be right-justified in a prescribed number of columns; `setiosflags` lets you choose fixed (`ios::fixed`) or scientific (`ios::scientific`) notation for floating-point numbers; `resetiosflags` lets you undo your choice; `setprecision` lets you specify the number of digits to be displayed to the right of the decimal point (with automatic rounding or zero padding).

▉ New C++ Constructs ▉

Construct	Effect
File Declarations	
`ifstream infil("data.txt", ios::in);` `ofstream outfil("out.txt", ios::out);`	Declares file variable `infil` and associates it with input file data.txt. Declares file variable `outfil` and associates it with output file out.txt.
Counting for Loop	
`for (num = 0; num <= 10; ++num) {` `    square = num * num;` `    cout << setw(5) << num <<` `        setw(7) << square << endl;` `}`	Displays 11 lines, each containing an integer from 0 to 10 and its square. Uses `setw` to align values in two columns.

Counting for Loop with a Negative Step

```cpp
for  (volts = 20; volts >= -20;
        volts -= 10) {
    current = volts / resistance;
    cout << setw(5) << volts << setw(8)
        << current << endl;
}
```

For values of volts equal to 20, 10, 0, -10, -20, computes value of current and displays volts and current. Uses setw to align values in two columns.

Sentinel-Controlled while Loop

```cpp
product = 1;
cout << "Enter " << SENVAL <<
    " to quit\n";
cout << "Enter first number=> ";
cin >> dat;
while (dat != SENVAL) {
    product *= dat;
    cout << "Next number=> ";
    cin >> dat;
}
```

Calculates the product of a list of numbers. The product is complete when the user enters the sentinel value (SENVAL).

Input-Failure-Controlled while Loop

```cpp
sum = 0;
infil >> num;
while (!infil.fail()) {
    sum += num;
    infil >> num;
}
```

Accumulates the sum of a list of numbers taken from an input file. The sum is complete when an input extraction operation fails.

File Close

```cpp
infil.close();
outfil.close();
```

Closes files associated with file variables infil and outfil.

PROGRAMMING PROJECTS

1. Manufacturing engineers use three principal measures of the roughness of the surface of an object. All are based on measurements at evenly spaced intervals along the surface, as diagrammed here, and labeled a, b, c, ...

Center line

Figure from Serope Kalpakjian, *Manufacturing Engineering and Technology*, 3rd ed. (Reading, Mass.: Addison-Wesley, 1995), p. 962.

Values above the centerline are positive; values below are negative. The three roughness indicators are:

Arithmetic mean value (R_a):

$$R_a = \frac{|a| + |b| + |c| + \cdots}{n}$$

Root-mean-square average (R_q):

$$R_a = \sqrt{\frac{a^2 + b^2 + c^2 + \cdots}{n}}$$

Maximum roughness height:

height from level of deepest trough to highest peak

Write a program that takes surface measurements from the file `surface.txt` and computes and displays these three surface roughness indicators.

Sample file `surface.txt`

```
−4.1 −2.2 −0.5 1.2 3.3 4.6 5.1 2.1 0.2 −3.6 −4.1  0.2 0.5 2.2 4.1
−0.2 −1.2 −3.3 −4.6 −5.0 −2.2  −1.1 0.8 3.2 −0.1 −4.8
```

2. The fact that most metals expand when heated and contract when cooled has serious implications when the dimensions of a piece of laboratory equipment are critical to an experiment. A typical aluminum bar that is *w* cm wide at 70°F will be

$$x = w + (t - 70) \times 10^{-4}$$

cm wide at a nearby temperature *t*. Write a program that prompts the user for the standard width of a bar at 70°F and for a tolerance for width variation. Then write to a file a table like the one below indicating the bar's width at temperatures from 60°F to 85°F in one-degree intervals and marking with a star the temperatures at which the bar's width is within the tolerance.

```
Ideal Bar Width (at 70 degrees F): 10.00000 cm
Tolerance for Width Variation: 0.00050

Temperature    Width    Within Tolerance
(degrees F)    (cm)

    60        9.99900
    61        9.99910
    62        9.99920
    63        9.99930
    64        9.99940
    65        9.99950           *
    66        9.99960           *
    67        9.99970           *
    68        9.99980           *
    69        9.99990           *
    70       10.00000           *

               . . .
    84       10.00140
    85       10.00150
```

3. Write a program that writes to a file a table that shows the height of a projectile launched straight up for each second from launch time (time zero) until the projectile hits the ground. The last entry in the table should show a projectile height of 0. The height after t seconds is given by:

$$s = v_0 t - \tfrac{1}{2} g t^2$$

where v_0 is the launch velocity in m/s and the gravitational constant g is 9.8 m/s^2. The program should prompt the user for the launch velocity. Here is a sample format for your table given a launch velocity of 60 m/s.

```
Projectile launched straight up at 60 m/s
Time (seconds)          Height (meters)
     0                       0.0
     1                      55.1
     2                     100.4
     3                     135.9
     4                     161.6
   . . .
    11                      67.1
    12                      14.4
    13                       0.0
```

4. A metallic conductor's resistivity almost always increases at higher temperatures. Over a temperature range of 0° to 100°C, the following equation approximates $\rho(T)$, a metal's resistivity, at temperature T,

$$\rho(T) = \rho_0[1 + \alpha(T - T_0)]$$

where ρ_0 is the metal's resistivity at reference temperature T_0. α is the metal's temperature coefficient of resistivity. Table 4.6 shows some representative α and ρ_0 values.

TABLE 4.6 Temperature Coefficients of Resistivity and Resistivities at Room Temperature (20°C)[1]

Substance	$\alpha[(°C)^{-1}]$	$\rho(\Omega \times m)$
Aluminum	0.00390	2.75×10^{-8}
Copper	0.00393	1.72×10^{-8}
Lead	0.00430	22.0×10^{-8}
Mercury	0.00088	95.0×10^{-8}
Silver	0.00380	1.47×10^{-8}
Tungsten	0.00450	5.25×10^{-8}

[1]Adapted from Hugh D. Young and Roger A. Freedman, *University Physics*, 10th ed. (Reading, Mass: Addison-Wesley, 2000), pp. 804-5.

Write a program that prompts the user for a reference temperature and for a metal's coefficient of resistivity and resistivity at that reference temperature and then writes to a file a table approximating the metal's resistivity at temperatures from 0°C to 100°C in 5-degree intervals. The sample table output below is for the metal copper.

```
Reference Temperature (Celsius): 20
Temperature Coefficient of Resistivity (1/C-degrees): 0.00393
Resistivity at Reference Temperature (Ohm-meters): 1.72000e-008

Temperature    Metal's Resistivity
(C degrees)       (Ohm-meters)
    0            1.58481e-008
    5            1.61861e-008
   10            1.65240e-008
   15            1.68620e-008

   . . .

   95            2.22697e-008
  100            2.26077e-008
```

5. The value for π can be determined by the series equation

$$\pi = 4 \times \left(1 - \frac{1}{3} + \frac{1}{5} - \frac{1}{7} + \frac{1}{9} - \frac{1}{11} + \frac{1}{13} - \dots\right)$$

Write an interactive program that asks the user how many terms of the series equation to use in approximating π. Then calculate and display the approximation. Here is a sample run:

```
PI Approximation Program

How many terms of the series should be included?
(The more terms, the better the approximation)
=> 3
Approximate value of pi is 3.466667
```

6. Write a program to assist in monitoring the gasoline supply in a refinery storage tank. Your program should alert the supervisor when the supply of gasoline in the tank falls below 10% of the tank's 80,000-barrel storage capacity. The supervisor is accustomed to dealing with the contents of the tank in terms of a number of barrels. However, the pump used to fill tanker trucks gives its measurements in gallons, so your program will need to do the necessary conversions. The petroleum industry's barrel equals 42 U.S. gallons. The program should first request that the operator enter the amount of gasoline currently in the tank. Then prompt the user to input the number of gallons pumped into a tanker and update the number of barrels still available. When the supply drops below the 10% limit, issue a warning and end the program. Here is a sample run:

```
Number of barrels currently in tank=> 8500.5
8500.50 barrels are available.

Enter number of gallons removed=> 5859.0
After removal of 5859.00 gallons (139.50 barrels),
8361.00 barrels are available.

Enter number of gallons removed=> 7568.4
After removal of 7568.40 gallons (180.20 barrels),
8180.80 barrels are available.

Enter number of gallons removed=> 8400.0
After removal of 8400.00 gallons (200.00 barrels),
only 7980.80 barrels are left.

*** WARNING ***
Available supply is less than 10 percent of tank's 80000.00-barrel
capacity.
```

7. When an object radiating light or other energy moves toward or away from an observer, the radiation will seem to shift in frequency. This phenomenon, called the Doppler shift, is frequently used in measuring indirectly the velocity or changes in velocity of an object or weather pattern relative to an observer. For example, a weather radar that attempts to find dangerous wind shear near airports relies on this phenomenon.

For a radar transmitting at frequency f_t, the difference in transmitted and received frequencies due to a target moving at speed v (m/s) relative to the radar—that is, directly toward or away from the radar—is given by

$$\frac{f_r - f_t}{f_t} = \frac{2v}{c}$$

where f_r is the received frequency and c is the speed of light (3×10^8 m/s). A weather service station at a major municipal airport is using a C-band Doppler radar ($f_t = 5.5$ GHz). During a severe thunderstorm, the following received frequencies are observed:

Time(s)	Frequency (GHz)
0	5.500000040
100	5.500000095
200	5.500000230
300	5.500001800
400	5.500000870
500	5.500000065
600	5.500000370

Write a program that scans these data and displays a table showing the data along with a third column displaying the Doppler velocities of the winds relative to the radar.

8. The pressure of a gas changes as the volume and temperature of the gas vary. Write a program that uses the Van der Waals equation of state for a gas,

$$\left(P + \frac{an^2}{V^2}\right)(V - bn) = nRT$$

to display, in tabular form, the relationship between the pressure and the volume of n moles of carbon dioxide at a constant absolute temperature (T). P is the pressure in atmospheres, and V is the volume in liters. The Van der Waals constants for carbon dioxide are $a = 3.592$ $L^2 \cdot$ atm/mol^2 and $b = 0.0427$ L/mol. Use 0.08206 L $\cdot$ atm/mol $\cdot$ K for the gas constant R. Inputs to the program include n, the kelvin temperature, the initial and final volumes in milliliters, and the volume increment between lines of the table. Your program will display a table that varies the volume of the gas from the initial to the final volume in steps prescribed by the volume increment. Here is a sample run:

```
Please enter at the prompts the number of moles of carbon
dioxide, the absolute temperature, the initial volume in
```

milliliters, the final volume, and the increment volume
between lines of the table.

```
Quantity of carbon dioxide (moles) => 0.02
Temperature (kelvin) => 300
Initial volume (milliliters) => 400
Final volume (milliliters) => 600
Volume increment (milliliters) => 50

0.0200 moles of carbon dioxide at 300 kelvin

Volume (ml)   Pressure (atm)
   400            1.2246
   450            1.0891
   500            0.9807
   550            0.8918
   600            0.8178
```

9. The greatest common divisor (gcd) of two integers is the product of the integers' common factors. Write a program that inputs two numbers and implements the following approach to finding their gcd. We will use the numbers –252 and 735. Working with the numbers' absolute values, we find the remainder of one divided by the other.

$$
\begin{array}{r}
0 \\
735\overline{)252} \\
0 \\
\hline
252
\end{array}
$$

Now we calculate the remainder of the old divisor divided by the remainder found.

$$
\begin{array}{r}
2 \\
252\overline{)735} \\
504 \\
\hline
231
\end{array}
$$

We repeat this process until the remainder is zero.

$$
\begin{array}{r}
1 \\
231\overline{)252} \\
231 \\
\hline
21
\end{array}
\qquad
\begin{array}{r}
11 \\
21\overline{)231} \\
21 \\
\hline
21 \\
21 \\
\hline
0
\end{array}
$$

The last divisor (21) is the gcd.

10. The Environmental Awareness Club of BigCorp, Int'l. is proposing that the company subsidize, at $.08 per passenger km, the commuting costs of employees who form carpools that meet a prescribed minimum passenger efficiency. Passenger efficiency P (in passenger · k/L) is defined as

$$P = \frac{ns}{l}$$

where n is the number of passengers, s is the distance traveled in km, and l is the number of liters of gasoline used.

Write a program that prompts the user for a minimum passenger efficiency and then processes a file of data on existing carpools (`carpool.txt`), displaying a table of all carpools that meet the passenger efficiency minimum. The file represents each carpool as a data line containing three numbers: the number of people in the carpool, the total commuting distance per five-day week, and the number of liters of gasoline consumed in a week of commuting. The data file ends with a line of zeros. Display your results in a table with this format:

```
CARPOOLS MEETING MINIMUM PASSENGER EFFICIENCY OF 25 PASSENGER KM / L
```

Passengers	Weekly Commute (km)	Gasoline Consumption(L)	Efficiency (pass km / L)	Weekly Subsidy($)
4	75	11.0	27.3	24.00
2	60	4.5	26.7	9.60
...				

User-Defined Functions

5

In Chapter 2 we studied one kind of function, a program unit designed to reduce the complexity of a large program system. We used the predefined library functions of header files **cmath** and **cstdlib** to perform operations for which C++ does not define operators. The majority of the cmath and cstdlib functions require one or more inputs (arguments) and return a single value as the function result. In this chapter you will study how to write and use such single-result functions, and you will investigate the definition of functions that compute multiple results.

In fact, you have already defined several functions, and they all had the same name—**main**. As you study the single-result functions presented in Section 5.1, you will notice that **main** is just such a function.

C++ allows the programmer to define more than one function with the same name as long as the compiler will be able to distinguish which version is being called. This chapter introduces the guidelines for defining such functions, and also presents rules for determining what names are visible in each part of a program. Classes whose time constraints do not permit coverage of all of this text's topics may elect to skip this scope rules discussion as well as the section that follows it, which presents functions that may call themselves.

5.1   Single-Result Functions

The math library functions that implement the $\sqrt{x}$, $|x|$, and x^y operations are very easy to use because you can place a function call in your code anywhere that the function's result will be needed. For example, the function call may be part of a complex expression

```
if (sqrt( pow( x1 - x2, 2 ) - pow ( y1 - y2, 2 )) > MaxDist)
```

or it may be the right operand of an assignment operator

```
rootX = sqrt( x );
```

or the right operand of an output stream insertion

```
cout << "The square root of " << x << " is " << sqrt( x ) <<
    endl;
```

You can define your own functions with similar characteristics.

function definition
program unit that associates with a function name a return type, a list of parameters, and a sequence of statements that manipulate the parameters to accomplish the function's purpose

EXAMPLE 5.1   Consider function mpg in Fig. 5.1. This function calculates the number of miles per gallon (rounded to the nearest mile) for one tank of gas. We could model this function as shown in Fig. 5.2. The function requires input of the odometer reading at the previous fill-up, the odometer reading at the current fill-up, and the number of gallons in the current tank. These inputs do not come from the keyboard; instead, they are provided as arguments in the call to the function:

$$\textit{arguments}$$

```
lastTankMpg = mpg( 10502.5, 10754.6, 10.0 );
```

function header
lines of code at the beginning of a function definition—includes the function return type, function name, and parameter list

Figure 5.1 gives the **function definition** for mpg. The lines

```
int mpg ( double oldOdom,   // previous odometer reading
          double newOdom,   // new odometer reading
          double gallons )
```

function body
block of statements that manipulate parameters to accomplish the function's purpose

are the **function header**, and the code enclosed in braces is the **function body**.
    A function such as mpg that returns a single result has these characteristics:

1. The function header begins with the data type of the function result. The result of mpg is of type int.

FIGURE 5.1 Definition of Function to Compute Miles Per Gallon

```
//
//  Calculate miles per gallon for a tank of gas
//     Pre:  oldOdom, newOdom, and gallons are nonnegative;
//           newOdom >= oldOdom
//
int mpg ( double oldOdom,   // previous odometer reading      ⎫
          double newOdom,   // new odometer reading           ⎬ Header  ⎫
          double gallons )                                    ⎭         ⎬ Definition
{                                                                       ⎪
   int ans = int( (newOdom - oldOdom) / gallons + 0.5 );      ⎫         ⎪
                                                              ⎬ Body    ⎭
   return ans;                                                ⎭
}
```

2. The function header includes in parentheses after the function name a list of declarations of formal parameters corresponding to the function inputs. The **formal parameter list** of mpg is

```
( double oldOdom, double newOdom, double gallons )
```

This list is the way that mpg receives the values of the arguments provided as input. In a formal parameter list, each parameter must be declared separately. For mpg, this would not be a valid formal parameter list:

```
( double oldOdom, newOdom, gallons ) // invalid
```

formal parameter list
parenthesized list of declarations of variables that correspond to arguments passed in a function call

3. The executable statements of the function include a `return` statement that communicates the result back to the statement that called the function.

The variable ans is called a **local variable** because it is declared within the function, and only the statements of the function can manipulate it. The initialization of ans demonstrates that an initializing expression can use formal parameters.

Notice that mpg begins with a block comment stating the purpose of the function and some assumptions about the values of the formal para-

local variable (of a function)
variable declared within the body of a function

FIGURE 5.2 Model of Function mpg

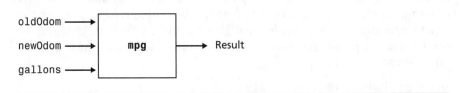

preconditions

conditions required of argument values to guarantee correct execution of a function body

meters (**preconditions**). This comment represents a contract between the function and any statement that calls it. The function promises to accomplish correctly its stated purpose provided that the arguments of all calls to it meet the stated preconditions.

We summarize the general format of the definition of a single-result function in the shaded box that follows.

Single-Result Function Format

```
/ /
/ /   Block comment with purpose and preconditions
/ /
resultDataType functionName ( parameter list )
{
      Function body includes
         Declarations of local variables
         Statements that manipulate parameters and local variables
         Return statement to send back result
}
```

Be careful to include a purpose/preconditions block comment at the beginning of every function you write. A carefully worded block comment combined with the function header provides all the information needed by the user of a function: the purpose, the function name, the type of the function result, the number of formal parameters and their data types, and any restrictions on the parameter values. If you break your program into many simple functions, you will often find that function purpose/precondition comments and explanations of variable meanings are the only program comments that you need.

Figure 5.3 shows a complete program file that includes function mpg and a main function that calls mpg with data provided by the program user. The figure ends with a sample run. Notice the order in which the various parts of the program are included: first the preprocessor directives, then a line labeled *Prototype*, followed by function main, and finally the definition of function mpg. This arrangement of program components is fairly typical. The C++ compiler expects to see either the definition or the **prototype** of a function before it encounters any calls to the function. By placing prototypes of all your own functions before function main and placing their definitions after function main, both main and all other functions will be able to call any other function. The prototype form that we show here is just a copy of the function header with a semicolon added at the end. Another valid prototype form omits the parameter names and shows only their types. Such a prototype for mpg would be

prototype

a statement declaring a function's return type, name, and list of parameter types

```
int mpg( double, double, double );
```

FIGURE 5.3 Program with User-Defined Function to Compute Miles Per Gallon

```cpp
//
// Define and test a function to compute miles per gallon
//
#include <iostream>
using namespace std;

int mpg ( double oldOdom, double newOdom, double gallons );
```
Prototype

```cpp
int main()
{
   double oldReading, newReading, gallons;
   int mPerGal;

   cout << "Previous odometer reading => ";
   cin >> oldReading;
   cout << "New odometer reading => ";
   cin >> newReading;
   cout << "Gallons added to tank to fill => ";
   cin >> gallons;
   mPerGal = mpg( oldReading, newReading, gallons);

   cout << "Car got " << mPerGal << " miles per gallon " <<
        "on last tank of gas." << endl;
   return 0;
}


//
//  Calculate miles per gallon for a tank of gas
//     Pre:  oldOdom, newOdom, and gallons are nonnegative;
//           newOdom >= oldOdom
//
int mpg ( double oldOdom,   // previous odometer reading
          double newOdom,   // new odometer reading
          double gallons )
{
   int ans = int( (newOdom - oldOdom) / gallons + 0.5 );

   return ans;
}
```
Definition

```
Previous odometer reading => 10543
New odometer reading => 10941
Gallons added to tank to fill => 11.2
Car got 36 miles per gallon on last tank of gas.
```

FIGURE 5.4 Execution of Call to mpg When oldReading = 10543, newReading = 10941, and gallons = 11.2

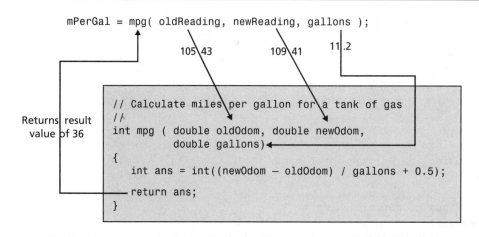

Figure 5.4 illustrates how the values of the arguments `oldReading`, `newReading`, and `gallons` are used as the values of mpg's formal parameters `oldOdom`, `newOdom`, and `gallons`. The arguments in the call are matched up in order with the formal parameters. The result calculated by `mpg` is returned to function `main` and displayed.

Function `main` from Fig. 5.3 is an example of a **driver**, a very simple program unit designed solely to allow testing of a single function.

driver
simple program unit that allows the user to call one or more functions with a variety of argument values

Function Data Area

Each time a function call is executed, the program allocates some memory for storing the function's data. Included are memory cells for both the function's formal parameters and local variables. The program reclaims the memory of the function data area when the function terminates; it allocates a new data area if the function is called again. Figure 5.5 traces the allocation of data areas for functions `main` and `mpg` as the program in Fig. 5.3 executes. Regions with dark shading represent memory that is available for the program to allocate to data areas; lightly shaded regions represent memory currently in use as a data area.

Initially, all of the memory shown is available for allocation (Fig. 5.5a). When execution of the program begins, the operating system calls function `main`. To carry out the call to `main`, a data area is allocated with space for main's variables `oldReading`, `newReading`, `gallons`, and `mPerGal`. As the user responds to main's prompting messages, main's input extraction operations store the values entered in `oldReading`, `newReading`, and `gallons` (Fig. 5.5b). When `main` calls `mpg`, space is allocated for mpg's three

FIGURE 5.5 Allocation of Function Data Areas in Memory

(a) Memory before execution

(b) After operating system calls main and main gets data

Data area for main		
oldReading	10543.0
newReading	10941.0
gallons	11.2
mPerGal	?

(c) After main calls mpg

Data area for main		
oldReading	10543.0
newReading	10941.0
gallons	11.2
mPerGal	?

Data area for mpg		
oldOdom	10543.0
newOdom	10941.0
gallons	11.2
ans	?

(d) After mpg returns

Data area for main		
oldReading	10543.0
newReading	10941.0
gallons	11.2
mPerGal	36

parameters (oldOdom, newOdom, and gallons) and one local variable (ans). The values of the arguments in the call to mpg are copied into the corresponding formal parameters (Fig. 5.4 and Fig. 5.5c). The assignment statement of mpg stores a value in ans, and this value is returned as the result of function mpg. At the return from mpg, its data area is deallocated (Fig. 5.5d). The values of oldOdom, newOdom, gallons, and ans will remain until the space is reused for another data area, but main has no way of accessing these variables.

Notice that it does not matter whether the names of the formal parameters match or do not match the names of the corresponding arguments. The memory cells in the data area for mpg are completely separate from those belonging to function main. Function main cannot reference oldOdom, newOdom, or ans, and a reference to gallons accesses main's own variable named gallons. Conversely, function mpg cannot reference oldReading, newReading, mPerGal, or the gallons variable in main's data area.

Source File Structure

For now, always organize your program source files according to the pattern shown in our examples. Begin with a block comment identifying the program's purpose, then include any #include preprocessor directives and any declarations of constants to be used by the whole program. Next, place prototypes of your functions followed by function main. Include definitions of your functions last, in any order you choose.

Argument List Correspondence

In Fig. 5.4 we saw that when executing a function call, the program assigns the values of the arguments to the formal parameters based on their order: The value of the first argument is assigned to the first formal parameter, the value of the second argument is assigned to the second formal parameter, and so on. An argument can be any expression (a single constant, a single variable, or a complex expression). For example, within function main of Fig. 5.3, this would be a legitimate (though not very useful) call to function mpg:

```
mPerGal = mpg( oldReading, pow(newReading, 2) / 3.0, 18.1 );
```

The value of variable oldReading would be stored in the first parameter, oldOdom, the value of the expression pow(newReading, 2) / 3.0 would be stored in the second parameter, newOdom, and the value 18.1 would be stored in the third parameter, gallons. Although you can use constants, variables, and expressions as arguments, always choose an argument of a data type that can be assigned to the corresponding formal parameter with no unexpected loss of information. If a floating point argument, such as 5.7, is passed to an integer formal parameter, the value assigned to the parameter will be 5. Assigning an integer argument to a floating-point parameter causes no such loss of information.

Logical Functions

In Section 3.2, we saw that C++ uses type bool to represent the logical (boolean) concepts true and false. A function can also return a boolean result. Such functions are often used to make conditions more readable.

EXAMPLE 5.2   Function even in Fig. 5.6 returns true if its integer argument is an even number; otherwise, it returns false. Function even is called in the following if statement, which could be used inside a loop to count even and odd numbers:

FIGURE 5.6 Function That Checks Whether a Value Is Even

```
//
// Indicates whether or not num is even (divisible by 2):
//   returns true if it is, false if not
//
bool even ( int num )
{
   bool ans = ((num % 2) == 0);
   return ans;
}
```

■

```
if (even( x ))
     ++evenNums;
else
     ++oddNums;
```

Section 5.1 Review Questions

1. What value would be returned by function **oneMore** for this call?

   ```
   oneMore( 92.84 )
   ```

   Definition of **oneMore**:

   ```
   int oneMore ( int num )
   {
      return (num + 1);
   }
   ```

2. Define a function that computes the performance coefficient of a refrigerator (*P*).

$$P = \frac{heat\ removed}{work\ done}$$

   For example, a refrigerator that expends 125 Btu's to remove 575 Btu's of heat has a performance coefficient of 4.6.

3. Define a function that rounds a number to a certain (nonnegative) number of decimal places. For example,

   ```
   round( −84.3517, 3 )
   ```

   would return −84.352. *Hint:* First store the number's sign as +1 or −1. Then work with the number's absolute value.

4. Define your own exponentiation function **power** that raises a type **double** value x to an integer power n. *Hint:* Calculate $x^{|n|}$ by repeated multiplication. Account for the sign of n by returning either your result or its reciprocal.

5.2 void Functions

Another useful kind of program unit is a function that displays a message. Since such a function does not return a value to the statement that calls it, it has a special return type called void. Figure 5.7 is a function that we could use to give more complete instructions to the user in a revised version of our sulfur dioxide emission program of Fig. 4.14. This function requires no input, so its formal parameter list is empty, represented in the function header by a set of parentheses. Notice that a void function like instruct includes no return statement.

Figure 5.8 shows the sulfur dioxide emission program as modified to use function instruct. Notice that the first executable statement of main is now

```
instruct();
```

A call to a void function is a separate statement in its own right: It cannot be embedded in a complex expression or used as the right operand of an assignment operator because the void function does not return a value.

Input Parameters in void Functions

void functions that require no arguments are of limited usefulness. However, one frequently needs void functions that display messages whose contents vary depending on the value of one or more input parameters.

Figure 5.7 Function That Displays User Instructions

```
//
// Display instructions for the user
//
void instruct()
{
    cout << "This program calculates the sulfur dioxide emission "
         << "rate for a coal sample — " << endl << "both without "
         << "scrubbing and with scrubbing that is 80% effective."
         << endl << endl;
    cout << "Respond to each prompt by typing a number and then "
         << "pressing the Enter key." << endl << endl;
}
```

FIGURE 5.8   Using a Function That Displays Instructions for the User

```cpp
//
//  Calculate sulfur dioxide emissions rate for a coal sample - without
//  scrubbing and with scrubbing that is 80% effective
//

#include <iostream>
using namespace std;

const double OXIDATION_FACTOR = 2.0;   // oxidizing n pounds of sulfur
                // produces about 2n pounds of sulfur dioxide
const double SCRUB_EFFICIENCY = 0.8;   // scrubbing combustion gases
                // reduces sulfur dioxide emissions by 80%

void instruct();

int main()
{
    int     sampleId;          // sample identification number
    double  sulfurContent,     // % of sample that is sulfur
            energyContent;     // number of Btu per pound
    char    badChar;           // character causing error in data

    // Display instructions
    instruct();

    // Get data on coal sample
    cout << "Enter sample identification number => ";
    cin >> sampleId;
    cout << "What percent of the sample is sulfur?  => ";
    cin >> sulfurContent;
    cout << "How many Btu's of energy from one pound of the sample? => ";
    cin >> energyContent;

    if (cin.fail()) {
        cin.clear();
        cin >> badChar;
        cout << endl << "Error in data.  First invalid character>> "
            << badChar << endl;
        cout << "Program aborted" << endl;
    } else {
        // Calculate emissions rate for burning this sample
        double poundsDioxide = sulfurContent / 100.0 * OXIDATION_FACTOR;
        double emissions = poundsDioxide * 1000000.0 / energyContent;
```

FIGURE 5.8   *(Continued)*

```
        // Calculate emissions rate with scrubbing
        double withScrubbing = emissions - emissions * SCRUB_EFFICIENCY;

        // Display results
        cout << "Sulfur dioxide emissions of coal sample " << sampleId <<
            " with sulfur content of " << endl;
        cout << "    " << sulfurContent << " percent and energy content of "
            << energyContent << " Btu per pound:" << endl;
        cout << "          Before scrubbing: " << emissions <<
            " pounds per million Btu" << endl;
        cout << "          After scrubbing:  " << withScrubbing <<
            " pounds per million Btu" << endl;
    }
    return 0;
}

//
// Display instructions for the user
//
void instruct()
{
    cout << "This program calculates the sulfur dioxide emission "
        << "rate for a coal sample - " << endl << "both without "
        << "scrubbing and with scrubbing that is 80% effective."
        << endl << endl;
    cout << "Respond to each prompt by typing a number and then "
        << "pressing the Enter key." << endl << endl;
}
```

EXAMPLE 5.3   Function `factor` in Fig. 5.9 displays a message showing the prime factors of the argument passed to its formal parameter n. For example, in response to the call

```
factor( 126 )
```

the function would display

```
126 = 2 x 3 x 3 x 7
```

Factoring an integer n requires repetition of the following steps:

1. Find the smallest prime factor of n (call it curFactor).
2. Display curFactor.
3. Divide n by curFactor.

This process continues as long as n is greater than 1.

Because Step 1 requires significant further refinement and is an operation that could be useful in other programs, we will define it as a separate function named smallDiv. By assuming that we have a working function smallDiv, we can predict the result of executing the call

```
factor( 126 );
```

which is traced in Table 5.1. The statement numbers refer to the numbers in circles next to lines of function factor in Fig. 5.9. ∎

FIGURE 5.9 void Function That Factors an Integer

```
//
// Displays a message showing the prime factors of n.
//    Example:  factor( 18 ) would display 18 = 2 x 3 x 3
//    Pre:  n > 1
//
void factor ( int n )
{
    // Displays beginning of message, including the smallest prime factor
①  int curFactor = smallDiv( n );
②  cout << n << " = " << curFactor;

    // Calculates and displays remaining factors preceded by x signs
③  for  (int toFactor = n / curFactor;
④          toFactor > 1;
⑤          toFactor /= curFactor) {
⑥      curFactor = smallDiv( toFactor );
⑦      cout << " x " << curFactor;
    }
⑧  cout << endl;
}
```

TABLE 5.1 Trace of factor(126) That Displays 126 = 2 x 3 x 3 x 7

Statement	n 126	toFactor ?	curFactor ?	Effect
1			2	smallDiv finds 126's smallest divisor > 1, and result is stored in curFactor
2				Displays 126 = 2
3		63		Stores 126 / 2 = 63 in toFactor
4				True: loop continues
6			3	Smallest divisor of 63 (> 1) stored in curFactor
7				Displays x 3
5		21		Stores 63 / 3 = 21 in toFactor
4				True: Loop continues
6			3	Smallest divisor of 21 (> 1) stored in curFactor
7				Displays x 3
5		7		Stores 21 / 3 = 7 in toFactor
4				True: Loop continues
6			7	Smallest divisor of 7 (> 1) stored in curFactor
7				Displays x 7
5		1		Stores 7 / 7 = 1 in toFactor
4				False: Loop exits
8				Completes output line

Subproblem: Function smallDiv

Function smallDiv must find the smallest prime divisor of a number n by trying each possible divisor, beginning with 2. If n is even, 2 is the divisor needed. If not, we will check only the odd integers beginning with 3. Throughout this textbook we reuse proven code whenever possible, so in smallDiv we will call function even that was developed in Section 5.1.

Algorithm

1. If n is even

   divisor is 2.

   else

Initialize `divisor` to 0 (meaning that no divisor has been found).
Initialize `trial` to 3.

2. As long as no divisor has been found, keep trying odd integers (`trial`). If a divisor is found, store it in `divisor`. If trial exceeds $\sqrt{n}$, store `n` in `divisor`.

3. Return `divisor`.

Figure 5.10 implements function `smallDiv`.

Section 5.2 Review Questions

1. Write an instructions function for the carbon monoxide emissions program of Fig. 4.7.

2. Rewrite the program from Fig. 4.10 so it displays the table of bacteria growth by repeated calls to a **void** function `displayGrowth`. The function should have a parameter representing time in hours.

FIGURE 5.10 Function to Find the Smallest Divisor Greater Than 1 of an Integer

```
#include <cmath>

//
// Finds the smallest divisor of an integer n between 2 and n
//    Pre: n > 1
//
int smallDiv( int n )
{
    int trial;     // current candidate for smallest divisor of n
    int divisor;   // smallest divisor of n; zero value means divisor
                   //    not yet found

    // Chooses initialization of divisor and trial depending on whether
    // n is even or odd
    if (even( n )) {
        divisor = 2;
    } else {
        divisor = 0;
        trial = 3;
    }

    // Tests each odd integer as a divisor of n until a divisor is found
    // or until trial is so large that it is clear that n is the smallest
    // divisor greater than 1
```

FIGURE 5.10   *(Continued)*

```
while (divisor == 0) {
    if (trial > sqrt( n ))
            divisor = n;
    else if ((n % trial) == 0)
            divisor = trial;
    else
            trial += 2;
}

// Returns problem result to calling statement
return divisor;
}
```

5.3   Functions with Output Parameters

The `return` statement can return only one value, so a function that needs to send back multiple results must use a different method of communicating them to the calling statement. In all our previous examples, when a call to a function is executing, the program creates a data area in memory in which to store the function's formal parameters and local variables, and initializes each formal parameter to the *value* of the corresponding argument in the call. This method of passing arguments is called **pass-by-value**. The function manipulates its own copy of each argument.

pass-by-value
method of passing an argument that evaluates the argument and stores this value in the corresponding formal parameter, so the function has its own copy of the argument value

    C++ defines a second method of passing arguments in which formal parameters actually reference the original copy of each argument. This method is named **pass-by-reference**, and it provides a mechanism for a function to return multiple results.

pass-by-reference
method of passing an argument that permits the function to refer to the memory holding the original copy of the argument

EXAMPLE 5.4   We need to define a function `addVect` that adds vectors **A** and **B** that are at right angles as illustrated here: **A** is a horizontal vector pointing to the right; **B** is a vertical vector pointing upward.

The resultant vector **A** + **B** is defined by its magnitude *m* and its direction, angle θ, so `addVect` could be modeled as shown in Fig. 5.11. Figure 5.12 de-

FIGURE 5.11 Model of a Function with Two Input Parameters and Two Output Parameters

FIGURE 5.12 Function addVect, Which Produces Two Results

```
//
//  Add vectors a and b that are at right angles:  a is horizontal,
//  b is vertical, a > 0, b > 0.  Express direction of
//  resultant in whole degrees.
//
void addVect( double& rMagnitude,     // output – magnitude of resultant
              int& rDirection,        // output – direction of resultant
                                      //             in whole degrees
              double a, double b)     // input – vectors at right angles

{
    double rDirRadians;  // direction of resultant in radians

    rMagnitude = sqrt( a * a + b * b );
    rDirRadians = atan( b / a );
    rDirection = int( 180 / PI * rDirRadians + 0.5 );
}
```

fines function addVect using reference parameters rMagnitude and rDirection to communicate results back to the calling statement. The first two parameters of addVect are value parameters used to bring into the function the magnitude of vector **A** and the magnitude of vector **B**. Notice that the type of function addVect is void, as it is for functions returning no result, and the function body does not include a return statement to send back a single value as we did in functions mpg and smallDiv.

Let's focus for a moment on the header of function addVect.

```
void addVect( double& rMagnitude,     // output – magnitude of resultant
              int& rDirection,        // output – direction of resultant
                                      //             in whole degrees
              double a, double b)     // input – vectors at right angles
```

A declaration of a reference parameter such as

```
double& rMagnitude
```

address

number that refers to a
particular memory cell

tells the compiler to generate code that stores in rMagnitude the **address** of the type double variable passed as the corresponding argument. Similarly, the compiler is to store in rDirection the address of the type int variable passed in a call to addVect.

Figure 5.13 shows a complete program, including a brief function main that calls addVect. This figure demonstrates the shorter format for the function prototype: The parameter names are omitted. Function addVect is defined as it was in Fig. 5.12. It is the responsibility of the function that *calls* addVect to provide variables into which the vector addition function can store the two parts of the result it computes. In Fig. 5.13, function main declares two variables to receive the results—a type double variable rMag and a type int variable rDir. Notice that main places no values in these variables prior to the call to function addVect: It is the job of addVect to define their values. This change of the values of memory cells in the data area of the calling function is the intended side effect of the call to function addVect.

FIGURE 5.13 Complete Vector Addition Program

```
//
//   Add two vectors that are at right angles to each other.
//
#include <iostream>
#include <cmath>
#include <iomanip>
using namespace std;

const double PI = 3.14159265358979;

void addVect( double&, int&, double, double );

int main()
{
    double aVect;
    double bVect;
    double rMag;
    int     rDir;

    cout << "Enter magnitude of horizontal vector A => ";
    cin  >> aVect;
    cout << "Enter magnitude of vertical vector B => ";
    cin  >> bVect;

    addVect( rMag, rDir, aVect, bVect );

    cout << setiosflags( ios::fixed ) << setprecision( 1 );
```

FIGURE 5.13 *(Continued)*

```
   cout << "A + B yields resultant vector of magnitude " << rMag <<
      endl << "and direction " << rDir << " degrees." << endl;
   return 0;
}


//
//  Add vectors a and b that are at right angles:  a is horizontal,
//  b is vertical, a > 0, b > 0.  Express direction of
//  resultant in whole degrees.
//
void addVect( double& rMagnitude,     // output — magnitude of resultant
              int& rDirection,        // output — direction of resultant
                                      //             in whole degrees
              double a, double b)     // input — vectors at right angles
{
   double rDirRadians;   // direction of resultant in radians

   rMagnitude = sqrt( a * a + b * b );
   rDirRadians = atan( b / a );
   rDirection = int( 180 / PI * rDirRadians + 0.5 );
}

Enter magnitude of horizontal vector A => 86.4
Enter magnitude of vertical vector B => 67.4
A + B yields resultant vector of magnitude 109.6
and direction 38 degrees.
```

Figure 5.14 shows the data areas for main and addVect as they are set up by the function call

```
addVect( rMag, rDir, aVect, bVect );
```

This statement causes the numbers stored in arguments aVect and bVect to be copied into the input parameters a and b. It also stores the addresses of arguments rMag and rDir in the corresponding reference parameters rMagnitude and rDirection. The small numbers in the memory locations, from which arrows originate in Fig. 5.14, represent possible actual addresses in memory. Because it makes no difference to our program which specific cells are used, we normally diagram an address stored in a memory cell simply as an arrow like the one from rMagnitude to rMag.

Notice that the function call does not distinguish between input and output arguments. It is part of the compiler's job to use its knowledge of a function's parameter list (information provided in the function's prototype) when it translates a call to a function. ■

FIGURE 5.14 Correspondence of Input and Output Parameters for
`addVect( aVect, bVect, rMag, rDir );`

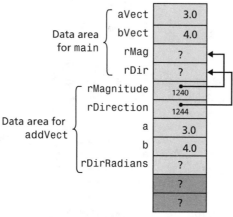

In Section 5.1 we studied the rules of argument correspondence for value parameters such as a and b in function `addVect`. Correspondence rules for reference parameters are even more restrictive. An argument passed to a reference parameter must be a *variable* of the type to which the parameter should refer. A parameter of type `int&` must be passed a variable of type `int`; a parameter of type `double&` must be passed a variable of type `double`, and so on.

So far, we have examined how to declare function outputs as reference parameters and how to choose appropriate corresponding arguments to include in the function call. Now consider the statements that manipulate the reference parameters to send back multiple results. In `addVect`, any use of `rMagnitude` or `rDirection` actually references `rMag` or `rDir`, the arguments in the call. Thus the statement

`rMagnitude = sqrt( a * a + b * b );`

stores a value in `rMag` of main, and the statement

`rDirection = int( 180 / PI * rDirRadians + 0.5 );`

stores a value in `rDir` of main.

Reference Parameters for Two-Way Communication

Sometimes a function uses a parameter both to receive information and to send information back. For example, you might model like this a function whose purpose is to correct the form of a common fraction, so that if the fraction is positive, both numerator and denominator are positive, and if a fraction is negative, only the numerator is negative.

In this case, both `num` and `denom` represent two-way communication paths. For example, the output from this code fragment

```
int n = -5;
int d = -2;
cout << n << " / " << d << " = ";
correctFrac(n, d);
cout << n << " / " << d << endl;
```

should be

```
-5/-2 = 5/2
```

Such input/output parameters are implemented just like output parameters—as references. Function `correctFrac` in Fig. 5.15 checks the sign of the product of the numerator and denominator as a quick means of determining the sign of the fraction. Then it uses the read/write access provided by its reference parameters to assign correct signed values to the numerator and denominator.

In this chapter, we have seen several kinds of functions, and we have seen how parameters are used in most of them. We have implemented input parameters as value parameters that bring information into a function, and we

FIGURE 5.15 Function That Uses Input/Output Parameters

```
#include <cstdlib>    // Defines abs

// Changes a fraction represented as an integer numerator and an
// integer denominator so numerator is negative only if fraction is
// negative, and denominator is always positive
void correctFraction ( int& num,    // input/
                       int& denom) //    output
{
   if (num * denom >= 0)
      num = abs(num);
   else
      num = -abs(num);
   denom = abs(denom);
}
```

TABLE 5.2 Kinds of Functions Seen So Far and Where to Use Them

Purpose	Function Type	Parameters	To Return Result
To compute or obtain as input a single numeric or character value.	Same as type of value to be computed or obtained.	Input parameters hold copies of data provided by calling function.	Function code includes a `return` statement with an expression whose value is the result.
To display output containing values of numeric or character arguments.	`void`	Input parameters hold copies of data provided by calling function.	No result is returned.
To compute multiple numeric or character results.	`void`	Input parameters hold copies of data provided by calling function. Output parameters are references to actual arguments.	Results are stored in the calling function's data area by assignment to reference parameters. No `return` statement is required.
To modify argument values.	`void`	Input/output parameters are references to actual arguments.	Results are stored in the calling function's data area by assignment to reference parameters. No `return` statement is required.

  Preferred functions—use if possible

have implemented output parameters as reference parameters that take multiple results back to the calling function. We have also used a single parameter as a two-way communication path to a function. Such an input/output parameter is implemented with a reference parameter, just like an output parameter. Table 5.2 compares the various kinds of functions and indicates the circumstances in which each kind should be used.

Preferred Kinds of Functions

Although all the function types we study in this chapter are useful in developing computer systems, we recommend that you use the first kind shown in Table 5.2 whenever possible. Functions that return a single value are the easiest functions for a program reader to follow. You will note that all the mathematical functions that we discussed in Section 2.6 are of this variety. Since such functions take only input arguments, the programmer is not concerned with using such complexities as reference parameters in the function definition. If the value returned by the function is to be stored in a variable, the reader sees an assignment operation in the calling statement. If a function has a meaningful name, the reader can usually get a good idea of what is happening in the calling function without feeling obliged to read the code of the called function.

Section 5.3 Review Questions

1. Write a function **separate** that has one type **double** input parameter and three output parameters—one that references a **char** variable, one that references an **int** variable, and one that references a **double** variable.

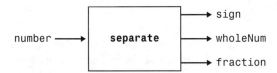

The function breaks its numeric input into three parts: the sign ('+', '−', or ' '), the whole number part, and the fractional part. Function **separate** should communicate its results through the output parameters. For example, if **number** were −87.25, **separate** would send back a **sign** of '−', a **wholeNum** of 87, and the **fraction** 0.25.

2. How would you call **separate** (see Question 1) to have the various parts of 105.72 stored in **signChar**, **whol**, and **frac**? What must be the declared types of **signChar**, **whol**, and **frac**?

3. Consider this function named **swap**, whose stated purpose is to exchange the values of its two type **double** arguments. Draw the data areas for driver function **main** and for **swap** as they would appear just before **swap** returns. Then explain why the output generated is

```
Before swap, x = 3.9    y = 12.7
After swap, x = 3.9     y = 12.7
```

How would you correct function **swap**?

```
void swap( double n1, double n2 );

int main()
{
    double x = 3.9, y = 12.7;
    cout << "Before swap, x = " << x << "   y = " << y << endl;
    swap( x, y );
    cout << "After swap, x = " << x << "    y = " << y << endl;
    return 0;
}
```

```
//
// Exchange the values of n1 and n2.
//
void swap( double n1, double n2 )
{
   double temp;

   temp = n1;
   n1 = n2;
   n2 = temp;
}
```

5.4 Overloaded Functions

In Sections 5.1–5.3, each function that we wrote had its own unique name. However, C++ also permits multiple definitions of the same function name, as long as the system can always determine which version is being called. Associating more than one definition with a function name is called **overloading**. Overloading functions improves code readability in cases where all versions of a function perform actions that are conceptually the same, even though the implementation details vary depending on the arguments' data types.

overloading functions

using the same name for more than one function

EXAMPLE 5.5   Consider a representation of a 24-hour clock as two integers—hours and minutes. We might wish to be able to advance the clock's time in several different ways—by adding minutes, by adding hours and minutes, or by adding hours and fractions of hours. Table 5.3 shows each of these possibilities.

The program in Fig. 5.16 uses overloaded functions to provide the ability to advance the clock in any of the ways illustrated in Table 5.3. All of the versions of advance take two input/output parameters of type int& to represent the time in hours and minutes. A call to advance with one additional int argument advances the clock by minutes, a call with two additional type int arguments will advance the clock by hours and minutes, and a call with an additional type double argument advances by hours. Function main of Fig. 5.16 allows the user to set the clock and then to select in which way to advance it. Function advance can be overloaded in all three ways shown, be-

TABLE 5.3 Three Ways of Advancing the Time on a Clock

Original Time	Advance	New Time
12:10	By 90 minutes	13:40
12:10	By 1 hour 30 minutes	13:40
12:10	By 1.5 hours	13:40

cause each version of advance has a distinct **signature**, the function name and its list of parameter types. The three signatures are:

signature
combination of a function's name and its parameter types

- ■ advance(int&, int&, int)
- ■ advance(int&, int&, int, int)
- ■ advance(int&, int&, double)

FIGURE 5.16 Overloading a Time-Advance Function for a 24-Hour Clock

```
// Implement a time—advance function three ways to allow advance by
// minutes, by minutes and hours, and by hours (including fractional
// hours).
#include <iostream>
using namespace std;

void advance (int& timeHr, int& timeMin, int minutes);  // by minutes
void advance (int& timeHr, int& timeMin, int hours, int minutes);
                                           // by hours and minutes
void advance (int& timeHr, int& timeMin, double hours); // by hours
void outputTime (int timeHr, int timeMin);

int main()
{
    int timeHour, timeMinute, howAdvance, hours, minutes;
    double hoursNfrac;

    cout << "Enter time as two integers separated by a space\n=> ";
    cin >> timeHour >> timeMinute;
    cout << "Time entered is ";
    outputTime(timeHour, timeMinute);
    cout << endl;
    cout << "Choose how you would like to advance clock\n" <<
        "(1) By minutes\n(2) By hours and minutes\n(3) By hours\n=> ";
    cin >> howAdvance;
    switch (howAdvance) {
    case 1:
        cout << "Enter minutes=> ";
        cin >> minutes;
        advance (timeHour, timeMinute, minutes);
        break;

    case 2:
        cout << "Enter hours and minutes, separated by a space=> ";
        cin >> hours >> minutes;
        advance (timeHour, timeMinute, hours, minutes);
        break;
```

FIGURE 5.16 *(Continued)*

```
   case 3:
      cout << "Enter hours=> ";
      cin >> hoursNfrac;
      advance (timeHour, timeMinute, hoursNfrac);
      break;

   default:
      cout << "Invalid choice\n";
   }
   cout << "Updated time: ";
   outputTime (timeHour, timeMinute);
   cout << endl;
   return 0;
}

//
//  Advance time by minutes
//
void advance (int& timeHr, int& timeMin, int minutes)
{
   int extraHrs = (timeMin + minutes) / 60;
   timeMin = (timeMin + minutes) % 60;
   timeHr = (timeHr + extraHrs) % 24;
}

//
//  Advance time by hours and minutes
//
void advance (int& timeHr, int& timeMin, int hours, int minutes)
{
   advance (timeHr, timeMin, hours * 60 + minutes);
}

//
//  Advance time by hours (including, possibly, fractions of hours)
//
void advance (int& timeHr, int& timeMin, double hours)
{
   int mins = int(hours * 60 + 0.5);
   advance (timeHr, timeMin, mins);
}

//
//  Display time as two integers separated by a colon.  Insert a
//  leading zero when the minutes value is less than 10.
```

FIGURE 5.16 *(Continued)*

```
//
void outputTime (int timeHr, int timeMin)
{
   cout << timeHr << ":";
   if (timeMin < 10)
      cout << "0";
   cout << timeMin;
}
```

Problematic Calls to Overloaded Functions

We have seen that when we call a function that takes input parameters, if the types of the arguments provided do not match exactly the types of the parameters, C++ will usually convert the arguments. For example, if we call the cmath library function pow like this

```
pow(x, 2)
```

the second argument, 2, will be converted to 2.0 for assignment to pow's second parameter, which is type double. However, when we call an overloaded function, sometimes C++ will be able to do such type conversions and sometimes not. For example, consider this call to function advance:

```
advance (timeHr, timeMin, 2.0, 35.0);
```

Even though there is no implementation of advance that expects two int variables and then two type double arguments, since there is only one implementation that takes four parameters and the reference parameter types match, C++ will convert the 2.0 and 35.0 to ints 2 and 35.

Consider now this code fragment:

```
float x = 2.5;
advance (timeHr, timeMin, x);
```

Although no implementation of advance expects two int variables followed by a float, and there are *two* implementations with three parameters, the compiler will still be able to translate this call. It chooses the version of advance where it can convert x to the correct type (double) without potential loss of information. It can therefore rule out the three-parameter version whose third parameter is int. However, had advance (by hours) been defined like this,

```
//
//  Advance time by hours (including, possibly, fractions of hours)
//
```

```
void advance (int& timeHr, int& timeMin, float hours)
{
    int mins = int(hours * 60 + 0.5);
    advance (timeHr, timeMin, mins);
}
```

with the third parameter of type float rather than double, then a call with a type double argument would generate a compiler error. Since there is the possibility of information loss either when converting double to float or double to int, the compiler cannot decide which version of advance to call.

Function Return Type Not a Part of Signature

We have seen that overloaded functions must have distinct signatures. Since the function's return type is not a part of the signature, C++ will not allow definition of functions that differ only in their return types. For example, consider how you would define a function that determines how much time has elapsed between two 24-hour clock times on the same day. Between 10:15 and 14:45, 270 minutes or 4.5 hours have elapsed. Although we might wish to be able to determine the elapsed time either in minutes or in hours, attempting to define an overloaded function, such as elapsedTime shown in Fig. 5.17, will generate a compiler error.

Section 5.4 Review Questions

1. Define two versions of an overloaded function **toCm** that converts either yards (which may have a fractional part) or whole inches to whole centimeters. One inch equals 2.54 cm.

FIGURE 5.17 Invalid Overloaded Functions

```
// Determine elapsed time in minutes (start time must precede end time
// on the same day)
int elapsedTime (int startHr, int startMin, int endHr, int endMin)
{
    return (endMin - startMin + (endHr - startHr) * 60);
}


// Determine elapsed time in hours (start time must precede end time
// on the same day)      Error: signature same as first version
double elapsedTime (int startHr, int startMin, int endHr, int endMin)
{
    return ((endMin - startMin + (endHr - startHr) * 60) / 60.0);
}
```

---

2. Assume that `hr` is 5 and `min` is 12 before each of these calls to `advance` executes. Indicate the new time that results from each call.

    a. `advance(hr, min, 2, 50);`

    b. `advance(hr, min, 420);`

    c. `advance(hr, min, 3.25);`

5.5   Introduction to Scope of Names

The **scope of a name** is the region of a program in which a name has a particular meaning. In C++, the basic region of a program is a **block** (compound statement)—a group of statements enclosed in braces.

```
{        statement₁
         statement₂
           . . .
         statementₙ
}
```

A name declared in a block is potentially "in scope" (has the declared meaning) from the point of declaration to the end of the block, and the name is said to be **local** to this block. In all the programs we have seen so far, every name's *potential* scope has been the same as its *actual* scope. We have also seen some names declared outside of any set of enclosing braces. For example, in Fig. 5.8, we declared

```
const double SCRUB_EFFICIENCY = 0.8;
```

outside of any block. We have routinely defined constants in this way. Also, the function prototypes we have studied in this chapter are the means of declaring a function name and have been placed outside any enclosing braces. For example, the prototype,

```
int myFun( double, double );
```

declares `myFun` to be the name of a function that takes two type `double` parameters and returns an integer result. Names declared outside any block are potentially in scope from their point of declaration to the end of the file in which they are declared, and are considered **global names**.

Let's consider what happens if the same name is declared both as a global name and as a name local to a block, as shown in the program fragment of Fig. 5.18. According to our discussion so far, x meaning "integer constant 35" is potentially visible from its point of declaration to the end of this file, and x meaning "type `double` variable" is potentially visible from its point of declaration to the closing } of the block in which it is declared. So, what is the meaning of x in this statement?

```
cout << x << endl;
```

scope of a name
portion of a program in which a particular declaration of a name is applicable

block
a sequence of statements enclosed in {} that introduces a new scope

local name
a name declared within the current block

global name
a name declared outside any block; potentially in scope from its declaration to the end of the file

FIGURE 5.18 Name Redeclared in an Inner Block

```cpp
const int x = 35;
const double PI = 3.14159265358979;

int main()
{
    double x;
    x = 9.7;
    cout << x << endl;
    return 0;
}
```

The x here is the type `double` variable, because a name local to a block takes precedence over a name from an outer region. Thus, we can summarize the notion of scope in two basic rules:

Scope Rules

1. A name that is declared local to a block is available in that block.
2. All other names are inherited from the immediately surrounding region.

So, although after the local declaration of x within function `main` of Fig. 5.15, x has the local meaning "type `double` variable," `PI` retains the global meaning "type `double` constant 3.14159265358979." One reason for our using a different naming convention for constants (names are all caps with underscores separating words) than for variables (names begin with a lowercase letter) is to avoid accidentally losing access to a global constant by redeclaring the name as a variable in another block.

Some C++ constructs cause variables to be local to a particular block even when the variables are not actually declared within the braces of the block. For example, in a function definition, the parameter names are considered local to the block containing the function code. In a `for` loop, if the loop control variable is declared in the `for` loop header, it is considered local to the block that is the loop body.

Figure 5.19 is a program that contains blocks nested within one another. Some of these scope-defining regions include more than just code between braces, as is indicated by the shading. For example, the loop control variable declared in the `for` loop header is considered local to the same block as the loop body. This variable x is visible from its point of declaration to the brace closing the `for` loop body. Within the `for` loop, the x that belongs to the outermost program region is not visible, since the `for` loop has its own local meaning for the name x. The shading also indicates that function names are local, not to their own blocks, but to the surrounding region. Function p's local names include parameter k and variable i. Function p cannot call function k: Since p has its own local meaning for the name k, it does not inherit access to function k from the surrounding region. Integer constant BOUND is visible in all three functions—main, p, and k. Global variable x is visible everywhere except within main's for loop. Table 5.4 summarizes the scope of the names in Fig. 5.19. You should be alert to the fact that some popular C++

FIGURE 5.19 Program with Nested Blocks for Study of Scope Rules

```cpp
#include <iostream>
using namespace std;

const int BOUND = 100;   // global constant
double x;                // global variable

int p( double );
int k( int );

int main()
{
    double m = 14.6;

    for  (int x = 0; x < BOUND; ++x) {
        int z;
        z = k( x );
        if (z == 0)
            cout << x << endl;
    }

    cout << p( m ) << endl;

    return 0;
}

int p( double k )
{
    x = k - 0.5;
    int i = k * 3;
    return i;
}

int k( int m )
{
    return (m % 10);
}
```

TABLE 5.4   Visibility of Names in Program from Fig. 5.19

Name	Visible in `main` (excluding `for` loop)	Visible in `main`'s `for` Loop	Visible in Function p	Visible in Function k
BOUND (global constant)	Yes	Yes	Yes	Yes
x (global variable)	Yes	No	Yes	Yes
p (function)	Yes	Yes	Yes	Yes
k (function)	Yes	Yes	No	Yes
m (variable in `main`)	Yes	Yes	No	No
x (loop counter)	No	Yes	No	No
z	No	Yes	No	No
k (p's parameter)	No	No	Yes	No
i	No	No	Yes	No
m (k's parameter)	No	No	No	Yes

compilers do not yet properly implement the C++ Standard's scope rules for `for` loops. For example, if we inserted the statement

```
cout << "x = " << x << endl;
```

just before function `main`'s return statement, the value displayed should be the value of global variable x. However, if the compiler does not yet properly implement the block defined by the `for` loop, the `for` loop's variables will be local to the enclosing block and the x displayed by our added statement will be the loop control variable.

Let us caution you about using a variable such as the x declared after constant BOUND. Although global variables are unavoidable in some applications, such unrestricted access to a variable is generally regarded as detrimental to a program's readability and maintainability. Global access conflicts with the principle that functions should have access to data on a need-to-know basis only, and then strictly through the documented interface as represented by the function prototype. However, the careful use of global constants is not a dangerous practice and can actually clarify the meaning of a program. In this textbook, our only use of a global variable is in this section on scope, but we use global constants routinely. We strongly recommend that you follow our example.

Section 5.5 Review Questions

1. Consider the following program outline. Create a table similar to Table 5.4 showing the visibility of names within each function and inner block.

```
int one( double, char );
```

```
int two( double, int );

const int LARGE = 100;

int main()
{
   char var1;
   ...
}

int one( double var1, char var2 )
{
   char alocal, one;
   ...
   for (int two = LARGE; two > 0; --two){
      ...
   }
   ...
}

int two( double one, int var1 )
{
   ...
}
```

Here are the headings to use in your table:

Name	Visible in Function main	Visible in one (excluding for loop)	Visible in one's for Loop	Visible in Function two

2. Consider the program in Fig. 5.13. Create a table similar to Table 5.4 showing the visibility of names.

5.6 Recursive Functions (Optional)

Many complex problems are easier to solve if we redefine them in terms of simpler versions of themselves. A programming language such as C++ supports this problem-solving approach by permitting a programmer to define recursive functions. A **recursive function** calls itself (see Fig. 5.20a) or is part of a potential cycle of calls (Fig. 5.20b). In the previous section, we saw that a function inherits from the immediately surrounding region any name that it does not declare local to its own block of code. The inherited names include the function's own name. If you review Table 5.4, you will see that functions p and k are both visible within their own blocks. This visibility permits recursive calls.

recursive function
a function that is part of a potential cycle of calls (f may call f or f calls g and g may call f)

FIGURE 5.20 Types of Recursive Functions

(a) Function f1
    calls itself.

(b) Function f1 calls function f2,
    which calls function f3, which
    sometimes calls function f1.

Defining a recursive solution to a problem requires that you do the following:

1. Find one or more instances of the problem that have very straightforward solutions. These instances are called **simple cases**.
2. Redefine all other instances of the problem in terms of cases that are closer to simple cases.

EXAMPLE 5.6 Computing $n!$ is a problem that lends itself to a recursive solution. We can identify two cases with the same very straightforward solution:

$$0! = 1$$
$$1! = 1$$

Let's consider other instances to see whether they can be redefined in terms of cases closer to our simple cases.

$$5! = 5 \cdot \underbrace{4 \cdot 3 \cdot 2 \cdot 1}_{4!}$$
$$5! = 5 \cdot 4!$$

Since 4 is closer to 1 (a simple case) than 5 is, $5 \cdot 4!$ is a redefinition of 5! that meets criterion 2 for a recursive solution. Similarly we can define 4!:

$$4! = 4 \cdot 3!$$

and 3!:

$$3! = 3 \cdot 2!$$

In general, we are redefining $n!$ as $n \cdot (n-1)!$ Since $n!$ is only defined for non-negative integers, we can summarize our recursive analysis as follows:

1. Simple cases

$$0! = 1$$
$$1! = 1$$

2. Other cases

$$n! = n \cdot (n-1)!$$

Figure 5.21 shows a recursive function implementing this definition of factorial. Function `factorial` demonstrates the basic algorithm typical of recursive solutions:

If this is a simple case,
   solve it.
else
   redefine the problem in terms of a simpler version of itself. ■

When you first work with recursive algorithms, you may find it awkward to rely on a function before you have even finished writing it! However, this is the key to designing recursive functions: You must first trust your function to solve a simpler version of the problem. Then you build the solution to the whole problem on the result from the simpler version.

Tracing a Recursive Function

Hand-tracing the execution of a recursive function is helpful in convincing yourself that recursion really works. We have already seen that every time a function call is executed, the program allocates space in memory for the function's parameters and local variables. Figure 5.22 traces execution of the function call

```
factorial( 3 )
```

FIGURE 5.21 Recursive Function factorial

```
//
// Calculate n!
//    Pre: n >= 0
//
int factorial ( int n )
{
   int ans;

   if (n <= 1)            // simple cases
         ans = 1;
   else                   // recursive redefinition needed
         ans = n * factorial( n - 1 );

   return ans;
}
```

Figure 5.22 shows that computation of factorial(3) requires three calls to factorial. Execution of the first call sets parameter n to 3. Because 3 <= 1 is false, n is assigned 3 * factorial(2), an expression that we cannot finish evaluating until the function call factorial(2) executes. Executing this call allocates a new data area and sets the new n to 2. Because 2 <= 1 is false, n is assigned 2 * factorial(1), another expression requiring evaluation of a call to factorial. Evaluating factorial(1) creates yet another data area, and stores 1 in the new parameter. Since 1 <= 1 is true, this call quickly returns 1 as its result. The heavy arrow in Fig. 5.22 shows the return of 1 as the value of factorial(1). As soon as this last call to factorial returns, its associated data area is reclaimed, and the only data areas still in use are the lightly shaded cells pictured in Fig. 5.23.

FIGURE 5.22 Memory Snapshot at Deepest Level of Recursion During Execution of factorial(3)

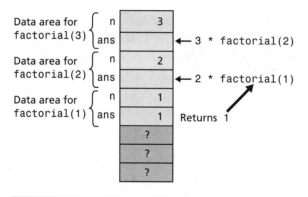

FIGURE 5.23 Memory Snapshot Just Prior to Second Return

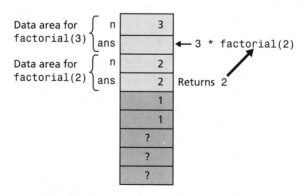

FIGURE 5.24 Memory Snapshot Just Prior to Final Return

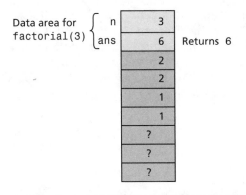

The snapshot of memory just prior to the second return shows that the expression for the value of ans has now been fully evaluated and factorial(2) is returning 2 as its result. Figure 5.21 is a snapshot of memory just prior to the final return, and it shows that the expression assigned to ans has been completely evaluated (3 * 2), and factorial(3) is returning 6 as its result.

Notice that returns from recursive calls occur in the reverse order of the function calls:

Calls

First   factorial(3)
Next   factorial(2)
Last   factorial(1)

Returns

First   factorial(1)
Next   factorial(2)
Last   factorial(3)

When and How to Trace Recursive Functions

Doing a trace by hand of multiple calls to a recursive function aids your understanding of how recursion works but is less useful when trying to develop a recursive algorithm. During algorithm development, it is best to trace a specific case simply by trusting any recursive call to return a correct value based on the function purpose. Then the hand trace can check whether this value is manipulated properly to produce a correct function result for the case under consideration.

If a recursive function's implementation is flawed, however, tracing its execution is an essential part of identifying the error. To accomplish this, you can use single-step execution of the program in your implementation's debugger or you can make the function self-tracing by inserting output statements showing entry to and exit from the function. Figure 5.25 shows a self-tracing version of function `factorial` along with output generated by the call

```
factorial( 4 )
```

FIGURE 5.25 Recursive Function factorial with Tracing Output: factorial(4)

```cpp
//
// Calculate n!
//    Pre: n >= 0
//    *** Display trace of function calls and returns
//
int factorial ( int n )
{
    int ans;

    cout << "Entering factorial with n = " << n << endl;

    if (n <= 1)              // simple cases
           ans = 1;
    else                     // recursive redefinition needed
           ans = n * factorial( n - 1 );

    cout << "factorial( " << n << " ) returning " << ans << endl;

    return ans;
}


Entering factorial with n = 4
Entering factorial with n = 3
Entering factorial with n = 2
Entering factorial with n = 1
factorial( 1 ) returning 1
factorial( 2 ) returning 2
factorial( 3 ) returning 6
factorial( 4 ) returning 24
```

FIGURE 5.26 Four Roots for the Equation $f(x) = 0$

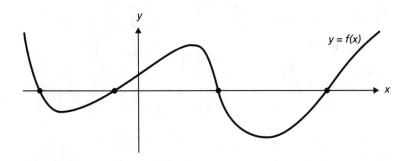

Roots of Equations

Many real-world problems can be solved by finding roots of equations. A value k is a *root* of an equation, $f(x) = 0$, if $f(k)$ equals zero. If we graph the function $f(x)$, as shown in Fig. 5.26, the roots of the equation are those points where the x-axis and the graph of the function intersect. The roots of the equation $f(x) = 0$ are also called the *zeros* of the function $f(x)$.

Consider this problem whose solution requires finding a function root. When firing a projectile at a target, one must determine the angle of elevation (θ) at which to fire the projectile. If we know the projectile's velocity (v) and both the distance (s) to the base of the target and the height (h) of the desired impact point on the target, we can write a function of θ that will evaluate to zero when θ is the desired angle of elevation. Using g as the acceleration of gravity, we know that

$$h = vt\sin\theta - \frac{1}{2}gt^2$$

and

$$t = \frac{s}{v\cos\theta}$$

Substituting and simplifying, we have

$$h = s\tan\theta - \frac{1}{2}g\left(\frac{s^2}{v^2\cos^2\theta}\right)$$

so a zero of the function

$$f(\theta) = s\tan\theta - \frac{1}{2}g\left(\frac{s^2}{v^2\cos^2\theta}\right) - h$$

will give us the correct angle of elevation. The bisection method is one way of approximating a root of the equation $f(\theta) = 0$.

Bisection Method

The bisection method repeatedly generates approximate roots until a true root is discovered or until an approximation is found that differs from a true root by less than *epsilon*, where *epsilon* is a very small constant (for example, 0.0001). The bisection method is well suited to a recursive implementation. In the next example we develop a recursive function to implement this method. Programming Project 8 at the end of this chapter calls for you to complete the solution of the projectile-firing problem for specific target data.

EXAMPLE 5.7   We need to develop a function that approximates a root of a function *f* on an interval containing an odd number of roots. When function *f* is called with the endpoints of such an interval, the function values will have different signs, as shown in Fig. 5.27.

Let us assume that *xLeft* to *xRight* is an interval on which a change of sign does occur and in which there is exactly one root. Furthermore, assume that the function *f(x)* is continuous on this interval. If we bisect this interval by computing its midpoint, *xMid*, using the formula

$$xMid = \frac{xLeft + xRight}{2.0}$$

there are three possible outcomes: $f(xMid)$ is zero, so *xMid* is the root; the root is in the left half of the interval, [*xLeft, xMid*]; or the root is in the right half of the interval, [*xMid, xRight*]. Figure 5.28 shows these three possibilities graphically. A fourth possibility is that the length of the initial interval is less than *epsilon*. In this case, any point in the interval is an acceptable root approximation.

Writing a recursive bisection algorithm is merely a matter of dividing the four possibilities into simple and complex cases. Using our generic recursive algorithm format, we have the following algorithm.

FIGURE 5.27   Change of Sign Implies an Odd Number of Roots

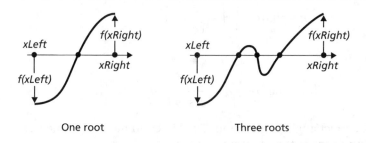

FIGURE 5.28 Three Possible Outcomes of Bisecting the Interval [*x*Left, *x*Right]

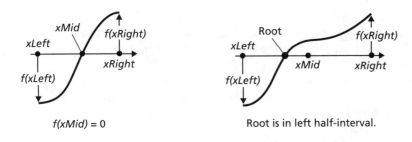

f(xMid) = 0   Root is in left half-interval.

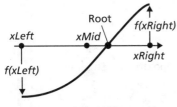

Root is in right half-interval.

Initial Algorithm

1. *If this is a simple case, solve it.*
   - 1.1 Simple Case 1   If the interval is shorter than epsilon, return the midpoint.
   - 1.2 Simple Case 2   If the function value at the midpoint is zero, return the midpoint.

   else redefine the problem in terms of a simpler version of itself.
   - 1.3 Bisect the interval and use a recursive call to look for the root in the half-interval that contains it.

Step 1.3 is sufficiently complicated that we must refine it before coding the function. We must find which half-interval contains the root by evaluating the function at the interval endpoints and checking to see whether the signs of the function values differ. A quick way to see whether the signs of two values differ is to compute their product. If the product is negative, the signs of the two values are different.

Refinement of Step 1.3:

1.3.1 If $f(xLeft) * f(xMid) < 0$
        1.3.2 Find the root by bisecting [*xLeft*, *xMid*]
   else
        1.3.3 Find the root by bisecting [*xMid*, *xRight*].

FIGURE 5.29 Bisection Method Implemented Recursively

```
//
// Implements the bisection method for approximating a root of a function f
// in the interval [xLeft, xRight].  Approximation is within epsilon of a true
// root.
//    Pre:  xLeft < xRight, epsilon > 0
//          Signs of f(xLeft) and f(xRight) are different, so interval
//          contains at least one root.
//
double bisect ( double xLeft,      // endpoints of interval in which to look
                double xRight,     //   for a root
                double epsilon)   // error tolerance
{
   double root;    // approximate root
   double xMid = (xLeft + xRight) / 2.0;  // Calculate midpoint of interval

   if (xRight — xLeft < epsilon)                  // Simple Case 1
        root = xMid;
   else if (f( xMid ) == 0.0)                     // Simple Case 2
        root = xMid;
   else if (f( xLeft ) * f( xMid ) < 0.0)         // Root in [xLeft, xMid]
        root = bisect( xLeft, xMid, epsilon );
   else                                           // Root in [xMid, xRight]
        root = bisect( xMid, xRight, epsilon );

   return root;
}
```

Figure 5.29 shows an implementation of this algorithm in function bisect.
To test the bisect function, we would place it in a file along with a definition of the function f for which we want to find roots. The file would include a main function that calls bisect with a variety of intervals and *epsilon* values. ∎

Section 5.6 Review Questions

1. List the recursive calls generated by the call

   bisect(2.5, 6.5, 0.001)

   if $f(x) = x^3 - 8x^2 - 35x + 150$

2. Add statements to function **bisect** to make it self-tracing like the version of **factorial** in Fig. 5.22.

3. Write a recursive exponentiation function that raises a type **double** value x to a nonnegative integer power n. Here is a recursive definition of x^n.

$x^n = 1$ for $n = 0$

$x^n = x \cdot (x^{n-1})$ for $n > 0$

5.7 Problem Solving with User-Defined Functions

Our next case study demonstrates how we can solve a large problem by solving its subproblems. We will reuse library functions when possible, and write our own functions for other problems.

COLLECTING AREA FOR SOLAR-HEATED HOUSE

CASE STUDY

Problem

Write a program that estimates the appropriate size for the collecting area of a solar-heated house. Determining collecting area size requires consideration of several factors, including the average number of heating degree days for the coldest month of a year (this is the product of the average difference between inside and outside temperatures and the number of days in the month), the heating requirement per square foot of floor space, the floor space, and the efficiency of the collection method. Your program will have access to two data files. File hdd.txt contains numbers representing the average heating degree days in the construction location for each of 12 months. File solar.txt contains the average solar insolation (rate at which solar radiation falls on one square foot of a given location) for each month. The first entry in each file represents data for January, the second is a data value for February, and so on.

Understanding the Problem

The formula for approximating the desired collecting area (A) is

$$A = \frac{heat\ loss}{energy\ resource}$$

In turn, *heat loss* is computed as the product of the heating requirement, the floor space, and the heating degree days. We compute the necessary *energy resource* by multiplying the efficiency of the collection method by the average solar insolation per day and the number of days.

We can now identify the problem's inputs, outputs, and scratch-pad variables.

Data Definition

Inputs

```
heatingDegreeDays // average heating degree days for coldest month
                     (integer)
solarInsolation   // average daily solar insolation for coldest month
                     (integer)
heatingRequirement// Btu/degree day ft² for planned type of construction
                     (integer)
efficiency        // % of solar insolation converted to usable heat
                     (integer)
floorSpace        // square feet (double)
```

Scratch Pad

```
energyResource    // usable solar energy available in coldest month
                     (double)
```

Outputs

```
heatLoss          // Btu's of heat lost by structure in coldest month
                     (double)
collectingArea    // approximate size (ft²) of collecting area needed
                     (double)
```

In all our previous programs, data for program inputs have all come from the same source—either the keyboard or a file. In this program we will use three input sources: the two data files and the keyboard. Thus, we must define two input stream variables.

```
hddFile           // accesses hdd.txt
solarFile         // accesses solar.txt
```

Algorithm Design

Initial Algorithm

1. Determine the coldest month and the average heating degree days for this month.
2. Find the average daily solar insolation per ft² for the coldest month.
3. Get from the user the other problem inputs: heatingRequirement, efficiency, and floorSpace.

4. Estimate the collecting area needed.

5. Display results.

We will design Steps 1 and 2 as separate functions: Function `fileMax` will find the largest value in a file and the position where the value was found: 1 if the first file element is the largest, 2 if the second is largest, and so on. Function `nthItem` will find the value in file `solar.txt` that corresponds to the coldest month. Steps 3 and 5 are quite straightforward, so only Step 4 calls for refinement here.

Refinement of Step 4

4.1 Calculate `heatLoss` as the product of `heatingRequirement`, `floorSpace`, and `heatingDegreeDays`.

4.2 Calculate `energyResource` as the product of `efficiency` (converted to hundredths), `solarInsolation`, and the number of days in the coldest month.

4.3 Calculate `collectingArea` as `heatLoss` divided by `energyResource`. Round result to nearest whole square foot.

We will develop a separate function for finding the number of days in a month (see Step 4.2).

Function fileMax: Problem

Find the largest value in a file of integers and the position where the largest is found (number the positions beginning with 1).

Understanding the Problem

To find the largest value in the file of integers, we will input all the values, comparing each new value to the largest seen so far. We will need to establish a counter variable whose value is 1 when we examine the file's first value, 2 when we input the second, and so on. Whenever we find a new largest value, we will copy the counter's current value into the output parameter representing position. Variables needed include:

Data Definition

Input Parameter

```
dataStream   // file from which to input data (ifstream&)
```

Scratch Pad

```
ct           // counter (int)
next         // next data value to examine (int)
```

Output Parameters

```
large       // largest data value seen so far (int)
maxPos      // position of largest value seen so far (int)
```

Notice that `dataStream` is to be passed by reference even though it is an input parameter. Always pass files as reference parameters.

Algorithm Design

Since the function has two result values, we could return both results through output parameters. However, C++ would also allow us to return one as the function value and the other through an output parameter. The function's name implies that the function's primary purpose is to find the maximum value. Therefore, we will return this maximum as the function result and send back the position through an output parameter.

Algorithm

1. Scan first value from `dataStream` into `large`, and initialize `maxPos` to 1.
2. Initialize `ct` to 2.
3. Scan a value from `dataStream` into `next`.
4. While input failure on `dataStream` has not been encountered, repeat
    5. If `next > large`
        6. Store `next` in `large`.
        7. Store `ct` in `maxPos`.
    8. Increment `ct`.
    9. Scan a value from `dataStream` into `next`.
10. Return `large`.

Other Functions

Functions `nthItem` and `daysInMonth` are quite simple, so we will show only their implementation. Figure 5.30 is an implementation of the entire program for approximating the necessary solar collecting area for solar heating of a certain structure in a given geographic area.

Section 5.7 Review Questions

1. Revise the solar collecting area program in Fig. 5.30 by writing and calling two additional functions: one that computes heat loss and one that computes the energy resource.
2. Write a revision of function **nthItem** that returns zero if the file contains fewer than **n** items.

FIGURE 5.30 Program to Approximate Solar Collecting Area

```
//
//  Estimate necessary solar collecting area for a particular type of
//  construction in a given location.
//

#include <iostream>
#include <fstream>
#include <cmath>
#include <iomanip>
using namespace std;

int daysInMonth( int);
int fileMax( ifstream&, int& );
int nthItem( ifstream&, int );

int main()
{
    int     heatingDegreeDays,  // average for coldest month
            solarInsolation,    // average daily solar radiation per
                                //   ft^2 for coldest month
            coldestMonth,       // number in range 1..12
            heatingRequirement, // Btu / degree day ft^2 for given type
                                //   of construction
            efficiency;         // % of solar insolation converted to
                                //   usable heat
    double floorSpace,          // ft^2
            heatLoss,           // Btu's lost in coldest month
            energyResource,     // Btu's heat obtained from 1 ft^2
                                //   collecting area in coldest month
            collectingArea;     // ft^2 needed to provide heat for
                                //   coldest month
    ifstream hddFile( "hdd.txt",  // average heating degree days for each
                    ios::in ),    //   of 12 months
            solarFile( "solar.txt",// average solar insolation for each of
                    ios::in );    //   12 months

    // Get from files average heating degree days for coldest month and
    //  corresponding average daily solar insolation
    heatingDegreeDays = fileMax( hddFile, coldestMonth );
    solarInsolation = nthItem( solarFile, coldestMonth );
    hddFile.close();
    solarFile.close();
```

Statement of Purpose

Standard Library & Namespace Inclusion

Function Prototypes

Variable Declarations

File Variable Declarations

Function Calls

File Close

FIGURE 5.30 *(Continued*

```
// Get from user specifics of this house
cout << "What is the approximate heating requirement (Btu / " <<
    "degree day ft^2)" << endl << "of this type of construction?" <<
    endl << "=> ";
cin >> heatingRequirement;
cout << "What % of solar insolation will be converted to usable heat?"
    << endl << "=> ";
cin >> efficiency;
cout << "What is the floor space (ft^2)?" << endl << "=> ";
cin >> floorSpace;

// Project collecting area needed
heatLoss = heatingRequirement * floorSpace * heatingDegreeDays;
energyResource = efficiency * 0.01 * solarInsolation *
            daysInMonth( coldestMonth );
collectingArea = int( heatLoss / energyResource + 0.5 );

// Display results
cout << setiosflags( ios::fixed ) << setprecision( 0 );
cout << "To replace heat loss of " << heatLoss << " Btu's in the " <<
    "coldest month (month " << coldestMonth << ")" << endl <<
    "with available solar insolation of " << solarInsolation <<
    " Btu / ft^2 / day, and an" << endl << "efficiency of " <<
    efficiency << "%, use a solar collecting area of " <<
    collectingArea << " ft^2." << endl;
return 0;
}
```

Function Definitions

```
//
// Given a month number (1 = January, 2 = February, ...,
// 12 = December ), return the number of days in the month
// (non-leap year).
//     Pre:  1 <= monthNumber <= 12
//
int daysInMonth( int monthNumber )
{
    int ans;

    switch (monthNumber) {
    case 2:  ans = 28;      // February
             break;
```

Statement of Purpose

Precondition

Function Header

FIGURE 5.30 *(Continued*

```
   case 4:                // April
   case 6:                // June
   case 9:                // September
   case 11: ans = 30;     // November
            break;

   default: ans = 31;
   }

   return ans;    ◄──────  Return Statement
}

//
//  Finds and returns the largest value in a file of integers, and assigns
//  to maxPos the index of this largest value (index of first value = 1).
//     Pre:  dataStream accesses a file of at least one integer
//                                                       Output Parameter
//
int fileMax( ifstream& dataStream, int& maxPos )
{
   int large, next;

   dataStream >> large;
   maxPos = 1;
   int ct = 2;
   for  (dataStream >> next;  !dataStream.fail();  dataStream >> next) {
       if (next > large) {
           large = next;
           maxPos = ct;
       }
       ++ct;
   }

   return large;
}

//
//  Finds and returns the nth integer in a file.
//     Pre:  dataStream accesses a file of at least n integers (n >= 1).
//                                         Input Parameter
//
int nthItem( ifstream& dataStream, int n)
{
   int item;
```

FIGURE 5.30   *(Continued*

```
   for  (int i = 1;  i <= n;  ++i)
       dataStream >> item;

   return item;
}
```

Input file hdd.txt

995   900   750   400   180   20   10   10   60   290   610   1051

Input file solar.txt

500   750   1100   1490   1900   2100   2050   1550   1200   900   500 500

Sample Run

```
What is the approximate heating requirement (Btu / degree day ft^2)
of this type of construction?
=> 9
What % of solar insolation will be converted to usable heat?
=> 60
What is the floor space (ft^2)?
=> 1200
To replace heat loss of 11350800 Btu's in the coldest month (month 12)
with available solar insolation of 500 Btu / ft^2 / day, and an
efficiency of 60%, use a solar collecting area of 1221 ft^2.
```

5.8   Software Designer Beware

Defining and calling functions with parameter lists provide many opportunities for mistakes. When you call a function that has an input parameter, make the corresponding input argument an expression of a type that can be assigned to the parameter without unexpected loss of information. When you call a function that has an output parameter, the corresponding argument must be either the same type as the parameter or the matching non-reference type. For example, if the function output parameter is of type double&, you may pass an argument that is of type double& or of type double, the corresponding nonreference type.

   If a function produces a single result, the function's prototype and header should declare it to be the type of the result, and the function definition should return the value using a return statement. It is easy to introduce errors in a function that produces multiple results. Every path through the function must assign a value to each output parameter, or in some instances, the program results will be incorrect.

The most common problem in a recursive function is that it may not terminate properly. For example, if the terminating condition that checks for a simple case is incorrect or incomplete, the function may call itself indefinitely or until all available memory is used up. Often, when a recursive function is not terminating, you will receive a run-time error message noting stack overflow or an access violation. Be sure to identify all simple cases and provide a terminating condition for each one. Also make sure that each recursive step redefines the problem in terms of arguments that are closer to simple cases so that recursive calls eventually lead to simple cases only.

In our examples of recursive functions that return a value, we have always used a local variable into which the function result is placed by the function's decision structure. Then we have ended the function's code with a `return` statement. Since C++ permits the use of the `return` statement anywhere in the function code, a function like `factorial` from Fig. 5.18 could also have been written as follows:

```
int factorial ( int n )
{
    if (n <= 1)            // simple cases
        return 1;
    else                   // recursive redefinition needed
        return (n * factorial( n - 1 ));
}
```

You should be aware that it is critical that every path through a nonvoid function lead to a `return` statement. In particular, the `return` statement that returns the value of the expression containing the recursive call to `factorial` is just as essential as the other `return` statement. However, when you adopt a multiple-return style, you can easily omit one of the necessary `return` statements.

Chapter Review

1. User-defined functions associate a function name with a group of statements that manipulate the function's parameters (if any) to accomplish the function's stated purpose.

2. A function's initial block comment, its statement of purpose, should include any preconditions—conditions required of argument values to guarantee correct execution.

3. Parameters enable a programmer to pass data to functions and to return multiple results from functions. The parameter list provides a highly visible communication

path between a function and its calling program. Using parameters enables a function to process different data each time it executes, thereby making it easy to reuse the function in other programs.

4. Parameters may be used for input to a function, for output from a function (sending back results), and for both input and output. An input parameter uses pass-by-value to send data into a function. The parameter's declared type is the same as the type of the data. Use pass-by-reference for output and input/output parameters. Reference parameters access variables in the calling function's data area. The actual argument corresponding to an input parameter may be an expression or a constant; the actual argument corresponding to an output or input/output parameter must be a variable.

5. Two or more functions can have the same name as long as each has a distinct signature, the combination of the function name and the list of parameter types.

6. The scope of an identifier dictates where it can be referenced. A parameter or local variable can be referenced anywhere in the block that declares it. A function name is visible from its declaration (the block prototype) to the end of the source file except within functions that have local variables or parameters of the same name. The same rule applies for a constant: it is visible beginning at its declaration.

7. A function is recursive if it calls itself or if it can be part of a circular chain of calls. Use recursive functions in situations where one or two instances of the problem are very simple to solve and where the remaining cases can be redefined in terms of cases that are closer to one of the simple cases.

New C++ Constructs

Function Example	Effect and Sample Call

Function That Returns a Single Result

```
// returns '+', '-', or ' ' depend-
// ing on whether x is positive,
// negative, or zero
char sign(double x)
{
   char signSymbol;

   if (x > 0)
      signSymbol = '+';
   else if (x == 0)
      signSymbol = ' ';
   else
      signSymbol = '-';
   return signSymbol;
}
```

Returns a character value indicating the sign of its type double argument.

```
double num;
char numSign;
. . .
numSign = sign(num);
```

Function Example	*Effect and Sample Call*

Function That Returns No Result

```
void printBoxed(int num)
{
    cout << "*********\n";
    cout << "*        *\n";
    cout << "*  " << setw(3)
        << num << "  *\n";
    cout << "*        *\n";
    cout << "*********\n";
}
```

Displays its type int input
argument inside a rectangle.

```
int score;
. . .
printBoxed(score + 2);
```

Function That Returns Multiple Results

```
void makeChange(int&    numTokens,  // output
                double& left,       // output
                double  change,     // input
                double  tokenVal)   // input
{
    numTokens = int(change / tokenVal);
    left = change – numTokens * tokenVal;
}
```

Determines how many of a certain bill
or coin (tokenVal) should be included
in change amount. This number is sent
back through the output parameter
numTokens. The amount of change
remaining to be made is sent back through
the output parameter left. The following
code assigns 3 to numTwenties and 11.50 to
remainingChange:

```
int numTwenties;
double remainingChange;
  . . .
makeChange(numTwenties,
    remainingChange, 71.50, 20.00);
```

Function with an Input/Output Parameter

```
void roundToNplaces(double& num,// input/
                                // output
                    int n) // input
{
    double tenToN = pow(10, n);
    int numTemp = int(num * tenToN + 0.5);
    num = numTemp / tenToN;
}
```

Rounds num to n decimal places.

```
double x = 35.1267;
roundToNplaces(x, 2);
```

Function Example	*Effect and Sample Call*
Overloaded Function	Returns correct absolute

```
int absVal(int num)
{
   if (num >= 0)
      return num;
   else
      return (-num);
}
double absVal(double num)
{
   if (num >= 0)
      return num;
   else
      return (-num);
}
```

Returns correct absolute values for types int and double.

double x = -38.4;
double absX = absVal(x);

PROGRAMMING PROJECTS

1. Write a collection of functions to do arithmetic with rational numbers (common fractions). Define functions getRational, displayRational, addRational, and subtractRational whose prototypes are

```
void getRational ( int& numer, int& denom );
void displayRational ( int numer, int denom );
void addRational ( int& ansNum, int& ansDenom, int num1, int
      denom1, int num2, int denom2);
void subtractRational ( int& ansNum, int& ansDenom, int num1,
      int denom1, int num2, int denom2);
```

Design main as a driver function that inputs pairs of rationals and displays for each pair the sum and difference. To produce results that are in reduced form, write and call a greatest common divisor (gcd) function (See Programming Project 4 from Chapter 4) and divide the numerator and denominator of each fraction by their gcd.

2. A hospital-supply company wants to market a program to assist with calculation of intravenous rates. Design and implement a program that interacts with the user as follows:

```
INTRAVENOUS RATE ASSISTANT

Enter the number of the problem you wish to solve.
      GIVEN A MEDICAL ORDER IN          CALCULATE RATE IN
```

(1) ml/hr & tubing drop factor	drops / min
(2) 1 L for n hr	ml / hr
(3) mg/kg/hr & concentration in mg/ml	ml / hr
(4) units/hr & concentration in units/ml	ml / hr
(5) QUIT	

```
Problem=> 1
Enter rate in ml/hr=> 150
Enter tubing's drop factor(drops/ml)=> 15
The drop rate per minute is 38.
```

```
Enter the number of the problem you wish to solve.
```

GIVEN A MEDICAL ORDER IN	CALCULATE RATE IN
(1) ml/hr & tubing drop factor	drops / min
(2) 1 L for n hr	ml / hr
(3) mg/kg/hr & concentration in mg/ml	ml / hr
(4) units/hr & concentration in units/ml	ml / hr
(5) QUIT	

```
Problem=> 2
Enter number of hours=> 8
The rate in milliliters per hour is 125.
```

```
Enter the number of the problem you wish to solve.
```

GIVEN A MEDICAL ORDER IN	CALCULATE RATE IN
(1) ml/hr & tubing drop factor	drops / min
(2) 1 L for n hr	ml / hr
(3) mg/kg/hr & concentration in mg/ml	ml / hr
(4) units/hr & concentration in units/ml	ml / hr
(5) QUIT	

```
Problem=> 3
Enter rate in mg/kg/hr=> 0.6
Enter patient weight in kg=> 70
Enter concentration in mg/ml=> 1
The rate in milliliters per hour is 42.
```

```
Enter the number of the problem you wish to solve.
```

GIVEN A MEDICAL ORDER IN	CALCULATE RATE IN
(1) ml/hr & tubing drop factor	drops / min
(2) 1 L for n hr	ml / hr
(3) mg/kg/hr & concentration in mg/ml	ml / hr
(4) units/hr & concentration in units/ml	ml / hr
(5) QUIT	

```
Problem=> 4
Enter rate in units/hr=> 1000
```

```
Enter concentration in units/ml=> 25
The rate in milliliters per hour is 40.

Enter the number of the problem you wish to solve.
     GIVEN A MEDICAL ORDER IN                CALCULATE RATE IN
(1) ml/hr & tubing drop factor              drops / min
(2) 1 L for n hr                            ml / hr
(3) mg/kg/hr & concentration in mg/ml       ml / hr
(4) units/hr & concentration in units/ml    ml / hr
(5) QUIT


Problem=> 5
```

Implement the following functions:

getProblem—Displays the user menu, then inputs and returns as the function value the problem number selected.

getRateDropFactor—Prompts the user to enter the data required for Problem 1, and sends this data back to the calling module via output parameters.

getKgRateConc—Prompts the user to enter the data required for Problem 3, and sends this data back to the calling module via output parameters.

getUnitsConc—Prompts the user to enter the data required for Problem 4, and sends this data back to the calling module via output parameters.

figDropsMin—Takes rate and drop factor as input parameters and returns drops/min (rounded to nearest whole drop) as function value.

figMlHr—Takes as an input parameter the number of hours over which one liter is to be delivered and returns ml/hr (rounded) as function value

byWeight—Takes as input parameters rate in mg/kg/hr, patient weight in kg, and concentration of drug in mg/ml and returns ml/hr (rounded) as function value

byUnits—Takes as input parameters rate in units/hr and concentration in units/ml, and returns ml/hr(rounded) as function value

Hint: Use a sentinel-controlled loop. Call getProblem once before the loop to initialize the problem number and again at the end of the loop body to update it.

3. A finite state machine (FSM) consists of a set of states, a set of transitions, and a string of input data. In the FSM of Fig. 5.31, the named ovals represent states and the arrows connecting the states represent transitions. The FSM is designed to recognize a list of C++ variable names (identifiers) and nonnegative integers, assuming that the items are ended by commas and that a period marks the end of all the data. Table 5.5 traces how the diagrammed machine would process a string composed of the digits 9

FIGURE 5.31   Finite State Machine for Numbers and Identifiers

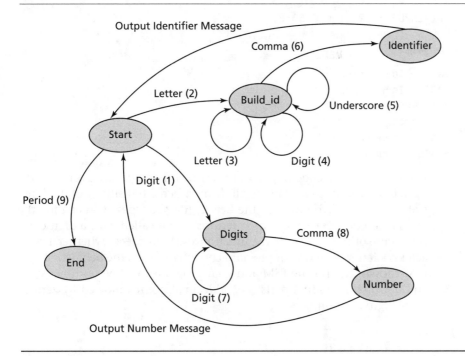

TABLE 5.5   Trace of Fig. 5.31 on Data "95,K9,."

State	Next Character	Transition
Start	9	1
Digits	5	7
Digits	,	8
Number		Output number message
Start	K	2
Build-id	9	4
Build-id	,	6
Identifier		Output identifier message
Start	.	9
End		

and 5, a comma, the letter K, the digit 9, a comma and a period. The machine begins in the Start state.

Write a program that represents the names of the states by their first initials. Your program should process a correctly formatted line of data, identifying each data item. Here is a sample of correct input and output.

Input:

```
rate,R2D2,48,2,time,555666,.
```

Output:

```
rate − Identifier
R2D2 − Identifier
48 − Number
2 − Number
time − Identifier
555666 − Number
```

Use the following code fragment in `main`, and design function `transition` to return the next state for all the numbered transitions of the finite state machine. If you include the header file `<cctype>`, you can use the library function `isdigit`, which returns true if called with a digit character, false otherwise. Similarly, function `isalpha` checks whether a character is a letter. When your program correctly models the behavior of the FSM shown, extend the FSM and your program to allow optional signs and optional fractional parts (i.e., a decimal point followed by zero or more digits) in numbers.

```cpp
do {
    if (currentState == 'I') {
        cout << " − Identifier\n";
        currentState = 'S';
    } else if (currentState == 'N') {
        cout << " − Number\n";
        currentState = 'S';
    }
    cin >> transitionChar;
    if (transitionChar != ',' && transitionChar != '.')
        cout << transitionChar;
    currentState = transition(currentState, transitionChar);
} while (currentState != 'E');
```

TABLE 5.6 Mathematical Models of Nonvertical Straight Lines

Model	Equation	Given
Two-point form	$m = \dfrac{y_2 - y_1}{x_2 - x_1}$	$(x_1, y_1), (x_2, y_2)$
Point-slope form	$y - y_1 = m(x - x_1)$	$m, (x_1, y_1)$
Slope-intercept form	$y = mx + b$	m, b

4. Table 5.6 summarizes three commonly used mathematical models of nonvertical straight lines.

Design and implement a program that permits the user to convert either two-point form or point-slope form into slope-intercept form. Your program should interact with the user as follows:

```
Select the form that you would like to convert to slope—intercept form:
1) Two—point form (you know two points on the line)
2) Point—slope form (you know the line's slope and one point)
=> 2
Enter the slope=> 4.2
Enter the x—y coordinates of the point separated by a space=> 1 1

Point—slope form
  y — 1.00 = 4.20(x — 1.00)

Slope—intercept form
  y = 4.20x — 3.20

Do another conversion (Y or N)=> Y

Select the form that you would like to convert to slope—intercept form:
1) Two—point form (you know two points on the line)
2) Point—slope form (you know the line's slope and one point)
=> 1
Enter the x—y coordinates of the 1st point separated by a space=> 4 3
Enter the x—y coordinates of the 2nd point separated by a space=> —2 1

Two—point form
          (1.00 — 3.00)
  m = ------------------
          (—2.00 — 4.00)

Slope—intercept form
  y = 0.33x + 1.66

Do another conversion (Y or N)=> N
```

Implement the following functions:

getProblem—Displays the user menu, then inputs and returns as the function value the problem number selected.

get2Pt—Prompts the user for the *x-y* coordinates of both points, inputs the four coordinates, and returns them to the calling function through output parameters.

getPtSlope—Prompts the user for the slope and *x-y* coordinates of the point, inputs the three values, and returns them to the calling function through output parameters.

SlopeIntcptFrom2Pt—Takes four input parameters, the *x-y* coordinates of two points, and returns through output parameters the slope (*m*) and *y*-intercept (*b*).

IntcptFromPtSlope—Takes three input parameters, the *x-y* coordinates of one point and the slope, and returns as the function value the *y*-intercept.

display2Pt—Takes four input parameters, the *x-y* coordinates of two points, and displays the two-point form line equation with a heading.

displayPtSlope – Takes three input parameters, the *x-y* coordinates of one point and the slope, and displays the point-slope form line equation with a heading.

displaySlopeIntcpt – Takes two input parameters, the slope and *y*-intercept, and displays the slope-intercept form line equation with a heading.

5. Write a program that displays base 10 positive integers converted to any base less than 10. Include a displayInBase function that implements this recursive algorithm.

    1. If decimalNumber < base

        2. Display decimalNumber.

    else

        3. Display decimalNumber / base in the new base.

            Note: integer division is intentional.

        4. Display decimalNumber % base.

Your driver program should ask the user for the desired base and then repeatedly input numbers to convert and display them in the new base.

6. When an aircraft or an automobile is moving through the atmosphere, it must overcome a force called *drag* that works against the motion of the vehicle. The drag force can be expressed as

$$F = \frac{1}{2}CD \times A \times \rho \times V^2$$

where *F* is the force (in newtons), *CD* is the drag coefficient, *A* is the projected area of the vehicle perpendicular to the velocity vector (in m^2), ρ is the density of the gas or fluid through which the body is traveling (kg/m^3), and *V* is the body's velocity. The drag coefficient *CD* has a complex derivation and is frequently an empirical quantity. Sometimes the drag coefficient has its own dependencies on velocities: For an automobile, the range is from approximately 0.2 (for a very streamlined vehicle) through about 0.5. For simplicity, assume a streamlined passenger vehicle is moving through air at sea level (where $\rho = 1.23$ kg/m³). Write a program that allows a user to input A and CD interactively and calls a function to compute and return the drag force. Your program should call the drag force function repeatedly and display a table showing the drag force for the input shape for a range of velocities from 0 m/s to 40 m/s in increments of 5 m/s.

7. Develop a collection of functions to solve simple conduction problems using various forms of the formula

$$H = \frac{kA(T_2 - T_1)}{X}$$

where H is the rate of heat transfer in watts, k is the coefficient of thermal conductivity for the particular substance, A is the cross-sectional area in m², T_2 and T_1 are the kelvin temperatures on the two sides of the conductor, and X is the thickness of the conductor in m.

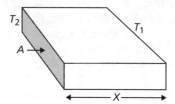

Define a function for each variable in the formula. For example, function calcH would compute the rate of heat transfer, calcK would figure the coefficient of thermal conductivity, calcA would find the cross-sectional area, and so on.

Develop a driver function that interacts with the user in the following way:

```
Respond to the prompts with the data known. For the unknown
quantity, enter a question mark (?).

Rate of heat transfer (watts) => 755.0
Coefficient of thermal conductivity (W/m-K) => 0.8
Cross-sectional area of conductor (m^2) => 0.12
Temperature on one side (K) => 298
Temperature on other side (K) => ?
Thickness of conductor (m) => 0.003


          kA (T2 - T1)
   H  =  ---------------
               X
```

Temperature on the other side is 274 K.

H = 755.0 W
k = 0.800 W/m–K
A = 0.120 m^2
T2 = 298 K
T1 = 274 K
X = 0.003 m

Hint: Extraction of the question mark when looking for a number will cause an input stream error. Be sure to clear the error and extract the question mark into a character variable before attempting additional input.

8. Use the recursive bisection function from Fig. 5.29 and a variant of function $f(\theta)$ from the "Roots of Equations" introduction (p. 195) in a program to approximate the necessary angle of elevation (radians) at which to launch a projectile traveling 250 m/s in order to impact a target 3300 m away at a height of 3 m. The approximation should be within 0.00001 of the actual angle. Use $g = 9.81$ m/s^2 as the gravitational acceleration. Your program should repeatedly prompt the user to enter endpoints of subintervals of the interval [0, $\pi/2$] radians until an interval is entered that contains an odd number of roots of f. Then call bisect with this interval and display the root returned.

Data Structures and Objects

6

In Chapters 1 to 5, we have studied C++'s representations of numbers, characters, and strings. However, the world we live in is full of objects far more complex than lists of numbers or words! In this chapter we study how to define our own data types to use in modeling objects. C++ provides two facilities for the software designer to use in creating composite types. The structure type is a facility also available in the parent language C. A structure type is a collection of data in which each individual component is referenced by its name. The components represent the attributes of an object.

The second C++ facility for creation of composite types, **class** definition, is the foundation of object-oriented programming in C++. Like a structure type definition, a class definition describes the attributes of a certain kind of object. Unlike a C-style structure type, a class definition also defines functions and operations that specify an object's behaviors. C++ structure types also allow for specification of object behaviors, but we do not cover that aspect of structure

class
mechanism for creating a new C++ type by combining a collection of data elements (attributes) and operations/functions defined on these data (behaviors)

types in this text. Structure type and class names are used in declarations of variables just as you use predefined type names such as `char`, `int`, and `double`. Just as C++ can convert numeric data from one type to another—either explicitly or implicitly in many contexts—C++ also allows the programmer to define new related classes in a way that permits implicit and explicit conversion from one to another. In this chapter we will study this conversion facility, and we will investigate how new classes are built on existing classes, a capability that promotes code reuse.

6.1   Structure Types

record
a collection of information about one entity

One common use of computers is for storing and searching a database of information. The elements of a database are **records**, collections of information about single entities. The record's structure is determined by the data type of the entity.

Before you can create or save a structured object, you must define the structure of its components. In this section we study one of several approaches available in C++—definition of a `struct`.

EXAMPLE 6.1   As part of a project for a manufacturer of metal machine parts, we are developing a database of pure metals. For each metal, we need to represent information like the following:

```
Name:  Chromium
Density:  7.19 g/cm3
Melting point:  1890°C
Tensile modulus:  289 GPa
Days to delivery: 19
```

structure type
a data type for a record composed of multiple components

We can define a **structure type** `Metal` to use in declaring a variable in which to store this information about the metal chromium. There must be variables to hold each of the components we have listed. The structure type `Metal` has five components. The first is a string variable in which to store the name of the metal. The next represents a quantity that has a fractional part, so it is type `double`. The last three components are of type `int`.

```cpp
struct Metal {
    string name;          // metal name
    double density;       // density (g/cm^3)
    int meltPt,           // melting point (Celsius)
        tensileMod,       // tensile modulus (GPa)
        daysDeliv;        // days to delivery
};
```

TABLE 6.1 Declarations That Use a Structure Type

Context of Declaration	Example
A Local Variable	`Metal oneMetal;`
Function Parameters—Reference and Value	`void manipMetal` `(Metal& newMetal,` `Metal oldMetal);`
Function Return Type	`Metal getMetal(ifstream&` `infile);` ■

This definition of type `Metal` describes the format of a `Metal` structure and the name and type of each component. A programmer is free to choose the same name for components of two different structure types, and this name can also be used for a single variable in the same scope. C++'s approach to referencing components will prevent confusion of such matching names.

The structure type definition itself allocates no memory. You must declare a variable to allocate space for a `Metal` structure. The name `Metal` can be used in exactly the same contexts where you can use the standard type names `int`, `bool`, `double`, etc.—to declare local variables and function parameters, and as a function return type. Table 6.1 illustrates these uses.

Accessing Structure Components

To reference a component of a structure, use the **member access operator**, the period.

Precede the period by the name of a structure type variable or a structure reference variable, and follow it by a component name. Figure 6.1 shows assignment of values to the components of the variable oneMetal that was declared in Table 6.1. The figure illustrates the state of the memory allocated for oneMetal after these assignments.

Data stored in a record like oneMetal can be manipulated just like any other data. For example, this statement

```
cout << "The tensile modulus of " << oneMetal.name << " is " <<
    oneMetal.tensileMod << " GPa.\n";
```

displays the sentence

```
The tensile modulus of Chromium is 289 GPa.
```

member access operator
a period placed between a structure type variable and a component name to create a reference to the component

Referencing Whole Structures

Use the name of a structure type variable with no member access operator to refer to the entire structure. For example, to pass the structure stored in vari-

FIGURE 6.1 Assigning Values to Components of Variable oneMetal

Variable oneMetal, a Structure
of Type Metal

`oneMetal.name = "Chromium";`	`.name`	Chromium
`oneMetal.density = 7.19;`	`.density`	7.19
`oneMetal.meltPt = 1890;`	`.meltPt`	1890
`oneMetal.tensileMod = 289;`	`.tensileMod`	289
`oneMetal.daysDeliv = 19;`	`.daysDeliv`	19

able `oneMetal` to a function `manipMetal` that expects a single parameter of type `Metal` or `Metal&`, use the function call

```
manipMetal( oneMetal );
```

Section 6.1 Review Questions

1. Define a structure type named **Point** that could store a point in the Cartesian plane. Include type **double** components named **x** and **y**.
2. Define a function **distance** that takes two type **Point** parameters (see Question 1) and calculates and returns the distance between them:

$$s = \sqrt{\left(x_2 - x_1\right)^2 + \left(y_2 - y_1\right)^2}$$

6.2   A Simple Class

We will begin our study of the C++ class definition facility by declaring a class that represents a point (x, y) in the Cartesian coordinate system. Declaring a class will create a type name that we can use in declaring a variable to represent a point. Figure 6.2 shows our class `Point`, the implementation of one of `Point`'s constructors, and a simple function `main` that uses a variable of type `Point`. We have labeled the figure with the terminology used to describe each aspect of the code.

Members

Just as a structure type is a collection of components, a class is a collection of members. `Point`, `getX`, `getY`, `x`, and `y` are all names of members of class

FIGURE 6.2 Declaring a Simple Class

```
1    #include <iostream>
2    using namespace std;
3
4    class Point { // point in Cartesian plane
5
6    public:
7       Point() {}
8       Point( double, double );
9
10      double getX() const { return x; }
11      double getY() const { return y; }
12
13   private:
14      double x, y;
15   };
16
17   //
18   // Create a Point object, initializing data members to parameter values
19   //
20   Point::Point( double xval, double yval )
21   {
22      x = xval;
23      y = yval;
24   }
25
26   int main()
27   {
28      Point pt1( 5.1, -4.7 );
29
30      cout << "The point is (" << pt1.getX() << ", " << pt1.getY() <<
31         ")\n";
32
33      return 0;
34   }
```

Class name → (line 4)

Access specifiers → (line 6)

Constructors → (lines 7–8)

Accessors → (lines 10–11)

Data members → (line 14)

Implementation of second constructor

Object declaration with initialization

Calls to accessor functions

Point. Point, getX, and getY are member functions, and x and y are data members. A critical difference between a structure type and a class is the use of the terms public and private. A class allows the definer to restrict access to some members by marking them private and to open access to other members by marking them public. The labels public: and private: are called **access specifiers**. In contrast, all the components of a structure type are public.

access specifiers
terms public and private that indicate the accessibility of class members

Data Members

data members
components of an object specified as separate variables within a class declaration

The **data members** x and y are the equivalents of a structure type's components. Class data members are typically marked `private`, which means that only member functions can reference them.[1] For example, since `main` is not a member function, these references would not be legal in `main`:

```
pt1.x        pt1.y        Illegal references in main
```

However, within member functions, the data members can be accessed by name. We see examples in member function `Point`,

```
x = xval;          // Lines 22 and 23
y = yval;
```

and in `getX` and `getY`.

```
return x;          // Line 10
return y;          // Line 11
```

Because member functions have automatic access to all of the current object's data members, their parameter lists are often empty.

Constructors

constructor
class member function with the same name as the class; provides mechanism for creating and initializing class objects

default constructor
a constructor that requires no arguments

Constructors are public member functions that are called when an object is created. Some constructors initialize their objects. Constructors always have the same name as the class. The constructor on line 7 of Fig. 6.2

```
Point() {}
```

is the **default constructor**. Every class has a default constructor that takes no arguments. `Point`'s default constructor leaves the data members uninitialized. Had it been written

```
Point() { x = 0; y = 0; }
```

it would initialize a point it creates to be (0, 0). A simple declaration of points such as

```
Point p1, p2;
```

calls the default constructor for each variable, allocating space as follows:

```
p1.x  [    ?    ]
  .y  [    ?    ]
p2.x  [    ?    ]
  .y  [    ?    ]
```

---

[1]Private members can also be referenced by member operators and friends, which we introduce later in the chapter.

On line 8 of Fig. 6.2, we have the prototype of a constructor for class Point that allows the programmer to declare a Point object and initialize its data members at declaration. Lines 17-24 are the definition of this constructor. The constructor takes the value of its first parameter, xval, and copies it into private data member x. Then it copies the second parameter into y. Line 28 of main calls this constructor:

```
Point pt1( 5.1, -4.7 );
```

and the allocated space is initialized as

```
pt1.x    5.1
  .y    -4.7
```

Accessors

An accessor is a public member function that allows any part of a program using the class to which the accessor belongs to look up the value of a private data member. Lines 10 and 11 of Fig. 6.2 define **accessor functions** getX and getY that return the values of x and y respectively.

```
double getX() const { return x; }
double getY() const { return y; }
```

To a user of getX, x becomes a "read-only" data member of a Point object—although any part of the program can *look at* the value of x, only the member functions can *change* x. Accessors getX and getY are **constant functions**, member functions that guarantee they will not alter any of the object's data members. The consts that follow their empty parameter lists

```
double getX() const { return x; }
double getY() const { return y; }
```

establish this guarantee. In the definition box that follows, *dataType* is the type of the member accessed and *DataMember* is the name of the member.

> Definition of an Accessor Function Within a Class Declaration
> *dataType* get*DataMember* () const { return *dataMember*; }

Line 30 of main demonstrates calls to accessors getX and getY from main, a nonmember function:

```
pt1.getX()
pt1.getY()
```

The next definition box shows how to call a public member function other than a constructor from a nonmember function.

accessor function
a public member function that provides "read-only" access to a private data member

constant function
a member function that promises not to change any of the object's data members

> Call to a Public Member Function from a Nonmember
> *objectName . functionName (argument list)*

Member Functions

Of the four member functions of class Point, three are fully defined within the class declaration:

```
Point() {}
double getX() const { return x; }
double getY() const { return y; }
```

For the fourth, the prototype is in the class declaration on Line 8 and the definition follows later.

Prototype

```
Point( double, double );
```

Definition

```
//
// Create a Point object, initializing data members to parameter
// values
Point::Point( double xval, double yval )
{
    x = xval;
    y = yval;
}
```

The programmer chooses one of these options for each member function. If the function's code is very short (a line or two), include its full definition in the class declaration. Otherwise, place only the prototype in the declaration and write the definition separately. When the definition is outside the class declaration, the function name must be preceded by the class name and the **scope resolution operator** : :.

scope resolution operator : :
binary operator whose left operand is a class and whose right operand is a member of the class

Section 6.2 Review Questions

1. Write a code fragment that would calculate and display the distance between points pt1 and pt2 that are objects of class **Point** defined in Fig. 6.2 Use the formula

$$s = \sqrt{\left(x_2 - x_1\right)^2 + \left(y_2 - y_1\right)^2}$$

2. Fill in the blanks with words or phrases to correctly complete these statements.
   a. Member functions _____ (use / do not use) an object name and class member selection operator to refer to other members of the default object.
   b. _____ provide the ability to declare an object just as you would declare a variable of a built-in type and to declare and initialize an object simultaneously.
   c. A member function that does not modify any object data members is a _____ function, and should therefore have a prototype and a header that end in _____.
   d. When a member function is defined outside a class declaration, in its header the function name is preceded by the _____ and the _____ operator.

3. Define a class to represent a cylinder. Data members are base radius and height (numbers) and units (string). Include a default constructor and a constructor that initializes all data members. Also define accessors for all data members. Here is a sample declaration:

```
Cylinder cyl1( 4.5, 12.0, "inches");
```

6.3 Analysis and Design of Classes

Now that we have a notion of the basic C++ syntax for a simple class, we will investigate the conceptual advantages of classes and present a design methodology suitable for development of more complex classes.

A close look at how C++ defines a type, such as `double`, will provide insight into what you should include in the definition of a class. Type `double` allows us to view a collection of data values—the bits of `double`'s mantissa and exponent in memory—as a single unified concept. The details of this collection of data values—how many bits are used for the mantissa and how many for the exponent, how a negative is stored—are of interest to the programmer only insofar as they impact the range and precision of legal values. Otherwise they are irrelevant to the programmer precisely *because* C++ provides adequate operations for manipulating `double` values. Figure 6.3 models type `double` by showing that the details of the type are completely hidden from the user, who always accesses the type by calling one of the predefined functions or operations. The figure illustrates some of the operations and functions that C++ defines for working with type `double`: the extraction and insertion operators for input/output, binary operators that add and multiply both type `double` and type `int`, and functions such as `sqrt`, `sin`, and `fabs` to perform operations for which no operators are defined. A type that is an internal representation hidden behind a collection of operations for access and manipulation of the data is called an **abstract data type** (ADT).

C++ lets you create your own abstract data types with the class definition facility. Object-oriented languages refer to an instance of an ADT as an object.

abstract data type (ADT)

a type whose internal representation is hidden behind a set of operations for access and manipulation

FIGURE 6.3 Type double and Its Predefined Operations

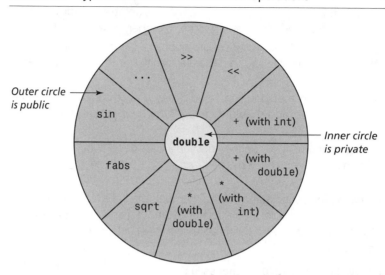

The C++ class definition facility allows you to define an object both in terms of its components (what it *is*) and its behavior (how it *acts* or *interacts* with other objects). In this section we design a class of objects representing drills such as the one pictured in Fig. 6.4. A drill is an object that would be modeled in a manufacturing engineering application. We will use the C++ class definition facility to implement our design in Section 6.4.

object-oriented analysis

process of identifying the attributes and behaviors of a class of objects

In Fig. 6.5, we apply to a drill the **object-oriented analysis** process described in Chapter 1. In the analysis phase, we identify the knowledge possessed by an object (its attributes), the questions it should be able to answer, and the services it provides. Because, in this initial example, we are developing one class of objects in isolation, we do not identify its relationships with other objects.

object-oriented design

process of determining types of attributes, prototypes and algorithms of behaviors, and accessibility of attributes and behaviors of a class of objects

The analysis in Fig. 6.5 is the input to the **design** phase of the development of our Drill class. Here we identify the types of the attributes and the parameter types and return types of the class-behavior functions. Figure 6.6 shows a model of a Drill comparable to Fig. 6.3's model of a double. The attributes in the internal circle are to be manipulated only by means of calls to the operations in the outer circle. C++ terms the hidden aspects (the inner circle) of the class private and the aspects known to all (the outer circle) public. Notice that the prototypes listed in Table 6.2 for the constructors of class Drill have no return type and have the same name as the class. In this phase we also decide which aspects of the class will be hidden from the other objects and functions that use the class and which will be accessible to all users.

FIGURE 6.4 Drill Object to Be Modeled

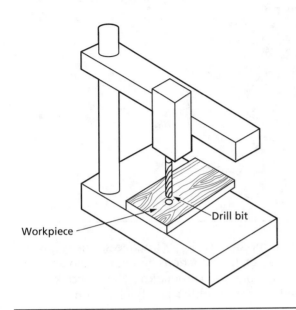

Material removal rate (mm³/s)

$$MRR = (\pi D^2/4)(f)(N/60)$$

Torque (W · s)

$$T = \frac{u(MRR)}{R}$$

D = bit diameter (mm)
f = feed (distance (mm) drill penetrates per revolution)
N = rpm
u = unit of power dissipated in drilling workpiece: W · s/mm³
R = rotational speed (radians/s)

Workpiece

Drill bit

FIGURE 6.5 Object-Oriented Analysis of a Drill

Attributes

What knowledge does it possess?
- Diameter (mm) of drill bit
- Feed rate—the distance (mm) that the drill bit penetrates the workpiece on each revolution
- Rotational speed (revolutions per minute)

Behavior

What questions should it be able to answer?
- At what rate does the drill remove the material from the object drilled (the workpiece)?
- What is the torque on the drill when cutting a certain workpiece material?

What services should it provide?
All class definitions must provide the service of construction—one or more mechanisms for declaring an object of this class. Our `Drill` class will provide two constructors—one that simply allocates space for the object on the stack and another that both allocates space and initializes the object's attributes.

FIGURE 6.6 Class Drill and Its Predefined Operations

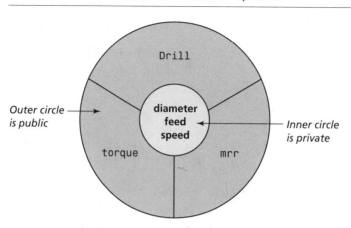

The design document must specify any object interfaces. The behaviors section describes the interfaces of the functions providing services and answering questions. These functions will automatically have access to the object's attributes, so we need parameters only when the function needs additional information. In a large object-oriented software system, the interfaces with other objects through these parameters would likely be the only ones necessary. However, to develop and test our `Drill` class in isolation, we also need an interface to the outside world, so in our design we have included facilities for input/output of `Drill` objects using the input extraction and output insertion operators.

Section 6.3 Review Questions

1. Design a class named **Ratio** to represent a common fraction as an integer numerator and integer denominator. Objects of this class should be able to modify themselves to reduce the fraction represented to lowest terms. Also plan for input/output of fractions. Do not forget to include constructors, one that initializes components and one that does not. Include in your answer an analysis document patterned after Fig. 6.5, an object model patterned after Fig. 6.6, and a design document in the format of Table 6.2.

2. Design a class named **Can** to represent a cylindrical aluminum can. Objects of this class should know their own (empty) weight in grams and their dimensions—base radius and height—in centimeters. When given the volume (cm³) of 1 gram of a product to be canned, objects of this class should be able to answer the question "How many whole grams of this product will fit in this can?" Do not forget to include constructors, one that takes parameters for initializing components and one that does not. Include in your answer an analysis document patterned after Fig. 6.5, an object model patterned after Fig. 6.6, and a design document in the format of Table 6.2.

TABLE 6.2 Design of Class Drill

Attributes

Name	Description	Type/Class	Accessibility
diameter	Drill bit diameter (mm)	double	private
feed	Distance (mm) that the drill bit penetrates on each revolution	double	private
speed	Drill bit rpm	double	private

Behaviors

Prototype	Description	Accessibility
double mrr()	Calculates material removal rate (mm³/sec) of drill	public
double torque (double)	Figures the torque (W·s) on the drill given the unit power (W·s/mm³) dissipated in cutting the workpiece material	public
Drill()	Constructor: Declares space for one Drill object, leaving components representing attributes uninitialized	public
Drill(double, double, double)	Constructor: Declares space for one Drill object, initializing attribute diameter to the value of the first parameter, attribute feed to the value of the second parameter, and attribute speed to the value of the third parameter.	public

Additional Interfaces

Interface with	Description
Outside world	Defines operators >> and << for I/O of Drill objects. Operator >> will take three type double values from the input source to initialize the attributes of a Drill object. Operator << will display the values of the attributes with labels.

6.4 Implementation of a Design as a Class

Figure 6.7 is an implementation of our Drill class that we have labeled with the terminology used to describe each aspect of the definition. The next few subsections focus on the class declaration and describe how various parts of this declaration implement our class design shown in Table 6.2. Later subsections describe in detail the definitions that follow the class declaration.

Constructors and Data Members

Class `Drill`'s constructors and data members are very similar to those of class `Point` in Fig. 6.2. They include a default constructor that allows an object declaration such as

```
Drill myDrill;
```

The second constructor, whose prototype is within the class declaration and whose definition follows the class declaration, provides the service of declaration with initialization:

```
Drill yourDrill( 5, 0.1, 500 );
```

Just as in class `Point`, the data members of class `Drill` have private accessibility. Since no accessors are defined, a nonmember function such as `main` cannot reference a `Drill` object's data members.

Prototypes of Member Functions

Most of the question-answering behavior of an object is implemented by member functions. We have seen that these functions belong to an object and are invoked by using the object name, the member access operator (.), and the function name. For example, here is a call to the material removal rate member function `mrr` of object `yourDrill`:

```
yourDrill.mrr()
```

The object name is not needed in the call if one member function calls another. For example, when function `torque` calls `mrr` in Fig. 6.7, the call is simply

```
mrr()
```

The class declaration shown in Fig. 6.7 includes prototypes of both member functions. Like the accessor functions of class `Point`, functions `mrr` and `torque` are constant functions, so their prototypes end with the qualifier `const`.

Access Specifiers

Our C++ class declaration indicates the accessibility of all members by marking the member declarations either `public` or `private`. Public members can be accessed by any part of the program where a legitimate reference can be made. As we noted earlier, member functions and constructors reference other members using only the names of the other members. Elsewhere, a member reference must include the name of the object to which the member belongs, so outside of the member functions and constructors, public members are accessible wherever their objects are in scope.

FIGURE 6.7 Class Drill for Drill Objects

```
include <iostream>
using namespace std;

const double PI = 3.141592654;
```

Class name

```
class Drill {
```

Access specifiers

```
public:
```

Constructors

```
    Drill() {}                              //Constructor 1—components uninitialized
    Drill( double, double, double );        //Constructor 2—components initialized
    double mrr() const;                     // material removal rate in mm^3/sec
    double torque( double )const;           // torque on drill given unit power
                                            // required to cut workpiece material
```

Prototypes of member functions

```
private:
    double   diameter,    // mm
             feed,        // mm / rev
             speed;       // rpm
```

Data members

```
    friend istream& operator>> ( istream&, Drill& );
    friend ostream& operator<< ( ostream&, const Drill& );
```

Prototypes of overloaded operators

```
};
```

Class Declaration

Constructor Definition

```
//
// Constructor 2:  initializes all components
//
Drill :: Drill( double drillDiam, double drillFeed, double drillSpeed )
{
    diameter = drillDiam;
    feed = drillFeed;
    speed = drillSpeed;
}
```

Member Function Definitions

```
//
// material removal rate:  mm^3 / sec
//
double Drill :: mrr() const
{
    return (PI * 0.25 * diameter * diameter * feed * speed / 60.0);
}
```

FIGURE 6.7 *(Continued)*

```
//
// torque (W . s) on drill based on unit power (W . s / mm^3) dissipated
// in cutting workpiece material
//
double Drill :: torque( double unitPower ) const
{
    double radSec;  // rotational speed in radians per second

    radSec = speed * 2 * PI / 60.0;
    return (unitPower * mrr() / radSec);
}
```

```
//
// Extract from input source the three components of a Drill object
//
istream& operator>> ( istream& is, Drill& dr )
{
    is >> dr.diameter >> dr.feed >> dr.speed;
    return is;
}


//
// Display a drill object, labeling all components
//
ostream& operator<< ( ostream& os, const Drill& dr )
{
    os << "Drill " << endl << "      diameter: " << dr.diameter << " mm" << endl
       << "      feed:     " << dr.feed << " mm/rev" << endl << "      speed:    "
       << dr.speed << " rpm" << endl;
    return os;
}
```

```
//
// Driver to declare and manipulate a drill object
//
int main()
{
    Drill  drillA;
    double unitPower;

    cout << "Describe a drill by entering diameter (mm), feed (mm/rev), "
         << "speed (rpm)" << endl << "=> ";
    cin  >> drillA;
```

FIGURE 6.7　*(Continued)*

```
        cout << "Enter average power unit for workpiece material (W . s / mm^3)"
             << endl << "=> ";
        cin  >> unitPower;

        cout << endl << drillA << endl;
        cout << "Drill's material removal rate is: " << drillA.mrr() <<
                " mm^3/sec" << endl;
        cout << "Torque on the drill when drilling the given workpiece material:"
             << "    " << drillA.torque( unitPower ) << " W . s" << endl;
        return 0;
}

Describe a drill by entering diameter (mm), feed (mm/rev), speed (rpm)
=> 10 0.2 800
Enter average power unit for workpiece material (W . s / mm^3)
=> 0.5

Drill
        diameter: 10 mm
        feed:     0.2 mm/rev
        speed:    800 rpm

Drill's material removal rate is: 209.439 mm^3/sec
Torque on the drill when drilling the given workpiece material:    1.25 W . s
```

Private members are accessible to all member functions and constructors. Additional code units can be given access to private members by designating them **friend**s of the class. We have done this in Fig. 6.7 for operators >> and <<. To reference a private member, a class's friend must use the object name, the member access operator, and the member name. Both operators and functions can be declared friends of a class.

In Fig. 6.7 we have grouped the members according to their accessibility, but C++ does not require this sequencing. Here is another class declaration that orders members alphabetically. It is equivalent to the declaration in Fig. 6.7, although not as easy to read.

friend
a nonmember operator or function given permission to access the private members of a class

```
class Drill {

private:
   double diameter;     // mm
public:
   Drill() {}           // Constructor 1 - components uninitialized
```

```
   Drill( double, double, double );   // Constructor 2 — components initialized
private:
   double feed;          // mm / rev
public:
   double mrr() const;  // material removal rate in mm^3 / sec
private:
   double speed;         // rpm
public:
   double torque( double ) const; // torque on drill given unit power required
                                  //    to cut workpiece material

friend istream& operator>> ( istream&, Drill& );
friend ostream& operator<< ( ostream&, const Drill& );


};
```

Prototypes of Operators

To assist us in thinking of a drill as a single unit rather than as a collection of pieces, the class declaration in Fig. 6.7 indicates the intent to define the operators << and >> so they can be used for input/output of drills. The form of a prototype for an operator is similar to the form of a function prototype. In this prototype,

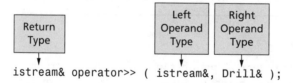

```
istream& operator>> ( istream&, Drill& );
```

istream& is the type of the value returned by the operator and (istream&, Drill&) is a list of the operand types: istream& is the type of the left operand; Drill& is the type of the right operand. Where a function prototype lists the function name, an operator prototype lists the keyword operator with the specific operator appended. We will present the reasons for using types istream& and ostream& when we discuss the definitions of these operators.

When we define operator >> and operator <<, we are overloading these operators, giving them more than one definition. Indeed, both >> and << already have multiple definitions. Consider this code fragment:

```
int   n;
char ch;

cin >> n >> ch;
```

If the input line is

5   5

then clearly the >> that takes the first 5 and stores it in the integer variable n is not performing the same operation as the second >> which takes the second 5 and stores it in the character variable ch. Both operations are receiving as input the character code for the digit 5. However, the first >> converts this character code to the integer 5 $(00 \ldots 00101_2)$ before storing it in n. Thus >> is actually the name of many different operations. The C++ compiler can determine which version of the >> code to invoke by checking the types of the operands. We discussed in Chapter 1 that the association of many operational definitions with one function or operator name is called **polymorphism** (see the "steak" example in Section 1.3) and is one of the special features supported by object-oriented programming languages such as C++.

polymorphism associating many forms of a function/operator definition with one name

Member Function Definitions

Following the constructor definitions in Fig. 6.7 are the definitions of member functions mrr and torque. They differ from nonmember function definitions in two regards:

1. In the function header, the function name is preceded by the class name and the scope resolution operator (::), and if the function never changes any of the object's data members, the header should end with the const qualifier.
2. The member function is always called in a context where there is a current object (this object is not an explicit parameter of the function). The function can reference this object's members by name.

Notice that mrr references components diameter, feed, and speed, and that torque references component speed and member function mrr.

Overloaded Operator Definitions

C++ requires that you define overloaded operators much as you define functions. The operator return types shown in Fig. 6.7 are references to objects of classes istream (keyboard or input files) and ostream (screen or output files). Always pass and return input/output sources and destinations by reference. The right operands of both operator>> and operator<< are references to Drill objects. It is obvious why operator>> requires a reference for its right operand: It intends to change the data members of this operand. Why operator<< calls for its right operand to be a reference is less obvious. The output insertion operator does not alter its right operand, so the use of the reference parameter seems unnecessary. Objects are frequently passed by reference simply for efficiency. Rather than using up time and space creating operator<<'s own personal copy of the object to be displayed, with a reference parameter the system can give the operator access to the original object. However, when you do use a reference parameter merely for efficiency, be sure to qualify it as const as you see in the prototype and definition of operator<<. The const qualifier notifies the compiler that the parameter's value will remain unchanged.

Consider how function main uses class Drill in Fig. 6.7. The first statement of main,

```
Drill drillA;
```

uses Constructor 1 to declare memory for a Drill object in which the three components are left uninitialized. Notice how the form of this statement matches the form of the declaration of type double variable unitPower that follows.

The next statement displays a prompting message by using the << operator four times. Figure 6.8 shows a step-by-step evaluation of this expression. Formerly we were concerned only with the statement's effect on the program output, the display of characters on the screen. However, the step-by-step evaluation demonstrates that the left operand of << is always an output destination and that the right operand is what is to be displayed. The value of an expression of the form

output destination << *data to display*

is the output destination, a reference to an object of type ostream. This fact enables us to write expressions consisting of sequences of << operations.

The next line of main,

```
cin >> drillA;
```

uses the definition of class Drill's friend operator >>. The system knows to call our definition of this operator rather than one of the standard definitions because the right operand is a Drill object. However, when executing the first statement of our Drill class definition of friend operator >>,

```
is >> dr.diameter >> dr.feed >> dr.speed;
```

the system will repeatedly use the standard definition of the binary operator >> that takes a type double right operand.

FIGURE 6.8 Step-by-Step Evaluation of Multiple << Operations

```
cout << "Describe a drill...(mm/rev), " << "speed (rpm)" << endl << "=> ";
     cout
                                           cout
                                                       cout
                                                                   cout
```

FIGURE 6.9 Step-by-Step Evaluation of Drill Display Statement with Output

```
                                              Displays
cout << endl << drillA << endl;       Starts a new line of output.
        cout                          Drill
            cout                          diameter: 10 mm
                                          feed:     0.2 mm/rev
                                          speed:    800 rpm
                                      Displays a blank line.
                          cout
```

The next two statements of `main` display a prompting message and input a numeric value for `unitPower`. The last three statements of `main` before the `return` use two of `drillA`'s member functions along with our friend operator `<<`. Figure 6.9 shows a step-by-step evaluation of

```
cout << endl << drillA << endl;
```

along with a trace of the output resulting from the operator evaluations assuming the data shown in the run at the end of Fig. 6.7. In this statement, evaluation of the shaded `<<` invokes the code of class `Drill`'s friend operator `<<` from Fig. 6.7. The other `<<`'s invoke standard definitions of the operator.

The next two statements display additional lines of output after computing the values of the calls

```
drillA.mrr()
```

and

```
drillA.torque( unitPower )
```

Section 6.4 Review Questions

1. Fill in the blanks with words or phrases to correctly complete these statements.
   a. The `const` qualifier should be used when declaring a parameter or an operand that is being passed by _____ merely for efficiency, not because the function/operator will change its value.
   b. When evaluating an expression of the form

      output stream `<<` *right operand*

      the compiler determines whether to use a standard definition of `<<` or an overloaded definition for a user-defined class by considering _____ .
2. Extend class `Drill` by defining an additional member function— `radSecSpeed`—that returns the drill's speed in radians per second. Why would

it be better to define this as a function rather than as an additional private component?

3. Here is a flawed implementation of the class **Ratio** that you were asked to design in Review Question 1 at the end of Section 6.3. Identify the errors in this implementation and correct them. The algorithm used to find the greatest common divisor of two integers is correct. Notice that **reduce** is an example of a member function that does change values of components; therefore its prototype and header should not end in **const**.

```
#include <iostream>
using namespace std;

class Ratio {

public:
    Ratio() {}       // Default constructor
    void reduce();   // reduces fraction

private:
    int num;      // numerator
    int denom;    // denominator

friend istream operator>> ( istream, Ratio );
friend ostream& operator<< ( ostream&, const Ratio& );

};

//
// Constructor that initializes components
//
Ratio :: Ratio( int numerator, int denominator )
{
    num = numerator;
    denom = denominator;
}

//
// Reduces fraction represented by a Ratio object by dividing num
// and denom by greatest common divisor
//
void reduce() const
{
    int n, m, r;
    n = num;
    m = denom;
```

```
    r = n % m;
    while (r != 0) {
        n = m;
        m = r;
        r = n % m;
    }
    num /= m;
    denom /= m;
}


//
// Extract from input source the two components of a Ratio
//
istream operator>> ( istream is, Ratio& oneRatio )
{
    is >> num >> denom;
    return is;
}


//
// Display a Ratio object as a common fraction
//
ostream& operator<< ( ostream& os, const Ratio& oneRatio )
{
    os << oneRatio.num ;
    if (oneRatio.denom != 1)
        cout << " / " << oneRatio.denom;
}


//
// Driver to declare and manipulate a Ratio object
//
int main()
{
    Ratio  aRatio;
    cout << "Enter numerator and denominator of a common fraction"
        << endl << "=> ";
    cin  >> aRatio;
    cout << endl  << "Fraction entered = " << aRatio << endl;
    reduce();
    cout << "Reduced fraction = " << aRatio << endl;

    return 0;
}
```

4. Write out an implementation of the class **Can** that you designed for Review Question 2 in Section 6.3. Write a main function that prompts for and inputs a **Can** object and then repeatedly inputs the volume of 1 gram of various products to be canned. Display how many whole grams of each product should fit in the can.

6.5 Accessors and Constructor Functions for Type Conversion

In our study of C++'s predefined types, we saw that one facility that assisted us in using the types was automatic conversion from one type to another. For example, C++ does not need to explicitly define operator * to handle multiplication of an int by a double. Instead, C++ converts the type int value to type double format and then uses its * operator that multiplies two doubles.

The differences between complex numbers and type double or int are comparable to the difference between int and double. The value 2 represents the same concept as 2.0, just as (2.5 + 0.0i) represents the same concept as 2.5, and (3.0 + 0.0i) is the same number as 3. Figure 6.10 defines class Complex in a manner that permits automatic conversion of type double to type Complex. By extension, since type int can be automatically converted to type double, we will also be able to convert from int to Complex.

FIGURE 6.10 Declaration, Implementation, and Use of Class Complex

```
#include <iostream>
#include <iomanip>
#include <cmath>
using namespace std;

class Complex {        // complex number object
public:
   Complex() {}                  // default constructor
   Complex( double, double );  // constructor that initializes real, imag
   Complex( double );          // constructor that permits conversion
                               //    from real to Complex
   double getReal() const { return real; }   // accessor
   double getImag() const { return imag; }   // accessor

private:
   double real;
   double imag;
friend istream& operator>> ( istream&, Complex& );
friend ostream& operator<< ( ostream&, const Complex& );
};
```

FIGURE 6.10   *(Continued)*

```
//
//  Constructor that initializes both data members
//
Complex :: Complex( double rl, double im )
{
   real = rl;
   imag = im;
}

//
//  Constructor that converts real to complex
//
Complex :: Complex( double rl )
{
   real = rl;
   imag = 0;
}

//
// Displays a parenthesized complex number, omitting imaginary part
// if its coefficient rounds (two decimal places) to zero
//      Example of format:   (−35.43 − 16.02i)
ostream& operator <<  ( ostream& os, const Complex& cnum )
{
   os << setiosflags( ios::fixed ) << setprecision( 2 );
   os << "(" << cnum.real;
   if (fabs(cnum.imag) < 0.005)
      os << ")";
   else if (cnum.imag > 0)
      os << " + " << cnum.imag << "i)";
   else
      os << " − " << fabs(cnum.imag) << "i)";
   return os;
}

//
// Inputs a complex number entered in the following format:
//      (−9.82 + 7i)
// Also accepts parenthesized real numbers with no imaginary part
//
istream& operator >> ( istream& is, Complex& cnum )
{
   char lparen, after, ichar, rparen;
   is >> lparen >> cnum.real >> after;
```

FIGURE 6.10   *(Continued)*

```
    if (after == ')'){
        cnum.imag = 0;
    } else {
        is >> cnum.imag >> ichar >> rparen;
        if (after == '-')
            cnum.imag = -cnum.imag;
    }
    return is;
}

int main()
{
    Complex c1, c2(9.3, -4.7), c3(18.0);  // Test three constructors
    double x = 17.6;
    int n;

    c1 = Complex(x); // Explicit conversion of double to Complex
    cout << "c1 = " << c1 << endl;
    cout << "c2 = " << c2 << endl;
    cout << "c3 = " << c3 << endl;

    cout << "Enter an integer and a number with a fractional part\n"
         << "separated by a space=> ";
    cin >> n >> x;
    c1 = x;  // Implicit conversion of double to Complex
    c2 = n;  // Implicit conversion of int to double to Complex
    cout << "c1 = " << c1 << endl;
    cout << "c2 = " << c2 << endl;

    cout << "Enter a parenthesized complex number=> ";
    cin >> c1;
    cout << "You entered " << c1 << endl;
    return 0;
}
```

Sample run:

```
c1 = (17.60)
c2 = (9.30 - 4.70i)
c3 = (18.00)
Enter an integer and a number with a fractional part
separated by a space=> -2  98.16
c1 = (98.16)
c2 = (-2.00)
Enter a parenthesized complex number=> (-19.2-40.1i)
You entered (-19.20 - 40.10i)
```

Class `Complex` has two private data members—`real` and `imag`. It has three member functions that are constructors: a default constructor that leaves both data members uninitialized, a constructor that takes two type `double` parameters and assigns the value of the first to `real` and the second to `imag`, and a constructor that takes a single type `double` parameter and assigns it to `real`, also assigning `imag` the value zero. It is this third constructor that permits automatic conversion of type `double` (and, by extension, type `int`) to type `Complex`.

Complex has two public member functions that are accessors, the functions named `getReal` and `getImag`. We saw in Section 6.2 that an accessor is a public function that allows any part of a program using the class to which the accessor belongs to look up the value of a private data member.

The driver function at the end of Fig. 6.10 shows declarations of object variables of class `Complex`:

```
Complex c1, c2(9.3, -4.7), c3(18.0);
```

The first variable declared (`c1`) uses the default constructor, and the second variable uses the constructor that takes two type `double` arguments. The third variable uses the constructor that takes one type `double` argument and gives c3 the value (18.0 + 0.0i). In the assignment to c1,

```
c1 = Complex(x);
```

we see another call to the third constructor to convert the type `double` value of x to an equivalent `Complex` number for assignment to c1.

The next three statements use the overloaded output insertion operator to display the values of `Complex` variables c1, c2, and c3.

```
cout << "c1 = " << c1 << endl;
cout << "c2 = " << c2 << endl;
cout << "c3 = " << c3 << endl;
```

The system automatically uses our definition of `<<` as a friend of class `Complex` when it detects that the right operand of each shaded `<<` is a `Complex` object.

The conversion constructor that we discussed above also provides the ability to carry out automatic (implicit) conversions. After the driver function of Fig. 6.10 prompts for and inputs two numbers, it assigns the second number (which is type `double`) to c1:

```
c1 = x;
```

Just as an assignment of an `int` expression to a type `double` variable causes an implicit conversion, this assignment of a `double` value to a `Complex` variable calls for an implicit conversion: C++ automatically calls the `Complex` conversion constructor that takes a single type `double` parameter. If no such constructor had been included for class `Complex`, however, the compiler would have marked this assignment statement as a syntax error with a message such as "Cannot convert `double` to `Complex`." The next assignment statement,

```
c2 = n;
```

requires C++ to perform two implicit conversions: First it converts the `int` value of n to a `double`, then it uses the one-parameter constructor of `Complex` to convert the `double` to a `Complex`.

Section 6.5 Review Questions

1. Fill in the blanks with words or phrases to correctly complete these statements.
   a. A(n) _____ is a member function that returns the value of a private data member of an object.
   b. To convert a value from type *A* to class *B*, the definition of _____ should include a constructor that takes a single parameter that is of _____.
2. Expand class **Ratio**, whose flawed implementation you were asked to correct in Review Question 3 of Section 6.4. Define a conversion constructor that converts an **int** such as 3 to a **Ratio** object (3/1).
3. Draw a nested-circle model of a **Complex** object (see Figs. 6.3 and 6.6).

6.6   Overloading Operators as Members

So far the only operators we have overloaded when defining new classes have been >> and <<. We can actually overload any of C++'s operators. For example, we might wish to overload the + and += operators to allow addition of two complex numbers.

Figure 6.11 overloads operators + and += as members of class `Complex`. You can implement a binary operator as a member of the class of its left operand, and the right operand will be passed as a parameter. We could not implement << or >> as a member of class `Drill` or of class `Complex` because the left operands of << and >> are streams, that is, objects that are instances of the iostream library classes `istream` and `ostream`. However, when we add two complex numbers

```
c1 + c2
```

the left operand is of type `Complex`, so the operator can be defined as a member.

Consider the prototypes and implementations of + and += shown in the shaded regions of Fig. 6.11. Notice that the form of a binary member operator is just like the form of a member function that requires one parameter in addition to the default object. The prototype begins with the type of value returned by the operator. Next comes the module name, and since the module defines an operator, the name is the keyword `operator` with + or += appended.

FIGURE 6.11 Program That Overloads Arithmetic Operators + and +=

```cpp
#include <iostream>
#include <iomanip>
#include <cmath>
using namespace std;

class Complex {

public:
    Complex() {}                    // default constructor
    Complex( double, double );  // constructor that initializes real, imag
    Complex( double );          // constructor that permits conversion
                                //    from real to Complex
    double getReal() const { return real; }   // accessor
    double getImag() const { return imag; }   // accessor
    Complex operator+ ( const Complex& ) const;
    Complex& operator+= ( const Complex& );

private:
    double real;
    double imag;

friend istream& operator>> ( istream&, Complex& );
friend ostream& operator<< ( ostream&, const Complex& );
};

// Constructors and operators >> and << omitted; same as in
// Figure 6.10

//
//  Adds two Complex numbers, returning the sum as a Complex object
//
Complex Complex :: operator+ ( const Complex& c2 ) const
{
      Complex sum(real + c2.real, imag + c2.imag);
      return sum;
}

//
// Adds the right operand (a Complex number) to the left operand
//
Complex& Complex :: operator+= ( const Complex& c2 )
{
```

FIGURE 6.11 *(Continued)*

```
        real += c2.real;
        imag += c2.imag;
        return *this;
}

int main()
{
        Complex c1, c2(9.3, -4.7), c3(18.0);
        double x(17.6);

        cout << "c2 = " << c2 << endl;
        cout << "c3 = " << c3 << endl;
        cout << "c2 + c3 = ";
        cout << (c2 + c3) << endl;
        c3 += c2;
        cout << "After c3 += c2, c3 = " << c3 << endl;

        c1 = Complex(0, 0.2) + x;
        cout << "c1 = " << Complex(0, 0.2) << " + " << x << " = "
           << c1 << endl;


        return 0;
}
```

Sample Run:

```
c2 = (9.30 - 4.70i)
c3 = (18.00)
c2 + c3 = (27.30 - 4.70i)
After c3 += c2, c3 = (27.30 - 4.70i)
c1 = (0.00 + 0.20i) + 17.60 = (17.60 + 0.20i)
```

After the name is the parenthesized parameter list. For a binary operator there is only one parameter, since the left operand is the default object to which this member operator belongs. In the implementations of operators + and +=, the parameter is named c2 to remind the reader that it represents the *second* operand. For both operators, this parameter is a constant reference to a Complex object, since neither operator needs to change the right operand.

The prototype and header of += differ from those of + in that they do not end in the keyword const. The compound assignment operator must change the value stored in its left operand, but the addition operator just looks at the value of the left operand without altering it.

The code of the + operator implementation is quite straightforward.

```
Complex sum( real + c2.real, imag + c2.imag );
return sum;
```

We simply call the `Complex` constructor that takes two parameters and pass it the sum of the real parts of the operands for the first argument and the sum of the imaginary parts for the second. The value of `Complex` object `sum` is returned as the operator result. Notice that we refer to the real and imaginary parts of the left operand (the default object) as `real` and `imag`, but to access the data members of the right operand that has been associated with parameter `c2`, we use the variable name and the member access operator as well as the data member name—`c2.real` and `c2.imag`.

Referring to the Whole Default Object: `*this`

Sometimes we need to refer to an entire object rather than just to a data member of an object. If the object is a parameter such as `c2` or a local variable like `sum` in `operator+`, we simply use the variable name (`c2` or `sum`) to refer to the entire object. However, if we need to refer to the entire *default* object within a member function or operator, there is no obvious name to use. C++ provides the predefined pointer `this` for such occasions. To reference the entire default object within a member module, use the expression

```
*this
```

The unary `*` operator follows the pointer that is the value of `this`, giving access to the default object. It is conventional for an assignment or compound assignment operator to return as its value a reference to the object assigned. For this reason, the result type of `+=` is `Complex&`, and the value returned is the default object. C++ automatically converts the value to a reference for consistency with the result type.

Figure 6.12 shows an alternative version of the Complex + operator that uses `*this`. The code fragment copies the first operand (the default object) into `sum` and then adds the real and imaginary parts of `c2` to `sum`.

> **`*this`**
> expression whose value within a member function or operator is the entire default object

FIGURE 6.12 `*this` Used to Reference the Entire Default Object

```
Complex Complex :: operator+ ( const Complex& c2 ) const
{
        Complex sum = *this;
        sum.real += c2.real;
        sum.imag += c2.imag;
        return sum;
}
```

Automatic Conversion of Operands

The driver function in Fig. 6.11 demonstrates the ability of C++ to convert operands of user-defined operators just as it converts them for system-defined operators. Consider the + operator in the statement

```
c1 = Complex(0, 0.2) + x;
```

The left operand of the + is the complex number resulting from an explicit call to the Complex constructor that takes two parameters. The right operand of the + is a variable of type double. A careful reading of Fig. 6.11 confirms that we never defined a Complex + operator that takes a type double right operand. So how is it that this assignment to c1 compiles and runs and generates a correct result? When C++ looks for a definition of a + operator that takes a type Complex left operand, it finds our + operator that takes two type Complex operands. It then applies to the value of x the Complex constructor that converts double to Complex and uses this result in figuring the value of

```
Complex( 0, 0.2 ) + x
```

C++ is always willing to look for a way to convert an actual argument to the type of a corresponding parameter. However, C++ will not convert the left operand to type Complex, so if the statement above were rewritten as

```
c1 = x + Complex(0, 0.2);
```

the compiler would display an error message. One way to avoid this error is to define + as a two-parameter friend operator rather than as a member of Complex.

Object Values or Object References

You may be puzzled why we define + with Complex& operands but have it return a Complex value as its result and why += has a Complex& result as well as Complex& operands. C++ offers great flexibility in these choices. Be aware, however, of two reasonable rules of thumb (the ones we are following):

1. Always pass object parameters/operands as references.
2. Never return an object reference as a function/operator value *unless* the reference was also a parameter/operand.

We follow Rule 1 for efficiency—to avoid the expenditure of time and space to make copies of object components. We follow Rule 2 to avoid returning a reference to memory that is no longer available. In the definition of operator +, for example, the declaration

```
Complex sum( real + C2.real, imag + c2.imag );
```

creates a new `Complex` object in the data area belonging to the current invocation of the operator (see Fig. 6.13). References to this memory will no longer be valid after the operator returns, so it makes no sense to return a reference to this object. In contrast, operator += does not create a new `Complex` object. Rather, it modifies a component of the object that is its left operand (see Fig. 6.14). The data area to which the left operand refers will continue to be available after operator += returns, so we return a reference to this object.

FIGURE 6.13 Return of Object Allocated on Stack by Operator+:

```
cout << (c2 + c3) << endl;
```

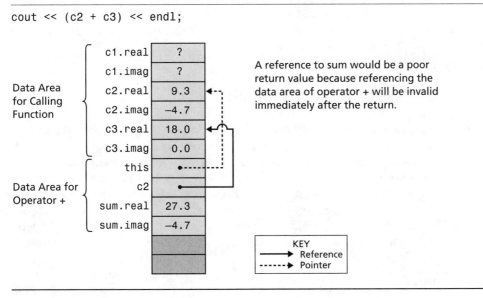

A reference to sum would be a poor return value because referencing the data area of operator + will be invalid immediately after the return.

FIGURE 6.14 Return of Reference to Object Parameter by Operator +=: c3 += c2;

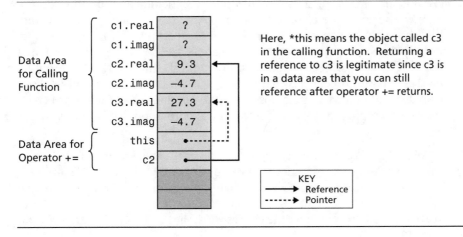

Here, *this means the object called c3 in the calling function. Returning a reference to c3 is legitimate since c3 is in a data area that you can still reference after operator += returns.

Section 6.6 Review Questions

1. Fill in the blanks with words or phrases to correctly complete this statement.

   A function should never return a(n) _____ to an object declared as a local variable of the function, because the space for this variable is no longer available after _____ .

2. Expand the complex number program of Fig. 6.11 by defining operators − and −= for class `Complex`. Test this version on several arithmetic expressions involving both addition and subtraction.

3. Although we have studied how to define + and += as members of class `Complex`, it is also possible to define them as friends. Show how you would change the class declaration and the implementations of + and += in Fig. 6.11 if you defined these operators as friends.

6.7 Class Reuse (Optional)

One major motivation for the use of an object-oriented programming language such as C++ is the ability to reuse code. Reuse of carefully designed, thoroughly tested modules of code can reduce development time and increase the reliability of new systems. C++ offers two primary methods for using existing classes of objects in building new ones. The first method builds on C++'s use of classes, like built-in types, and allows you to build new classes that have component objects of other class types. The functions and operators you have already defined can be applied to the components of objects of the new class. The second method allows you to derive new classes from existing classes. To determine which of these methods is appropriate, identify whether the existing class is a *part of* the new class or is a more specific *kind of* the existing class.

Figure 6.15 shows examples of "part-of" and "kind-of" hierarchies. When class *B* is *part of* class *A*, class *A*'s definition will include one or more components whose types are class *B*. For example, a class modeling the view of a Tree, shown in the "part-of" hierarchy of Fig. 6.15, would include components of class `Root`, class `Trunk`, class `Branch`, and so on. In contrast, when modeling a `Tree` object based on the "kind-of" hierarchy of the figure, `Needleleaf` would be a class derived from `Tree`: It would have all of Tree's attributes and behaviors plus possibly some specialized attributes or behaviors. The example that follows demonstrates both approaches to class reuse.

EXAMPLE 6.2   We can model a position on earth as a latitude and a longitude. Latitudes and longitudes are both directed angles such as 20° 40′ 5″ S, 75° 20′ 0″ E. In this example we will analyze the problem of modeling global locations and design a collection of classes to represent such locations. Since a location is a static concept, the classes we design will include attributes and

FIGURE 6.15 "Kind-of" and "Part-of" Hierarchies

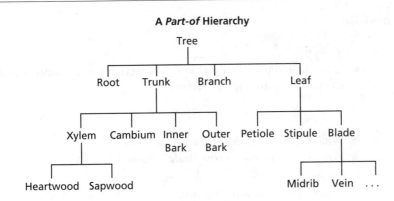

A *Part-of* Hierarchy

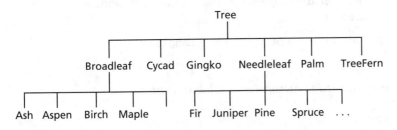

A *Kind-of* Hierarchy

standard services, such as construction and attribute access, but will incorporate no other behavior. However, if we wished to represent a location in multiple formats, we could later add member functions to convert from one format to another. For example, sometimes longitudes are represented by a single number, a signed value in radians whose magnitude ranges from 0 to π and whose sign indicates direction. We will propose addition of such a member function as part of Programming Project 7.

Figure 6.16 first identifies the attributes and behaviors of a global location (class GlobalLocation). Then, since the attributes are not normally represented as single values, we identify the attributes and behaviors of a class for representing latitudes and longitudes (DirectedAngle). We then recognize that a DirectedAngle is actually a special case of a more common notion—the measure of an angle—and we note the attributes and behaviors of class AngularDistance.

Next, we design the classes GlobalLocation, DirectedAngle, and AngularDistance (see Table 6.3). GlobalLocation is the first class we have created whose components are not of a standard type. Both its components latitude and longitude are objects of class DirectedAngle. Thus a

FIGURE 6.16 Object-Oriented Analysis of GlobalLocation and Its Component Classes

---

GlobalLocation—Class modeled

Attributes

What knowledge does it possess?	■ Latitude, longitude (angles with a direction and a measurement in degrees, minutes, and seconds)

Behavior

What questions should it be able to answer?	■ What is the location's latitude? (accessor) ■ What is the location's longitude? (accessor)
What services should it provide?	Constructors ■ Default (with no initialization) ■ Initialization with two directed angles ■ Initialization with latitude degrees, minutes, seconds, and direction and longitude degrees, minutes, seconds, and direction

Relationships with Other Classes	Two attributes are of type `DirectedAngle`

DirectedAngle—Type of latitude, longitude attributes of GlobalLocation

Attributes

What knowledge does it possess?	■ Angle measurement (in degrees, minutes, seconds—the attributes of class `AngularDistance`) ■ Direction (a character)

Behavior

What questions should it be able to answer?	None
What services should it provide?	Constructors ■ Default (with no initialization) ■ Initialization with all attributes specified ■ Initialization with direction, degrees, minutes specified (seconds defaults to 0) ■ Initialization with only direction and degrees specified (minutes and seconds default to 0)

Relationships with Other Classes	■ Part of `GlobalLocation` ■ Kind of `AngularDistance` (`DirectedAngle` is a derived class)

FIGURE 6.16 *(Continued)*

AngularDistance—Generic angle measurement of which DirectedAngle is a special case

Attributes

What knowledge does it possess?	■ Degrees—measurement in whole degrees ■ Minutes—fraction of a degree (one minute = $\frac{1}{60}$ degree) ■ Seconds—fraction of a minute (one second = $\frac{1}{60}$ minute)

Behavior

What questions should it be able to answer?	None
What services should it provide?	Constructors ■ Default (with no initialization) ■ Initialization with all attributes specified

Relationships with Other Classes	Base class from which `DirectedAngle` is derived

`DirectedAngle` object is *part of* a `GlobalLocation` object. Our design of classes `DirectedAngle` and `AngularDistance` reflects the fact that a `DirectedAngle` is a *kind of* `AngularDistance`. Thus class `DirectedAngle` is derived from **base class** `AngularDistance`.

base class
a previously defined class whose members are inherited by another class

TABLE 6.3 Design of Classes GlobalLocation, AngularDistance, and DirectedAngle

Class GlobalLocation

Attributes

Name	Description	Type/Class	Accessibility
latitude	a directed angle in degrees, minutes, seconds	DirectedAngle	private
longitude	a directed angle in degrees, minutes, seconds	DirectedAngle	private

Behaviors

Prototype	Description	Accessibility
const DirectedAngle& getLatitude() const	"Read-only" access to latitude data member	public
const DirectedAngle& getLongitude() const	"Read-only" access to longitude data member	public

TABLE 6.3 *(Continued)*

Prototype	Description	Accessibility
`GlobalLocation()`	Constructor: Declares space for one `Global-Location` object, leaving data members representing attributes uninitialized	public

`GlobalLocation(`
`  const DirectedAngle&,`
`  const DirectedAngle&`
`)`
	Constructor: Declares space for one `Global-Location` object, initializing attribute `latitude` to the value of the first parameter, and attribute `longitude` to the value of the second parameter.	public

`GlobalLocation( int,`
`int, int, char, int,`
`int, int, char )`
	Constructor: Declares space for one `Global-Location` object, initializing the elements of the `latitude` data member with the first four parameters and the elements of the `longitude` data member with the last four.	public

Additional Interfaces

Interface with	Description
Outside world	Overload operators >> and <<.

Class AngularDistance: Base Class for DirectedAngle

Attributes

Name	Description	Type/Class	Accessibility
`degrees`	integer representing number of degrees ($1 = \frac{1}{360}$ of a circle)	int	protected
`minutes`	integer representing number of minutes ($1 = \frac{1}{60}$ of a degree)	int	protected
`seconds`	integer representing number of seconds ($1 = \frac{1}{60}$ of a minute)	int	protected

Behaviors

Prototype	Description	Accessibility
`AngularDistance()`	Constructor: Declares space for one `AngularDistance` object, leaving data members representing attributes uninitialized	public
`AngularDistance( int,` `    int, int )`	Constructor: Declares space for one `AngularDistance` object, initializing attribute `degrees` to the value of the first parameter, attribute `minutes` to the value of the second parameter, and attribute `seconds` to the value of the third.	public

TABLE 6.3 *(Continued)*

Additional Interfaces

Interface with	Description
Outside world	Overload operators >> and <<.

Class DirectedAngle: Derived from AngularDistance

Attributes

Name	Description	Type/Class	Accessibility
degrees, minutes, seconds	Inherited from AngularDistance		
direction	Character N (north), S (south), E (east), or W (west)	char	private

Behaviors

Prototype	Description	Accessibility
DirectedAngle()	Constructor: Declares space for one DirectedAngle object, leaving data members representing attributes uninitialized	public
DirectedAngle(int, char)	Constructor: Declares space for one DirectedAngle object, initializing attribute degrees to the value of the first parameter, attribute direction to the value of the second parameter, and setting attributes minutes and seconds to 0.	public
DirectedAngle(int, int, char)	Constructor: Declares space for one DirectedAngle object, initializing attribute degrees to the value of the first parameter, attribute minutes to the value of the second parameter, attribute direction to the value of the third parameter, and setting attribute seconds to 0.	public
DirectedAngle(int, int, int, char)	Constructor: Declares space for one DirectedAngle object, initializing attribute degrees to the value of the first parameter, attribute minutes to the value of the second parameter, attribute seconds to the value of the third parameter, and attribute direction to the value of the fourth parameter.	public

TABLE 6.3 *(Continued)*

Additional Interfaces

Interface with	Description
Outside world	Overload operators >> and <<.

derived class

a class whose declaration indicates that it is to inherit the members of a previously defined base class

protected

access specifier comparable to `private` used in base classes to permit derived classes' member functions to access base class's nonpublic members

A **derived class** inherits components and member functions from the base class. However, it does not inherit the base class's constructors. Notice that in our design, we have indicated the accessibility of the components of class `AngularDistance` as `protected`. Access specifier **protected** has essentially the same meaning as `private` except that members and friends of a derived class are permitted to access the protected members inherited from the base class. For this reason, `protected` should be used only in classes intended to be base classes from which other more specialized classes will be derived.

Figure 6.17 implements our design of classes `GlobalLocation`, `Directed Angle`, and `AngularDistance`. Since `GlobalLocation` has components of type `DirectedAngle`, `DirectedAngle` is declared before `GlobalLocation`. Since `DirectedAngle` is derived from `AngularDistance`, `AngularDistance` is declared before `DirectedAngle`. In Fig. 6.17, we have shaded the aspects of the code that pertain to the implementation of a base class and a derived class. We have used boldface type to highlight reuse of one class as a component of another. Notice that in the first line of the declaration of derived class `DirectedAngle`, the class name is followed by a colon, the access specifier `public`, and the name of the base class.

Look carefully at the definitions of the constructors of class `DirectedAngle`, derived from class `AngularDistance`. With the exception of the default constructor, each definition begins by initializing the components inherited from base class `AngularDistance`:

```
DirectedAngle :: DirectedAngle( int deg, char dir )
  :AngularDistance( deg, 0, 0 )

DirectedAngle :: DirectedAngle( int deg, int min, char dir )
  :AngularDistance( deg, min, 0 )

DirectedAngle :: DirectedAngle( int deg, int min, int sec,
                                    char dir )
  :AngularDistance( deg, min, sec )
```

Notice that in the definition of the `AngularDistance` class, the data members `degrees`, `minutes`, and `seconds` are classified as `protected`. We see the

FIGURE 6.17 Building New Classes Using Existing Classes

Base Class Declaration

```
#include <iostream>
using namespace std;

class AngularDistance {  // Represents an angle measurement
                         // in degrees, minutes, and seconds


public:
   AngularDistance() {}              // default constructor
   AngularDistance( int, int, int ); // constructor that initializes
                                     //    all components
protected:
   int degrees, minutes, seconds;
friend ostream& operator<< ( ostream&, const AngularDistance& );
friend istream& operator>> ( istream&, AngularDistance& );
```

Base Class

```
};
```

Derived Class Declaration

```
class DirectedAngle : public AngularDistance {  // Represents a
                      // directed angle; direction may be
                      // 'N', 'S', 'E', or 'W'
public:
   DirectedAngle() {}                    // Default constructor
   DirectedAngle( int, char );           // Constructor that initializes
                                         //    degrees, direction (other
                                         //    components set to 0)
   DirectedAngle( int, int, char );      // Constructor that initializes
                                         //    degrees, minutes, direction
                                         //    (seconds set to 0)
   DirectedAngle( int, int, int, char ); // Constructor that initializes
                                         //    all components
private:
   char direction;  // 'N'(north), 'S'(south), 'E'(east), or 'W' (west)
friend ostream& operator<< ( ostream&, const DirectedAngle& );
friend istream& operator>> ( istream&, DirectedAngle& );

};

class GlobalLocation {  // Represents a location as two directed angles:
                        // a latitude and a longitude
public:
   GlobalLocation() {}                              // Default constructor
```

FIGURE 6.17 *(Continued)*

```
    GlobalLocation( const DirectedAngle&,       // Constructor that initializes
                    const DirectedAngle& );     //    latitude and longitude
    GlobalLocation( int, int, int, char,        // Constructor that initializes
                    int, int, int, char );      //    latitude and longitude one
                                                //    attribute at a time
  const DirectedAngle& getLatitude() const { return latitude; }   // Accessor
  const DirectedAngle& getLongitude() const { return longitude; } // Accessor
private:
  DirectedAngle latitude, longitude;
friend ostream& operator<< ( ostream&, const GlobalLocation& );
friend istream& operator>> ( istream&, GlobalLocation& );
};


//
// Constructor that initializes all three components of an angle
// measurement—degrees, minutes, and seconds
//
AngularDistance :: AngularDistance( int deg, int min, int sec )
{
   degrees = deg;
   minutes = min;
   seconds = sec;
}


//
//  Displays an angular distance with labels:  20 45'10"
//
ostream& operator<< ( ostream& os, const AngularDistance& angle )
{
   os << angle.degrees << " " << angle.minutes << "'" << angle.seconds
      << "\"";  // \" puts a quotation mark in the quoted string
   return os;
}


//
//  Inputs an angle measurement as three integers: degrees, minutes,
//  seconds
//
istream& operator>> ( istream& is, AngularDistance& angle )
{
   is >> angle.degrees >> angle.minutes >> angle.seconds;
   return is;
}
```

FIGURE 6.17 *(Continued)*

```
//
// Constructor that initializes degrees and direction components
// of a directed angle to parameter values; initializes other components
// to zero
//
DirectedAngle :: DirectedAngle( int deg, char dir )
   :AngularDistance( deg, 0, 0 )        ◄——  Member initialization list

{
   direction = dir;
}


//
// Constructor that initializes degrees, minutes, and direction components
// of a directed angle to parameter values; initializes other components
// to zero
//
DirectedAngle :: DirectedAngle( int deg, int min, char dir )
    :AngularDistance( deg, min, 0 )     ◄——  Member initialization list

{
   direction = dir;
}


//
// Constructor that initializes all components of a directed
// angle to parameter values
//
DirectedAngle :: DirectedAngle( int deg, int min, int sec,
                                   char dir )
    :AngularDistance( deg, min, sec )   ◄——  Member initialization list
{
   direction = dir;
}


//
//  Displays a directed angle with labels:  20 45'10" E
//
ostream& operator<< ( ostream& os, const DirectedAngle& angle )
{
   os << angle.degrees << " " << angle.minutes << "'" << angle.seconds
      << "\" " << angle.direction;
   return os;
}
```

FIGURE 6.17 *(Continued)*

```
//
// Inputs a directed angle as three integers (degrees, minutes, seconds)
// and a character (N, S, E, or W for direction)
//
istream& operator>> ( istream& is, DirectedAngle& angle )
{
   is >> angle.degrees >> angle.minutes >> angle.seconds >> angle.direction;
   return is;
}


//
// Constructor that initializes a GlobalLocation object with a latitude
// and a longitude
//
GlobalLocation :: GlobalLocation ( const DirectedAngle& lat,
                                   const DirectedAngle& lon )
{
   latitude = lat;
   longitude = lon;
}


//
// Constructor that initializes a GlobalLocation object with the
// components of a latitude and a longitude
//
GlobalLocation :: GlobalLocation ( int latDeg, int latMin, int latSec,
                                   char latDir, int longDeg, int longMin,
                                   int longSec, char longDir )
{
   latitude = DirectedAngle( latDeg, latMin, latSec, latDir );
   longitude = DirectedAngle( longDeg, longMin, longSec, longDir );
}


//
// Display a global location as a latitude and longitude
//
ostream& operator<< ( ostream& os, const GlobalLocation& where )
{
   os << where.latitude << ", " << where.longitude;
   return os;
}
```

FIGURE 6.17 *(Continued)*

```
//
// Input a global location as a latitude (3 integers for degrees,
// minutes, and seconds and a character for direction) and a
// longitude.  Sample input: 10 30 0 N  84 30 0 W
//
istream& operator>> ( istream& is, GlobalLocation& where )
{
    is >> where.latitude >> where.longitude;
    return is;
}

int main()
{
    GlobalLocation loc1, loc2;

    cout << "Enter a global location as a latitude and longitude."
         << endl << "Example: 10 30 0 N  84 30 0 W" << endl << "=> ";

    cin >> loc1;

    cout << "Location entered was: " << loc1 << endl;
    cout << "   Latitude:  " << loc1.getLatitude() << endl;
    cout << "   Longitude: " << loc1.getLongitude() << endl;

    loc2 = GlobalLocation( 17, 50, 0, 'S', 178, 0, 0, 'E' );

    cout << "Location assigned was: " << loc2 << endl;
    cout << "   Latitude:  " << loc2.getLatitude() << endl;
    cout << "   Longitude: " << loc2.getLongitude() << endl;

    loc2 = GlobalLocation( DirectedAngle( 18, 51, 'N' ),
                           DirectedAngle( 180, 'E') );

    cout << "Location assigned was: " << loc2 << endl;
    cout << "   Latitude:  " << loc2.getLatitude() << endl;
    cout << "   Longitude: " << loc2.getLongitude() << endl;

    return 0;
}
```

FIGURE 6.17 *(Continued)*

Sample Run

```
Enter a global location as a latitude and a longitude.
Example: 10 30 0 N  84 30 0 W
=> 20 40 5 S  75 20 0 E
Location entered was: 20 40'5" S, 75 20'0" E
   Latitude:  20 40'5" S
   Longitude: 75 20'0" E
Location assigned was: 17 50'0" S, 178 0'0" E
   Latitude:  17 50'0" S
   Longitude: 178 0'0" E
Location assigned was: 18 51'0" N, 180 0'0" E
   Latitude:  18 51'0" N
   Longitude: 180 0'0" E
```

advantages of this access specifier in the definition of DirectedAngle's friend operator, <<, which accesses both DirectedAngle's own data member, direction, and the protected components that DirectedAngle inherits from base class AngularDistance—degrees, minutes, and seconds.

Function main of this program demonstrates the use of most of the constructors and operators defined. First we assign a value to loc1 by using GlobalLocation's friend operator >>. Then we display this location twice, once using the operator << that is GlobalLocation's friend, and once by two uses of the operator << that is DirectedAngle's friend. We provide this operator with its right operand by using class GlobalLocation's accessor functions getLatitude and getLongitude. Notice the use of const in the prototypes and definitions of these accessors. In keeping with our policy of passing and returning objects by reference whenever possible, getLatitude and getLongitude are returning references to the latitude and longitude components of a GlobalLocation object. However, the intent of an accessor is to give "read-only" access to a component. If the return type of the accessor were simply DirectedAngle&, then a function could use this reference to modify the component's contents. By returning type const DirectedAngle&, we notify the compiler that the data member returned cannot be changed.

After displaying loc1 as two directed angles, we construct a GlobalLocation object to store in loc2 by calling GlobalLocation's eight-parameter constructor function. Finally, we test GlobalLocation's two-parameter constructor by calling DirectedAngle's three- and two-parameter constructors and then passing the DirectedAngle objects to GlobalLocation. ■

Section 6.7 Review Questions

1. Identify the following hierarchies as *part-of* or *kind-of*.

(a)

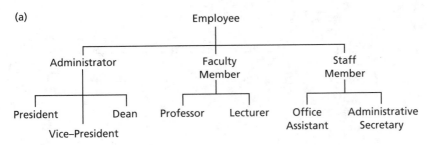

(b)

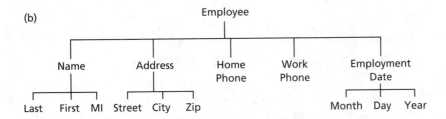

2. Define a class, `RectangularSolid`, whose data members are `length`, `width`, and `height` (in mm). Derive a `RectSolidObject` class that is a kind of `RectangularSolid` but also specifies the object's mass in grams.

3. Define a `Triangle` class whose data members are two angles and a side (the included side measured in mm). Use class `AngularDistance` from Fig. 6.17 and expand it by adding a member function that returns a type `double` value representing the angle measured in radians. Also define a member function for `Triangle` named `threeSides` that has reference parameters through which it communicates to the caller the lengths of the `Triangle` object's three sides. Why is it preferable to define such a member function rather than to store the lengths of the other two sides as additional data members?

6.8 Software Designer Beware

When you overload functions and operators, be sure that each version has a distinct signature (the function/operator name and its list of parameter types). For example, you could not add both of the following constructors,

```
//
// Constructor 3:  initializes drillDiam and drillSpeed only
//
Drill :: Drill( double drillDiam, double drillSpeed )
```

```
{
    diameter = drillDiam;
    speed = drillSpeed;
}


//
// Constructor 4:  initializes drillDiam and drillFeed only
//
Drill :: Drill( double drillDiam, double drillFeed)
{
    diameter = drillDiam;
    feed = drillFeed;
}
```

to the definition of the `Drill` class of Fig. 6.7 because their signatures are identical:

> Function name: `Drill`
>
> List of parameter types: (`double, double`)

If you overload the `<<` and `>>` operators for a new class, be sure to return the `istream&` or `ostream&` object operand as the operator value. It is this return value that lets you build an expression that uses the operator multiple times.

Carefully analyze your class definitions to determine where to use the `const` qualifier. Verify that each member function that does not change object components is declared `const`—both in its prototype and in its definition. Also be sure to declare as `const` any object reference parameters that are strictly inputs to a function or to an operation and any reference parameters used as return types that are intended to give "read-only" access to the object.

Design a class so you cannot store conflicting data. For example, if you want a class to provide access to a data member value in two formats (for example, in degrees and in radians), store the component in only one format and provide a member function to convert the data to another format.

Chapter Review

1. Like C, C++ provides a facility for defining a structure type composed of multiple named components. A structure component is accessed by placing the member access operator, a period, between the structure variable name and the component name.

2. C++ provides a second facility for naming a new type, class definition. Defining a class permits creation of an object, which combines a collection of data elements (attributes) and operations defined on these data (behaviors).

3. Object attributes are implemented as class data members whose accessibility is usually private—i.e., fully accessible only to class members and friends.

4. Object behaviors and services are implemented as class member operators and functions, which are usually public—i.e., callable from any part of the program that can make a valid reference to the operator or function.

5. Except within member functions and operators, accessible object members are referenced by placing the member access operator, a period, between the object name and the member name.

6. All classes provide the service of construction, which allows creation, initialization, and sometimes conversion of objects.

7. C++ permits overloading of operators with the same restrictions as for overloading of functions: each version must have a unique signature, a combination of the operator name and the list of operand types.

8. Overloaded operators can be implemented as members of a class when the first operand is an object of that class.

9. Usually, function parameters that are objects should be declared as reference parameters for efficiency. Parameters that are strictly input parameters should be declared as constant references.

10. A derived class inherits the members of its base class. The derived class member functions and friends can access only the public and protected members inherited.

New C++ Constructs

Construct	Effect

Definition of a Structure Type
``
struct Point3D {
    double x, y, z;
};
``
	A structure type `Point3D` is defined with components that can store the x, y, and z coordinates of a point in three dimensions.

Declaration and Use of Variables to Hold Point3D Structures
``
Point3D refPt, copyRef;
refPt.x = 0.0;
refPt.y = 4.5;
refPt.z = -12.7;
copyRef = refPt;
``
	`refPt` and `copyRef` are structured variables of type `Point3D`. Each component of `refPt` is assigned a value. Then the whole structure is copied into `copyRef`.

Class Declaration
``
class Ratio {
 	
public:
    Ratio() {}
    Ratio(int, int);
    void reduce();
    Ratio operator+ (const Ratio&)
        const;
``
	Declares class `Ratio`, a class of objects that represent common fractions. The class includes two constructors, a member function for reducing a common fraction to lowest terms, and a member addition operator.

```
private:
    int num;   // numerator
    int denom; // denominator
};
```

Object Declaration

`Ratio oneRatio;` — Declares `oneRatio` to be an object, an instance of class `Ratio`.

Member Function Header

`void Ratio :: reduce()` — First line of implementation of `reduce`, a function that is a member of class `Ratio`.

Member Operator Header

```
Ratio Ratio :: operator+
    ( const Ratio& r2 ) const
```
Beginning of implementation of the + operator for addition of two `Ratio` objects. The operator changes neither the parameter r2 nor the default object.

PROGRAMMING PROJECTS

1. Develop a class `Rational` that represents rational numbers as two integers, a numerator and a denominator. Include a default constructor, a constructor that takes two `int` parameters (numerator and denominator), and a constructor that takes one `int` parameter (the numerator) and initializes the denominator to 1. Include a member function `reduce` that reduces the fraction to lowest terms and guarantees that if the rational number is negative, the numerator *only* is negative, and if the rational number is nonnegative, *neither* numerator nor denominator is negative. Make `reduce` a private function and call it anywhere a rational number is created that might not be in lowest terms. Since reducing a fraction requires you to divide numerator and denominator by their greatest common divisor, look at the gcd algorithm given in Programming Project #9 of Chapter 4. Here is an example of a situation where `reduce` is needed:

   `Rational r1(6, -4);`

   If your two-parameter constructor simply assigned its first parameter to the numerator and its second to the denominator, you would have a fraction that was not in standard form. By calling `reduce` from this constructor, you can assure that the fraction stored in this case will be –3/2 rather than 6/-4.

Overload the >> and << operators as friends. The input extraction operator should input two integers separated by a slash. Discard the slash—there is no need to store it in the Rational object. The output insertion operator should display –3/1 as –3 and 0/n as 0. Define +, –, *, and / as public member operators. These should all return results of type Rational.

Here is a code fragment to include in function main of your implementation:

```
Rational r1, r2(-5), r3(8, -10);
Rational sum(0), product(1);
cout << "r2 = " << r2 << endl;
cout << "r3 = " << r3 << endl;
cout << "r2 + r3 = " << (r2 + r3) << endl;
cout << "r2 - r3 = " << (r2 - r3) << endl;
cout << "r2 * r3 = " << (r2 * r3) << endl;
cout << "r2 / r3 = " << (r2 / r3) << endl;
cout << "r3 * 2 = " << (r3 * 2) << endl;   // How?
cout << "Enter 5 rational numbers.  Sample rational number:"
     << " -5/2\n";
for (int i = 0;  i < 5;  ++i) {
   cout << "=> ";
   cin >> r1;
   sum = sum + r1;
   product = product * r1;
}
cout << "The sum is " << sum << endl;
cout << "The product is " << product << endl;
```

Notice the line marked // How? You will find that this statement compiles and executes despite the fact that you have not defined a * operator that takes a Rational left operand and an int right operand. If you were to trace this line in the debugger, you would discover that it calls the one-parameter constructor to convert 2 to the Rational 2/1 and then calls the * operator for two Rationals.

2. Develop a class AirborneLocation that represents the locations of airplanes with respect to a reference airplane. Each AirborneLocation object should include data members for an aircraft ID—a string of letters and numbers such as AZ719CD4; aircraft type, the character M or C indicating military or civilian; and a position (x, y, z) where x, y, and z are the distances in km (east-west, north-south, up-down) from the reference aircraft (x, y, and z are signed quantities where positive means east, north, or up; negative means west, south, or down). Overload the >> and

<< operators for class `AirborneLocation`. The >> should expect data in the format shown in the sample data file given. The << should output all data members with labels. This operator should translate the signed x, y, and z into their meanings: (-8, 4, 1.5) would be "8 km west, 4 km north, 1.5 km up." Include a member function `distance` that calculates how far the plane is from the reference airplane: $\sqrt{x^2 + y^2 + z^2}$. Use an input-failure-driven loop to input all the `AirborneLocation` objects, and write to an output file the descriptions of each along with their distances from the reference airplane. After processing all locations, display on the screen the objects representing the airplane nearest to the reference airplane and the one farthest from it.

Sample Data File

```
AF719CD4  SR-71-Blackbird  M   95.2  20.4   3.5
UA950AL2  Boeing-747X      C  -38.1 -45.9  -1.1
NW777BB1  Airbus-A3XX      C   55.7 -50.2   0.3
AF994ZZ7  ER-111A-Raven    M  -87.6  14.5   2.0
TW121TX3  Boeing-757       C   10.8 -96.5   1.5
```

3. Design and implement a class `Quadratic` to represent a quadratic function, a function of the form

$$f(x) = ax^2 + bx + c$$

Include private data members for coefficients a, b, and c. Define a default constructor and a constructor that initializes a, b, and c to the values of its three parameters. Overload the input extraction operator to input a `Quadratic` object as three coefficients. Overload the output insertion operator to display the quadratic in this form:

```
-2x^2 - 4x + 35
```

Define a member function to evaluate the function at a value for x provided as a parameter, returning the value calculated as the function result. Also define a member function that displays the two real roots of the quadratic or an appropriate message if the function has a double root or no real roots. You will use the quadratic formula in this function:

$$rt = \frac{-b \pm \sqrt{b^2 - 4ac}}{2a}$$

4. Define a class `Vect` to represent a vector as a magnitude r and a direction `theta`. Store `theta` as an angle (in radians) in the range [0, 2π). Define a default constructor function and two initializing constructor functions: one that takes two type `double` operands, and one that takes a single `Vect` operand. Overload the >> and << operators to input and output vectors with the angles expressed in degrees and minutes. Define mem-

ber functions xComponent and yComponent that resolve the vector into its x component ($r \cos \theta$) and its y component ($r \sin \theta$). Overload operators + and += to add vectors: First find the x and y components of the sum and apply the Pythagorean theorem to determine the magnitude of the resultant vector. Check the signs of the x and y components to determine the quadrant of the resultant vector, and use the relation

$$\tan \theta = \frac{y_{sum}}{x_{sum}}$$

to find the direction of the vector. Since class Vector directions should fall in the range $[0, 2\pi)$, you will need to adjust the angle computed by the arctangent function atan if the vector is not in quadrant I. The necessary adjustments follow:

Quadrant of Vector	Sign of y_{sum}/x_{sum}	Add to Angle
II	–	π
III	+	π
IV	–	2π

5. Design and implement a class to model a battery. A battery object should know its voltage, how much energy it is capable of storing, and how much energy it is currently storing (in joules). Include the following member functions:

powerDevice: Given the current of an electrical device (amps) and the time the device is to be powered by the battery (seconds), this function determines whether the battery's energy reserve is adequate to power the device. If so, the function updates its energy reserve by subtracting the energy consumed and returns the value true. Otherwise it returns the value false and leaves the energy reserve unchanged.

maxTime: Given the current of an electrical device, the function returns the number of seconds the battery can operate the device before it is fully discharged. This function does not modify the energy reserve.

reCharge: This function sets the battery's component representing the present energy reserve to its maximum capacity.

Use the following equations in your design:

$p = vi$ p = power in watts (W)
             v = voltage in volts (V)
$w = pt$ i = current in amps (A)
             w = energy in joules (J)
             t = time in seconds (s)

For this simulation, neglect any loss of energy in the transfer from battery to device.

Create a main function that tests your class by creating an object to model a 12-V automobile battery with a maximum energy storage of 5×10^6 J. Use the battery to power a 4-A light for 15 minutes. Then find out how long the battery's remaining energy could power an 8-A device. After recharging the battery, ask again how long it could operate an 8-A device.

6. Define a class `Auto` to represent an automobile in a cross-country driving simulation program. Include components for an integer ID number, the odometer reading, the manufacture and purchase dates (define another class called `Date`), the official highway fuel economy rating in kilometers per liter, and the gas tank (define a class `Tank` with components for the tank's capacity and current fuel level, giving both in liters). Include default constructors and constructors that initialize all components—one that takes all single-number parameters and one that takes object parameters for the two dates and the tank and single numbers for the other components. Overload << and >> for all three new classes, ensuring that the definitions of << and >> for `Auto` use the definitions of << and >> for `Date` and `Tank`. Define a member function called `fillUp` for class `Tank` and a member function called `drive` for class `Auto`. Function `fillUp` should copy the tank capacity value into the current fuel level component and return a type `double` value indicating the number of liters required to fill the tank. Function `drive` should take the number of kilometers driven as an input argument and should adjust the odometer reading and the tank's current fuel level component. Write a driver function that fills several `Auto`-class variables in ways designed to test the three classes' various constructor functions and the overloaded >> and << operators. Also include calls to `fillUp` and `drive`.

7. Expand the `GlobalLocation` program of Fig. 6.17 to allow computation of the distance (in km) between two locations on earth. This distance (s) is calculated as

$$s = 2 \cdot r \cdot \sin^{-1} \sqrt{ \sin^2 \left(\frac{\phi_0 - \phi_1}{2} \right) + \cos \phi_1 \cos \phi_0 \sin^2 \left(\frac{\lambda_0 - \lambda_1}{2} \right) }$$

where r is the earth's radius (approximately 6365 km), (ϕ_0, λ_0) represents (latitude, longitude) of one location, and (ϕ_1, λ_1) is the other location. The formula assumes that latitudes and longitudes are in radians with north latitudes and east longitudes being positive, and south latitudes and west longitudes negative.[1]

Define a class `RadianLocation` that represents a location using the formula's conventions, and include a constructor for `RadianLocation`

[1] John P. Snyder, "Map Projections—A Working Manual," *U.S. Geological Survey Professional Paper 1395*, 1987.

that will convert a `GlobalLocation` object. Also define a new member function for `DirectedAngle` that returns a type `double` value representing the directed angle as a signed value in radians.

8. Design and implement a class to model an ideal transformer. If you have a single iron core with wire 1 coiled around the core N_1 times and wire 2 wound around the core N_2 times, and if wire 1 is attached to a source of alternating current, then the voltage in wire 1 (the input voltage V_1) is related to the voltage in wire 2 (the output voltage V_2) as

$$\frac{V_1}{V_2} = \frac{N_1}{N_2}$$

and the relationship between the input current I_1 and the output current I_2 is

$$\frac{I_1}{I_2} = \frac{N_2}{N_1}$$

A transformer object should store N_1, N_2, V_1, and I_1, and should provide member functions `vOut` and `iOut` to compute the output voltage and current. Also provide member functions to set each of the transformer's components to produce a desired output voltage or current. For example, member function `setN1forV2` should take a desired output voltage as a parameter and should change the object component representing N_1 to produce the desired voltage. Member function `setI1forI2` should take a desired output current as a parameter and change the object component representing I_1 to produce the desired current. Also define `setV1forV2`, `setN2forV2`, `setN1forI2`, and `setN2forI2`. Either overload `<<` for transformer output or define accessor functions for the components representing V_1, I_1, N_1, and N_2 to facilitate output.

Arrays and Strings

7

In previous chapters we processed lists of data by taking one data value at a time from the input stream, processing the value fully, and then replacing the value by the next item in the data stream. We never stored all the data of a list in memory at the same time. Our inability to work with earlier data values after seeing the entire list has severely limited the analysis we could do of the data. For example, if we had data representing monthly rainfall for a year and we wished to create a table categorizing each month as rainy (rainfall 20% higher than average), dry (rainfall 25% lower than average), or average, our program would need to look at the list of rainfall data at least twice because it could not determine a month's category until after it had figured the average rainfall. We, therefore, would need to store all the data in memory at once.

This chapter presents a C++ **data structure**—a collection of related data values—that allows storage of an entire list of data in memory cells accessed using one name.

data structure
a collection of related data values associated with one name

7.1 Arrays for List Storage

array

a data structure in which all elements are the same type

An **array** is a collection of adjacent memory cells associated with a single variable name. All the individual values, called *array elements*, must be of the same data type. A statement that declares an array tells the compiler the type of the elements, the name of the array variable, and the number of elements.

EXAMPLE 7.1   The statement

```
double precip[12];
```

declares a 12-element array of type `double` values and names the list `precip`. The size of the array is 12.

array subscript

an expression in square brackets after an array name; indicates which array element to access

To store data in `precip` and to process these data, we use the array name and an **array subscript** in square brackets identifying a single array element. We refer to the initial element of `precip` as `precip[0]` (read precip-sub-zero). The next element is `precip[1]`, and `precip[11]` is the last element. The subscript can be any integer expression whose value is in the range from zero to one less than the array size. Figure 7.1 is a picture of array `precip` filled with data.

Table 7.1 shows some statements that access the data in `precip`, given the values of i and j shown:

Figure 7.2 shows the new contents of `precip` after execution of the valid statements in Table 7.1. If the final statement of Table 7.1 were executed, `precip[2]` would be changed to the value stored in the memory cell after `precip[11]`.

FIGURE 7.1 Array precip in Memory

precip[0]	5.8
precip[1]	4.2
precip[2]	6.7
precip[3]	7.3
precip[4]	6.1
precip[5]	3.2
precip[6]	2.1
precip[7]	1.9
precip[8]	2.4
precip[9]	4.5
precip[10]	4.9
precip[11]	5.3
	?

TABLE 7.1 Statements Using the Data in precip

`cout << "precip[4] = " << precip[4] << endl;`	Displays the value of `precip[4]` (6.1) with a label.
`cout << precip[9] - precip[8] << endl;`	Displays the difference between `precip[9]` and `precip[8]` (2.1).
`precip[0] = 5.6;`	Stores 5.6 in `precip[0]`.
`precip[j - 1] = precip[i];`	Copies 2.1 (`precip[6]`) into `precip[1]`.
`cout << precip[i + j] << endl;`	Displays 2.4 (`precip[8]`).
`cout << precip[i] + precip[j] << endl;`	Displays 8.8 (2.1 + 6.7).
`cout << precip[i++] << endl;`	Displays 2.1 (`precip[6]`) and then increments `i` to 7.
`cout << precip[i] << endl;`	Displays 1.9 (`precip[7]`).
`for (int i = 0; i < 12; ++i)` `    cout << precip[i] << endl;`	Displays entire precip list, one element per line.
`precip[j] = precip[12];`	`precip[12]` is an **out-of-range** (invalid) **reference**.

out-of-range reference reference to an array element with a subscript < 0 or >= the array size

FIGURE 7.2 New Contents of Array precip

precip[0]	5.6
precip[1]	2.1
precip[2]	6.7
precip[3]	7.3
precip[4]	6.1
precip[5]	3.2
precip[6]	2.1
precip[7]	1.9
precip[8]	2.4
precip[9]	4.5
precip[10]	4.9
precip[11]	5.3
	?

EXAMPLE 7.2   Two 50-element arrays are declared as follows:

```
const int NUM_QUESTIONS = 50;
char     answer[NUM_QUESTIONS];
double   pctRight[NUM_QUESTIONS];
```

Each of the fifty elements of `answer` can be used to store a single character, perhaps a letter representing the correct answer to a multiple-choice question. The values in array `pctRight` are floating point numbers. If these arrays are used in a program that is grading and analyzing the results of a multiple-choice test, `answer[0]` could represent the correct answer to the first question and `pctRight[0]` could be the percentage of students who correctly answered that question. Because the data in `answer[i]` and `pctRight[i]` relate to the same question, `answer` and `pctRight` are **parallel arrays**. Possible values follow.

parallel arrays

two or more same-size arrays that store related information

Initialization

You may initialize an array in its declaration. You have the option of omitting the size of an array that you initialize fully, since the compiler can deduce the size from the initialization list. For example, the following statement declares a 15-element array of integer constants and initializes it with the prime numbers less than 50:

```
const int primesLt50[] = {2, 3, 5, 7, 11, 13, 17, 19, 23, 29,
                          31, 37, 41, 43, 47};
```

Section 7.1 Review Questions

1. What is the difference in meaning between **stress4** and **stress[4]**?
2. Answer these questions about the declaration

   ```
   int value[10];
   ```

   a. How many array elements are there?
   b. What is the data type of one element?
   c. How do you refer to the initial element? to the final element?

7.2 Sequential Access of Array Elements

Programs that use arrays must frequently access each element in sequence. For example, such access is necessary when filling an array with input data and when displaying its contents. A counting for loop is an ideal structure to use for sequential access of array elements. By setting the loop counter to run from zero to one less than the array size, we can use the counter as our array subscript to access each element in turn.

EXAMPLE 7.3 The program in Fig. 7.3 solves the problem described in the chapter introduction: After figuring the average monthly rainfall in a year based on a list of 12 monthly rainfall values, it creates a table categorizing each month as rainy (rainfall 20% higher than average), dry (rainfall 25% lower than average), or average. The program uses an array to store all the

FIGURE 7.3 Program that Uses an Array to Store a Year of Monthly Rainfall Figures

```
//
//  Process one year's list of monthly rainfall in mm.  Find the
//  average monthly rainfall (rounded to the nearest millimeter) and
//  then classify each month as average, rainy (at least 20% more rain
//  than average), or dry (25% less rain than average or drier).
//  Display a table with the month, the rainfall data, and the classi-
//  fication.  Also display the average rainfall.
//

#include <iostream>
#include <iomanip>
using namespace std;

const int    NUM_MONTHS = 12;
const double RAINY_RATE = 0.20;   // 20% more rain than average
const double DRY_RATE = 0.25;     // 25% less rain than average

int main()
{
   int rainfall[NUM_MONTHS];  // monthly rainfall (mm)
   int sumRain = 0;
   int i;

   // Fill rainfall array
   cout << "Enter monthly rainfall in mm, beginning with January."
        << endl;
```

FIGURE 7.3 *(Continued)*

```
for  (i = 0;   i < NUM_MONTHS;   ++i) {
    cout << "Month " << setw( 2 ) << i + 1 << "=> ";
    cin >> rainfall[i];
}

// Calculate average rainfall and "Dry" and "Rainy" cutoffs
for  (i = 0;   i < NUM_MONTHS;   ++i)
    sumRain += rainfall[i];
double averageRain = int (double(sumRain) / NUM_MONTHS + 0.5);
double dryCut = averageRain - DRY_RATE * averageRain;
double rainyCut = averageRain + RAINY_RATE * averageRain;

// Classify months as Dry, Average, or Rainy and display results
cout << endl << "The year's average monthly rainfall was " <<
    averageRain << " mm." << endl << endl;
cout << "Month  Rainfall(mm)  Classification" << endl
    << "_____  _____  _____" << endl;
for  (i = 0;   i < NUM_MONTHS;   ++i) {
    cout << setw( 4 ) << i + 1 << setw( 11 ) << rainfall[i];
    if (rainfall[i] >= rainyCut)
        cout << setw( 17 ) << " Rainy " << endl;
    else if (rainfall[i] <= dryCut)
        cout << setw( 17 ) << "  Dry  " << endl;
    else
        cout << setw( 17 ) << "Average" << endl;
}

return 0;
}
```

```
Enter monthly rainfall in mm, beginning with January.
Month  1 => 95
Month  2 => 100
Month  3 => 120
Month  4 => 130
Month  5 => 135
Month  6 => 145
Month  7 => 155
Month  8 => 185
Month  9 => 190
Month 10 => 160
Month 11 => 130
Month 12 => 120
```

FIGURE 7.3 *(Continued)*

```
The year's average monthly rainfall was 139 mm.

Month   Rainfall(mm)  Classification
_____   _____  _____

  1           95           Dry
  2          100           Dry
  3          120          Average
  4          130          Average
  5          135          Average
  6          145          Average
  7          155          Average
  8          185           Rainy
  9          190           Rainy
 10          160          Average
 11          130          Average
 12          120          Average
```

data in memory so it can look at the list of rainfall data twice—once to figure the average rainfall and once to display each month's category.

The program uses three counting `for` loops to access the array elements in sequence. The first fills the array with data entered by the user. The second adds each element in turn to `sumRain` in preparation for computing the average. The final `for` loop displays a line of the table of results on each iteration. This final loop demonstrates one of the drawbacks of C++ arrays: Because the subscripts always run from zero to one less than the array size, they may not correspond to the way we might naturally number the array elements. In this example, rainfall for January is stored in `rainfall[0]` even though we normally think of January as month 1. You will note that the expression that we display as the month number is `i + 1`, one more than the current value of the loop counter.

Notice that we can use a subscripted variable anywhere that we could use a simple variable of the same type. In the rainfall program, we use subscripted variables as input destinations,

```
cin >> rainfall[i];
```

as sources of output,

```
cout << setw( 4 ) << i + 1 << setw( 11 ) << rainfall[i] << ...
```

and in expressions.

```
sumRain += rainfall[i];
(rainfall[i] >= rainyCut)
(rainfall[i] <= dryCut)
```
■

Partially Filled Arrays

When we declare an array variable, the size must be a constant expression. Frequently, however, we don't know in advance exactly how many array elements we will be processing. For this reason, we often declare an array size larger than we believe is necessary and then only partially fill the array. When we run out of data, we must keep track of how many array elements were filled and use this value as the array's effective size.

Figure 7.4 shows a program that fills an array with a list of data terminated by a sentinel and then displays all the array elements. We don't use a counting loop for data input in this program because we don't know in advance how many times the loop should execute. However, we also need a counter to use as an array subscript, so we initialize this counter (i) to zero before entering the while loop and add 1 to it after input of each array value. We must be sure not to **overflow** the array by attempting to store data beyond the final element, but we also must leave the input loop as soon as we input the sentinel, so our loop repetition condition is fairly complicated. The loop must exit if either of these conditions is true:

array overflow
an attempt to store data in an array element with a subscript >= the array size

1. `i >= MaxSize` (Execution of another input would overflow the array.)
2. The last input was the sentinel.

Therefore our "stay-in-the-loop" condition must be the negation of

```
i >= MAX_SIZE || list[i-1] == SENTINEL
```

Applying DeMorgan's theorem, we find that our "stay-in" condition is

```
i < MAX_SIZE  &&  list[i-1] != SENTINEL
```

FIGURE 7.4   Filling an Array Using a Sentinel Loop

```
//
//   Partially or completely fill an array with data terminated by
//   a sentinel
//
#include <iostream>
#include <fstream>
#include <iomanip>
using namespace std;

const int MAX_SIZE = 20;
const double SENTINEL = -99.0;

int main()
{
```

FIGURE 7.4 *(Continued)*

```
double list[MAX_SIZE];
int    i = 0;
int    actSize;
double checkSent;
ifstream infile( "list.txt", ios::in );

// Fill array from data file
infile >> list[i++];
while  (i < MAX_SIZE  &&  list[i-1] != SENTINEL)
    infile >> list[i++];

if (list[i-1] == SENTINEL) {
    actSize = i - 1;
} else {
    actSize = MAX_SIZE;
    infile >> checkSent;
    if (checkSent != SENTINEL)
        cout << "Too much data in file. First " << MAX_SIZE
             << " items used." << endl;
}
infile.close();

// Display array contents
cout << "The list is: " << endl << setiosflags( ios::fixed )
    << setprecision( 2 );
for  (i = 0;  i < actSize;  ++i)
    cout << setw( 10 ) << list[i] << endl;
return 0;
}
```

Contents of list.txt

```
1420.587
32.1
16.48
-99.0
```

Output

```
The list is:
   1420.59
     32.10
     16.48
```

When the loop exits, if `list[i−1]` is not the sentinel, then there may be too much data in the input file. On the other hand, there may be just enough data to fill the array. To be sure, we need to extract one more value from the input stream. If the value is not the sentinel, then the program notifies the user that some data are being ignored.

After loop exit, we set `actSize` to represent the number of array elements actually filled. Then in subsequent steps, when we need to access each array element in sequence, we can use a counting `for` loop as we do to display the array in Fig. 7.4.

FIGURE 7.5 Tracking Station in Canberra, Australia (Courtesy of the Jet Propulsion Laboratory, California Institute of Technology.)

Passing Individual Array Elements as Arguments

We have noted that an individual array element can be used anywhere a simple variable of the same type would be valid. In our next example we see array elements used as input and output arguments in a call to a function that converts a 24-hour-clock time to a different time zone.

EXAMPLE 7.4   When spacecraft are launched on their missions, tracking stations around the globe must know when to send commands to each spacecraft. For spacecraft far from the earth, three stations—in Madrid, in Canberra (see Fig. 7.5), and at a site called Goldstone in the California Mojave Desert—share the tracking duty. Each tracking site operates 24 hours a day, seven days a week, and sends commands to many spacecraft in the course of a day. The mission controllers who plan the spacecraft activities, however, do not want to keep track of three different time zones. Therefore everything the tracking stations need to do is spelled out in "universal time (coordinated)," or UTC, which happens to be local time in Greenwich, England. The tracking stations then must figure out at what local time to send a command based on this universal time. For example, a tracking station whose local time is 8 hours behind universal time would convert UTC day 40, time 248 (2:48 A.M. on February 9: day 40 = 31 days of January + 9 of February) to local day 39, time 1848 (6:48 P.M. on February 8).

The program outlined in Fig. 7.6 is intended to convert a list of spacecraft contact times from universal time to local time. The figure includes the prototype of a function that converts an integer time on a 24-hour clock to a time in a different time zone. The function takes the original time and the time change as input parameters and computes the different-time-zone time as an output parameter, also modifying if necessary the day number that is an input/output parameter. Adding 1 to the day value indicates a change to the following day; subtracting 1 indicates a change to the previous day. We show only the program outline. You will be asked to complete the program in the Review Questions at the end of this section.

Notice that in the `timeChange` function to which we pass the elements of `utc`, `local`, and `day`, there is no indication that the function expects to manipulate an array. It simply expects to receive two integer values and two references to integers, and it does not matter to `timeChange` whether these are simple integer variables or elements of an integer array. In the main function's `for` loop that converts the list of times, the argument list in the function call

```
timeChange( utc[i], timeDiff, local[i], day[i] );
```

supplies the value of an element of array `utc` and the value of variable `timeDiff` as input arguments along with references to corresponding elements of local (an output argument) and day (an input/output argument).

FIGURE 7.6 Outline of Program to Convert List of Times to New Time Zone

```cpp
//
//  Converts a list of universal times to a list of local times
//

#include <iostream>
using namespace std;

const int TSIZE = 20;

void timeChange ( int, int, int&, int& );

int main()
{
    int utc[TSIZE];      // list of universal times
    int timeDiff;        // time difference in hours
    int local[TSIZE];    // list of local times
    int day[TSIZE];      // list of corresponding day numbers
    int i;

    // Code to fill utc, day, timeDiff with data
        ...

    // Conversion of universal times to local times
    for  (i = 0;  i < TSIZE;  ++i)
        timeChange( utc[i], timeDiff, local[i], day[i] ); // Notice that
                            // passing an array element by value uses the same
                            // notation as passing an element by reference

    // Further processing
        ...
}


//   Converts a 24-hour-clock time in one time zone to an
//   equivalent time in another zone where the time differs from
//   the first zone by timeDiff hours.  The effect of the time
//   change on the day is recorded in dayNum:  no change => same
//   day, 1 added => next day, 1 subtracted => previous day
void timeChange ( int time, int timeDiff, int& newTime,
                int& dayNum) ...
```

TABLE 7.2 Partial Trace of for Loop Calling timeChange with Time Difference of –8

Statement	i	utc[i]	local[i]	day[i]	Effect

for (i=0; i<TSIZE; ...
    timeChange
        (utc[i], timeDiff,
        local[i], day[i])
	0	605	?
			
			2205
				62
				
				61
					0 < 20 is true.
					
					605 is converted to 2205 the previous day, storing 2205 in the ith element of local and decrementing the ith element of day.

Increment and test i
(... i<TSIZE; ++i) {
    timeChange
        (utc[i], timeDiff,
        local[i], day[i]);
	1	720	?
			
			2320
				62
				
				61
					1 < 20 is true.
					
					720 is converted to 2320 the previous day, storing 2320 in the ith element of local and decrementing the ith element of day.

Increment and test i
(... i<TSIZE; ++i) {
    timeChange
        (utc[i], timeDiff,
        local[i], day[i]);
	2	915	?
			
			115
				62
				
				62
					2 < 20 is true.
					
					915 is converted to 115 the same day, storing 115 in the ith element of local.

. . . See Fig. 7.7					

Table 7.2 traces the first few calls to timeChange, assuming these contents of utc and day.

Array utc

utc[0]	utc[1]	utc[2]	utc[3]	utc[4]	
605	720	915	1041	1255	. . .

Array day

day[0]	day[1]	day[2]	day[3]	day[4]	
62	62	62	62	62	. . .

The time 605 on day 62 represents 6:05 A.M. on March 3 in a nonleap year (31 days in January + 28 in February + 3 in March). Figure 7.7 shows the data areas of functions main and timeChange as they appear just before

FIGURE 7.7   Data Areas of Functions main and timeChange Just Before Return from Third Call

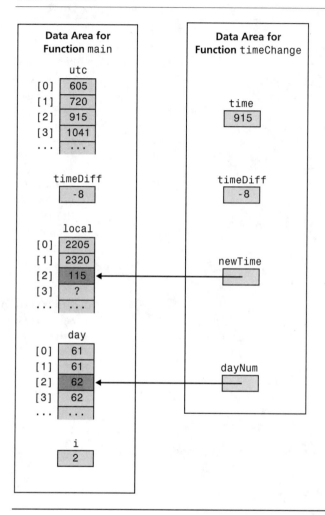

the return from the third call to timeChange. Clearly, the conversion code needed to complete function timeChange must contain assignment statements beginning

```
newTime = ...
dayNum = ...
```

These statements use the references in newTime and dayNum to send the function results back to the calling function.   ■

Section 7.2 Review Questions

1. Declare a 10-element integer array named **nCube**, and use a counting **for** loop to fill it with the values 1, 8 (2^3), 27 (3^3), . . . , 1000 (10^3).

2. Declare two 40-element arrays **id** and **gpa**. Each element of **id** is to contain a four-digit integer identification number, and each element of **gpa** will hold a grade-point average. Write a code fragment to fill these arrays from a file named **stuavg.txt**. The file consists of 40 lines of data. Each line has one student ID and that student's gpa. *Hint:* Use only one **for** loop.

3. Complete the time-change program of Fig. 7.6 so that it displays a table listing the universal times and the converted times, both with day numbers. Assume the input data comes from a file named utc.txt.

7.3 Using Whole Arrays as Parameters

Until now, we have usually distinguished between input and output parameters by using reference types for output and input/output parameters and nonreference types for input parameters. When we studied classes, however, sometimes we passed objects that were input arguments by reference, simply to conserve the time and space that would be required to make a full copy of the object in the function's data area.

C++ does not even give the programmer the option of automatic copying of a whole array used as an input argument. Rather, when an array name with no subscript appears in the argument list of a function call, what is actually stored in the function's corresponding formal parameter is the address of the initial array element. Subscripting operations can be applied to the formal parameter to access all of the array's elements. However, the function is manipulating the original array, not its own personal copy, so an assignment to one of the array elements by a statement in the function changes the contents of the original array. To notify the C++ compiler that an array is only an input to a function and that the function does not intend to modify the array, we can include the const qualifier in the declaration of the array parameter. Thus from the function's perspective, the array contents are constant, and the compiler can mark as an error any attempt to change an array element within the function.

EXAMPLE 7.5 Function highest in Fig. 7.8 can be called to find the largest value in an array. Array list, its input parameter, can be either completely or partially filled, because the function uses its second input parameter to determine how many elements of list to examine.

Let's focus on Fig. 7.8's declaration of the formal parameter list in function highest:

```
const int list[]
```

FIGURE 7.8   Function to Find the Largest Element in an Array

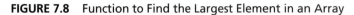

```
//
//  Find the largest value in the first size elements of an array
//  of integers.
//     Pre: size >= 1
//
int highest( const int list[], int size )
{
   int high;

   high = list[0];

   for  (int i = 1;  i < size;  ++i)
      if (list[i] > high)
        high = list[i];

   return high;
}
```

The type qualifier const alerts both the reader of the code and the compiler that list is an input argument only. Notice that this parameter declaration does not state how many elements are in list: The brackets ([ ]) are empty. Because C++ does not allocate space in memory for copying the array, the compiler does not need to know the size of the array parameter. In fact, since the size is unknown, we have the flexibility of passing to the function an array of any number of integers. ∎

EXAMPLE 7.6   Photochemical oxidants are one of the components of air pollution for which the federal government has established a clean-air standard. The program in Fig. 7.9 takes input of photochemical oxidant concentrations for each day of one month. It displays the highest concentration recorded, calling function highest to find this value. Then the program prompts for entry of the clean-air standard and calls another function to count how many days the photochemical oxidant concentration exceeded the standard.

Figure 7.10 shows a memory snapshot for the call to highest from function main, which is repeated here, given the data shown in the sample run at the end of Fig. 7.9:

```
cout << "The highest reading recorded was " <<
      highest( concentration, days ) << " micrograms/m^3." << endl;
```

Notice that what is stored in list is actually the address of concentration[0]. ∎

FIGURE 7.9 Program that Checks Photochemical Oxidant Pollution Levels

```cpp
#include <iostream>
using namespace std;

int highest( const int [], int );
int numAboveCut( const int [], int, int );

const int MAX_DAYS = 31;

//
// Process one month's list of highest daily concentration levels of
// photochemical oxidants:  determine highest reading, and number of
// days when level exceeded federal clean-air standard.
//
int main()
{
    int concentration[MAX_DAYS];
    int days;
    int fedStandard;

    cout << "How many days in this month? => ";
    cin  >> days;
    cout << "Enter photochemical oxidant concentrations (micrograms/m^3)"
       << " for each day." << endl;
    for  (int i = 0;  i < days;  ++i)
       cin >> concentration[i];
    cout << "The highest reading recorded was " <<
       highest( concentration, days ) << " micrograms/m^3." << endl;
    cout << "What level is the federal standard? => ";
    cin  >> fedStandard;
    cout << "During this month, the federal standard for photochemical "
       << "oxidants" << endl << "was exceeded on " <<
       numAboveCut( concentration, days, fedStandard ) << " days." << endl;
    return 0;
}

//
//  Find the largest value in the first size elements of an array of
//  integers
//     Pre: size >= 1
//
```

FIGURE 7.9   *(Continued)*

```cpp
int highest( const int list[], int size )
{
   int high;

   high = list[0];

   for  (int i = 1;  i < size;  ++i)
      if (list[i] > high)
         high = list[i];

   return high;
}


//
// Count how many of the first size elements of list are greater than
// cutoff.
//
int numAboveCut( const int list[], int size, int cutoff )
{
   int num = 0;

   for  (int i = 0;  i < size;  ++i)
      if (list[i] > cutoff)
         ++num;

   return num;
}
```

```
How many days in this month? => 30
Enter photochemical oxidant concentrations (micrograms/m^3) for each day.
80 83 79 180 190 200 220 220 200 200 198 225 199 183 160 119
162 180 122 121 121 119 80 83 79 119 121 121 122 119
The highest reading recorded was 225 micrograms/m^3.
What level is the federal standard? => 160
During this month, the federal standard for photochemical oxidants
was exceeded on 13 days.
```

C++ permits an alternative form of the declaration of an array parameter. The declaration

```
const int* list
```

is often used in place of

```
const int list[]
```

FIGURE 7.10 Memory During Function Call highest (concentration, days)

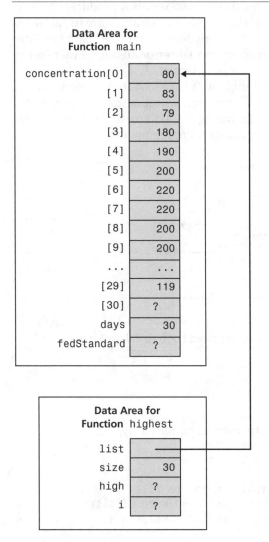

You should recognize either form as a declaration of an array input parameter. We will continue to use the [ ] notation for array parameters, but Appendix B's list of standard functions routinely uses the * notation, as is common in reference manuals.

EXAMPLE 7.7 We often need to partially fill an array with a list of data terminated by a sentinel, as we demonstrated with file input in Fig. 7.4. Therefore, a robust function that accomplishes this purpose would be a very reusable code module. Figure 7.11 models function `fillToSentinel`, showing the input parameters it requires and the two results it produces. We will return the filled size of the array as the function value and store the array result through an output parameter. This function, which takes data from the keyboard, is designed to exit with an appropriate error message if there is too much data or if there is an error in the data format.

As implemented in Fig. 7.12, function `fillToSentinel` demonstrates a standard approach to writing a C++ function whose result is a new array. Such a function typically requires the calling function to declare space for the array and to pass the array variable as an output argument. ■

FIGURE 7.11 Model of Function fillToSentinel

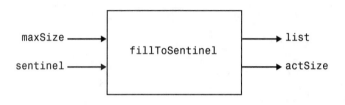

FIGURE 7.12 More Robust Function That Uses a Sentinel-Controlled Loop to Fill an Array

```cpp
#include <iostream>
using namespace std;

//
//  Partially or completely fills an array with data terminated by
//  a sentinel.  Returns filled size as function value.
//     Pre:  maxSize > 0
//
int fillToSentinel ( double list[],      // output – array to fill
                     int    maxSize,     // input – declared size of list
                     double sentinel ) // input – sentinel value
{
   int    i = 0;
   int    actSize;    // filled size of array
   double checkSent;
   char   badChar;

   cin >> list[i++];

   while  (i < maxSize  && !cin.fail()  &&
           list[i–1] != sentinel)
       cin >> list[i++];
```

FIGURE 7.12   *(Continued)*

```
if (cin.fail()) {
     cin.clear();
     cin >> badChar;
     cout << "Error in data format at => " << badChar <<
          " <<<" << endl;
     actSize = i - 1;
     cout << "First " << actSize << " items used." << endl;
} else if (list[i-1] == sentinel) {
     actSize = i - 1;
} else {
     actSize = maxSize;
     cin >> checkSent;
     if (checkSent != sentinel)
          cout << "Too much data.  First " << maxSize <<
               " items used. " << endl;
}

return actSize;
}
```

Arrays with Object Elements

For simplicity, we have limited our examples thus far to arrays whose elements are all `int` or `double`. However, a single element of an array can be of *any* type, including user-defined types. The only requirement is that all array elements be the *same* type.

EXAMPLE 7.8   In Figs. 6.10–11 we developed a class `Complex` with overloaded input, output, +, and += operators. Figure 7.13 shows how to input an array of complex numbers and use a function to figure its sum.

Section 7.3 Review Questions

1. Write a C++ function that searches a type `int` array parameter `list` to find the location of the first occurrence of a specified value, `target`. The function's third input parameter is the size of `list`. Return the subscript of the first occurrence of `target`. If the target is not found, return the value of the constant `NOT_FOUND`:

   ```
   const int NOT_FOUND = -1;
   ```

   Implement this linear search algorithm, which uses the type `bool` variable `found` to indicate whether the target has been found.

   1. Note that the target has not yet been found (initialize `found` to false).

FIGURE 7.13 Summing an Array of Complex Numbers

```
//
//  Enter and add up a list of ten complex numbers
//
//  Class Complex from Fig. 6.10-11 and necessary #include statement omitted

const int MAX_SIZE = 10;
Complex sumList( const Complex[], int );

int main()
{
   Complex complexList[MAX_SIZE];
   cout << "Enter " << MAX_SIZE << " parenthesized complex numbers\n";
   for (int i = 0;  i < MAX_SIZE;  ++i) {
      cout << "=> ";
      cin >> complexList[i];
   }
   cout << "The sum is " << sumList( complexList, MAX_SIZE ) << endl;

   return 0;
}

//
//  Add up a list of n complex numbers
//
Complex sumList( const Complex list[], int n )
{
   Complex sum(0);
   for (int i = 0;  i < n;  ++i)
      sum += list[i];
   return sum;
}
```

2. Initialize a counter to 0, so subscripting begins with the initial array element.
3. Repeat as long as the target has not been found and the counter is still in range:
   4. If the current element is the target
      5. Change **found** to true.
   else
      6. Increment the counter.
7. If the target is found
   8. Return the counter.
else
   9. Return **NOT_FOUND**.

2. Write a C++ function that adds corresponding elements of two type `double` arrays of the same size, filling another array with the pairwise sums. Make this array an output parameter. Provide the arrays' size as an input parameter. How would you change your function so it would add corresponding elements of two type complex arrays?

7.4   Strings Revisited

In our earlier work we have used both string variables and string constants. In this section, we investigate the representational difference between the quoted string `"Sample string"` and the named string constant `SAMPLE`:

```
const string SAMPLE = "Sample string";
```

We also meet a small subset of the operators and member functions defined by class `string`.

Cstrings and Class string

Quoted strings in C++ are not actually represented as objects of class `string`: rather, they are stored as arrays of characters terminated by the **null character** `'\0'`. Such character arrays represent all strings in C++'s parent language, C, so we call null-character-terminated character arrays Cstrings to distinguish them from objects of class `string`. Here is the character-array representation of the quoted string `"Sample string"`.

null character
character `'\0'` that marks the end of a Cstring

[0]	[1]	[2]	[3]	[4]	[5]	[6]	[7]	[8]	[9]	[10]	[11]	[12]	[13]
s	a	m	p	l	e		s	t	r	i	n	g	\0

The data type of this quoted string is `const char []` or `const char *`, since it is a one-dimensional array of characters whose values cannot be changed. Consider the declaration

```
const string SAMPLE = "Sample string";
```

The data type of `SAMPLE` (`const string`) is different from the data type of the initializing value (`const char *`). However, class `string` includes a constructor that converts character-array Cstrings to string objects, so the conversion happens automatically.

Unfortunately, there is no mechanism for automatic conversion of type `string` to type `const char *`. An example where such a conversion would be needed is in declaring and opening a file using a string variable as the file name. The compiler will give you an error message such as "`No operator available that can convert string to const char *`" on the last line of this code fragment:

```
string filename;
cout << "Enter name of input file=> ";
cin >> filename;
ifstream infile(filename, ios::in); // syntax error
```

c_str

string class member function that returns the character-array Cstring equivalent of a string object

Fortunately, the string class defines a member function c_str that does the required conversion, so you can replace the last line of the fragment above by

```
ifstream infile(filename.c_str(), ios::in);
```

Aligning String Output

We can use a call to setw from the iomanip library to establish a minimum field width for a string that is output:

```
cout << "***" << setw(8) << "Short" << "*** << setw(3)
    << "Strings" << "***" << endl;
```

The output is

```
***    Short***Strings***
```

The string "Short" is displayed right-justified in a field of eight columns. The string "Strings" is longer than the specified field width, so the field is expanded to accommodate it exactly with no padding. We are more accustomed to seeing lists of strings displayed left-justified rather than right-justified. Consider the two lists in Fig. 7.14.

Left-Justification

To left-justify values output to a stream, use an expression like this:

stream << setiosflags(ios::left)

To turn off left-justification, use

stream << resetiosflags(ios::left)

FIGURE 7.14 Right- and Left-justification of Strings

Right-Justified	Left-Justified
George Washington	George Washington
John Adams	John Adams
Thomas Jefferson	Thomas Jefferson
James Madison	James Madison

FIGURE 7.15 Right- and Left-justification

```
Buckley         29%
Donovan         25%
Allen           21%
Ferguson        11%
Lugar            7%
```

Both functions `setiosflags` and `resetiosflags` are part of the iomanip library. If `candidate` is a string variable and `votePct` is an integer variable, repeated execution of this statement will create two columns of output, as shown in Fig. 7.15. The first column is left-justified, and the second is right-justified.

```
cout << setiosflags( ios::left ) << setw( 15 ) << candidate <<
    resetiosflags( ios::left ) << setw( 4 ) << votePct << "%" << endl;
```

String Operators and Functions

A complete discussion of all the member functions and operators of the string class is beyond the scope of this text. However, Table 7.3 lists a collection of frequently used facilities, and Appendix D covers additional operations. Fig. 7.16 demonstrates the use of the += concatenation operator from the table. It also uses two new file input functions.

Function `getline` takes three parameters—an input stream, a string variable, and a single character, viewed as a delimiter. The function copies all characters from the input stream into the string variable until it encounters the delimiter. `getline` takes the delimiter from the input stream and discards it rather than storing it in the string. In Fig. 7.16, the statement

```
getline(infile, last, ',');
```

takes from the current line of `infile` all characters up to the first comma and stores them in string variable `last`. The comma is discarded. The third argument to `getline` is optional. If it is omitted, `'\n'` is used as the delimiter. If `getline` encounters end of file before seeing the delimiter, it stores all remaining characters in its string argument.

The loop in Fig. 7.16 that processes one address at a time uses the stream member function `get`.

```
// build rest of line, separating pieces by single blanks and
// stopping at newline character
infile >> addressPt;
address = addressPt;
```

TABLE 7.3 Selected String Class Member Functions and Operators

Function/ Operator	Sample Call from string object str	Purpose	Result if str is "daisy" and str2 is "hyacinth"
=	str = str2;	Assigns str a copy of the value of str2	str becomes "hyacinth"
+=	str += str2;	Concatenates value of str2 on the end of str	str becomes "daisyhyacinth"
== !=	str == str2 str != str2	Comparison for equality/inequality	Value of first comparison: false Value of second comparison: true
<, >, <=, >=	str < str2	Lexicographical comparisons. If str and str2 contain alphabetic letters of the same case, str < str2 evaluates to true if str would precede str2 in an alphabetized list.	true
[] at	str[i] str.at(i)	Both give read/write access to the ith character of str (first character is at position 0). at aborts program on an out-of-range reference.	If i is 3, value is 's' (type char result)
substr	str.substr(start, n)	Returns an n-character substring of str, beginning with the character at position start.	If start is 1 and n is 3, then result is "ais"
length	str.length()	Returns the number of characters in str	5

FIGURE 7.16 File Processing Using String Data

```cpp
// Processes file in which each line consists of name, birth date,
// and address, with a newline character immediately following
// the address:
//    LastName, FirstName MiddleName  Mo/Day/Yr  Address
// Displays the information of each record in a sentence.
#include <iostream>
#include <fstream>
#include <string>
using namespace std;

const string MONTHS[12] = { "January", "February", "March", "April",
  "May", "June", "July", "August", "September", "October", "November",
  "December" };

int main()
{

    string filename, first, last, middle, addressPt, address;
    int birthMon, birthDay, birthYr;
    char nextChar;

    cout << "Enter name of input file=> ";
    cin >> filename;
    ifstream infile(filename.c_str(), ios::in);

    getline(infile, last, ','); // input comma-terminated name
    while( !infile.fail() ) {
        infile >> first;
        infile >> middle;

        // input slash-separated date : 10/31/1949
        infile >> birthMon >> nextChar >> birthDay >> nextChar >> birthYr;

        // build rest of line, separating pieces by single blanks and
        // stopping at newline character
        infile >> addressPt;
        address = addressPt;
        infile.get(nextChar);
        while (!infile.fail() && nextChar != '\n'){
          infile >> addressPt;
          address += (" " + addressPt);
          infile.get(nextChar);
        }
```

FIGURE 7.16 *(Continued)*

```
            // display information in a sentence
            cout << endl << first << " " << middle << " " << last <<
                " was born on " << MONTHS[birthMon - 1] << " " <<
                birthDay << ", " << birthYr << endl << " and lives at "
                << address << "." << endl;
            getline(infile, last, ',');
        }
        infile.close();
        return 0;
}
```

Input file address.txt

```
Adams, Mary Ann        10/25/1953  17152 Glendo Rd. NW, Kearney, NE
Hardy, Brian Vaughan   1/3/1974    412 S. 38th St., Laramie, WY
Johnson, Jeri K.       2/17/1943   1849 N. 9th St., Loveland, CO
Ruiz, Trinity Amber    2/22/1984   335 W. Washington St., Evansville, IN
```

Screen output:

Enter name of input file=> a:address.txt

Mary Ann Adams was born on October 25, 1953
 and lives at 17152 Glendo Rd. NW, Kearney, NE.

Brian Vaughan Hardy was born on January 3, 1974
 and lives at 412 S. 38th St., Laramie, WY.

Jeri K. Johnson was born on February 17, 1943
 and lives at 1849 N. 9th St., Loveland, CO.

Trinity Amber Ruiz was born on February 22, 1984
 and lives at 335 W. Washington St., Evansville, IN.

```
infile.get(nextChar);
while (!infile.fail() && nextChar != '\n'){
    infile >> addressPt;
    address += (" " + addressPt);
    infile.get(nextChar);
}
```

Member function get stores in its character argument the very next character in the input stream. Unlike the >> operator, get does not skip **whitespace characters** such as blanks, newlines, and tabs, so when we reach the end of the line, get will copy the newline character into nextChar.

whitespace characters
characters used for indentation and vertical spacing: blanks, tabs, newlines, carriage returns, and formfeeds

Section 7.4 Review Exercises

Write C++ code to accomplish each of the following goals:

1. Write a message indicating whether strings **name1** and **name2** match.
2. Store in the string variable **word** either the value of **w1** or of **w2**. Choose the value that comes first alphabetically.
3. Store in **mtch** matching initial portions of **s1** and **s2**. For example, if **s1** is "placozoa" and **s2** is "placement", **mtch** becomes "plac". If **s1** is "joy" and **s2** is "sorrow", **mtch** becomes the empty string.

7.5 Classes with Array Components

Now that we know how C++ represents lists of data, we can define more interesting classes that include array components. In our next case study we develop a more general version of our program of Fig. 7.9 that compared a month of photochemical oxidant levels to the U.S. clean-air standard.

EPA REPORTS ON POLLUTANT LEVELS

CASE STUDY

Problem

The U.S. government has established clean-air standards for a variety of pollutants. The Environmental Protection Agency (EPA) has assigned us the task of developing a representation for pollutant records that will simplify creation of reports that include, by month, the highest levels of the pollutant recorded each day, the highest level in the month, and the number of days during the month when the pollutant level exceeded the federal standard. The data for the report will come from a file containing the name of the pollutant, the federal standard (number and units), and monthly lists of daily high readings, each list preceded by the month number and year when the data was collected.

Understanding the Problem

Developing a representation for a pollutant record that will simplify reporting involves identifying the attributes to store and the services that must be provided for efficient report creation. Since all information in the report is collected monthly, it seems appropriate to develop a class for an object that is one monthly record. Figure 7.17 shows our analysis, and Table 7.4 our design of this class.

We omit the algorithm development for the member functions, since both call helper functions developed earlier in the chapter. Figure 7.18 shows our implementation of class `MonthRecord` along with a main program that uses the class in processing a data file of monthly records for one pollutant, a file that begins with the name of the pollutant and its federal clean-air standard. Following the code of the implementation is a sample data file and a run of the program.

The main function begins by prompting the user for the name of the data file. It stores this name in the string variable `infileName` and then declares

FIGURE 7.17 Object-Oriented Analysis of a MonthRecord for a Pollutant

Attributes

What knowledge does it possess?

Time of observations
- month (name and number)
- year

Observations
- levels – list of highest readings for each day of the month
- number of readings (number of days in the month)
- unit of measurement for readings

Behavior

What questions should it be able to answer?
- What is the highest level for the month?
- On how many days did the level exceed the federal standard?

What services should it provide?
- Default constructor
- Constructor that initializes unit of measurement

Interface with outside world?

Operators needed
- to extract MonthRecords from file
- to write MonthRecords to report file

TABLE 7.4 Design of Class MonthRecord

Attributes

Name	Description	Type/Class	Accessibility
monthName	month of observations	string	private
monthNum	observation month (1-12)	int	private
year	year of observations	int	private
levels	list of highest observed level of pollutant for each day of month	int[31]	private
numDays	number of days in month	int	private
concentrationUnit	unit of measurement—e.g. micrograms/m^3	string	private

Behaviors

Prototype	Description	Accessibility
int highestLevel() const	Returns high pollutant level for the month. Doesn't alter object.	public
int daysAboveMax(int) const	Returns number of days this month the level has exceeded federal standard, which is provided as a parameter. Doesn't alter object.	public
MonthRecord()	Default constructor	public
MonthRecord(const string&)	Constructor: initializes unit of measurement (needed because unit is not part of file data for each month)	public

Additional Interfaces

Interface with	Description
outside world	Defines >> to extract MonthRecord data (other than unit of measurement) from file
	Defines << to output MonthRecord data in report format

variable infile as an object of class ifstream. Notice that such a call to if-stream actually activates a constructor function of this class defined by the fstream library. Next, the program extracts from the input file the pollutant name (a string on one line that may contain spaces), the federal clean-air standard (an integer), and the units used in measuring the pollutant. After

FIGURE 7.18 Program to Process a One-Month Record of a Pollutant

```cpp
#include <iostream>
#include <iomanip>
#include <fstream>
#include <string>
using namespace std;

int highest( const int*, int );
int numAboveCut( const int*, int, int );
int daysInMonth( int );

const string MONTHS[12] = { "January", "February", "March", "April",
    "May", "June", "July", "August", "September", "October", "November",
    "December" };
const int MAX_DAYS = 31;

class MonthRecord {    // pollutant levels for one month

public:
    MonthRecord() {}
    MonthRecord( const string& );
    int highestLevel() const;
    int daysAboveMax( int ) const;
private:
    string monthName;
    int   monthNum;
    int   year;
    int   numDays;
    int   levels[MAX_DAYS];
    string concentrationUnit;
friend ostream& operator<< ( ostream&, const MonthRecord& );
friend istream& operator>> ( istream&, MonthRecord& );

};

//
// Process a file containing monthly lists of highest daily
// concentration levels of a pollutant.  For each month determine
// highest reading and number of days when level exceeded federal
// clean-air standard.
//    Pre:  File format is
//          pollutant name (first line)
//          federal standard (an integer and a one-word string
```

FIGURE 7.18 *(Continued)*

```
//            indicating units)
//       month records consisting of month number, year, and list of
//            pollutant concentrations—one level for each day of the
//            month
//
int main()
{
   string infileName;
   string pollutant;
   string unit;
   int    fedStandard;

   // Open data file and extract and echo pollutant name and federal
   // standard
   cout << "Enter name of data file => ";
   cin  >> infileName;
   ifstream infile( infileName.c_str(), ios::in );
   getline(infile, pollutant);
   infile >> fedStandard >> unit;
   cout << endl << setw( 24 ) << "Records of " << pollutant << endl;
   cout << setw( 30 ) << "Federal standard = " << fedStandard <<
       " " << unit << endl << endl << endl;

   // Extract and process MonthRecords from data file until end of file
   // or error encountered
   MonthRecord current( unit );

   for  (infile >> current;  !infile.fail();  infile >> current) {
      cout << current;
      cout << "Highest level of " << pollutant << " = " <<
          current.highestLevel() << " " << unit << endl;
      cout << "Level exceeded federal standard " <<
          current.daysAboveMax( fedStandard ) << " days." << endl <<
          endl << endl;
   }

   if (!infile.eof())
      cerr << infileName << ": Data file format error\n";

   infile.close();
   return 0;
}
```

FIGURE 7.18 *(Continued)*

```cpp
MonthRecord :: MonthRecord( const string& unit )
{
    concentrationUnit = unit;
}


//
// Finds highest value in levels array
//
int MonthRecord :: highestLevel() const
{
    return highest( levels, numDays );
}


//
// Counts how many elements of levels exceed the federal standard
//
int MonthRecord :: daysAboveMax( int standard ) const
{
    return numAboveCut( levels, numDays, standard );
}


//
// Displays one MonthRecord with labels
//
ostream& operator<< ( ostream& os, const MonthRecord& rec )
{
    os << "Levels (" << rec.concentrationUnit << ") for " <<
        rec.monthName << " " << rec.year << endl;
    for  (int i = 0;  i < 15;  ++i)
        os << setw( 5 ) << rec.levels[i];
    os << endl;
    for  (i = 15;  i < rec.numDays;  ++i)
        os << setw( 5 ) << rec.levels[i];
    os << endl;

    return os;
}


//
// Extracts one MonthRecord from text file.  File represents a
// MonthRecord as a month number (1..12), year, and then one
// concentration level for each day of the month.
//
```

FIGURE 7.18 *(Continued)*

```cpp
istream& operator>> ( istream& is, MonthRecord& rec )
{
    is >> rec.monthNum >> rec.year;
    if (!is.fail()) {
        rec.monthName = MONTHS[rec.monthNum - 1];
        rec.numDays = daysInMonth( rec.monthNum );
        for (int i = 0;  i < rec.numDays;  ++i)
            is >> rec.levels[i];
    }

    return is;
}


//
//  Find the largest value in the first size elements of an array of
//  integers
//
int highest( const int list[], int size )
{
    int high;

    high = list[0];

    for  (int i = 1;  i < size;  ++i)
        if (list[i] > high)
            high = list[i];

    return high;
}


//
// Count how many of the first size elements of list are greater than
// cutoff.
//
int numAboveCut( const int list[], int size, int cutoff )
{
    int num = 0;

    for  (int i = 0;  i < size;  ++i)
        if (list[i] > cutoff)  ++num;

    return num;
}
```

FIGURE 7.18 *(Continued)*

```
//
//  Return the number of days in the month (non-leap-year) based on
//  the month number (1 = January, ... 12 = December)
//  Pre:  1 <= monthNumber <= 12
//
int daysInMonth( int monthNumber )
{
   int days;

   switch (monthNumber) {
   case 4:                  // April, June, September, November have 30
   case 6:
   case 9:
   case 11:  days = 30;
             break;

   case 2:   days = 28; // February has 28
             break;

   default:  days = 31; // The others have 31.
   }

   return days;
}
```

Contents of photoox.txt

```
photochemical oxidants
160    micrograms/m^3

2 2001
 60   65   80   80   85 110 110 120 130 140 150 155 150 140 130
125 120 120 110 100   95   95 100 110 120 100   90 100

6 2001
 80   83   79 180 190 200 220 220 200 200 198 225 199 183 160
119 162 180 122 121 121 119   80   83   79 119 121 121 122 119
```

One Run

```
Enter name of data file => photoox.txt
```

FIGURE 7.18 *(Continued)*

```
            Records of photochemical oxidants
        Federal standard = 160 micrograms/m^3


Levels (micrograms/m^3) for February 2001
   60   65   80   80   85  110  110  120  130  140  150  155  150  140  130
  125  120  120  110  100   95   95  100  110  120  100   90  100
Highest level of photochemical oxidants = 155 micrograms/m^3
Level exceeded federal standard 0 days.



Levels (micrograms/m^3) for June 2001
   80   83   79  180  190  200  220  220  200  200  198  225  199  183  160
  119  162  180  122  121  121  119   80   83   79  119  121  121  122  119
Highest level of photochemical oxidants = 225 micrograms/m^3
Level exceeded federal standard 13 days.
```

displaying this information with labels, the program calls the MonthRecord constructor function that takes a single string parameter. The constructor gives us space for a MonthRecord object named current and initializes its concentrationUnit component to the parameter value.

The program then executes an input-failure-controlled for loop that repeatedly calls the overloaded >> operator that is a friend of class MonthRecord. This operator extracts from the data file values for the monthNum and year components of current. It stores in current the string naming the month and the number of days in the month, then extracts that number of pollutant concentration levels from the data file and stores them in current levels component.

In the body of the main function's for loop, the code activates the overloaded friend operator << to display with labels a representation of the current object and then calls current's member functions, highestLevel and daysAboveMax, to determine the highest pollutant concentration for the month and the number of days that the pollutant level exceeded the government standard.

Section 7.5 Review Questions

1. Consider the following output statements taken from Fig. 7.18. For each shaded occurrence of the << operator, indicate which definition will be applied: << for

type **double**, << for type **int**, << for strings, << for Cstrings, << overloaded for class **MonthRecord**.

In function main

```
cout << current;                                              (a)
cout << "Highest level of " << pollutant << " = " <<         (b) (c) (d)
    current.highestLevel() << " " << unit << endl;
cout << "Level exceeded federal standard " <<                (e)
    current.daysAboveMax( fedStandard ) << " days." <<
    endl << endl << endl;
```

In definition of MonthRecord friend operator <<

```
os << "Levels (" << rec.concentrationUnit << ") for "        (f) (g) (h)
    << rec.monthName <<   " " << rec.year << endl;
for (int i = 0;  i < 15;  ++i)
    os << setw( 5 ) << rec.levels[i];                         (i)
os << endl;
for (i = 15;  i < rec.numDays;  ++i)
    os << setw( 5 ) << rec.levels[i];
os << endl;
```

2. Suppose you are defining a class named **Array** to represent lists of up to 100 type **double** values. You want to allow input of such a list from a file that contains first the list length and then the list values. You also want to be able to output the list (filled values only) and to create a new **Array** object and initialize its value to a copy of another **Array**, copying only the filled elements and the size. Here is the declaration of such a class. Write out implementations of the copy constructor and of operators **>>** and **<<**.

```
const int MAX_SIZE = 100;
class Array {
public:
    Array(){}
    Array(const Array&);   // copy constructor
private:
    int size;
    double list[MAX_SIZE];
friend istream& operator>> (istream&, Array&);
friend ostream& operator<< (ostream&, const Array&);
};
```

3. Revise class **Array** from Question 2 by adding two member functions, **sum** and **average**. Function **sum** should calculate and return the sum of the filled elements of **list**, and **average** should return their average. Both functions should commit to not altering the default object (i.e., they are *constant* functions). *Hint:* Call **sum** from **average**.

7.6 Dynamically Allocated Array Components

In the pollutant records program of Fig. 7.18, the component of class MonthRecord that was an array had an integer constant size. This was reasonable
because the maximum number of days in a month is known and individual
month lengths do not vary greatly. Defining class MonthRecord as

```
class MonthRecord {    // pollutant levels for one month

public:
   MonthRecord() {}
   MonthRecord( const string& );
   int highestLevel() const;
   int daysAboveMax( int ) const;
private:
   string monthName;
   int   monthNum;
   int   year;
   int   numDays;
   int   levels[MAX_DAYS];
   string concentrationUnit;
friend ostream& operator<< ( ostream&, const MonthRecord& );
friend istream& operator>> ( istream&, MonthRecord& );

};
```

when we called one of the MonthRecord constructor functions, enough space
was allocated on the stack to store an entire MonthRecord object, including
the contents of its array components. Figure 7.19 shows the memory required for one such object.

FIGURE 7.19 A MonthRecord Object with a Fixed-Size Array Component

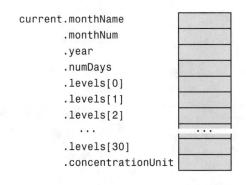

```
current.monthName
        .monthNum
        .year
        .numDays
        .levels[0]
        .levels[1]
        .levels[2]
           ...
        .levels[30]
        .concentrationUnit
```

Sometimes there is such great variation in the size of an array component of an object that it is an enormous waste of memory to routinely set aside space on the stack for the largest sized array conceivable. For example, if you are defining an object to represent a class roll in a university whose class sizes range from 5 to 500, it is wasteful to set aside room for a list of 500 in every instance. C++ does provide an alternative to such a wasteful practice. In our next example, we demonstrate this alternative.

EXAMPLE 7.9　Figure 7.20 is a program that opens a file representing a class roll, extracts from the file the number of students in the class, and then declares a `ClassRoll` object for this number of students. The constructor function that is called sets the object's `numStudents` component and allocates space for an array of student IDs with exactly the right number of elements. Then the program uses the `>>` operator that is a friend of class `ClassRoll` to fill the remaining data members, including the newly allocated array.

FIGURE 7.20　Program Using a ClassRoll Class with a Dynamically Allocated Array Component

```
#include <iostream>
#include <fstream>                          Preprocessor Directives
#include <iomanip>
#include <string>
using namespace std;

class ClassRoll {
                                    Constructors
public:
    ClassRoll() { numStudents = 0; } // Allocate empty class roll
    ClassRoll( int );
                            Data Members
private:
    string dept;          // abbreviation for department offering course
    int    courseNum;     // course number
    string days;          // abbreviation for days when class meets
    int    time;          // 24-hour clock time when class begins
    int    numStudents;   // number of students in class
    int*   students;      // list of student i.d.'s        Prototypes of
    friend ostream& operator<< ( ostream&, const ClassRoll& );  Overloaded
    friend istream& operator>> ( istream&, ClassRoll& );        Operators
};
```

Class Declaration

FIGURE 7.20 *(Continued)*

```
//
//  Process a file containing a class roll in this format:  number of
//  students, course i.d. (department and number), days (TR, MWF,
//  MTWRF, etc.), and meeting time on 24-hour clock (810 = 8:10 a.m.),
//  i.d.'s of all students.  Program extracts one class roll
//  from the user-designated data file and displays it.
//
int main()
{
   string infileName;
   int    size;

   cout << "Enter name of class roll data file => ";
   cin >> infileName;
   ifstream infile( infileName.c_str(), ios::in );
   infile >> size;
   ClassRoll thisClass( size );
   infile >> thisClass;
   cout << thisClass;
   infile.close();

   return 0;
}
```

> ***Constructor Definition***

```
//
// Allocate ClassRoll object with dynamic array data member that
// will store classSize i.d.'s
//
ClassRoll :: ClassRoll( int classSize )
{
   students = new int [classSize];
   numStudents = classSize;
}
//
```

> ***Operator Definitions***

```
// Display one ClassRoll object with labels on stream os
//
ostream& operator<< ( ostream& os, const ClassRoll& cl )
{
   os << "Course:   " << cl.dept << " " << cl.courseNum << endl;
   os << "Meeting times: " << cl.days << " " << cl.time << endl;
   os << setw( 45 ) << "CLASS ROLL" << endl;
```

FIGURE 7.20 *(Continued)*

```
for  (int i = 0;  i < cl.numStudents;  ++i)
    os << setw(42) << cl.students[i] << endl;

return os;
}

//
// Fill a ClassRoll object from stream is
//
istream& operator>> ( istream& is, ClassRoll& cl )
{
    is >> cl.dept >> cl.courseNum >> cl.days >> cl.time;

    for  (int i = 0;  i < cl.numStudents;  ++i)
        is >> cl.students[i];

    return is;
}
```

Contents of clsroll.txt

```
5
COSC 3440
TR    1210
2333
1555
4321
4637
4892
```

One run

```
Enter name of class roll data file => clsroll.txt
Course:  COSC 3440
Meeting times: TR 1210
                                CLASS ROLL
                                   2333
                                   1555
                                   4321
                                   4637
                                   4892
```

Let's focus on how class `ClassRoll` implements the dynamically allocated array component. Here is the class definition:

```cpp
class ClassRoll {
public:
    ClassRoll() { numStudents = 0; }
    ClassRoll( int );
private:
    string dept;        // abbreviation for department offering
                        // course
    int    courseNum;   // course number
    string days;        // abbreviation for days when class meets
    int    time;        // 24-hour clock time when class begins
    int    numStudents; // number of students in class
    int*   students;    // list of student i.d.'s
friend ostream& operator<< ( ostream&, const ClassRoll& );
friend istream& operator>> ( istream&, ClassRoll& );
};
```

The data member declaration

```cpp
int* students;
```

tells the C++ compiler that `students` is to represent the address of an integer. Since any array name with no subscript represents the address of the array's initial element, the name of any integer array is also of type `int*`.

Consider the program's call to constructor function `ClassRoll`:

```cpp
ClassRoll thisClass( size );
```

Before running the two lines of code of the constructor function, the `thisClass` object appears in memory as depicted in Fig. 7.21. After execution

FIGURE 7.21 Data Area of ClassRoll Constructor Before Dynamic Array Allocation

infileName	class1.txt
size	5
thisClass.dept	?
thisClass.courseNum	?
thisClass.days	?
thisClass.numStudents	?
thisClass.students	?

pointer
address of a memory location

heap
region of memory used for data structures dynamically allocated and deallocated by operators new and delete

stack
region of memory used for allocation of function data areas; allocation of variables on the stack occurs automatically when a block is entered, and deallocation occurs when the block is exited

of the code of `ClassRoll`, the object `thisClass` appears in memory as is shown in Fig. 7.22. The `students` component of `thisClass` now contains a **pointer** to a five-element dynamically allocated array. A pointer is a memory address, in this case the address of the initial element of the new array. Notice that the area in which the array is allocated is called the **heap**. This storage area is separate from the **stack**, the region of memory in which function data areas are allocated and reclaimed as functions are entered and exited.

The individual elements of the dynamically allocated array are accessed as `thisClass.students[0]`, `thisClass.students[1]`, `thisClass. students [2]`, `thisClass.students[3]`, `thisClass.students[4]`. The entire array (represented by the address of its initial element) can be passed to a function with the reference `thisClass.students`. Thus, from the standpoint of how the `students` component is manipulated once it is allocated and filled, there is no difference between an array declared to be a fixed size in a class definition and an array that is dynamically allocated with `new`.

Returning Cells to the Heap

A call to the operator `delete[ ]` returns an array of memory cells to the heap so the memory can be reused later in response to `new`. For example,

```
delete[] students;  // statement in a member function
```

FIGURE 7.22   Data Area of ClassRoll Constructor After Dynamic Array Allocation

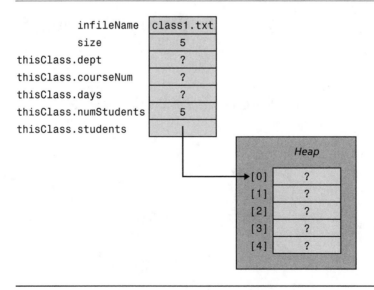

returns to the heap the array of cells whose initial address is in the `students` component of a `ClassRoll` object. Unlike memory allocated in function data areas on the stack, cells in the heap are not automatically released upon the return of the function that caused the memory to be allocated. If we wanted to use our `ClassRoll` class in a program that processed a list of class rolls of different sizes, we could provide an additional member function to resize the array of students included in a `ClassRoll` variable. Here is such a function:

```
//
//  Change the size of the array of student i.d.'s:  return to
//  the heap the space used by the current array.  Then allo-
//  cate a new array of the desired size.
//
void ClassRoll :: resize( int classSize )
{
   delete[] students;
   students = new int [classSize];
   numStudents = classSize;
}
```

Destructors

When an object that includes a dynamically allocated data member passes out of scope, the space allocated for it on the stack is automatically reclaimed. However, the space on the heap remains allocated, but inaccessible, unless we provide a **destructor** for the class. A destructor is a member function that is called automatically when an object is passing out of scope. For example, in Fig. 7.20, `ClassRoll` object `thisClass` passes out of scope when function `main` returns. At that time, the stack space that had been used for `main`'s local variables `infileName`, `size`, and `thisClass` is reclaimed. In order to also reclaim the heap space reserved for `thisClass`, we would define the destructor shown in Fig. 7.23 and add its prototype to the public member function prototypes in the class declaration for `ClassRoll`. The name of

destructor
member function named `~ClassName` that is called automatically when an object is passing out of scope

FIGURE 7.23 Destructor for Class ClassRoll

```
ClassRoll :: ~ClassRoll()
{
   if (numStudents > 0)
      delete [] students;
}
```

a class destructor is always formed by appending the class name to the tilde sign (~). Notice that our release of space is conditional on the value of num-Students being greater than zero. The need to be sure that there was actually space allocated for this object's array before we tried to release it is the reason we initialized numStudents to zero in the default constructor:

```
class ClassRoll {
public:
    ClassRoll() { numStudents = 0; }
    ...
```

Section 7.6 Review Questions

1. Draw the memory set-up that results from execution of each version of the program fragment that follows:

<table>
<tr><td>Version 1</td><td>Version 2</td></tr>
</table>

```
       Version 1                          Version 2
class List{                       class List {

public:                           public:
    List() {}                         List() {size = 0;}
private:                              List( int );
                                      ~List();
                                  private:
    int size;                         int size;
    int values[4];                    int* values;
}                                 };

int main()                        int main()
{                                 {
    List one;                         List one( 4 );
    ...                               ...
}                                 }


                                  List :: List( int listSize );
                                  {
                                      values = new int [listSize];
                                      size = listSize;
                                  }
```

2. Extend the class roll program of Fig. 7.20 so it can input and display class rolls until input of a new class size fails. Notice that handling the first class roll is different from processing the rest: For the first class roll, you must declare a **ClassRoll** object variable and allocate enough space to accommodate its student list. For all the other class rolls, you can reuse the existing variable, simply resizing its student list component.

7.7 Software Designer Beware

The most common error in manipulating arrays is an out-of-range reference, which occurs when a subscript value is used that is outside the range indicated by the array declaration or allocation statement. For the arrays fixedList and dynamicList,

```
int  fixedList[30];
int* dynamicList;
dynamicList = new int [40];
```

a subscript-range error occurs if fixedList is referenced with a subscript greater than 29 or less than 0, and there is a similar error if dynamicList is referenced with a subscript greater than 39 or less than 0. If the value of i is 100, a reference to fixedList[i] might cause a run-time error such as access violation. More often, though, an out-of-range reference is not flagged as a run-time error, and the program simply produces incorrect results. Preventing such erroneous references is the responsibility of software designers. Subscript-range errors are typically caused by an incorrect subscript expression, a loop counter error, or an endless loop.

If an out-of-range reference occurs inside a counting loop, check that the subscript expression is in range for both the initial and final values of the loop counter. If the error occurs in another kind of loop, verify that the loop control variable is being updated as required. If the subscripting variable is incremented on each iteration, and the loop is repeated more often than it should be, a subscript-range error will result. This might be caused by omitting the loop-control-variable update or by placing the update inside a condition.

Be sure to use proper forms when declaring array input and output parameters. Output parameter arrays are not declared as reference parameters, because an array is always passed as the address of the initial element.

When you declare a class that contains a dynamically allocated data member, be sure to include a destructor to return space to the heap when an object passes out of scope. Check every constructor for the class and every function or operator that may change the size of the list. Be certain that space is allocated to accommodate a size change and that space no longer needed is returned to the list of free space.

Chapter Review

1. A data structure is a grouping of related data items in memory.
2. An array is a data structure used to store a collection of data items of the same type.
3. To reference an individual array element, place a square-bracketed subscript immediately after the array name.

4. Reference the initial element of a one-dimensional array `list` as `list[0]`. If `list` has *n* elements, reference the last element as `list[n−1]`.

5. A **for** loop whose counter runs from 0 to one less than an array's size enables you to reference all the elements of an array in sequence by using the loop counter as the array subscript.

6. When an array is declared as a local variable of a function, space for all its elements is allocated in the function data area.

7. When an array is declared as a parameter of a function, space is allocated in the function data area for only the address of the initial element of the argument array passed.

8. The name of an array with no subscript is a pointer to the initial array element.

9. A function that produces an array result should require the calling function to pass an output argument array in which to store the result.

10. The C++ string class defines many operators and functions, including facilities for input, output, single-character access, substring access, comparison, and concatenation of strings.

11. An array component of an object can either have a fixed maximum size or can be dynamically allocated using **new**, so that the maximum size can be determined at run time.

12. A class that includes a dynamically allocated data member should define a destructor to return any space allocated on the heap when an object passes out of scope.

■ New C++ Constructs ■

Construct	Effect
Array Declarations	
Local Variables	
```const int MAX_ELE = 12;``` ```double nums[MAX_ELE];``` ```int monthTotals[MAX_ELE] =``` ``` {0, 0, 0, 0, 0, 0, 0, 0, 0,``` ``` 0, 0, 0};```	Allocates space for 12 type **double** values in array nums. Declared size must be a constant. Allocates space for 12 type **int** values in monthTotals and initializes each to zero.
Input Parameter	
```void printAlpha``` ``` (const string alpha[],``` ``` const int m[],``` ``` int aSize, int mSize)``` ``` or``` ```... (const string* alpha, ...```	States that function printAlpha uses arrays alpha and m as input parameters only—printAlpha will not change their contents.

Output or Input/Output Parameter

```
void fill(double nums[], int n)
            or
... (double* nums, …
```

States that function `fill` can both look at and modify the argument array passed to `nums`.

Dynamic Memory Allocation

```
int* nums;
```

`nums` is a pointer variable of type pointer to `int`

```
nums = new int [40];
```

A new ten-element array of integers is allocated on the heap, and its starting address is stored in `nums`.

Array References

```
if (data[0] < 39.8)
```

Compares value of initial element of array `data` to 39.8.

```
for (i = 0;  i < 30;  ++i)
   data[i] /= 2.0;
```

Divides each element of array `data` by 2, changing the array contents.

Class with Dynamically Allocated Array and Destructor

```
class DoubleList
{
  public:
    DoubleList() { maxSize = 0 }
    DoubleList(int);
    ~DoubleList(); //Destructor
  private:
    double* list;
    int maxSize;
    int size;
};

DoubleList :: DoubleList (int n)
{
  list = new double[n];
  maxSize = n;
  size = 0;
}

DoubleList :: ~DoubleList()
{
  if (maxSize > 0)
    delete [] list;
}
```

Declares a class suitable for representing a list of type `double` values. The `list` data member is dynamically allocated, and a destructor is defined to return space to the heap when a `DoubleArray` object passes out of scope.

PROGRAMMING PROJECTS

1. Write a C++ function selectSort that will sort an array of *n* integers in ascending order. Here is a selection sort algorithm that is so named because for each array position it selects the correct value to place there and swaps it with the value currently in that position.

   1. Repeat for each array position toFill from 0 to *n* – 2.

       2. Let smallPos be the subscript of the smallest value in array elements toFill.. *n* – 1.

           3. If smallPos ≠ toFill, swap list[smallPos] and list[toFill].

   We can refine Step 2:

   2.1   Initialize smallPos to toFill.

   2.2   Repeat for pos ranging from toFill to *n* – 1.

       2.3   If list[pos] is smaller than list[smallPos]

           2.4 Copy the value of pos into smallPos.

   Also write a main function that inputs a list of numbers and displays the list before and after sorting.

   Test your program on a list in random order, on a list that is already in order, and on a list sorted in descending order.

2. Implement the Array class whose declaration follows. Then test your implementation using function main shown.

```
const int MAX_SIZE = 30;
const double SENTINEL = -999;
class Array
{
  public:
    Array() {}
    Array( const Array& );
    double& operator[] (int i);
    double getEle(int i) const;
    int getSize() const;
  private:
    double data[MAX_SIZE];
    int size;
  friend istream& operator>> (istream&, Array&);
  friend ostream& operator<< (ostream&, const Array&);
};
```

   Base your input extraction operator on the algorithm used in Fig.7.4.

```
int main()
{
```

```
      Array a;
      int i;
      cout << "Enter up to " << MAX_SIZE << " numbers followed by "
          << SENTINEL << endl;
      cin >> a;
      cout << "Original list: " << a << endl;
      Array aDoubled(a);
      for (i = 0; i < aDoubled.getSize(); ++i)
          aDoubled[i] *= 2;
      cout << "Doubled list: " << aDoubled << endl;
      cout << "Reversed original list: ";
      for (i = a.getSize() - 1; i >= 0; -i)
          cout << setw(6) << a.getEle(i);
      cout << endl;
      return 0;
  }
```

3. Microbiologists estimating the number of bacteria in a sample that contains bacteria that do not grow well on solid media may use a statistical technique called the *most probable number* (MPN) method. Each of five tubes of nutrient medium receives 10 ml of the sample. A second set of five tubes receives 1 ml of sample per tube, and in each of a third set of five tubes, only 0.1 ml of sample is placed. Each tube in which bacterial growth is observed is recorded as a positive, and the numbers for the three groups are combined to create a triplet such as 5-2-1, which means that all five tubes receiving 10 ml of sample showed bacterial growth, only two tubes in the 1-ml group showed growth, and only one of the 0.1-ml group was positive. A microbiologist would use this combination-of-positives triplet as an index in a table like Table 7.5 to determine that the most probable number of bacteria per 100 ml of the sample is 70, and 95% of the samples yielding this triplet contain between 30 and 210 bacteria per 100 ml.

   Write a C++ program to implement the following algorithm for generating explanations of combination-of-positives triplets.

   1. Load the MPN table from a file into four parallel arrays:
      - an array of strings combOfPositives
      - three integer arrays—mpn, lower, and upper
   2. Repeatedly get from the user a combination-of-positives triplet, find its subscript in combOfPositives, and use this subscript on mpn, lower, and upper to generate a message such as:

      ```
      For 5-2-1, MPN = 70; 95% of samples contain between 30 and
      210 bacteria / ml.
      ```

   Define and call the following functions.

TABLE 7.5 Table of Bacterial Concentrations for Most Probable Number Method[1]

Combination of Positives	MPN Index/100 ml	95% Confidence Limits	
		Lower	Upper
4-2-0	22	9	56
4-2-1	26	12	65
4-3-0	27	12	67
4-3-1	33	15	77
4-4-0	34	16	80
5-0-0	23	9	86
5-0-1	30	10	110
5-0-2	40	20	140
5-1-0	30	10	120
5-1-1	50	20	150
5-1-2	60	30	180
5-2-0	50	20	170
5-2-1	70	30	210
5-2-2	90	40	250
5-3-0	80	30	250
5-3-1	110	40	300
5-3-2	140	60	360

[1] *Microbiology, An Introduction*, 7th Ed. by Gerard J. Tortora, Berdell R. Funke, and Christine L. Case, Benjamin Cummings, 2001, p. 177.

loadMpnTable

Parameters

maxSize (input)

Arrays combOfPositives, mpn, lower, upper (output)

Purpose

Open file, fill output parameter arrays, close file. Return actual array size as function result.

search

Parameters:

Array combOfPositives, target string (input)

Purpose:

Return subscript where target found in array or –1 if not found.

4. A resistor is a circuit device designed to have a specific resistance value between its ends. Resistance values are expressed in ohms (Ω) or kilo-

FIGURE 7.24 Bands Encoding the Resistance Value of a Resistor

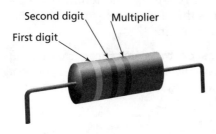

ohms (kΩ). Resistors are frequently marked with colored bands that encode their resistance values, as shown in Fig. 7.24. The first two bands are digits, and the third is a power-of-ten multiplier.

Table 7.6 shows the meanings of each band color. For example, if the first band is green, the second is black, and the third is orange, the resistor has a value of $50 \times 10^3 \Omega$ or 50 kΩ. The information in Table 7.6 can be stored in a C++ program as a constant array of strings.

```
const string COLOR_CODES[10] = {"black", "brown", "red",
    "orange", "yellow", "green", "blue", "violet", "gray",
    "white"};
```

Notice that "red" is COLOR_CODES[2] and has a digit value of 2 and a multiplier value of 10^2. In general, COLOR_CODES[n] has digit value n and multiplier value 10^n.

Write a program that prompts for the colors of Band 1, Band 2, and Band 3, and then displays the resistance in kilo-ohms. Include a helper

TABLE 7.6 Color Codes for Resistors[2]

Color	Value as Digit	Value as Multiplier
Black	0	1
Brown	1	10
Red	2	10^2
Orange	3	10^3
Yellow	4	10^4
Green	5	10^5
Blue	6	10^6
Violet	7	10^7
Gray	8	10^8
White	9	10^9

[2]Adapted from *Sears and Zemansky's University Physics*, 10th Ed. by Hugh D. Young and Roger A. Freedman, Addison-Wesley, 2000, p. 807.

function search that takes three parameters—the list of strings, the size of the list, and a target string, and returns the subscript of the list element that matches the target or returns –1 if the target is not in the list. Here is a short sample run:

```
Enter the colors of the resistor's three bands, beginning with
the band nearest the end.  Type the colors in lowercase
letters only, NO CAPS.
Band 1 => green
Band 2 => black
Band 3 => yellow
Resistance value:  500 kilo-ohms
Do you want to decode another resistor?
=> y
Enter the colors of the resistor's three bands, beginning with
the band nearest the end.  Type the colors in lowercase
letters only, NO CAPS.
Band 1 => brown
Band 2 => vilet
Band 3 => gray
Invalid color: vilet
Do you want to decode another resistor?
=> n
```

5. Define a class Element to represent one element from the periodic table of elements. Data members should include the atomic number (an integer), the name, chemical symbol, and class (one-word strings), a numeric component for the atomic weight, and a seven-element array of integers for the number of electrons in each shell. Here are the components of an Element-class object representing sodium:

```
11  Sodium Na alkali_metal  22.9898  2 8 1 0 0 0 0
```

Define a default constructor and a constructor that takes one parameter representing the atomic number. Define a type int accessor function getAtomicNumber and a type string accessor getName, and overload the >> and << operators as friends of Element. Write a main function that tests all the features of the class.

6. Numeric addresses for computers on the wide area network Internet are composed of four parts separated by periods, of the form *xx.yy.zz.mm*, where *xx*, *yy*, *zz*, and *mm* are positive integers. Locally, computers are usually known by a nickname as well. You are designing a program to process a list of Internet addresses, identifying all pairs of computers from the same locality (i.e., with matching *xx* and *yy* components). Create a class called InternetAddress with components for the four integers and a fifth component to store an associated nickname. Your program should extract a list of *any* number of addresses and nick-

names from a data file whose name is provided by the user. The first line of the file should be the number of addresses that follow. Here is a sample data set:

```
3
111.22.3.44    platte
555.66.7.88    wabash
111.22.5.66    green
```

Dynamically allocate an array to hold the indicated number of InternetAddress objects. Fill the array, and then display a list of messages identifying each pair of computers from the same locality. In the messages, the computers should be identified by their nicknames. Here is a sample message:

```
Machines platte and green are on the same local network.
```

   Include in your class definition friend operators >> and << and a sameNetwork member function that takes a second InternetAddress object as a parameter and returns true if the two addresses are on the same local network and false otherwise. Follow the messages by a display of the full list of addresses and nicknames.

7. If n points are connected to form a closed polygon as shown below, the area A of the polygon can be computed as

$$A = \frac{1}{2}\left|\sum_{i=0}^{n-2}(x_{i+1} + x_i)(y_{i+1} - y_i)\right|$$

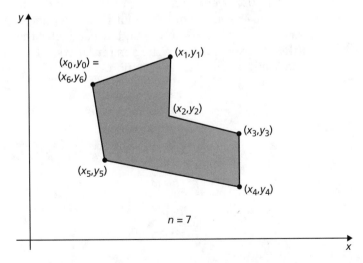

Notice that although the illustrated polygon has only six distinct corners, n for this polygon is 7 because the algorithm expects that the last point, (x_6, y_6), will be a repeat of the initial point, (x_0, y_0). Define a class

ClosedPolygon that represents the (x, y) coordinates of the connected points as two dynamically allocated arrays of type double values. Overload the >> and << operators to allow input/output of this class, and define a member function for the class that calculates the polygon area.

For one test, use this data set that defines a polygon whose area is 25.5 square units.

x	y
4	0
4	7.5
7	7.5
7	3
9	0
7	0
4	0

8. Many engineering applications require "normalizing" an n-element vector V. Each element w_i of the normalized vector W is defined as follows:

$$w_i = \frac{v_i}{\sqrt{\sum_{i=0}^{n-1} v_i^2}}$$

Write a C++ program that defines a class Vector that allocates stack space for vectors of up to ten elements, and stores the actual vector size as a component of the class. Overload the >> operator to allow sentinel-terminated input of a vector. Also overload the << operator. Then define a function normalize that takes a class Vector input parameter and a class Vector output parameter, and stores in the output parameter the normalized version of the input parameter. Write a main function that thoroughly tests your class and the normalize function.

Multidimensional Arrays

8

8.1 Creating and Using Multidimensional Arrays

8.2 Matrix Operations

8.3 Linear Systems
   Case Study: Solving a System of Linear Equations

8.4 Dynamic Allocation of Two-Dimensional Array Components

8.5 Software Designer Beware

Chapter Review

Many engineering applications require modeling of tables of data, grids, matrices, graphs, and all kinds of images—photographic, radar, x-ray, ultrasound, infrared, and magnetic resonance. For this type of modeling we need arrays with two or more dimensions: multidimensional arrays. This chapter presents C++'s tools for creating these data structures.

8.1 Creating and Using Multidimensional Arrays

The creation and use of a two-dimensional array is demonstrated in the following example. First we create an array whose exact dimensions are known in advance. Then we write a comparable program that uses a two-dimensional array whose dimensions can vary within fixed limits.

EXAMPLE 8.1 Peabody Public Utilities tracks the status of its power service throughout the city with a 3×4 grid in which each cell represents power service status in one sector. When power is available everywhere, all grid values are 1. A grid value of 0 indicates an outage somewhere in the sector.

The declaration

```
int powerGrid[3][4]
```

allocates a grid of twelve cells, three rows of four columns as shown in Fig. 8.1. To reference a grid element, you specify the array name, the row subscript in [ ] brackets, and the column subscript in [ ] brackets. Since there are three rows and four columns, the row subscripts range from 0 to 2; the column subscripts range from 0 to 3. The element highlighted in Fig. 8.1 is in row 1, column 3. The grid shown indicates power outages by zeros in `powerGrid[1][0]`, `powerGrid[2][0]`, and `powerGrid[2][1]`.

Figure 8.2 shows a class definition for `Grid` that includes a component `powerGrid`. The class also defines member functions `powerOK` and `whereOff`, and overloads operators `>>` and `<<`. Function `powerOK` checks whether all grid values are 1. If they are, the function returns true, and false otherwise. Function `whereOff` displays the row and column subscripts of all cells that have a power outage. To do this, it checks the value of each cell in the grid. When you need to access every element of a two-dimensional array, use two nested counting loops like you see in the definition of function `whereOff` in Fig. 8.3:

```
for  (i = 0;  i < GRID_ROWS;  ++i)
    for  (j = 0;  j < GRID_COLS;  ++j)
        if (powerGrid[i][j] != 1)
            cout << "   (" << i << "," << j << ")" << endl;
```

FIGURE 8.1 A Two-Dimensional Array That Represents a Power Grid

FIGURE 8.2 Class Definition for a Two-Dimensional Grid

```
const int GRID_ROWS = 3;  // number of rows
const int GRID_COLS = 4;  // number of columns

class Grid {  // object type for monitoring power status

public:
   Grid() {}
   bool powerOK() const;    // returns true if all sectors have power
   void whereOff() const;   // displays subscripts of sectors
                            //   where power is off
private:
   int powerGrid[GRID_ROWS][GRID_COLS];
friend ostream& operator<< ( ostream&, const Grid& );
friend istream& operator>> ( istream&, Grid& );
};
```

Because whereOff considers first all the elements of the first row, then the elements of the second row, and so on, the outer loop's counter is the row subscript and the inner loop's counter is the column subscript. If you need to consider all of the first column, then the second column, and so on, make the outer loop's counter the column subscript.

Figure 8.3 shows the code of the entire power grid program. The implementations of both friend operators >> and << take Grid references as their right operands. Although the reference parameter is essential for >> since the operator stores data in the object passed, the << operator could have been defined so that its right operand was passed by value. However, then the entire Grid object would be copied into operator <<'s local data area, quite an expenditure of time and space. We have elected to pass the Grid parameter by reference here for reasons of efficiency and we have marked the reference const to indicate that operator << will not modify the grid's contents.

FIGURE 8.3 Program that Uses a Grid to Monitor Power Availability

```
//
// Program to track the status of power service throughout the city
// with a 3 x 4 grid in which each cell represents power service
// status in one sector.  When power is available everywhere,
// all grid values are 1.  A grid value of 0 indicates an outage
// somewhere in the sector.
//
```

FIGURE 8.3 *(Continued)*

```cpp
#include <iostream>
#include <fstream>
#include <iomanip>
#include <string>
using namespace std;

const int GRID_ROWS = 3;  // number of rows
const int GRID_COLS = 4;  // number of columns

class Grid {  // object type for monitoring power status

public:
   Grid() {}
   bool powerOK() const;  // returns true if all sectors have power
   void whereOff() const; // displays subscripts of sectors
                          //   where power is off
private:
   int powerGrid[GRID_ROWS][GRID_COLS];
friend ostream& operator<< ( ostream&, const Grid& );
friend istream& operator>> ( istream&, Grid& );
};

int main()
{
   Grid pubServ;
   string inFileName;

   cout << "Enter name of data file => ";
   cin  >> inFileName;
   ifstream infile( inFileName.c_str(), ios::in );

   infile >> pubServ;
   infile.close();
   cout << "Current grid" << endl;
   cout << pubServ << endl;
   if (pubServ.powerOK())
      cout << "Power is on throughout grid." << endl;
   else
      pubServ.whereOff();
   return 0;
}
```

FIGURE 8.3 *(Continued)*

```
//
//  Returns true if power on (value = 1) in all sectors
//
bool Grid :: powerOK() const
{
   bool ok = true;
   int i, j;

   for (i = 0;  i < GRID_ROWS  &&  ok;  ++i)
      for (j = 0;  j < GRID_COLS  &&  ok;  ++j)
         if (powerGrid[i][j] != 1)
            ok = false;

   return ok;
}


//
//  Displays coordinates of Grid cells where power is off
//
void Grid :: whereOff() const
{
   int i, j;

   cout << "Power is off in grid cells:"  << endl;

   for (i = 0;  i < GRID_ROWS;  ++i)
      for (j = 0;  j < GRID_COLS;  ++j)
         if (powerGrid[i][j] != 1)
            cout << "    (" << i << "," << j << ")" << endl;
   cout << endl;
}


//
//  Writes a Grid to an output stream with each row on a
//  separate line
//
ostream& operator<< ( ostream& os, const Grid& gr )
{
   int i, j;

   for (i = 0;  i < GRID_ROWS;  ++i) {
      for (j = 0;  j < GRID_COLS;  ++j)
```

FIGURE 8.3 *(Continued)*

```
        os << "    " << gr.powerGrid[i][j];
      os << endl;
   }
   return os;
}

//
//  Fills a Grid with data from an input stream
//
istream& operator>> ( istream& is, Grid& gr )
{
   int i, j;

   for  (i = 0;  i < GRID_ROWS;   ++i)
      for  (j = 0;  j < GRID_COLS;  ++j)
         is >> gr.powerGrid[i][j];

   return is;
}
```

Data file gridbad.dat

```
1  1  1  1
0  1  1  1
0  0  1  1
```

One run

```
Enter name of data file => gridbad.dat
Current grid
  1  1  1  1
  0  1  1  1
  0  0  1  1

Power is off in grid cells:
   (1,0)
   (2,0)
   (2,1)
```

The program in Fig. 8.3 processes *only* grids of three rows and four columns. Figure 8.4 shows a more flexible version of the same program. This second version sets a maximum grid size and assumes that the grid data file begins with a line indicating the number of rows and columns in the grid.

The overloaded >> operator takes the data and fills as much of the grid as is needed. This version of the program is both more flexible (allowing the grid size to vary) and more robust. The program of Fig. 8.3 assumes that the data file contains valid data, but the version of Fig. 8.4 is designed to signal input failure both in the event of encountering end of file or nonnumeric data and in situations when the data file contains a matrix that is too big for the avail-

FIGURE 8.4 Program That Uses a Varying-Size Grid to Monitor Power Availability

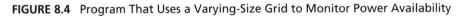

```cpp
//
// Program to track the status of power service throughout the city
// with a grid of maximum size MaxRows x MaxCols in which each cell
// represents power service status in one sector.  When power is
// available everywhere, all grid values are 1.  A grid value of
// 0 indicates an outage somewhere in the sector.
//

#include <iostream>
#include <fstream>
#include <iomanip>
#include <string>
using namespace std;

const int MAX_ROWS = 6;   // maximum number of rows
const int MAX_COLS = 6;   // maximum number of columns

class Grid {  // object type for monitoring power status

public:
   Grid() {}
   bool powerOK() const;   // returns true if all sectors have power
   void whereOff() const;  // displays subscripts of sectors
                           //   where power is off
private:
   int gridRows;
   int gridCols;
   int powerGrid[MAX_ROWS][MAX_COLS];
friend ostream& operator<< ( ostream&, const Grid& );
friend istream& operator>> ( istream&, Grid& );
};

int main()
{
   Grid pubServ;
   string inFileName;
```

FIGURE 8.4 *(Continued)*

```
   cout << "Enter name of data file => ";
   cin  >> inFileName;
   ifstream infile( inFileName.c_str(), ios::in );

   infile >> pubServ;
   infile.close();
   cout << "Current grid" << endl;
   cout << pubServ << endl;
   if (pubServ.powerOK())
      cout << "Power is on throughout grid." << endl;
   else
      pubServ.whereOff();
   return 0;
}


//
//   Returns true if power on (value = 1) in all sectors
//
bool Grid :: powerOK() const
{
   bool ok = true;
   int i, j;

   for  (i = 0;  i < gridRows  &&  ok;  ++i)
      for  (j = 0;  j < gridCols  &&  ok;  ++j)
         if (powerGrid[i][j] != 1)
            ok = false;

   return ok;
}


//
//   Displays coordinates of Grid cells where power is off
//
void Grid :: whereOff() const
{
   int i, j;

   cout << "Power is off in grid cells:"  << endl;

   for  (i = 0;  i < gridRows;  ++i)
      for  (j = 0;  j < gridCols;  ++j)
         if (powerGrid[i][j] != 1)
            cout << "   (" << i << "," << j << ")" << endl;
   cout << endl;
}
```

FIGURE 8.4 *(Continued)*

```
//
//  Writes a Grid to an output stream with each row on a
//  separate line
//
ostream& operator<< ( ostream& os, const Grid& gr )
{
   int i, j;

   for  (i = 0;  i < gr.gridRows;  ++i) {
      for  (j = 0;  j < gr.gridCols;  ++j)
         os << "   " << gr.powerGrid[i][j];
      os << endl;
   }
   return os;
}


//
//  Gets the number of rows and columns from the input stream.  If
//  gridRows <= MAX_ROWS and gridCols <= MAX_COLS, fills gr with data
//  from file.  Otherwise signals failure on stream is and sets grid
//  size to 0 x 0.
//
istream& operator>> ( istream& is, Grid& gr )
{
   int i, j;

   is >> gr.gridRows >> gr.gridCols;
   if (is.fail()) {
      gr.gridRows = 0;
      gr.gridCols = 0;
   } else if (gr.gridRows > MAX_ROWS || gr.gridCols > MAX_COLS) {
      is.setstate( ios::failbit );
      gr.gridRows = 0;
      gr.gridCols = 0;
   } else {
      for  (i = 0;  i < gr.gridRows;  ++i)
         for  (j = 0;  j < gr.gridCols;  ++j)
            is >> gr.powerGrid[i][j];
      if (is.fail()) {
         gr.gridRows = 0;
         gr.gridCols = 0;
      }
   }
   return is;
}
```

FIGURE 8.4   *(Continued)*

Data file gridbadd.txt

```
3  4
1  1  1  1
0  1  1  1
0  0  1  1
```

One run

```
Enter name of data file => gridbadd.txt
Current grid
  1  1  1  1
  0  1  1  1
  0  0  1  1

Power is off in grid cells:
   (1,0)
   (2,0)
   (2,1)
```

able space. This latter case requires the program to explicitly signal a failure on the input stream `is`, which it does with this call to `is`'s member function `setstate`:

```
is.setstate( ios::failbit )
```

Although it is possible to dynamically allocate a two-dimensional array in C++ as an array of addresses of dynamically allocated one-dimensional arrays, the memory management involved is nontrivial and requires quite a bit of execution time. Therefore, unless there is enormous variation in the sizes of the grids you must process, it usually makes sense to simply allow sizes to vary within fixed limits, as shown in Fig. 8.4. We will study dynamic allocation of two-dimensional arrays in Section 8.4.

Section 8.1 Review Questions

1. Assuming the class definition of **Grid** of Fig. 8.4, define a **Grid** member function named **col2Row1** that displays first the second column and then the first row of the **powerGrid** data member.

2. Revise version 2 of the power grid program (Fig. 8.4) so that function `main` prompts the user to enter the grid dimensions and calls a two-parameter constructor function that sets the `gridRows` and `gridCols` components after verifying that they fall within the set limits. Add to `main` a prompting message telling the user how to enter the grid values interactively, then revise >> so it just fills the `powerGrid` component.

3. Revise version 1 of the power grid program (Fig. 8.3) so the `Grid` class definition includes a member function `columnSums` that stores in an array output parameter the sum of each column's values. Here is this member function's prototype:

```
void columnSums( int [] ) const;
```

8.2 Matrix Operations

A matrix is a two-dimensional mathematical object such as the one depicted in Fig. 8.5. The individual elements of a matrix are indicated by row and column subscripts as shown in Fig. 8.6. Notice that mathematicians and engineers traditionally use row subscripts ranging from 1 to the number of rows, and column subscripts ranging from 1 to the number of columns.

Matrices are used in modeling a wide variety of concepts. The power grid in our electric company problem of Section 8.1 is a matrix. You can use matrices to model network connections of all types—telephone, ethernet, transportation. Matrices also model specific transformations applicable to three-dimensional objects, transformations such as translation and rotation.

FIGURE 8.5 A Four × Three Matrix *M*

$$
M = \begin{bmatrix} 5 & 0 & 1 \\ 2 & 1 & 0 \\ 6 & 4 & 3 \\ 0 & 1 & 0 \end{bmatrix}
$$

FIGURE 8.6 Individual Element Names in *M*

$$
M = \begin{bmatrix} m_{11} & m_{12} & m_{13} \\ m_{21} & m_{22} & m_{23} \\ m_{31} & m_{32} & m_{33} \\ m_{41} & m_{42} & m_{43} \end{bmatrix}
$$

FIGURE 8.7 A Wire-Frame Representation of a Solid Object as a List of Three-Dimensional Coordinates

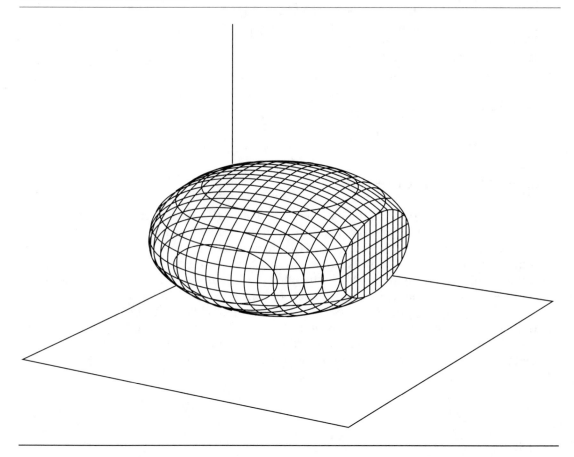

We use matrices to solve simultaneous equations and to represent finite state machines that recognize strings of characters as valid program entities such as reserved words, variable names, numbers, and so on.

Matrix Multiplication

Matrix multiplication is a common operation in applications that use matrices. We repeatedly multiply matrices representing network connections in order to discover which network nodes are reachable from other network nodes. To rotate a three-dimensional wire-frame object like the one illustrated in Fig. 8.7, we multiply the coordinates of each surface reference point by an appropriate rotation matrix.

Before multiplying two matrices, you must verify that the matrices are conformable: The number of columns of the first matrix must match the number of rows of the second matrix. Consider these matrices M_1 and M_2:

$$M_1 = \begin{bmatrix} 5 & 0 & 1 \\ 2 & 1 & 0 \\ 6 & 4 & 3 \\ 0 & 1 & 0 \end{bmatrix} \qquad M_2 = \begin{bmatrix} 2 & 0 \\ 1 & 4 \\ 1 & 3 \end{bmatrix}$$

We can compute the matrix product $M_1 \times M_2$ because M_1 has 3 columns and M_2 has 3 rows. However, we could not compute $M_2 \times M_1$. The product $M_1 \times M_2$ will have as many rows as M_1 (4), and as many columns as M_2 (2). Figure 8.8 shows the product $M_1 \times M_2$. The *ij*th element of the product matrix is calculated by forming the inner product of row *i* of M_1 and column *j* of M_2. This product is the sum of the products of corresponding elements of the two vectors. The shaded portions of Fig. 8.8 show the computation of one element of the product matrix.

Figure 8.9 is a program that implements a class `Matrix` that allows run-time variation of the dimensions of a `Matrix` object within fixed limits. The class defines `int` components `rows` and `cols` along with a component, `mat`, that is a matrix of the maximum size allowed.

Class `Matrix` implements a `*=` member operator that multiplies the default object matrix by another matrix on the right. The operator changes the default object to represent the matrix product, and like the `+=` operator defined for class `Complex` in Fig. 6.11, our `Matrix` `*=` operator uses the pointer `this` to return as the operator value a reference to the object assigned.

Function `main` of Fig. 8.9 asks the user for the names of two data files containing matrices. The expected file format is one line with the matrix di-

FIGURE 8.8 Calculation of Matrix Product $M_1 \times M_2$

$$\underset{M_1}{\begin{bmatrix} 5 & 0 & 1 \\ 2 & 1 & 0 \\ 6 & 4 & 3 \\ 0 & 1 & 0 \end{bmatrix}} \times \underset{M_2}{\begin{bmatrix} 2 & 0 \\ 1 & 4 \\ 1 & 3 \end{bmatrix}} = \underset{M_1 \times M_2}{\begin{bmatrix} 11 & 3 \\ 5 & 4 \\ 19 & 25 \\ 1 & 4 \end{bmatrix}}$$

$$\begin{array}{ccccr} 6 & \times & 2 & = & 12 \\ 4 & \times & 1 & = & 4 \\ 3 & \times & 1 & = & +3 \\ \hline & & & & 19 \end{array}$$

FIGURE 8.9 Program That Multiplies Two Matrices

```
//
//  Program that multiplies one matrix by another; matrices' maximum
//  sizes are MAX_ROWS x MAX_COLS
//

#include <iostream>
#include <fstream>
#include <iomanip>
#include <string>
using namespace std;

const int MAX_ROWS = 6;
const int MAX_COLS = 6;

class Matrix {  //  Represents a varying-size matrix that
                //  can be input from a file
public:
   Matrix() {}
   Matrix( int, int, int );  // Constructor that initializes matrix
                             // size and sets all valid elements to
                             // given initial value
   Matrix& operator*=( const Matrix& );
private:
   int   rows;
   int   cols;
   int   mat[MAX_ROWS][MAX_COLS];
friend ostream& operator<< ( ostream&, const Matrix& );
friend istream& operator>> ( istream&, Matrix& );
};

//
//  Inputs two matrices from files designated by the user.
//  Forms and displays their product.
//
int main()
{
   Matrix m1;
   Matrix m2;
   string file1Name;
   string file2Name;

   cout << "Name of file containing first matrix => ";
   cin >> file1Name;
   ifstream infilOne( file1Name.c_str(), ios::in );
```

FIGURE 8.9 *(Continued)*

```
   infilOne >> m1;
   infilOne.close( );

   cout << "Name of file containing second matrix => ";
   cin >> file2Name;
   ifstream infilTwo( file2Name.c_str(), ios::in );
   infilTwo >> m2;
   infilTwo.close( );

   if (!infilOne.fail() && ! infilTwo.fail()) {
      cout << endl << "Matrix 1" << endl << endl << m1 << endl << endl;
      cout << "Matrix 2" << endl << endl << m2 << endl << endl;
      m1 *= m2;
      cout << "Matrix 1 x Matrix 2 = " << endl << endl << m1 <<
          endl << endl;
   } else {
      cout << "Error in input" << endl;
   }
   return 0;
}


//
//  Constructor that initializes a Matrix object of size initRows
//  x initCols, setting matrix elements to initValue
//
Matrix :: Matrix( int initRows, int initCols, int initValue )
{
   rows = initRows;
   cols = initCols;

   for  (int i = 0;  i < rows;  ++i)
       for  (int j = 0;  j < cols;  ++j)
           mat[i][j] = initValue;
}


//
//  Multiplies m1 by m2 if these matrices are conformable.
//  Otherwise, displays an error message and sets m1's size
//  to 0 x 0
//
Matrix& Matrix :: operator*=(const Matrix& m2 ) // input
{
   int val, i, j, k;
   Matrix prod;
```

FIGURE 8.9 *(Continued)*

```
   if (cols != m2.rows) {
      cout << "Matrices are not conformable." << endl;
      prod.rows = 0;
      prod.cols = 0;
   } else {
      prod.rows = rows;
      prod.cols = m2.cols;
      for  (i = 0;  i < prod.rows;  ++i)
          for  (j = 0;  j < prod.cols;  ++j) {
              val = 0;
              for  (k = 0;  k < cols;  ++k)
                  val += mat[i][k] * m2.mat[k][j];
              prod.mat[i][j] = val;
          }
   }
   *this = prod;
   return *this;
}

//
//  Writes to the output stream the contents of matrix m,
//  one row at a time
//
ostream& operator<< ( ostream& os, const Matrix& m )
{
   for  (int i = 0;  i < m.rows;  ++i) {
      for  (int j = 0;  j < m.cols;  ++j)
          cout << setw( 5 ) << m.mat[i][j];
      cout << endl;
   }
   return os;
}


//
//  Gets the number of rows and columns from the input
//  stream. If rows <= MAX_ROWS and cols <= MAX_COLS,
//  fills m with data from file; otherwise signals failure
//  on stream is. In the event of input failure, sets m size
//  to 0 x 0
//
istream& operator>> ( istream& is, Matrix& m )
{
   int i, j;
```

FIGURE 8.9 *(Continued)*

```
    is >> m.rows >> m.cols;
    if (is.fail()) {
        m.rows = 0;
        m.cols = 0;
    } else if (m.rows > MAX_ROWS  ||  m.cols > MAX_COLS) {
        is.setstate( ios::failbit );
        m.rows = 0;
        m.cols = 0;
    } else {
        for  (i = 0;  i < m.rows;  ++i)
            for  (j = 0;  j < m.cols;  ++j)
                is >> m.mat[i][j];
        if (is.fail()) {
            m.rows = 0;
            m.cols = 0;
        }
    }
    return is;

}

Name of file containing first matrix => mat1.txt
Name of file containing second matrix => mat2.txt

Matrix 1

    10    1    2    3
     2    4    6    8
     7    1    1    1


Matrix 2

     1    0
     0    1
     1    0
     0    1


Matrix 1 x Matrix 2 =

    12    4
     8   12
     8    2
```

row-major storage

placing the elements of the initial row of a two-dimensional array in memory first, followed by the elements of the next row, and so on

mensions and then the matrix values in **row-major** order. Function `main` calls operator `>>`, which gets the matrix dimensions from the file, and then fills the matrix from the data file. After input of both m1 and m2, the main function uses operator `*=` to compute the matrix product.

Section 8.2 Review Questions

1. Revise the matrix multiplication program of Fig. 8.9 so that it uses just one input file and repeatedly inputs pairs of matrices and displays each pair and their product. Use a loop that exits on input failure.

2. Extend class **Matrix** of Fig. 8.9 by defining two versions of a member operator `+=`. One version should take a type **int** right operand and should add this value to every element of the matrix. The second version should take another matrix as the right operand and should add to the left operand corresponding elements of the right operand. If the two matrices are of different sizes, `+=` should display an error message and set the size of the left operand to 0×0.

3. Revise the matrix multiplication program of Fig. 8.9 by overloading the `*=` operator to permit multiplication of a matrix by a scalar. For example, if **m1** is

$$\begin{bmatrix} 0 & 1 & 1 \\ 0 & 2 & 0 \\ 0 & 1 & 1 \end{bmatrix} \quad \text{then } \texttt{m1 *= 5} \text{ should assign to } \texttt{m1} \quad \begin{bmatrix} 0 & 5 & 5 \\ 0 & 10 & 0 \\ 0 & 5 & 5 \end{bmatrix}$$

8.3 Linear Systems

Systems of linear equations are used to model a wide range of phenomena, including seismic data, schedules for flight crews and airplanes, and relationships among sectors of a nation's economy, to name just a few. In our next case study, we develop a program to solve systems of linear equations using an algorithm that is a variant of one discovered by the 19th century German mathematician, Carl Friedrich Gauss. First, let's investigate some basic linear algebra terminology.

EXAMPLE 8.2   A *linear equation* in the variables $x_1, x_2, \ldots, x_n$ can be written as

$$c_1 x_1 + c_2 x_2 + \ldots + c_n x_n = y$$

where the coefficients c_i and the value y are numeric constants. A *linear system* is a group of linear equations that use the same variables. A solution of a system of linear equations is a list of values for $x_1, x_2, ..., x_n$ that makes each linear equation a true statement. For example, for the system

$$x_1 + x_2 + x_3 = 8$$
$$3x_1 - 2x_3 = 2$$
$$2x_1 + 5x_2 + 4x_3 = 23$$

$x_1 = 4$, $x_2 = -1$, $x_3 = 5$ is a solution since

$$4 + (-1) + 5 = 8$$
$$3(4) - 2(5) = 2$$
$$2(4) + 5(-1) + 4(5) = 23$$

are all true statements.

Our original system of equations could be written as the matrix product

$$
\begin{array}{ccc}
C & X & Y
\end{array}
$$
$$
\begin{bmatrix} 1 & 1 & 1 \\ 3 & 0 & -2 \\ 2 & 5 & 4 \end{bmatrix} \times \begin{bmatrix} x_1 \\ x_2 \\ x_3 \end{bmatrix} = \begin{bmatrix} 8 \\ 2 \\ 23 \end{bmatrix}
$$

Matrix C is the coefficient matrix. Our solution system of equations could be written as the matrix product

$$
\begin{bmatrix} 1 & 0 & 0 \\ 0 & 1 & 0 \\ 0 & 0 & 1 \end{bmatrix} \times \begin{bmatrix} x_1 \\ x_2 \\ x_3 \end{bmatrix} = \begin{bmatrix} 4 \\ -1 \\ 5 \end{bmatrix}
$$

Our goal is to develop a procedure for transforming the original linear system into the solution system. ■

Augmented Matrix

A common representation of a system of linear equations is an **augmented matrix**. All but the last column of the matrix represent the coefficients of the linear system. The last column is the vector of constants, Y. Thus, the augmented matrix for our example system is

$$
\begin{bmatrix} 1 & 1 & 1 & 8 \\ 3 & 0 & -2 & 2 \\ 2 & 5 & 4 & 23 \end{bmatrix}
$$

augmented matrix
representation of a linear system as a concatenation of the coefficient matrix and the vector of constants

where the unshaded portion is the coefficient matrix C and the shaded portion is the vector of constants Y. The augmented matrix for our solution system is

$$\begin{bmatrix} 1 & 0 & 0 & 4 \\ 0 & 1 & 0 & -1 \\ 0 & 0 & 1 & 5 \end{bmatrix}$$

This augmented matrix is said to be in *reduced echelon form*, because:

1. The first nonzero entry in each nonzero row is 1.
2. Each leading 1 is the only nonzero value in its column.
3. Each row's leading 1 is to the right of the leading 1's of all the preceding rows.

The leading 1's of the solution system's augmented matrix are in "pivot positions."

A *pivot position* in an augmented matrix is a position a_{ii} that is the location of a leading entry in the matrix's reduced echelon form.

Our algorithm for transforming the original linear system matrix into the solution system matrix can use any of the elementary row operations:

> **Elementary Row Operations**
>
> Replacement: Add to one row a multiple of another row.
>
> Interchange: Interchange two rows.
>
> Scaling: Multiply all entries in a row by a nonzero constant.

In the case study that follows, we develop a program that implements a Matrix class that offers the service of transforming the augmented matrix of a linear system into the solution matrix if a unique solution exists.

CASE STUDY   SOLVING A SYSTEM OF LINEAR EQUATIONS

Problem

Adapt the implementation of class Matrix in Fig. 8.9 so the class provides the service of solving a system of n linear equations represented as an augmented matrix of size $n \times (n+1)$. The program should input an augmented matrix and transform it into a matrix in reduced echelon form. If a unique solution is found, the program should display it. Allow n to range from 2 to 10.

Data Definition

Constants

```
MAXN    10
MINN    2
```

Inputs

```
fileName        // name of file containing augmented matrix
                // representing linear system (string)
augMatrix       // augmented matrix (Matrix)
```

Scratch Pad

```
infile          // input stream (ifstream)
uniqueSolution// whether or not a unique solution exists
```

Outputs

Solution or message indicating there is no unique solution.

Algorithm Design

Initial Algorithm

1. Get fileName and open stream infile.
2. Input augMatrix.
3. If infile.fail()
    3.1 Display an error message.
   else
    3.2 Display augMatrix.
    3.3 Transform augMatrix to a solution if possible, setting unique-Solution.
    3.4 If there is a unique solution, display it; otherwise report that there is no unique solution.

We will design separate class Matrix member functions for Steps 3.3 and 3.4.

Member Function transformMatrix: Problem

Use elementary row operations to transform an augmented matrix for a system of n linear equations into reduced echelon form, determining if there exists a unique solution to the linear system.

Data Definition (transformMatrix)

Parameters

None needed other than the data members of the default object—two-dimensional array `mat` (element-type `double`) and its filled dimensions, `rows` and `cols` (`int`).

Scratch Pad

```
uniqueFound     // indicates whether or not a unique solution
                //   is found (bool)
p               // pivot position counter (int)
r, c            // row and column counters (int)
mult            // multiplier when adding a multiple of one
                //   row to another  (double)
```

Algorithm Design (transformMatrix)

Since the function has two results, one of which is the transformed matrix, we return the value of `uniqueFound` as the function's return value, and we modify the default object to send back the solution matrix. After consulting a linear algebra textbook, we devise the following algorithm.

1. Assume a unique solution exists (initialize `uniqueFound` to true).
2. Repeat for each pivot position p except the last as long as a unique solution may exist
   - 2.1 Find a nonzero value in column p, updating `uniqueFound`, and place this pivot value in `mat[p][p]` by exchanging rows if necessary.
   - 2.2 If there is a nonzero pivot, scale the pivot row to place a 1 in the pivot position. Then perform row operations to place a zero in column p of each row below row p.
3. If a unique solution may exist and value in last pivot position (`mat[n–1][n–1]`) is nonzero
   - 3.1 Scale last row.
   - 3.2 Working backward from row n – 1 to row 1, use row operations to place zeroes in the column above each pivot element.
   - else
   - 3.3 Assign false to `uniqueSolution`.
4. Return `uniqueSolution`.

Steps 2 and 3 need some refinement before we write the code.

Refinement of Steps 2 and 3

2. Repeat for p = 0 to n-2 while `uniqueSolution`
   - 2.1 Find a nonzero value in column p, updating `uniqueSolution`, and place this pivot value in `mat[p][p]` by exchanging rows if necessary.
     - 2.1.1 Let r = p.

2.1.2 While r < n – 1 and mat[r][p] is 0, increment r.

2.1.3 If mat[r][p] is 0, there is no nonzero pivot, so

    2.1.3.1 Set uniqueSolution to false.

    else if r doesn't equal p

    2.1.3.2 Exchange rows r and p of mat.

2.2 If there is a nonzero pivot, scale the pivot row to place a 1 in the pivot position. Then perform row operations to place a zero in column p of each row below row p:

2.2.1 If there is a unique solution

    2.2.1.1 Scale row p of mat.

    2.2.1.2 For each row after p, add an appropriate multiple of row p to place a zero in column p.

3. If there may be a unique solution and value in last pivot position (mat[n–1][n–1]) isn't 0

3.1 Scale row n – 1 of mat.

3.2 Working backward from row n – 1 to row 1, use row operations to place zeroes in the column above each pivot element.

3.2.1. Repeat for p = n – 1 down to 1, subtracting 1 after each iteration

    3.2.1.1 Repeat for r = p – 1 down to 0, subtracting 1 after each iteration

        3.2.1.1.1 Let mult be the negative of mat[r][p]

        3.2.1.1.2 Add to row r the product of mult and row p

Other Functions

Member function displaySolution and helper functions scale and swap are sufficiently straightforward that we show only their implementations. Note, however, that scale and swap are called with individual rows of our two-dimensional matrix. Accessing an element of a two-dimensional matrix requires two subscripts. If only one is provided, we are accessing a row. Figure 8.10 shows the implementation of our matrix transformation design.

FIGURE 8.10 Matrix Transformation to Solve a Linear System

```
//
//   Program that solves a system of linear equations using
//   an augmented matrix
//

#include <iostream>
#include <fstream>
#include <iomanip>
#include <string>
```

← *Preprocessor directives*

FIGURE 8.10 *(Continued)*

```
using namespace std;

const int MAXN = 10;
const int MINN = 2;

void scale (double r[], int rsize);
void swap (double oneList[], double twoList[], int size);

class Matrix {  //  Represents a matrix whose size can vary
                //  up to MAXN x (MAXN + 1)
public:
   Matrix() {}
   bool transformMatrix();  // finds solution to object's
                            // system of linear equations
   void displaySolution( ostream& ) const;
private:
   int    rows;
   int    cols;
   double mat[MAXN][MAXN + 1];
friend ostream& operator<< ( ostream&, const Matrix& );
friend istream& operator>> ( istream&, Matrix& );
};

//
//  Inputs an augmented matrix from a file designated by the user.
//  Finds and displays unique solution if one exists.
//
int main()
{
   Matrix augMatrix;
   string fileName;
   bool uniqueSolution;

   cout << "Name of file containing augmented matrix => ";
   cin >> fileName;
   ifstream infile( fileName.c_str(), ios::in );
   infile >> augMatrix;

   if (infile.fail()) {
      cout << "\nInvalid file format\n";
   } else {
      cout << "\nAugmented Matrix\n" << augMatrix << endl;
```

Labels pointing to code:
- *Constant declarations* → `const int MAXN = 10;` / `const int MINN = 2;`
- *Function prototypes* → `void scale...` / `void swap...`
- *Class Declaration* (bracket around class Matrix block)
- *Constructor* → `Matrix() {}`
- *Prototypes of member functions* → `bool transformMatrix();` region
- *Data members* → `int rows;`
- *Prototypes of overloaded operators* → `friend ostream&...` / `friend istream&...`

FIGURE 8.10 *(Continued)*

```
      uniqueSolution = augMatrix.transformMatrix();
      if (uniqueSolution) {
         cout << "Solution\n";
         augMatrix.displaySolution(cout);
      } else {
         cout << "There is no unique solution.\n";
      }
   }
   infile.close();

   return 0;
}
```

Operator definitions

```
//
//  Writes to the output stream the contents of matrix m,
//  one row at a time
//
ostream& operator<< ( ostream& os, const Matrix& m )
{
   for  (int i = 0;  i < m.rows;  ++i) {
      for  (int j = 0;  j < m.cols;  ++j)
         cout << setw( 9 ) << m.mat[i][j];
      cout << endl;
   }
   return os;
}


//
//  Gets the number of rows from the input stream;
//  Assumes one more column than rows. Fills a two-
//  dimensional array
//
istream& operator>> ( istream& is, Matrix& m )
{
   int i, j;

   is >> m.rows;
   if (m.rows >= MINN && m.rows <= MAXN) {
      m.cols = m.rows + 1;
      for  (i = 0;  i < m.rows;  ++i)
         for  (j = 0;  j < m.cols;  ++j)
            is >> m.mat[i][j];
```

FIGURE 8.10 *(Continued)*

```
      } else {
         is.setstate( ios::failbit );
      }
      return is;

   }
```

```
   //                                    Member function definitions
   //  Transforms augmented matrix into solution matrix if unique
   //  solution exists.  Function value indicates whether solution
   //  found.
   //
   bool Matrix :: transformMatrix()
   {
      int p,         // pivot position
          r, c;      // row and column counters
      double mult;
      bool uniqueSolution = true;

      //  Repeat for each pivot position except the last
      for (p = 0; p < rows − 1 && uniqueSolution; ++p) {

         // Find a nonzero pivot
         for ( r = p; r < rows − 1 && mat[r][p] == 0; ++r) {}

         // Perhaps there is no nonzero pivot
         if (mat[r][p] == 0)
            uniqueSolution = false;

         // Swap rows if necessary to place nonzero pivot
         // in pivot position p
         else if (r != p)
            swap(mat[r], mat[p], cols);

         // Scale pivot row and eliminate coefficients below pivot
         if (uniqueSolution) {
            scale(mat[p], cols);
            for (r = p+1;  r < rows; ++r) {
               mult = −mat[r][p];
               for (c = p; c < cols; ++c)
                  mat[r][c] += mult * mat[p][c];
            }
```

FIGURE 8.10 *(Continued)*

```
      }
   }

   // If there's still a possible solution, scale final row
   // and, working backwards, eliminate coefficients above
   // each pivot position
   if (uniqueSolution && mat[rows − 1][rows − 1] != 0) {
      scale(mat[rows − 1], cols);
      for (p = rows − 1; p > 0; −−p)
         for (r = p−1;  r >= 0; −−r) {
             mult = −mat[r][p];
             for (c = p; c < cols; ++c)
                 mat[r][c] += mult * mat[p][c];
         }
   } else {
      uniqueSolution = false;
   }

   return uniqueSolution;
}


//
//  Display last column of matrix, labeling first value x<1>, second
//  x<2>, and so on
//
void Matrix :: displaySolution( ostream& out ) const
{
   for (int i = 0; i < rows; ++i)
      out << "x<" << i + 1 << "> = " << mat[i][cols − 1] << "    ";
   out << endl;
}
```

Helper function definitions

```
//
//  Divide each element of r by the first nonzero element of r
//
void scale (double r[], int rsize)
{
   int i;
   double divisor;

   // Find first nonzero element
   for (i = 0; i < rsize &&  r[i] == 0; ++i) {}
```

FIGURE 8.10 *(Continued)*

```
    // If there is a nonzero element, divide the rest of the row by it
    if (i < rsize) {
      divisor = r[i];
      for (int j = i; j < rsize; ++j)
        r[j] /= divisor;
    }
}


//
//   Interchange contents of two lists
//
void swap (double oneList[], double twoList[], int size)
{
   double temp;

   for (int i = 0;  i < size;  ++i) {
      temp = oneList[i];
      oneList[i] = twoList[i];
      twoList[i] = temp;
   }
}
```

Input File linear.txt

```
3
1  1  1  8
3  0 -2  2
2  5  4 23
```

Sample Run

```
Name of file containing augmented matrix => linear.txt

Augmented Matrix
          1        1        1        8
          3        0       -2        2
          2        5        4       23

Solution
x<1> = 4    x<2> = -1    x<3> = 5
```

Section 8.3 Review Questions

1. Revise class `Matrix` from Fig. 8.10 by adding a member function `outputLinear` that outputs an augmented matrix to a stream in the form of a list of linear equations. For example, for our augmented matrix from Example 8.2, `outputLinear` should output

   ```
   1x_1 + 1x_2 + 1x_3 = 8
   3x_1 + 0x_2 - 2x_3 = 2
   2x_1 + 5x_2 + 4x_3 = 23
   ```

2. Revise class `Matrix` from Fig. 8.10 by adding a copy constructor. The constructor should take a parameter of type `const Matrix&` and should copy the argument matrix into the constructed object. Be sure you copy values of only the *filled* elements of the matrix.

8.4 Dynamic Allocation of Two-Dimensional Array Components

In Section 7.5 we studied how to allocate space for an array on the heap, a technique that allows you to delay setting the maximum array size until runtime. Similarly, for a two-dimensional array you can set the maximum number of rows and columns at runtime by allocating space on the heap. However, the process for multidimensional arrays is more complicated, because the new operator can allocate directly only single structures or one-dimensional arrays, but not arrays of two or more dimensions. To allocate a two-dimensional array on the heap is a two-step process:

1. Use new to dynamically allocate a one-dimensional array of pointers, one for each row. Operator new returns a pointer to this pointer array.
2. Repeat for each row: Use new to dynamically allocate a one-dimensional array of elements, one element for each column of the two-dimensional array. Store the pointer returned by new in this row's element of the array allocated in Step 1.

Figure 8.11 implements the dynamic allocation process for class `Matrix` as a member function that assumes that the `rows` and `cols` data members represent the dimensions of the array to be dynamically allocated.

Fig. 8.12 illustrates the heap-dynamic allocation process. The pointers in this figure are dashed or solid to indicate their types. As shown in the figure's key, the solid pointer stored in object `aMatrix` on the stack is of type `double **`, but the dashed pointers are of type `double *`. Notice the consistency of the typing: the pointer's type is always formed by appending a `*` to the type of the array element to which the pointer gives access.

Figure 8.13 shows a revised version of class `Matrix` from Fig. 8.9 that includes a one-parameter copy constructor that calls function `createMat` to

FIGURE 8.11   Dynamic Allocation of the Two-Dimensional Array Component of a Matrix Object

```
//
//   Allocates space on the heap for an array of pointers.
//   Stores in each element the pointer to a dynamically
//   allocated array of type double values.  This space
//   represents a rows x cols matrix.
//   Precondition:  rows > 0 and cols > 0
//
void Matrix :: createMat()
{
   mat = new double* [rows];
   for  (int i = 0;  i < rows;  ++i)
      mat[i] = new double [cols];
}
```

dynamically allocate a matrix whose dimensions are determined by the dimensions of the matrix parameter. The figure shows a destructor as well as a helper function `deleteMat` that reverses the allocation process, first returning to the heap the space for each row, and then returning the space for the array of pointers. Notice that our class declaration specifies that helper functions `createMat` and `deleteMat` are both private members. The helper functions are needed by any public member function or operator that *initializes* or *changes* the dimensions of a matrix (see the two initializing constructors and operators >> and *=), but there is no need for a client program to call them directly. Aspects of Fig. 8.13 that relate to the dynamic allocation of matrices on the heap are highlighted with gray shading. We have so highlighted the modification to the default constructor that sets the dimensions

FIGURE 8.12   Allocating a Two-Dimensional (3 × 4) Array on the Heap

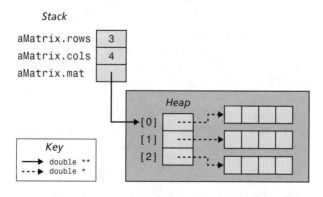

FIGURE 8.13 Matrix Multiplication Program With Array Data Member Allocated on the Heap

```cpp
//
//  Program that multiplies two dynamically allocated matrices
//

#include <iostream>
#include <fstream>
#include <iomanip>
#include <string>
using namespace std;

class Matrix {   //  Represents a dynamically allocated matrix that
                 //  can be input from a file and multiplied by
                 //  another matrix
public:
    Matrix() { rows = 0; cols = 0;} // default constructor
    Matrix(const Matrix&);   // copy constructor
    ~Matrix();  // destructor
    Matrix& operator*= (const Matrix&);   // matrix product operator
private:
    int    rows;
    int    cols;
    double** mat;
    void createMat();  // dynamic allocation function
    void deleteMat();  // release of dynamic memory

    friend ostream& operator<< ( ostream&, const Matrix& );
    friend istream& operator>> ( istream&, Matrix& );

};

//
//  Inputs two matrices from files designated by the user.
//  Forms and displays their product.
int main()
{
    Matrix m1;
    Matrix m2;

    string file1Name, file2Name;

    cout << "Name of file containing first matrix >>> ";
    cin >> file1Name;
```

FIGURE 8.13 *(Continued)*

```cpp
ifstream infilOne( file1Name.c_str(), ios::in );
infilOne >> m1;
infilOne.close();

cout << "Name of file containing second matrix >>> ";
cin >> file2Name;
ifstream infilTwo( file2Name.c_str(), ios::in );
infilTwo >> m2;
infilTwo.close();

Matrix mProd( m1 );
mProd *= m2;
cout << "Matrix 1" << endl << endl << m1 << endl << endl;
cout << "Matrix 2" << endl << endl << m2 << endl << endl;
cout << "Matrix 1 x Matrix 2 = " << endl << endl << mProd <<
    endl << endl;

return 0;

}


//
// Copy constructor allocates space on heap for an array of
// pointers.  Stores in each element the pointer to a dynamically
// allocated array of type double values.  This space represents
// a matrix of the same dimensions as m's mat data member.
// Copies m into new object.
//
Matrix :: Matrix (const Matrix& m)
{

    rows = m.rows;
    cols = m.cols;
    createMat();
    for (int i = 0; i < rows; ++i)
        for (int j = 0; j < cols; ++j)
            mat[i][j] = m.mat[i][j];


}
```

FIGURE 8.13 *(Continued)*

```
//
// Destructor returns dynamically allocated space to the heap.
//
Matrix :: ~Matrix()
{
      deleteMat();
}
```

```
//
//  Allocates space on the heap for an array of pointers.
//  Stores in each element the pointer to a dynamically
//  allocated array of type double values.  This space
//  represents a rows x cols matrix.
//
void Matrix :: createMat()
{
   mat = new double* [rows];
   for  (int i = 0;  i < rows;  ++i)
      mat[i] = new double [cols];
}
```

```
//
//  Releases space allocated on the heap for a 2D array that

//  represents a rows x cols matrix.
//
void Matrix :: deleteMat()
{
      if (rows > 0 && cols > 0) {
         for (int i = 0; i < rows; ++i)
            delete [] mat[i];
         delete [] mat;
         rows = 0;
         cols = 0;
      }
}
```

```
//
//  Writes to the output stream the contents of matrix m,
//  one row at a time
//
ostream& operator<< ( ostream& os, const Matrix& m )
{
   for  (int i = 0;  i < m.rows;  ++i) {
```

FIGURE 8.13   *(Continued)*

```
      for  (int j = 0;  j < m.cols;  ++j)
            cout << setw( 9 ) << m.mat[i][j];
      cout << endl;
   }
   return os;
}


//
//  Gets the number of rows and columns from the input
//  stream; dynamically allocates and fills a two-
//  dimensional array
//
istream& operator>> ( istream& is, Matrix& m )
{
   int i, j;

   if (m.rows > 0 && m.cols > 0)
         m.deleteMat();

   is >> m.rows >> m.cols;
   m.createMat();
   for  (i = 0;  i < m.rows;  ++i)
      for  (j = 0;  j < m.cols;  ++j)
          is >> m.mat[i][j];
   return is;

}


//
//  Forms and returns the matrix product of the default object
//  matrix and m2 if these matrices are conformable.  Otherwise returns
//  the default object unchanged
//
Matrix& Matrix :: operator*= ( const Matrix& m2 )
{
   int val, i, j, k;
   Matrix m1 (*this);
   if (m1.cols != m2.rows) {
      cout << "Matrices are not conformable." << endl;
   } else {
      deleteMat();
      rows = m1.rows;
      cols = m2.cols;
      createMat();
```

FIGURE 8.13 *(Continued)*

```
    for  (i = 0;  i < rows;  ++i)
        for  (j = 0;  j < cols;  ++j) {
            val = 0;
            for  (k = 0;  k < m1.cols;  ++k)
                val += m1.mat[i][k] * m2.mat[k][j];
            mat[i][j] = val;
        }
    }
    return *this;
}
```

to zero. It is essential that an object record its size from the moment of creation so that modules that change matrix sizes can detect whether there is space that must be returned to the heap.

From the user's perspective, the program in Fig. 8.13 executes exactly like the program in Fig. 8.9, except that the program imposes no specific limits on matrix dimensions. That is not to say, however, that there *are* no limits. The target computer is finite, so there are *always* limits on the size of the matrices that can be represented!

The implementation of the matrix multiplication operator *= gives an example of an object with a dynamically allocated component that passes out of scope when the operator returns. The `Matrix` object m1, which is initialized as a copy of the default object matrix in its declaration, passes out of scope when *= returns. The space for its dynamically allocated data member mat is returned to the heap by destructor ~Matrix. Had we neglected to define ~Matrix, the space on the heap would have remained allocated, but would have been inaccessible for the rest of the program.

Section 8.4 Review Questions

1. Which parts of the program from Fig. 8.4 would change if it allocated the **powerGrid** data member of class `Grid` on the heap?
2. Write revised code for the parts you identified in Question 1.

8.5 Software Designer Beware

In this chapter we have demonstrated the use of multidimensional array parameters only in cases where the array is a data member of an object. We strongly recommend packaging multidimensional arrays and their dimensions in class definitions as we did with our `Grid` and `Matrix` objects. We have demonstrated two types of varying-size matrices:

1. stack-based allocation with fixed maximum sizes
2. heap-dynamic allocation with dimensions determined at run-time

If you need a very flexible matrix class, you should purchase a professionally developed class to handle dynamic memory allocation and deallocation.

Chapter Review

1. A multidimensional array is an array of two or more dimensions. A two-dimensional array is often called a matrix or grid.
2. To reference an individual element of a multidimensional array, place immediately after the array name a square-bracketed subscript for each dimension.
3. Nested **for** loops provide sequential access to multidimensional array elements. To access a two-dimensional array one element at a time by rows (row-major access), use the counter of the outer loop as the row subscript. To access by columns (column-major access), use the counter of the outer loop as the column subscript.
4. You can implement a varying-sized two-dimensional array data member of a class by using allocation on the stack of a fixed maximum number of rows and columns or by using a pointer to a one-dimensional array of pointers on the heap, with each of the list of pointers accessing a dynamically allocated one-dimensional array representing one row. Use of the heap-dynamic option requires defining a destructor to return to the heap each row and then the array of pointers when the object goes out of scope.

■ New C++ Constructs ■

Construct	Effect
Two-Dimensional Array Declaration `int matrix[2][3];`	Allocates storage for six type `int` items (2 rows of 3 columns) in two-dimensional array `matrix`: `matrix[0][0]`, `matrix[0][1]`, `matrix[0][2]`, `matrix[1][0]`, `matrix[1][1]`, `matrix[1][2]`.

Two-Dimensional Array Reference
`for (i = 0; i < 2; ++i) {`
`   for (j = 0; j < 3; ++j)`
`      cout << setw(6) << matrix[i][j];`
`   cout << endl;`
`}`
	Displays contents of `matrix` in 2 rows and 3 columns.

Two-Dimensional Array Data Member

Stack-Based

```
const int MAX_ROWS = 8,
   MAX_COLS = 8;
class MatrixFixed {
public:
   MatrixFixed() {}
private:
   int rows, cols;
   double mat[MAX_ROWS][MAX_COLS];
friend ostream& operator<<
   (ostream&, const MatrixFixed&);
friend istream& operator>>
   (istream&, MatrixFixed&);
}
```

Class declaration includes a 2-dimensional array data member with eight rows and eight columns. Actual matrix size can vary up to 8×8 by partially filling data member mat and setting data members rows and cols to indicate actual size of filled portion.

Heap-Dynamic

```
class MatrixDyn {
public:
   MatrixDyn() {rows = 0;
      cols = 0;}
   MatrixDyn(int, int);
   ~MatrixDyn();
private:
   int rows, cols;
   double ** mat;
friend ostream& operator<<
   (ostream&, const MatrixFixed&);
friend istream& operator>>
   (istream&, MatrixFixed&);
}

MatrixDyn :: MatrixDyn( int r,
                        int c)
{
   rows = r;
   cols = c;
   mat = new double * [rows];
   for (int i = 0; i < rows; ++i)
      mat[i] = new double [cols];
}
```

Class declaration includes a data member for a pointer to a 2-dimensional array. Constructor with two int parameters (array dimensions) allocates space on the heap for the matrix. Destructor ~Matrix returns to the heap the space for the dynamically allocated array data member.

```
MatrixDyn :: ~MatrixDyn()
{
  if (rows > 0 && cols > 0} {
    for (int i = 0; i < rows; ++i)
        delete [] mat[i];
    delete [] mat;
  }
}
```

PROGRAMMING PROJECTS

1. Revise class `Matrix` from Fig. 8.9 by adding member function `power`. This member function should take an integer input parameter n and a `Matrix` output parameter `mToTheN`. If the default object is a square matrix (same number of rows as columns), `power` should store in `mToTheN` the default matrix raised to the nth power. Raising a square matrix M to a power n is defined as the product of n copies of M:

identity matrix

a square matrix with 1s on the diagonal and 0s elsewhere.

$$I_3 = \begin{bmatrix} 1 & 0 & 0 \\ 0 & 1 & 0 \\ 0 & 0 & 1 \end{bmatrix}$$

$M^0 = I$ (I is the **identity matrix**—1s on the diagonal, 0s elsewhere)

$M^n = \underbrace{M \cdots M}_{n}$ for $n \geq 1$

If `power` is called with a non-square matrix or if n is negative, set the output parameter to the empty matrix (0×0).

2. Design a class `PtMassSys` to represent a collection of point masses, and develop and test a member function `centerGrav` to calculate and return the center of gravity of the system. Each point mass consists of a 3-D location and an associated mass, such as

Location: (6, 0, –2)   Mass: 3g

In a system of point masses, let $p_1, p_2, \ldots p_n$ be the n 3-D points and $m_1, m_2, \ldots m_n$ be their associated masses. If m is the sum of the masses, the center of gravity C is calculated as

$$C = \frac{1}{m}(m_1 p_1 + m_2 p_2 + \ldots + m_n p_n)$$

Include in your class private data members to represent a location matrix (an $n \times 3$ matrix in which each row is a point), a one-dimensional array of masses, and the number of point masses, n. Allow n to vary from 3 to 10. Overload the input extraction operator so it will store a data file such as this one

Sample Data File

```
4
5  -4   3   2
4   3  -2   5
-4  -3  -1   2
-9   8   6   1
```

as

```
location        5  -4   3
                4   3  -2
               -4  -3  -1
               -9   8   6

mass            2
                5
                2
                1

n               4
```

Your main function should repeatedly input and process data sets from an input file until an input operation fails. For each point-mass-system data set, display the location matrix, the mass vector, n, and the center of gravity.

3. The *inverse* of square matrix A is denoted A^{-1} and has the following property:

$$A(A^{-1}) = I = A^{-1}(A)$$

where I is the identity matrix with the same dimensions as A (see Project 1). Not all matrices are invertible—for some, no inverse exists. However, if a matrix is invertible, the inverse can be calculated using a structure similar to the class we developed for solving systems of linear equations in the case study of Section 8.3.

To find the inverse of invertible matrix A, create an augmented matrix with A on the left and I_n on the right: $[A \ I_n]$. Perform elementary row operations on this augmented matrix to transform matrix A into reduced echelon form. If the transformation is successful, the augmented matrix will now represent $[I_n \ A^{-1}]$. For example, if

$$A = \begin{bmatrix} 1.0 & 3.0 & -1.0 \\ 0.0 & 1.0 & 2.0 \\ -1.0 & 0.0 & 8.0 \end{bmatrix}, \text{ the initial augmented matrix is}$$

$$\begin{bmatrix} 1.0 & 3.0 & -1.0 & 1.0 & 0.0 & 0.0 \\ 0.0 & 1.0 & 2.0 & 0.0 & 1.0 & 0.0 \\ -1.0 & 0.0 & 8.0 & 0.0 & 0.0 & 1.0 \end{bmatrix}$$

After reducing the matrix to row echelon form, the result is

$$\begin{bmatrix} 1.0 & 0.0 & 0.0 & 8.0 & -24.0 & 7.0 \\ 0.0 & 1.0 & 0.0 & -2.0 & 7.0 & -2.0 \\ 0.0 & 0.0 & 1.0 & 1.0 & -3.0 & 1.0 \end{bmatrix}, \text{ so } A^{-1} \text{ is } \begin{bmatrix} 8.0 & -24.0 & 7.0 \\ -2.0 & 7.0 & -2.0 \\ 1.0 & -3.0 & 1.0 \end{bmatrix}$$

Verify that $A(A^{-1}) = I = A^{-1}(A)$

Complete the definition of class `MatrixInv` whose declaration follows.

```
const int MAXN = 5;
class MatrixInv
{
public:
  MatrixInv() {}
  bool invertMatrix ( MatrixInv& ) const;
private:
  int n;
  double mat[MAXN][MAXN];
friend istream& operator>> ( istream&, MatrixInv& );
friend ostream& operator<< ( ostream&, const MatrixInv& );
};
```

Member function `invertMatrix` should store in its `MatrixInv&` output parameter the inverse of the default object, if the inverse exists. The function's return value will be true if the inverse exists, false otherwise. You will be able to detect the absence of an inverse in the same way we detected the absence of a unique solution when solving systems of linear equations. The augmented matrix described above will be stored in a local variable of `invertMatrix`.

Test your code on the 3×3 matrix shown as an example above and also on these matrices:

$$\begin{bmatrix} -9 & 2 \\ 5 & -1 \end{bmatrix} \qquad \begin{bmatrix} 1 & -2 & -1 \\ -1 & 5 & 6 \\ 5 & -4 & 5 \end{bmatrix} \qquad \begin{bmatrix} 6 & 10 & -5 \\ -6 & -9 & 5 \\ -1 & -2 & 1 \end{bmatrix}$$

4. A robot that can rotate on a pedestal has a sensor that measures Cartesian coordinates (x', y') relative to the robot itself. It is desired, however, to know object coordinates (x, y) relative to the fixed coordinate system in which the robot rotates. If the robot is rotated counterclockwise through the angle θ relative to the fixed system,

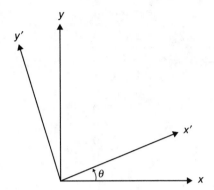

then coordinates in the fixed system are related to the robot's coordinate system by the following transformation:

$$\begin{bmatrix} x \\ y \end{bmatrix} = M \begin{bmatrix} x' \\ y' \end{bmatrix}$$

where M is the matrix

$$M = \begin{bmatrix} \cos\theta & -\sin\theta \\ \sin\theta & \cos\theta \end{bmatrix}$$

Write a program that takes positions in the (x', y') system (as measured by the sensor) and reports the equivalent coordinates in the fixed (x, y) coordinate system for user-input values of θ between 0 and π radians.

5. The transpose of a matrix is formed by interchanging the matrix's rows and columns. Thus the transpose of matrix

$$A = \begin{bmatrix} 2 & 4 \\ 6 & 8 \\ 10 & 12 \end{bmatrix} \qquad \text{is} \qquad A^t = \begin{bmatrix} 2 & 6 & 10 \\ 4 & 8 & 12 \end{bmatrix}$$

Expand the definition of class Matrix to include a transpose member function, and use this function in your solution to the following problem.

The organizers of an in-house software engineering conference for a small consulting company are trying to minimize scheduling conflicts by scheduling the most popular presentations at different times. First the planners survey the ten participants to determine which of the five presentations they want to attend. Then they construct a matrix A in which a 1 in entry ij means that participant i wants to attend presentation j.

	Presentation				
Participant	1	2	3	4	5
1	1	0	1	0	1
2	0	0	1	1	1
3	1	0	0	0	0
4	0	1	1	0	1
5	0	0	0	0	0
6	1	1	0	0	0
7	0	0	1	0	1
8	0	1	0	1	0
9	1	0	1	0	1
10	0	0	0	1	0

Next, the planners calculate the transpose of A (A^t) and the matrix product A^tA. In the resulting matrix, entry ij is the number of participants wishing to attend both presentation i and presentation j.

$$A^tA = \begin{bmatrix} 4 & 1 & 2 & 0 & 2 \\ 1 & 3 & 1 & 1 & 1 \\ 2 & 1 & 5 & 1 & 5 \\ 0 & 1 & 1 & 3 & 1 \\ 2 & 1 & 5 & 1 & 5 \end{bmatrix}$$

Notice that A^tA is symmetric ($a_{ij} = a_{ji}$ for all i, j), so the entries below the main diagonal (entries ij where $i > j$) need not be calculated (see shaded region). If we supply zeros for the unnecessary entries, the resulting matrix is termed an *upper triangular matrix*. The entries on the main diagonal (a_{ii}) represent the total participants wanting to attend presentation i.

  Write a program that creates a class `Matrix` object from a data file of participant preferences. Then display how many participants wish to attend each presentation. Finally, find the three largest numbers in the entries above the diagonal of A^tA, and display up to three pairs of presentations that the conference committee should avoid scheduling opposite one another. You will display fewer than three pairs if one (or more) of the three largest numbers is 1.

6. Figure 8.14 represents the flow of fluid in a system of pipes. The arrows indicate the direction of fluid flow, and the numbers just past each intersection indicate the portion of the fluid taking that path. For example, of the fluid reaching P_1, 40% flows to P_3 and 60% flows to P_2. Thus

$$x_1 = 0.4n_1$$
$$x_2 = 0.2(0.6n_1 + n_2) = 0.12n_1 + 0.2n_2$$
$$x_3 = 0.8(0.6n_1 + n_2) = 0.48n_1 + 0.8n_2$$

FIGURE 8.14   Fluid Flow in System of Pipes

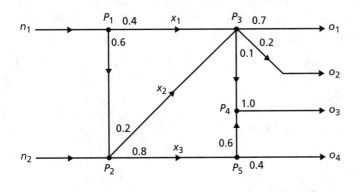

We can represent this system of linear equations as the matrix equation

$$X = AN$$

where

$$X = \begin{bmatrix} x_1 \\ x_2 \\ x_3 \end{bmatrix} \qquad A = \begin{bmatrix} 0.40 & 0 \\ 0.12 & 0.2 \\ 0.48 & 0.8 \end{bmatrix} \qquad N = \begin{bmatrix} n_1 \\ n_2 \end{bmatrix}$$

Similarly,

$$O = BX$$

where

$$O = \begin{bmatrix} o_1 \\ o_2 \\ o_3 \\ o_4 \end{bmatrix} \qquad B = \begin{bmatrix} 0.7 & 0.7 & 0 \\ 0.2 & 0.2 & 0 \\ 0.1 & 0.1 & 0.6 \\ 0 & 0 & 0.4 \end{bmatrix}$$

Thus, the vector of outputs from the system is computed as the product of three matrices:

$$O = B(AN)$$

Write a program that takes from a data file a vector of input flows N and additional matrices A, B, C, . . . , and computes the pipe system outputs by forming the matrix product . . . $C(B(AN))$.

7. Directed graphs (digraphs) are often used as models of communications networks. One of the most useful representations of an n-vertex digraph is an $n \times n$ adjacency matrix. Consider these three representations of the same digraph:

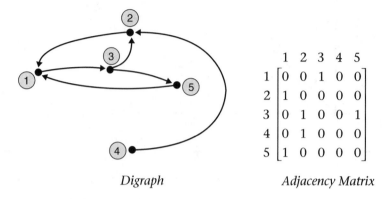

		1	2	3	4	5
1		0	0	1	0	0
2		1	0	0	0	0
3		0	1	0	0	1
4		0	1	0	0	0
5		1	0	0	0	0

Digraph   *Adjacency Matrix*

Vertices: {1, 2, 3, 4, 5}

Edges: { (1,3), (2, 1), (3, 2), (3,5), (4,2), (5,1)}

> *Lists of Vertices and Edges*

In the adjacency matrix, a 1 in entry ij means there is an edge from vertex i to vertex j. Write a program that defines a class `Digraph` with private components `vertices` and `edges`, and a class `AdjacencyMatrix` similar to class `Matrix`. Include constructor functions that permit automatic conversion from each representation to the other, and overload >> and << for both classes. You may assume that the vertices of an n-vertex graph will be numbered from 1 to n, so a file representation of the digraph shown could be

```
5
1   3
2   1
3   2
3   5
4   2
5   1
```

Remember that your matrix subscripts will be one less than the corresponding vertex numbers. Allow for up to eight vertices.

8. Write a program that finds and displays a rough representation of an object in a gray-scale image. A *gray-scale image* is a digitized version of a black-and-white photograph. The image is a grid in which each pixel (picture element) is represented by an integer in the range 0 (white) to a

maximum determined by the number of shades of gray recognized by the imaging system. This maximum number represents black.

Include in your program a definition of two two-dimensional array classes: intImage and charImage. The array elements of an intImage object are to be integers representing a gray-scale image in a system with 256 shades of gray (0 = white, 255 = black). The array elements of a charImage object are either '*' (representing darker pixels) or ' ' (representing lighter pixels). Overload >> and << for both image classes. In addition to the default constructor for class charImage, define a charImage constructor that takes a single intImage parameter and creates a charImage object in which all intImage pixels ≥ a threshold of 128 are represented by asterisks, and all lower values are represented by blanks.

Also include in the intImage class a member function robertsCross that applies the Roberts Cross operator to the image. The *Roberts Cross operator* is a simple gradient operator that is applied to a matrix of pixels to find changes in intensity. In every 2×2 neighborhood, the value of rc[i][j] is

$$maximum(|img[i][j] - img[i + 1][j + 1]|, |img[i + 1][j] - img[i][j + 1]|)$$

For example,

$$given\ img = \begin{bmatrix} 150 & 152 & 160 & 159 \\ 22 & 149 & 155 & 156 \\ 24 & 25 & 152 & 155 \\ 23 & 22 & 22 & 151 \end{bmatrix} \quad rc = \begin{bmatrix} 130 & 11 & 4 & 0 \\ 125 & 130 & 4 & 0 \\ 2 & 130 & 133 & 0 \\ 0 & 0 & 0 & 0 \end{bmatrix}$$

$$|149 - 152| = 3, \qquad |25 - 155| = 130, \qquad Maximum(3, 130) = 130$$

The shaded regions demonstrate the calculation of rc[1][1]. Note that we zero-fill the final column and row of rc to yield a matrix that is the same size as the original.

Using the same example, here are img and rc converted to charImage objects:

In the charImage object on the left, all the dark pixels of img are represented as asterisks and all the light pixels are represented as blanks, yielding a very rough picture of the original image. The diagonal line that appears in the charImage object on the right represents the boundary between the light and dark pixels of the original image. Try your program on a file of pixels representing an image with a dark square and triangle on a light background.

Input and Output Streams

9

This chapter summarizes what we have studied about the use of input and output streams and explores this topic in greater depth. You will learn how text files, keyboard input, and screen output are represented, and how to recover from stream errors. Understanding these concepts will allow you to write more robust C++ programs. You will also learn how to use a text file to represent a searchable database.

9.1   Text Files

text file

a named collection of characters residing in secondary storage

The files that we have used as input to programs since Chapter 4 and the output files created by our programs are all **text files**, named collections of characters saved in secondary storage (e.g., on a disk). To mark the end of a text file, the program creating it places an end-of-file character, which we will denote <eof>, after the last character of the file. As you create a file using a word processor, pressing the <Enter> key inserts a newline character (represented by C++ as '\n') in the file.

The following lines represent a text file consisting of two lines of letters, blank characters, and the punctuation characters . and !.

```
This is a text file!<newline>
It has two lines.<newline><eof>
```

Each line ends with <newline>, and <eof> follows the last <newline> in the file. For convenience in examining the file's contents, we listed each line of the file (through <newline>) as a separate line, although this would not be the case in the actual disk file. Conceptually, the disk file consists of a sequence of characters occupying consecutive storage locations on a track of the disk, as shown here:

```
This is a text file!<newline>It has two lines.<newline><eof>
```

The first character of the second line (I) follows directly after the last character of the first line (<newline>). Because all textual input and output data are actually a continuous stream of character codes, we often refer to a data source or destination as an **input stream** or an **output stream**. These general terms can be applied to files, to the terminal keyboard and screen, and to any other sources of input data or destinations of output data.

input stream

a continuous sequence of character codes coming from an input device or input file

output stream

a continuous sequence of character codes sent to an output device or output file

The character '\n' is one of several escape sequences defined by C++ to represent special characters. Table 9.1 shows some of the most commonly used escape sequences. Because all the escape sequences begin with a backslash (\), to represent the actual backslash character in a C++ program, you must use two: '\\'. The '\r' sequence differs from the newline ('\n') in that it moves the cursor to the beginning of the current line of output, not to the beginning of the next line. You can move the cursor back one space by using the '\b' sequence. Using '\r' or '\b' gives a program the ability to create a file containing more than one character in one line position. In Example 9.1, we will demonstrate the use of '\r' and '\f'.

Mixing Whole-Line and Whitespace-Delimited Input

We have studied the use of the input extraction operator >> for input of numbers, single characters, and strings. In every case, the >> skips over whitespace (blanks, tabs, newlines, etc.) before inputting a value and then stops input at the next whitespace character after the value, leaving the delimiting

TABLE 9.1 Meanings of Common Escape Sequences

Escape Sequence	Meaning
'\n'	new line
'\t'	tab
'\f'	form feed (new page)
'\r'	return (go back to column 1 of current output line)
'\b'	backspace
'\\'	backslash character
'\"'	quote character

newline or blank on the input line. Be aware that if you mix the use of >> with calls to function getline, you may be surprised by the results. Consider this code fragment:

```
string data;
int n1, n2;
...
infile >> n1 >> n2;
getline( infile, data );
```

If the data in the file accessed by infile is

```
35 108
some text
```

then the data stream will be

35 108<newline>some text<newline>

After execution of

```
infile >> n1 >> n2;
```

the value of n1 will be 35, and n2 will be 108. The next item to be input from the stream will be <newline>.

35 108<newline>some text<newline>
    ↑

When the call to getline is executed, the <newline> will be encountered immediately, and the empty string ("") will be stored in data. To input the line "some text", we need first to get past the rest of the text line that contained the numbers 35 and 108. One way to accomplish this is to call getline twice, once to input the rest of the first line of data and then again to input the following line. Another possibility is to use the input stream member function `get` to bring in the newline character. This function that we met in Section 7.4 stores the next character from the stream in its type `char` output argument:

```
infile.get(oneChar);
```

The disadvantage of this option is that it would not get rid of the rest of the first line of data if the line included a few blanks before the newline character.

The Keyboard and Screen

In interactive programming, C++ associates the names of system stream objects with the terminal keyboard and screen. The object `cin` represents the keyboard's input stream. Two system stream objects are associated with the screen: (1) the "normal" output stream `cout` and (2) the "error" output stream `cerr`.

Normally, when typing at a keyboard, we enter one line of data at a time, pressing <Enter> to indicate the end of a data line. Pressing this key inserts the newline character in system stream `cin`. Usually in interactive programming, we use a sentinel value to indicate the end of data rather than attempting to place the eof character in system stream `cin`. However, the eof character could be used. No single key stroke gives a representation of <eof>, so most systems use the control key followed by a letter (for example, computers that run the UNIX or Macintosh operating systems use the strokes <control-d>; IBM PC-compatibles use <control-z>).

Inserting characters in the output streams `cout` and `cerr` causes the characters to appear on the screen in an interactive program. Inserting `endl` or the character `'\n'` in one of these streams causes output of a <newline>: a sequence of characters that moves the cursor to the start of the next line of the screen.

Classes ifstream and ofstream

In Chapter 4 we presented declaration of program-controlled input and output streams using `ifstream` and `ofstream`. Both `ifstream` and `ofstream` are names of classes defined in the fstream library. Figure 9.1 shows a portion of the stream I/O class hierarchy that C++ defines. Notice that `ifstream` objects are more specialized kinds of `istream` objects and that `ofstream` objects inherit from class `ostream`. Our declarations of input and output files are actually calls to constructor functions defined by classes `ifstream` and `ofstream`.

You will recall that when we overload the `>>` and `<<` operators, the left operand is always a reference to an `ostream` or an `istream` object. The standard input stream `cin` is an object of class `istream`, and output streams `cout` and `cerr` are `ostream` objects.

In our examples so far of file I/O, we have always used constructors that

FIGURE 9.1 Portion of C++ Stream I/O Class Hierarchy

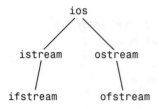

both declare a file stream variable and attach it to an open file. However, it is also possible to do this in two steps, as demonstrated in Table 9.2. In the two-step case, we declare the file variable using the default constructor and then attach the variable to a file by calling stream member function open. If you later wished to close this file and reattach your file variable to a different file, you could do so by following your call to function close by another call to open. Since member function open, as shown in Table 9.2, will position the file pointer at the beginning of the file, if you close an input file and re-open the same file, your next input will come from the beginning of the file.

In Example 9.1, we review several file input/output concepts presented previously and we demonstrate the use of escape sequences '\r' and '\f'.

EXAMPLE 9.1 When a group of people are working on revisions to a document, it is helpful to have a copy of the document in which the lines are numbered. The program in Fig. 9.2 produces such a listing. It places 50 document lines on each page and begins each page with a header that displays the file name (underlined) and the listing page number.

Function main of the line-numbering program uses an endfile-controlled while loop that extracts lines of text from the input file one at a time using the function getline. The loop body displays the line number and text line and then checks whether the line number is evenly divisible by LINES_PER_PAGE. If so, it begins a new page by outputting the '\f' formfeed escape sequence and calls function header to display a new page header. Function header writes out the file name followed by the '\r' return control sequence,

TABLE 9.2 Input and Output File Declaration and Opening

One-Step Approach	Two-Step Approach
`ifstream infil("data.txt", ios::in);`	`ifstream infil;` `infil.open("data.txt");`
`ofstream outfil("out.txt", ios::out);`	`ofstream outfil;` `outfil.open("out.txt");`

FIGURE 9.2 Program That Numbers the Lines of a Text File

```
//
//  Create a listing of a file in which each line is numbered, and each
//  page has a heading showing the file name and the page number.

#include <iostream>
#include <fstream>
#include <iomanip>
#include <string>
#include <cstdlib>
using namespace std;

const int LINES_PER_PAGE = 50;
void header( ofstream&, const string&, int );

int main()
{
   string line;             // one line from input file
   string inName, outName;  // names of input and output files
   int  lineNum = 1;        // listing line number
   int  pageNum = 1;        // listing page number

   cout << "Create listing of which file?   ";
   cin >> inName;
   cout << "Put listing in which file?   ";
   cin >> outName;

   ifstream in( inName.c_str(), ios::in );
   ofstream out( outName.c_str(), ios::out );

   header( out, inName, pageNum++ );
   getline( in, line );
   while (!in.fail()) {
      out << setw( 4 ) << lineNum << "  " << line << endl;
      if (lineNum % LINES_PER_PAGE == 0) {
         out << '\f';
         header( out, inName, pageNum++ );
      }
      ++lineNum;
      getline( in, line );
   }
   cout << "Listing of " << inName << " on " << outName << " complete."
      << endl;
```

FIGURE 9.2 *(Continued)*

```cpp
   in.close();
   out.close();

   return 0;

}

//
//  Output a page header consisting of file name (underlined) and
//  page number.
//
void header( ofstream& out, const string& name, int page )
{
   int nameLen;
   int width;

   nameLen = name.length();
   width = 70 - nameLen;

   out << name << '\r';
   for  (int i = 0;  i < nameLen; ++i)
      out << '_';
   out << setw( width ) << "Page " << page << endl << endl;
}
```

Sample Listing File

<u>a:\solar.cpp</u>   Page 1

```cpp
    1  //
    2  //  Estimate necessary solar collecting area for a particular type of
    3  //  construction in a given location.
    4  //
    5
    6  #include <iostream>
    7  #include <fstream>
    8  #include <iomanip>
    9  #include <cmath>
   10  using namespace std;
   11
   12  int daysInMonth( int);
   13  int fileMax( ifstream&, int& );
   14  int nthItem( ifstream&, int );
```

FIGURE 9.2   *(Continued)*

```
      . . .
49      cin >> efficiency;
50      cout << "What is the floor space (ft^2)?" << endl << ">>> ";
```

<form feed>

<u>a:\solar.cpp</u>   Page 2

```
51      cin >> floorSpace;
52
53      //  Project collecting area needed
54      heatLoss = heatingRequirement * floorSpace * heatingDegreeDays;
55      energyResource = efficiency * 0.01 * solarInsolation *
56                      daysInMonth( coldestMonth );
```

which returns to the beginning of the line on which the file name appears. Function header's for loop then writes one underscore ('_') for each character in the file name, underlining the name. Finally the function writes out the string "Page " right-justified in a field whose width is based on the length of the file name. This string is followed by the page number.   ■

Section 9.1 Review Questions

1. Assume these declarations for the problem that follows:

```
double   x;
int      n;
char     ch;
string   str;
```

Indicate the contents of these variables after each of the following input operations is performed. Assume that the file accessed by **ifstream** variable **indata** consists of the data shown and that each lettered group of operations occurs at the beginning of a program before any other data have been taken from the file.

123 3.145 xyz<newline>35 z<newline> . . .

a. indata >> n >> x >> str >> ch;

b. indata >> n >> x;
   indata >> str >> ch;

c. indata >> x >> n >> ch >> str;

d. `getline(indata, str);`
   `indata >> n >> ch;`

9.2 Stream Error Detection

In previous chapters, we have always assumed that our declarations of input and output streams were successful in creating objects attached to open input or output files. In fact, there are many reasons why creation of such an object might fail. There might exist no input file of the given name in the directory where C++ looks for the file. The user might have no authorization to create a file in the directory specified for an output file, or the target disk might be full. To construct a more robust program, we could check for failure on the input or output stream immediately after our calls to the `if-stream` and `ofstream` constructors. Figure 9.3 shows a more robust version of function `main` of our listing-creation program of Fig. 9.2. This version checks whether the input and output stream objects have been successfully associated with open files, and if they have not, it displays an error message and calls the `cstdlib` library function `exit` to terminate the program prematurely. The argument 1 in the call to `exit` indicates that the program termination is due to an error; an argument value of 0 would imply that the call to `exit` was the normal means of program termination.

FIGURE 9.3 More Robust Main Function for Program That Numbers the Lines of a Text File

```
int main()
{
   string line;              // one line from input file
   string inName, outName;   // names of input and output files
   int  lineNum = 1;              // listing line number
   int  pageNum = 1;              // listing page number

   cout << "Create listing of which file?  ";
   cin >> inName;
   cout << "Put listing in which file?  ";
   cin >> outName;

   ifstream in( inName.c_str(), ios::in );

   if (in.fail()) {
      cerr << "Unable to open " << inName << " for input." << endl;
      exit( 1 );
   }
```

FIGURE 9.3 *(Continued)*

```
ofstream out( outName.c_str(), ios::out );
if (out.fail()) {
   cerr << "Unable to open " << outName << " for output." << endl;
   exit( 1 );
}
header( out, inName, pageNum++ );
getline( in, line );
while (!in.fail()) {
   out << setw( 4 ) << lineNum << "   " << line << endl;
   if (lineNum % LINES_PER_PAGE == 0) {
      out << '\f';
      header( out, inName, pageNum++ );
   }
   ++lineNum;
   getline( in, line );
}
cout << "Listing of " << inName << " on " << outName << " complete."
     << endl;
in.close();
out.close();
return 0;
}
```

Error Recovery

In numerous programs we have used the `fail` stream member function to detect an input failure from either the keyboard or from an input file. Sometimes it is advantageous to recover from such an error and continue processing. Even if the error is not one from which the program can fully recover, being able to do just a little more input after an input failure may enable you to give a much more useful error message before terminating the program.

After a failure has occurred on a stream, there can be no more input from the stream until the failure flag has been cleared, using stream member function `clear`. The code fragment in Fig. 9.4 repeatedly prompts for an integer between 0 and 10 until the user complies. The loop recovers from *any* faulty input by detecting the error, clearing the failure flag, issuing a descriptive error message that includes the result of inputting the rest of the line a character at a time until the newline character is encountered, and reprompting.

Table 9.3 summarizes the stream error detection and recovery functions we have met in this chapter and in previous chapters.

FIGURE 9.4 Loop That Recovers From Any Faulty Input

```
int num;
bool again;
char badChar;
do {
   cout << "Enter an integer between 0 and 10=> ";
   cin >> num;
   if (cin.fail()) {
      again = true;
      cin.clear();
      cerr << "Invalid data: ";
      for  (cin.get(badChar); !cin.fail() && badChar != '\n';
           cin.get(badChar))
         cerr << badChar;
      cerr << ", try again.\n";
   } else if (num < 0 || num > 10) {
      again = true;
      cerr << "Data out of range: " << num << ", try again.\n";
   } else {
      again = false;
   }
} while (again);
```

Sample run:

```
Enter an integer between 0 and 10=> three
Invalid data: three, try again.
Enter an integer between 0 and 10=> -5
Data out of range: -5, try again.
Enter an integer between 0 and 10=> 11
Data out of range: 11, try again.
Enter an integer between 0 and 10=> 10
```

Section 9.2 Review Questions

1. Define a function that prompts for and inputs a number and returns this number as the function value (type **double**). The function should recover from any input error and continue prompting until valid input is received. Sample run:

```
Enter a number=> Ten
Invalid input:  Ten
Enter a number=> 48
```

2. Write a function **outputEmptySet** that takes a single output file parameter and outputs to that file the symbol Ø (a zero overstruck with a slash).

TABLE 9.3 Commonly Used Stream Error Detection Functions

Function	Purpose	Example

eof	Returns true if an input operation on the stream has encountered end-of-file.
	
	Commonly used *after* detecting failure because some systems detect eof after final *successful* input.
		```getline(infile, data);```
		```while (!infile.eof()) {```
		``` ...```
		``` getline(infile, data);```
		```}```

fail	Returns true if an operation on the stream has failed.	```if (cin.fail() && !cin.eof())```
		``` cout << "Invalid data" <<```
		``` " encountered" << endl;```

clear	Restores a stream that has had an input failure to a state permitting additional input.	```cin.clear()```
setstate	Signals a failure on a stream.	```infile.setstate(ios::failbit)```

9.3 Formatting Text Output

Table 9.4 reviews the C++ facilities we have seen for formatting text output.

TABLE 9.4 Formatting Text Output

Format Desired	Facilities to Use	Header File to Include	Example	Output (□ means space)

Integer right-justified in a field of w columns	setw(w)	iomanip	```n = 15; q = 410;```
			```m = 5;```
			```cout << setw(4) << n```
			``` << setw(5) << q <<```
			``` endl << setw(4) <<```
			``` m << endl;```
				□□15□□410
				□□□5

Floating point number right-justified in a field of w columns with d digits to right of decimal point	setw(w)
	setiosflags (ios::fixed)
	setprecision (d)
		iomanip	```x = 38.816;```
			```y = -1.0;```
			```cout << setiosflags```
			``` (ios::fixed)```
			``` << setprecision(2);```
			```cout << setw(8) <<```
			``` << x << endl <<```
			```setw(8) << y <<```
			```endl;```
				□□□38.82
				□□□-1.00

TABLE 9.4 *(Continued)*

Format Desired	Facilities to Use	Header File to Include	Example	Output (☐ means space)
Value left-justified in a field of w columns	setiosflags (ios::left) setw(w)	iomanip	str = "Joan"; n = 5; cout << setiosflags (ios::left) << setw(10) << str << n << endl;	Joan☐☐☐☐☐☐5
Turn off left-justification	resetiosflags (ios::left)	iomanip		
Integer in base 8, base 16, or base 10	oct hex dec	iomanip	n = 26; cout << n << " " << oct << n << " " << hex << n << " " << dec << n << endl;	26☐ 32☐ 1a☐ 26

Section 9.3 Review Questions

1. Complete the following program so that it could produce the report shown. (The line of digits is *not* part of the report.) Assume that file **data.txt** has each value on a separate line with no leading blanks:

```
Oil

billion barrels
25
2.97
...
```

Review the Section 9.1 warnings about mixing input with >> and with `getline`.

```
FOSSIL FUEL         UNIT            RESERVES(1988)   ANNUAL PRODUCTION

Oil                 billion barrels       25              2.970
Natural gas         trillion cubic feet  192             16.600
Coal                billion tons         480              0.959
12345678901234567890123456789012345678901234567890123456789012345678901234567890
```

```
#include <iostream>
#include _____
#include _____
#include _____
using _____

int main()
{   string fuel[3];
    string unit[3];
    int  reserves[3];
    double production[3];
    int i;
    string restOfLine;

    ifstream in( "data.txt", ios::in );
    ofstream out( "report.txt", ios::out );
    ...
    for  (i = 0;  i < 3;  ++i) {
        getline(in, fuel[i]);
        getline(in, unit[i]);
        in >> reserves[i] >> production[i];
         ...
    }

        ...
```

9.4 Searching a Database

Solutions of many engineering problems require searching for materials or manufactured components that satisfy a list of constraints. For example, you might need to find a metal for an engine part that must bear heavy stresses at high temperatures. You would like to minimize the part's weight, and you have a limit on the number of days you can wait for delivery. Searching for candidate metals can be accomplished very quickly if you have computerized access to a file of records about available materials.

Such a large file of data organized in records that are searchable by subject or keyword is called a **database**. In this section, we will develop a program that searches a database to find all records that match a set of requirements.

database

a large electronic file of information that can be quickly searched using subjects or keywords

METALS DATABASE INQUIRY[1]

Problem

Metals Unlimited is a mail-order metal supply company that maintains its inventory as a computer file in order to facilitate answering questions regarding that database. Questions of interest might include the following:

- What metals are available that can withstand pressures of 135 gigapascals (1 gigapascal [GPa] = 1 kilonewton/mm^2)?
- What are the characteristics (density, melting point, tensile modulus) of vanadium?
- What metals whose melting points are at least 1400°C can be delivered within 15 days of the order date?

These questions and others can be answered if we know the correct way to ask them.

Analysis

A database inquiry program has two phases: setting the search parameters and searching for records that satisfy those parameters. In our program, we will assume that all the structure components can be involved in the search. The program user must enter low and high bounds for each field of interest. Let's illustrate how we might set the search parameters to answer the question, *What metals whose melting points are at least 1400°C can be delivered within 15 days of the order date?*

Since we know that all Metals Unlimited materials can be delivered within 90 days, that no metal's density exceeds 20 g/cm^3, that all metals melt at temperatures below 4000°C, and that no metal can withstand pressures in excess of 420 GPa, we can use the following menu-driven dialogue to set the search parameters:

```
Select by letter a search parameter to set, or enter q to
accept parameters shown.

Search Parameter                             Current Value
  [a]  Low bound for name                        aaaa
  [b]  High bound for name                       zzzz
  [c]  Low bound for density  (g/cm^3)              0
  [d]  High bound for density (g/cm^3)             20
  [e]  Low bound for melting point  (degrees C)     0
  [f]  High bound for melting point (degrees C)  4000
```

[1]Adapted from *C Program Design for Engineers*, by Jeri R. Hanly and Elliot B. Koffman with Joan C. Horvath.

```
[g]  Low bound for tensile modulus  (GPa)        0
[h]  High bound for tensile modulus (GPa)       420
[i]  Low bound for days to delivery              0
[j]  High bound for days to delivery            90

Selection> e
New low bound for melting point> 1400

Select by letter a search parameter to set, or enter q to
accept parameters shown.

Search Parameter                          Current Value
  [a]  Low bound for name                       aaaa
  [b]  High bound for name                      zzzz
  [c]  Low bound for density  (g/cm^3)            0
  [d]  High bound for density (g/cm^3)           20
  [e]  Low bound for melting point  (degrees C) 1400
  [f]  High bound for melting point (degrees C) 4000
  [g]  Low bound for tensile modulus  (GPa)       0
  [h]  High bound for tensile modulus (GPa)     420
  [i]  Low bound for days to delivery             0
  [j]  High bound for days to delivery          90

Selection> j
New high bound for days to delivery> 15

Select by letter a search parameter to set, or enter q to
accept parameters shown.

Search Parameter                          Current Value
  [a]  Low bound for name                       aaaa
  [b]  High bound for name                      zzzz
  [c]  Low bound for density  (g/cm^3)            0
  [d]  High bound for density (g/cm^3)           20
  [e]  Low bound for melting point  (degrees C) 1400
  [f]  High bound for melting point (degrees C) 4000
  [g]  Low bound for tensile modulus  (GPa)       0
  [h]  High bound for tensile modulus (GPa)     420
  [i]  Low bound for days to delivery             0
  [j]  High bound for days to delivery          15

Selection> q
```

Data Definition

Inputs

```
params      // structure containing high and low bounds for all search
            //  parameters (user-defined type SearchParams)
invFileName // name of inventory file (string)
```

Scratch Pad

```
inventory    // variable to access database file (ifstream)
```

Outputs

all metals from the file that satisfy the search parameters

Algorithm Design

Initial Algorithm

1. Open inventory file.
2. Get search parameters.
3. Display all metals that satisfy the search parameters.
4. Close inventory file.

We will implement Steps 2 and 3 as separate functions getParams and displayMatch, so the refinement of our initial algorithm will be the development of algorithms for these functions.

Implementation

Figure 9.5 outlines the implementation of our database program, showing all the constants representing parameter bounds along with two necessary structure types. The first, Metal, is one we presented in Chapter 6 when we first looked at structures. The second, SearchParams, is designed to represent the parameter bounds associated with one query of the database. Our initial algorithm appears as function main.

Function getParams: Problem

This function must initialize the output parameter to values that allow the widest possible search and then let the user change parameters to narrow the search.

Data Definition (getParams)

Parameter

```
params // output parameter to be set by this function (SearchParams&)
```

FIGURE 9.5 Outline and Function main for Metals Database Inquiry Program

```
//
//  Displays all metals in the database that satisfy the search
//  parameters specified by the program user.
//
#include <iostream>
#include <fstream>
#include <string>
#include <iomanip>
using namespace std;

const double MAX_DENSITY = 20.0;   // maximum density (g/cm^3)
const int MAX_MELT_PT = 4000;      // maximum melting point (degrees C)
const int MAX_TENS_MOD = 420;      // maximum tensile modulus (GPa)
const int MAX_DAYS = 90;           // maximum days to delivery

struct Metal {                     // metal structure type
     string name;
     double density;               // g/cm^3
     int    meltPt,                // melting point in degrees C
            tensMod,               // tensile modulus in GPa
            daysToDeliv;           // days from order to delivery
};

struct SearchParams {       // search parameter bounds structure type
     string lowName, highName;
     double lowDensity, highDensity;
     int    lowMeltPt, highMeltPt,
            lowTensMod, highTensMod,
            lowDays, highDays;
};

// Insert prototypes of other functions needed

//
//  Prompts the user to enter changes to the search parameters
//
void getParams(SearchParams& params);

//
//  Displays records of all metals in the inventory that satisfy search
//  parameters.
//
void displayMatch(ifstream& database, const SearchParams& params);
```

FIGURE 9.5 *(Continued)*

```cpp
int main()
{
    string invFileName;    // name of inventory file
    SearchParams params;

    //  Get name of inventory file and open it, if possible
    cout << "Enter name of inventory file> ";
    cin >> invFileName;
    ifstream inventory(invFileName.c_str(), ios::in);

    if (!inventory.fail()) {

        //  Get the search parameters
        getParams(params);

        //  Display all metals that satisfy the search parameters
        displayMatch(inventory, params);

        //  Close the inventory file
        inventory.close();

    } else {

        cerr << "Cannot open file " << invFileName << ".\n";
    }

    return 0;
}
```

Scratch Pad

```
choice // user's menu choice (char)
```

Algorithm Design (getParams)

1. Initialize params to permit widest possible search.
2. Display menu and get response to store in choice.
3. Repeat while choice is not 'q'
    3.1   Select appropriate prompt and get new parameter value
    3.2   Display menu and get response to store in choice.

Implementation (getParams)

We omit the implementation of function getParams because we assign it as an exercise in Review Question 3 at the end of this section. However, Figure 9.6 shows the code for helper functions initializeParams and menuChoose which implement steps 1 and 2 of the algorithm.

Function displayMatch: Problem

This function must examine each file record with a name between the low and high bounds for names. We assume that the records in the database file are ordered so the names are alphabetized. If a record satisfies the search parameters, it is displayed. The function must also display a message if no matches are found.

Data Definition (displayMatch)

Parameters

```
database    // access to file of Metal records (ifstream&)
params      // search parameters to satisfy (const SearchParams&)
```

Scratch Pad

```
nextMetal   // current metal from database (Metal structure)
noMatches   // indicates if no matches found (bool)
```

Algorithm Design (displayMatch)

1. Initialize noMatches to true.
2. Advance to the first metal record in database whose name is within the set search range.
3. While the current name is still within the search range, repeat
   3.1 If the search parameters match, display the metal and set noMatches to false.
   3.2 Get the next metal record.
4. If there were no matches, display a "No metals available" message.

Implementation (displayMatch)

Figure 9.6 includes the code of function displayMatch and its helper function match needed for the condition in Step 3.1, along with an implementation of an overloaded input extraction operator needed for Steps 2 and 3.2. The function show that implements the display aspect of Step 3.1 is left as an exercise at the end of this section. Also shown in Fig. 9.6 are implementations of functions initializeParams and menuChoose mentioned above.

FIGURE 9.6 Functions initializeParams, menuChoose, displayMatch and match, and Operator >>

```cpp
//
//  Initialize parameters to allow widest possible search
//
void initializeParams(SearchParams& params)
{
    params.lowName = "aaaa";
    params.highName = "zzzz";
    params.lowDensity = 0;
    params.highDensity = MAX_DENSITY;
    params.lowMeltPt = 0;
    params.highMeltPt = MAX_MELT_PT;
    params.lowTensMod = 0;
    params.highTensMod = MAX_TENS_MOD;
    params.lowDays = 0;
    params.highDays = MAX_DAYS;
}


//
//  Displays a lettered menu with the current values of search parameters.
//  Returns the letter the user enters.  A letter in the range a..j selects
//  a parameter to change;  q quits, accepting search parameters shown.
//
char menuChoose(const SearchParams& params) // input - current search
                                            // parameter bounds
{
    char choice;

    cout.precision(2);
    cout << "\nSelect by letter a search parameter to set, " <<
        "or enter q to\naccept parameters shown.\n\n";
    cout << "Search Parameter                             " <<
        "Current Value\n";
    cout << " [a]  Low bound for name                     " <<
        params.lowName << endl;
    cout << " [b]  High bound for name                    " <<
        params.highName << endl;
    cout << " [c]  Low bound for density  (g/cm^3)        " <<
        setw(5) << params.lowDensity << endl;
    cout << " [d]  High bound for density (g/cm^3)        " <<
        setw(5) << params.highDensity << endl;
    cout << " [e]  Low bound for melting point  (degrees C)    " <<
        setw(4) << params.lowMeltPt << endl;
```

FIGURE 9.6 *(Continued)*

```
   cout << " [f]  High bound for melting point (degrees C)    " <<
      setw(4) << params.highMeltPt << endl;
   cout << " [g]  Low bound for tensile modulus  (GPa)        " <<
      setw(3) << params.lowTensMod << endl;
   cout << " [h]  High bound for tensile modulus (GPa)        " <<
      setw(3) << params.highTensMod << endl;
   cout << " [i]  Low bound for days to delivery              " <<
      setw(3) << params.lowDays << endl;
   cout << " [j]  High bound for days to delivery             " <<
      setw(3) << params.highDays << endl << endl ;
   cout << "Selection> ";
   for  (cin >> choice;
        !(choice >= 'a' && choice <= 'j' || choice == 'q');
        cin >> choice) {
      cout << "Re-enter selection> ";
   }

   return (choice);
}


//
//  Displays records of all metals in the inventory that satisfy search
//  parameters.
//
void displayMatch(ifstream& database,          // database file
                  const SearchParams& params)  // search parameter bounds
{
   Metal nextMetal;          // current metal from database
   bool   noMatches = true; // flag indicating if no matches have been found

   // Advances to first record with a name the same as or that
   // alphabetically follows the lower bound
   for  (database >> nextMetal;
        !database.fail() && params.lowName > nextMetal.name;
        database >> nextMetal)
      {}

   // Displays a list of the metals that satisfy the search
   // parameters
   cout << "\nMetals satisfying the search parameters:\n";
   while (!database.fail() && nextMetal.name <= params.highName)  {
      if (match(nextMetal, params)) {
         noMatches = false;
```

FIGURE 9.6 *(Continued)*

```
            show(nextMetal);
        }
        database >> nextMetal;
    }

    // Displays a message if no metals found
    if (noMatches)
        cout << "Sorry, no metals available.\n";
}

//
//  Determines whether metal satisfies all search parameters
//
bool match(const Metal& metal,      // input – metal record to check
           const SearchParams& params) // input – parameters to satisfy
{
    return (params.lowDensity <= metal.density  &&
            params.highDensity >= metal.density &&
            params.lowMeltPt <= metal.meltPt    &&
            params.highMeltPt >= metal.meltPt   &&
            params.lowTensMod <= metal.tensMod  &&
            params.highTensMod >= metal.tensMod &&
            params.lowDays <= metal.daysToDeliv &&
            params.highDays >= metal.daysToDeliv);
}

//
//  Input one metal from stream is
//
istream& operator>> (istream& is, Metal& m)
{
    is >> m.name >> m.density >> m.meltPt >> m.tensMod >> m.daysToDeliv;
    return is;
}
```

Section 9.4 Review Questions

1. What values would you use as search parameter bounds to answer the questions listed at the beginning of this section?

2. Which function in our database search program determines whether a particular record satisfies the search parameters? Why does function **match** not need to check a metal's **name** field?

3. Write the functions `getParams` and `show` described in the metals database inquiry program. The algorithm for function `getParams` is on page 395, and Fig. 9.6 shows helper functions `initializeParams` and `menuChoose`, which implement Steps 1 and 2 of the algorithm. Function `show` should display all components of its `const Metal&` parameter with labels.

9.5   Software Designer Beware

Remember to declare an `ifstream` object for every input file you want to process and an `ofstream` object for every output file. If you permit the program user to enter the name of a file to process, you will have two variables identifying the file—one storing its name (a string) and one representing the stream object. It is essential to remember that the only operation in which the file name is used is the call to the stream constructor. Keep in mind that creating an output stream object typically results in a loss of any existing file with the same name.

Before attempting input from or output to a stream, always use the `fail` function to test whether the stream object has been successfully associated with an open file. Provide an explicit error message that includes the file name if the file open is unsuccessful.

C++ expects the programmer to check for input stream errors. You should assume that any numeric input operation could result in an error. Always attempt to recover from the error or, at least, terminate the program with an error message that points out the text line that caused the error. In either case, you will need to detect the error by calling input stream member function `fail`, to clear the error by a call to `clear`, and then to input the rest of the line of text that contains the error by calling function `getline`.

Chapter Review

1. Text files are continuous streams of character codes that can be viewed as broken into lines by the newline character.

2. Processing text files requires the transfer of sequences of characters between disk storage and main memory.

3. The C++ input file class `ifstream` is a specialized kind of `istream`, and the output file class `ofstream` is a specialized kind of `ostream`, so parameters of types `istream` and `ostream` can be matched with arguments of types `ifstream` and `ofstream` respectively.

4. Standard libraries iostream, fstream, and iomanip provide many facilities for stream manipulation, error detection and recovery, and output formatting.

5. A simple database can be implemented as a text file in which all records are of the same user-defined structure type.

▰ New C++ Constructs ▰▰▰▰▰▰▰▰▰▰▰▰▰▰▰▰▰▰▰▰

Construct	*Effect*
Failure Flag Clear Function `infile.clear();`	Clears failure flag set by encountering end of file on `infile`, by a failed input operation, or by a call to `setstate`. Clearing the flag allows further input from `infile`.
Failure Flag Set Function `infile.setstate(ios::failbit);`	Sets `infile`'s failure flag, permitting a user-defined input function or operator to indicate that an input from the file was not in the proper format for a user-defined type.
Exit Function `exit(1);`	Prematurely terminates execution due to an error. From cstdlib library.

PROGRAMMING PROJECTS

1. Write a void function that merges the contents of two text files containing chemical elements sorted by atomic number and produces a sorted file of elements. The function's parameters are references to the two input streams and the output stream. Each text file line will contain an integer atomic number followed by the element name, chemical symbol, and atomic weight. Here are two sample lines:

   ```
   11   Sodium    Na    22.99
   20   Calcium   Ca    40.08
   ```

   The function can assume that one file does not have two copies of the same element and that the binary output file should have this same property. *Hint:* When one of the input files is exhausted, do not forget to copy the remaining elements of the other input file to the result file.

2. Develop a database inquiry program to search a file of aircraft data sorted in descending order by maximum cruise speed. Each aircraft record should include the name (up to 25 characters), maximum cruise speed (in km/h), wing span and length (in m), the character M (for military) or C (for civilian), and a descriptive phrase (up to 80 characters). Your sys-

tem should implement a menu-driven interface that allows the user to search on all components except the descriptive phrase. Here are data for three aircraft to start your database:

```
SR-71 Blackbird          (name)
3500                     (max cruise speed)
16.95  32.74  M          (wing span, length, military/civilian)
high-speed strategic reconnaissance      (descriptive phrase)


EF-111A Raven
2280
19.21  23.16  M
electronic warfare


Concorde
2140
25.61  62.2  C
supersonic airliner
```

3. You are developing a database of measured meteorological data for use in weather and climate research. Define a structure type MeasuredData with components siteIdNumber (a four-digit integer), windSpeed, day-OfMonth, and temperature. Each site measures its data daily, at noon local time. Write a program that inputs a file of MeasuredData records and determines the site with the greatest variation in temperature (defined here as the biggest difference between extrema) and the site with the highest average wind speed for all the days in the file. You may assume that there will be at most ten sites. Test the program on the following July daily data collected over one week at three sites:

ID	Day	Wind Speed (knots)	Temperature (deg C)
2001	10	11	30
2001	11	5	22
2001	12	18	25
2001	13	16	26
2001	14	14	26
2001	15	2	25
2001	16	14	22
3345	10	8	29
3345	11	5	23
3345	12	12	23
3345	13	14	24
3345	14	10	24
3345	15	9	22
3345	16	9	20

3819	10	17	27
3819	11	20	21
3819	12	22	21
3819	13	18	22
3819	14	15	22
3819	15	9	19
3819	16	12	18

4. A sparse matrix is one in which a large number of the elements are zero. Define a SparseMatrix class for a compressed representation of a two-dimensional sparse matrix of integers. Include components rows and cols (matrix dimensions), numNonZero (number of nonzero elements), and nonZeroList (numNonZero-element array in which each element is of class SparseEle, a class with three components: row subscript, column subscript, and value). Overload >> and << operators to allow file I/O of sparse matrices. The file representation should be compressed: The first line should be the matrix dimensions, the second the number of nonzero elements, and the remaining lines should each have three numbers—row subscript, column subscript, and value of one nonzero entry. Also define a constructor for class SparseMatrix that takes a single class Matrix operand (see Fig. 8.9) and creates an equivalent SparseMatrix object.

5. Develop a small airline reservation system. Define a class FlightRecord with the following components:
   a. Flight number (including airline code)
   b. City of departure
   c. Destination
   d. Date and time of departure
   e. Date and time of arrival
   f. Number of first-class seats still available
   g. Number of first-class seats sold
   h. Number of coach seats still available
   i. Number of coach seats sold

   Define a class FlightDatabase that includes a component that is an array of FlightRecord objects. The database of flight information should be kept in a file. Your program should define member functions make-Reservation, cancelReservation, and findFlightData for class FlightDatabase. Functions makeReservation and cancelReservation should take data interactively from the user and modify the FlightDatabase object accordingly. Function findFlightData should also take data in interactively and should display the entire FlightRecord object of the flight desired. Your program should also provide a facility for creating a FlightDatabase object from the data in a file and should overload the << and >> operators for class FlightRecord.

6. Develop a measurement conversion program that can take a measurement in one unit (e.g., 4.5 miles) and convert it to another (e.g., kilometers). Your program should take a database of conversion information from an input file before accepting conversion problems entered interactively by the user. The user should be allowed to specify units either by name (e.g., kilograms) or by abbreviation (e.g., kg). Define a class Unit-Measure with components for the unit's name, abbreviation, category (e.g., mass, distance, volume), and a representation of the unit in terms of the chosen standard unit for its class. This standard unit will be determined by the database file. Here is a brief sample database file:

```
miles        mi        distance      1609.3
kilometers   km        distance      1000
yards        yd        distance      0.9144
meters       m         distance      1
kilograms    kg        mass          1
grams        g         mass          0.001
slugs        slugs     mass          0.1459
```

This sample file uses the meter as the standard unit of distance and the kilogram as the standard unit of mass. Overload the >> operator for class UnitMeasure, and make sure that this operator's definition allows it to recover from a numeric input error: If it encounters a nonnumeric value on input of the number in the last column, >> should display an error message showing the line in which the error was encountered and should then attempt input of the record on the next line.

Introduction to Numerical Methods

10

10.1 Finding Roots of Functions
10.2 Fundamental Statistics
10.3 Numerical Differentiation
10.4 Numerical Integration
10.5 Solving First-Order Differential Equations
10.6 Software Designer Beware
Chapter Review

Numerical analysis is the study of methods for calculating useful solutions to problems expressed mathematically. It is natural to implement such methods on a computer, since they frequently call for repeated numerical computations. We have met examples of numerical methods in earlier chapters:

- Root approximation through repeated bisection of an interval (Section 5.5)
- Solving a system of linear equations by matrix operations (Section 8.3)
- Inverting a matrix (Chapter 8, Programming Project 3)

Numerical methods calculate approximate solutions to a problem rather than exact solutions. Sometimes we use approximation techniques even when we also know how to implement a symbolic solution that will yield an exact result. Of course, if we plan to use our result in performing additional computations, we jeopardize the "exactness" of the value as soon as we store it as a finite-precision, floating point number. Moreover, if an exact solution to a problem were, say $2\sqrt{2}$, we would need to approximate the value of $\sqrt{2}$ before we could make further use of the result. Thus, if calculating an exact solution requires more computer time than computing a good approximate solution, it often makes sense to just compute an approximation in the first place.

numerical analysis
the study of methods for approximating solutions to mathematical problems

This chapter focuses on writing C++ functions to implement a variety of elementary numerical methods. Several of the chapter's programming projects call for you to integrate your study of these methods with your understanding of object-oriented programming by creating classes with member functions that perform numerical approximations.

Before reading this chapter, take a moment to review the discussion of numeric error in Section 2.4. All of the numerical methods we will discuss are affected by representational error and by cancellation error.

10.1 Finding Roots of Functions

We saw in Section 5.5 that solutions of the equation

$$f(x) = 0$$

are called roots or zeros of the function f. In Example 5.6 we searched for such a root by beginning with an interval $[x_{left}, x_{right}]$ known to contain a root because the signs of $f(x_{left})$ and $f(x_{right})$ were different, then repeatedly considering shorter intervals still known to contain a root. When a numerical method is successful in finding an acceptable root approximation, it is said to have **converged** to a root. Failure to find such a root is called **divergence**. One issue that is important to the user of a numerical method is the speed of convergence. This bisection method is usually slower to converge to a root than the root-finding method that we examine next.

convergence
success of a numerical method using a sequence of approximations to find an acceptable solution to a problem

divergence
failure of a numerical method to find an acceptable solution to a problem by means of a sequence of approximations

Newton's method
root-finding method that approximates f (the function whose root is sought) by a tangent to the curve of f in a region close to a root

Newton's Method

The Newton–Raphson method (often called **Newton's method**) of finding a root of a function is based on using a tangent line as an approximation of $f(x)$ near points at which the function value is zero. To apply the method, guess an initial approximation to a root of

$$f(x) = 0$$

Call your guess x_0. Then calculate the next approximation x_1 using the formula

$$x_1 = x_0 - \frac{f(x_0)}{f'(x_0)}$$

where $f'(x_0)$ is the first derivative of f at x_0. In general, compute each new approximation x_{n+1} from the previous approximation x_n by applying the formula

Newton's Method

$$x_{n+1} = x_n - \frac{f(x_n)}{f'(x_n)}$$

We will use Fig. 10.1 to illustrate the derivation of this formula that calculates x_{n+1} based on x_n and on functions f and f'. The figure shows a heavy line that is tangent to the curve $y = f(x)$ at the point $(x_n, f(x_n))$. The slope of this line (m) is the value of f's first derivative evaluated at x_n:

$$m = f'(x_n)$$

Alternatively, since m is also the slope of the line connecting $(x_n, f(x_n))$ and $(x_{n+1}, 0)$, we could define it as the change in y divided by the change in x:

$$m = \frac{0 - f(x_n)}{x_{n+1} - x_n}$$

Replacing m by $f'(x_n)$ and performing some algebraic manipulations,

$$f'(x_n) = \frac{-f(x_n)}{x_{n+1} - x_n}$$

$$f'(x_n)(x_{n+1} - x_n) = -f(x_n)$$

$$x_{n+1} - x_n = \frac{-f(x_n)}{f'(x_n)}$$

$$x_{n+1} = x_n - \frac{f(x_n)}{f'(x_n)}$$

we derive the iterative formula for Newton's method.

FIGURE 10.1 Illustration of Derivation of Newton's Method Formula

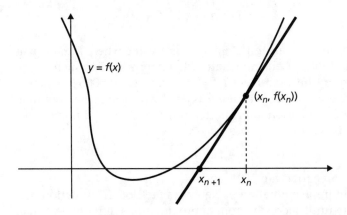

TABLE 10.1 Using Newton's Method to Approximate a Root of $f(x) = x^3 + 3x^2 - 6x - 8$

n	x_n (guess = 1.0)	x_n (guess = 1.5)
0	1.00000	1.50000
1	4.33333	2.20512
2	2.97476	2.01814
3	2.27097	2.00016
4	2.03033	2.00000
5	2.00044	2.00000
6	2.00000	2.00000
7	2.00000	2.00000

Let's apply Newton's method to approximate a root of

$$f(x) = x^3 + 3x^2 - 6x - 8$$

We know there must be a root between $x = 0$ ($f(0) = -8$) and $x = 3$ ($f(3) = 27 + 27 - 18 - 8 = 28$), so let's try guesses of 1.0 and 1.5. We generate Table 10.1 using

$$f'(x) = 3x^2 + 6x - 6$$

This table illustrates that for initial guesses that are close to a root, Newton's method can converge very rapidly, as it does for the guesses 1.5 and 1.0. When $x = 2.0$, $x^3 + 3x^2 - 6x - 8$ does indeed equal zero.

However, some initial guesses do not lead to rapid convergence to a root. We can anticipate where the areas of difficulty would lie by looking again at our iterative formula:

$$x_{n+1} = x_n - \frac{f(x_n)}{f'(x_n)}$$

Clearly we are in trouble if our initial guess x_0 is a value where $f'(x_0)$ equals or approaches zero. Table 10.2 demonstrates what happens when such an initial guess is chosen. In this example, $f'(x) = 3x^2 + 6x - 6 = 0.000528$ when $x_0 = 0.732$. In this instance, our initial guess was far closer to an actual root than is our Newton's approximation after six iterations. Because the polynomial we are calling f factors into

$$(x - 2)(x + 1)(x + 4)$$

we know that our three roots are 2, –1, and –4.

Figure 10.2 is an implementation of Newton's method as a function that continues to iterate until successive root approximations differ by less than

TABLE 10.2 A Guess That Causes Newton's Method to Perform Poorly

n	x_n (guess = 0.732)
0	0.73200
1	−19681.
2	−13261.
3	−8840.9
4	−5894.3
5	−3929.9
6	−2620.2
7	−1747.2

FIGURE 10.2 Function That Implements Newton's Method of Finding a Root of *f*

```
//
//  Uses Newton's method to approximate a root of function f (assumes
//  fPrime is first derivative of f);  sets converges to false if
//  convergence not achieved in MAX_ITER iterations.
//
double newton( double xGuess, double okError, bool& converges )
{
    const int MAX_ITER = 25;

    double xN, xNplus1, absDiff;
    int    iter = 0;

    xN = xGuess;
    do {
        ++iter;
        xNplus1 = xN − f( xN ) / fPrime( xN );
        absDiff = fabs( xN − xNplus1);
        xN = xNplus1;
    } while (absDiff >= okError  &&  iter < MAX_ITER);

    if (absDiff < okError) {
        converges = true;
        return xN;
    } else {
        cout << "Newton's method did not converge to a root of f "
            << "in " << MAX_ITER << endl << "iterations using an initial"
            << " guess of " << xGuess << endl;
        converges = false;
        return xGuess;
    }
}
```

the value of parameter okError. However, the implementation also calls for iterative approximation to cease if convergence to an acceptable approximation is not achieved in 25 iterations. Figure 10.3 shows a program to test function newton. Functions f and fPrime are defined as in our examples on which Tables 10.1 and 10.2 are based. The figure ends with five runs of the program. The first two use the initial guesses illustrated in Table 10.1, and the third uses a guess that is very close to a root of f'. The last two runs demonstrate the method's ability to find the polynomial's other two roots.

FIGURE 10.3   Program That Tests Function newton

```cpp
#include <iostream>
#include <iomanip>
#include <cmath>
using namespace std;

double f( double );   // function whose root is sought
double fPrime( double ); // f'
double newton( double, double, bool&);

int main()
{
   const double MAX_ERROR = 0.00001;
   double rootGuess;
   bool    rootFound;
   double rootApprox;

   cout << "Enter an initial guess for a root of f => ";
   cin >> rootGuess;
   rootApprox = newton( rootGuess, MAX_ERROR, rootFound );
   cout << setiosflags( ios::fixed ) <<
       setprecision( 5 );
   if (rootFound) {
      cout << "Starting with an initial guess of " << rootGuess <<
         ", Newton's method " << endl << "approximates a root of f at "
         << rootApprox << endl;
      cout << "f( " << rootApprox << " ) = " << f(rootApprox) << endl;
   }
   return 0;
}


// Definition of function newton goes here
```

FIGURE 10.3 *(Continued)*

```
//   3      2
//   x   + 3x    - 6x - 8
//
double f( double x )
{
    return ( x * x * x + 3 * x * x - 6 * x - 8 );
}


//     2
//   3x   + 6x  -  6
//
double fPrime( double x )
{
    return ( 3 * x * x + 6 * x - 6 );
}
```

Five Runs with Different Guesses

```
Enter an initial guess for a root of f => 1.0
Starting with an initial guess of 1.00000, Newton's method
approximates a root of f at 2.00000
f( 2.00000 ) = 0.00000


Enter an initial guess for a root of f => 1.5
Starting with an initial guess of 1.50000, Newton's method
approximates a root of f at 2.00000
f( 2.00000 ) = 0.00000


Enter an initial guess for a root of f => .7321
Newton's method did not converge to a root of f in 25
iterations using an initial guess of 0.7321


Enter an initial guess for a root of f => 0
Starting with an initial guess of 0.00000, Newton's method
approximates a root of f at -1.00000
f( -1.00000 ) = 0.00000


Enter an initial guess for a root of f => -10
Starting with an initial guess of -10.00000, Newton's method
approximates a root of f at -4.00000
f( -4.00000 ) = 0.00000
```

FIGURE 10.4 Meaning of the Secant Method Root-Approximation Formula

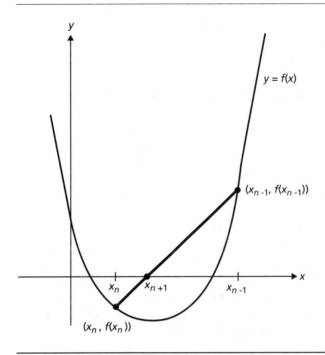

Secant Method

secant method

root-finding method that approximates f (the function whose root is sought) by a line joining two points known to be on the curve of f

The **secant method** is another iterative approach to approximating roots of functions. Its formula computes x_{n+1} based on x_n and x_{n-1}:

Secant Method

$$x_{n+1} = \frac{x_{n-1}\big(f(x_n)\big) - x_n\big(f(x_{n-1})\big)}{f(x_n) - f(x_{n-1})}$$

The method's name comes from the fact that x_{n+1} is the point at which a line through $(x_{n-1}, f(x_{n-1}))$ and $(x_n, (f(x_n))$ crosses the x axis (see Fig. 10.4). Programming Project 1 asks you to implement this numerical method.

Section 10.1 Review Questions

1. Determine the results displayed by these calls to function **newton** of Fig. 10.2

```
cout << setprecision( 5 ) << setiosflags( ios::fixed );
cout << newton( 1.0, 0.0001, found ) << endl;
```

```
cout << newton( -1.0, 0.0001, found ) << endl;
cout << newton( 10.0, 0.0001, found ) << endl;
cout << newton( -10.0, 0.0001, found ) << endl;
```

if functions **f** and **fPrime** are defined as

$$f(x) = 2x^2 - 2x - 1.5$$
$$f'(x) = 4x - 2$$

2. Using $x_0 = 1.5$ and $x_1 = 1.0$, complete the following table using the secant method. Use $f(x) = x^3 + 3x^2 - 6x - 8$, the same function on which Table 10.1 is based.

x_0	1.5
x_1	1.0
x_2	
x_3	
x_4	
x_5	
x_6	
x_7	
x_8	
x_9	
x_{10}	

10.2 Fundamental Statistics

This section develops C++ functions for a few of the fundamental statistics commonly used by engineers and scientists for analysis and description of sets of data.

Arithmetic Mean

The most popular single-number characterization of a set of data is the **arithmetic mean**, or average. Figure 10.5 is a C++ function that returns the arithmetic mean of a list of numbers stored in an array. This function is very straightforward: It simply adds up the list of data and divides by the number of items:

arithmetic mean ($\bar{x}$)
average of the values in a data set

Arithmetic Mean
$$\bar{x} = \frac{\sum x_i}{n}$$

The notation $\bar{x}$ is commonly used to denote the average of all x_i in a data set.

FIGURE 10.5 Function That Computes an Arithmetic Mean

```
//
//   Computes the arithmetic mean (average) of the first size
//   elements of list
//      Pre:  size > 0
//
double arithmeticMean( const double list[], int size )
{
   int i;
   double sum = 0;

   for  (i = 0;  i < size;  ++i)
       sum += list[i];

   return (sum / size);
}
```

FIGURE 10.6 Two Sets of Quiz Scores with the Same Arithmetic Mean

Quiz 1	Quiz 2
10	7
9	7
7	6
5	6
4	5
1	5

Standard Deviation

Of course, quite different data sets can have the very same arithmetic mean. Consider the two lists of quiz scores shown in Fig. 10.6, both of which have the mean 6.0. The scores for Quiz 1 are much more spread out than the Quiz 2 scores. The **standard deviation** of a data set is a measure of the spread of the values.

standard deviation (s)
a statistic that measures the spread of the values in a data set

To find the standard deviation of a data set, you do the following calculations:

1. Subtract the mean from each data value to determine the value's deviation from the mean.
2. Square each deviation.

3. Average the squared deviations.
4. Take the square root of this average.

Thus the formula for the standard deviation of an n-element data set is

> **Standard Deviation**
>
> $$s = \sqrt{\frac{\sum (x_i - \bar{x})^2}{n}}$$

Looking back at Fig. 10.6, we can now calculate the standard deviations of the two sets of quiz scores:

Quiz 1

$$s = \sqrt{\frac{(10-6)^2 + (9-6)^2 + (7-6)^2 + (5-6)^2 + (4-6)^2 + (1-6)^2}{6}}$$

$$= \sqrt{\frac{4^2 + 3^2 + 1^2 + (-1)^2 + (-2)^2 + (-5)^2}{6}} = \sqrt{\frac{56}{6}} \approx 3.055$$

Quiz 2

$$s = \sqrt{\frac{(7-6)^2 + (7-6)^2 + (6-6)^2 + (6-6)^2 + (5-6)^2 + (5-6)^2}{6}}$$

$$= \sqrt{\frac{1^2 + 1^2 + 0^2 + 0^2 + (-1)^2 + (-1)^2}{6}} = \sqrt{\frac{4}{6}} \approx 0.816$$

Thus the standard deviation of the more spread-out set of quiz scores is higher than the standard deviation of the other set of scores. Figure 10.7 shows a function that implements our standard deviation formula.

Linear Regression

Engineers are often called upon to predict the outcome of a certain event based on their past experiences. Most practical applications, however, involve a large number of variables that influence the analysis of possible outcomes. Statisticians call the outcome that one wishes to predict the **dependent variable** and the variables influencing or providing explanation of the outcome the **independent variables**. **Regression analysis** is the study of the relationship between the dependent and independent variables. It proceeds by first selecting a model to link the variables and then fitting this

dependent variable
outcome of a certain event that one tries to predict using regression analysis

independent variable
a variable that influences or explains the outcome of a certain event

regression analysis
analysis of the relationship between dependent and independent variables

FIGURE 10.7 Function That Computes Standard Deviation

```cpp
#include <cmath>

//
//  Calculates standard deviation of first size elements of any list
//      Pre:  size > 0
//
double stDev( const double list[], int size )
{
    double mean;              // arithmetic mean
    double dev;               // deviation of one list element from mean
    double devSqrSum = 0;     // sum of squares of deviations
    int    i;

    mean = arithmeticMean( list, size );   // function defined in Fig. 10.5

    for  (i = 0;  i < size;  ++i) {
        dev = list[i] − mean;
        devSqrSum += dev * dev;
    }

    return (sqrt( devSqrSum / size ));
}
```

model to the data. If the model fits well enough to be considered useful, it can then be used to predict the value of the dependent variable in light of given values for the independent variables.

linear regression

analysis that models as a straight line the relationship between a single dependent variable and a single independent variable

In the simplest form of regression analysis, **linear regression**, a single dependent variable y is related to a single independent variable x, and the relationship is modeled as a straight line,

$$y = mx + b$$

where m (the slope) and b (the y-intercept) are constants called the *linear regression coefficients*. When we fit the model to the data, we seek the line that is the best abstraction for our collection of (x, y) data points.

Figure 10.8 illustrates one step in the most commonly used approach to determining this line—the method of *least squares*. A small class of six students takes a calculus midterm. While recording their scores, the professor notices that the students' standardized mathematics aptitude scores are also available and so decides to try to predict the midterm score of a seventh student, who was absent. The following are the aptitude and midterm scores of the six who were present:

Aptitude	Midterm
50	47
60	41
75	75
77	65
86	88
96	89

Figure 10.8 displays the six points defined by the coordinates (x_i, y_i), where x_i is the ith student's math aptitude score and y_i is the ith student's calculus midterm score. Each d_i is the deviation between y_i, an actual y, and the y value predicted by the regression line $y = mx + b$. Calculation of m and b uses these formulas:

$$\text{Linear Regression Coefficients}$$

$$m = \frac{\sum (x_i - \bar{x})(y_i - \bar{y})}{\sum (x_i - \bar{x})^2}$$

$$b = \bar{y} - m\bar{x}$$

FIGURE 10.8 Fitting a Least-Squares Regression Line to a Data Set

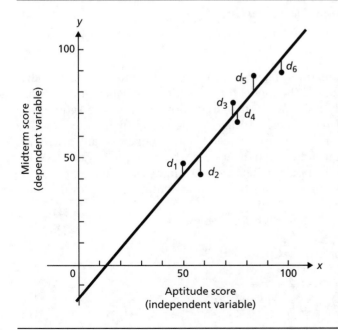

TABLE 10.3 Calculating Regression Coefficients m and b for Aptitude/Midterm Regression Study

	x_i	y_i	$x_i - \bar{x}$	$y_i - \bar{y}$	$(x_i - \bar{x})(y_i - \bar{y})$	$(x_i - \bar{x})^2$
	50	47	−24	−20.5	492	576
	60	41	−14	−26.5	371	196
	75	75	1	7.5	7.5	1
	77	65	3	−2.5	−7.5	9
	86	88	12	20.5	246	144
	96	89	22	21.5	473	484
Sum					1582	1410
Mean	74	67.5				

$$m = \frac{1582}{1410} \approx 1.122$$

$$b = 67.5 - (1.122)74 \approx -15.528$$

The absent calculus student had a math aptitude score of 81. Table 10.3 shows the intermediate calculations and the equations that the professor used to predict a midterm score of

$$y = 1.122(81) - 15.528 \approx 75$$

In the Review Questions, you will implement the formulas for m and b in a function with two output parameters.

Correlation

correlation coefficient (r)
a statistic indicating how well a line models the relationship between a dependent variable and an independent variable

In our description of regression analysis, we noted that after fitting a model to the data, we should use the model for predicting the behavior of the dependent variable only if the model fits "well enough." This subsection presents a statistic called the **correlation coefficient**, which measures the strength of the linear relationship between y and x. Engineers and scientists often use correlation techniques to determine why a complex system is failing. They look for a relationship between the times when problems occur and some other measurable quantities such as temperature, pressure, humidity, or wind velocity.

The correlation coefficient r is calculated as:

Correlation Coefficient

$$r = \frac{n\sum x_i y_i - \sum x_i \sum y_i}{\sqrt{n\sum x_i^2 - \left(\sum x_i\right)^2}\sqrt{n\sum y_i^2 - \left(\sum y_i\right)^2}}$$

FIGURE 10.9 A Sample of Patterns of Data Distribution

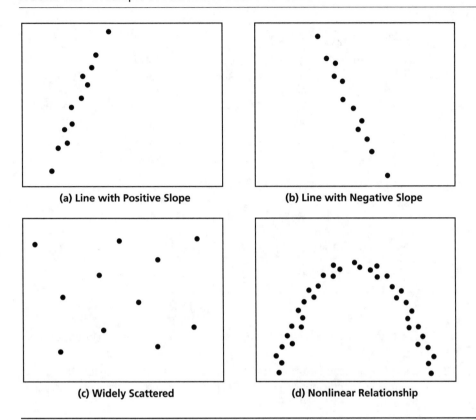

(a) Line with Positive Slope

(b) Line with Negative Slope

(c) Widely Scattered

(d) Nonlinear Relationship

This statistic always falls in the range $-1 \ldots 1$. A value close to 1 results when the data are all close to a line with positive slope, as illustrated in Fig. 10.9(a). A correlation coefficient close to -1 indicates that the data are close to a line with negative slope (see Fig. 10.9b). Widely scattered data (Fig. 10.9c) and data for variables related in a nonlinear fashion (Fig. 10.9d) yield correlation coefficients near 0. Table 10.4 shows the calculation of the correlation coefficient for the data relating aptitude and midterm scores.

Section 10.2 Review Questions

1. Define a C++ function named **linRegress** that uses the least-squares line fitting method to approximate the slope (*m*) and *y*-intercept (*b*) of a line fitted to a data set defined by an array of *y* values, an array of corresponding *x* values, and the size of the arrays. Use reference parameters to return the linear regression co-

TABLE 10.4 Calculating Correlation Coefficient r for Aptitude/Midterm Regression Study

	x_i	y_i	$x_i y_i$	x_i^2	y_i^2
	50	47	2350	2500	2209
	60	41	2460	3600	1681
	75	75	5625	5625	5625
	77	65	5005	5929	4225
	86	88	7568	7396	7744
	96	89	8544	9216	7921
Sum	444	405	31552	34266	29405

$$r = \frac{(6)(31552) - (444)(405)}{\sqrt{(6)(34266) - (444)^2}\sqrt{(6)(29405) - (405)^2}}$$

$$= \frac{9492}{\sqrt{8460}\sqrt{12405}} \approx 0.93$$

efficients (m and b) calculated. Write a main function that tests `linRegress` on the data from Table 10.3.

2. Define a C++ function `correl` that calculates and returns as the function value the correlation coefficient of a set of (x, y) points defined by arrays of x and y values and their size.

10.3 Numerical Differentiation

Engineers and scientists frequently deal with functions for which they have no formulas. Rather, the function is represented as a collection of data points. For example, Table 10.5 represents the distance traveled by a vehicle as a function of time. If we would like to know the vehicle's velocity at any of the times t, we would need to estimate the rate of change of the distance function over time. This rate of change of f is called the first derivative of f, dy/dx, or f'. If function f were represented by an equation, we could apply the

TABLE 10.5 Distance Traveled by a Vehicle as a Function of Time

t (min)	0	1	2	3	4	5	6
$f(t)$ (km)	0	0.3	1.2	2.7	4.5	6.3	8.1

techniques of elementary calculus to find the first derivative. In the absence of an equation defining f, we can approximate the value of $f'(t)$ as the slope of the line through the points $(t - h, f(t - h))$ and $(t + h, f(t + h))$ where h is a constant representing the difference between successive t values. In Fig. 10.10, we see the line segment whose slope is used to approximate $f'(2)$.

Thus, we can approximate $f'(1)$, $f'(2)$, $f'(3)$, $f'(4)$, and $f'(5)$ using the central difference formula

Central Difference Formula

$$f'(t) \approx \frac{f(t+h) - f(t-h)}{2h}$$

However, the best approximation of $f'(0)$ that we can compute is the slope of the line through $(0, f(0))$ and $(1, f(1))$, a slope calculated by the forward difference formula:

Forward Difference Formula

$$f'(t) \approx \frac{f(t+h) - f(t)}{h}$$

FIGURE 10.10 Approximating $f'(2)$ Using Central Difference Formula

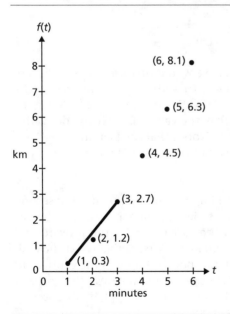

TABLE 10.6 Approximation of First Derivative

t (min)	0	1	2	3	4	5	6
$f(t)$ (km)	0	0.3	1.2	2.7	4.5	6.3	8.1
$f'(t)$ (km/min)	0.3	0.6	1.2	1.65	1.8	1.8	1.8

We can use the backward difference formula to approximate $f'(6)$. Table 10.6 shows the approximation of $f'(t)$ for the function of Table 10.5.

Backward Difference Formula

$$f'(t) \approx \frac{f(t) - f(t-h)}{h}$$

Whereas the first derivative gives the rate of change of one variable with respect to another, the second derivative can be thought of as an acceleration—the rate of change of the velocity in the previous example. A second derivative based on three values—$f(t-h)$, $f(t)$, and $f(t+h)$—can be approximated using the following formula:

Second Derivative Formula

$$f''(t) \approx \frac{f(t+h) - 2f(t) + f(t-h)}{h^2}$$

To check the validity of this formula, we would first find the equation of a parabola through the three points, $(t-h, f(t-h))$, $(t, f(t))$, and $(t+h, f(t+h))$. The equation shown is the second derivative of the parabola. Since the parabola is close to f near the point $(t, f(t))$, the value of its second derivative at t is a reasonable approximation of $f''(t)$. Notice that calculation of each second derivative value requires knowledge of three data points.

EXAMPLE 10.1 The program in Fig. 10.11 approximates the first and second derivatives of a function represented by a series of data points such as the distance function of Table 10.5. The fPrime function uses the forward and backward difference formulas to approximate the first derivative at the endpoints of the list of data values. For interior points it applies the central difference formula. Function fDoublePrime approximates the second derivative of the function represented by array fOfT by applying the second derivative formula to all the interior data points. ∎

FIGURE 10.11 Numerical Approximation of First and Second Derivatives

```cpp
#include <iostream>
#include <iomanip>
using namespace std;

const int MAX = 7;

void fPrime( double [], const double [], int );
void fDoublePrime( double [], const double [], int );

int main()
{
   double fOfT[] = { 0, 0.3, 1.2, 2.7, 4.5, 6.3, 8.1 };
   double fstDeriv[MAX];
   double scndDeriv[MAX];
   int    i;

   // Display heading, data, first and second derivatives
   cout << "    Approximation of f' and f''" << endl;
   cout << "t(min)           ";

   for  (i = 0;  i < MAX;  ++i)
      cout << setw( 8 ) << i;
   cout << endl;

   cout << "f(t) (km)        ";
   cout << setiosflags( ios::fixed ) << setprecision( 2 );
   for  (i = 0;  i < MAX;  ++i)
      cout << setw( 8 ) << fOfT[i];
   cout << endl;

   cout << "f'(t) (km/min)    ";
   fPrime( fstDeriv, fOfT, MAX );
   for  (i = 0;  i < MAX;  ++i)
      cout << setw( 8 ) << fstDeriv[i];
   cout << endl;

   cout << "f''(t) (km/min/min)";
   cout << setw( 8 ) << " ";
   fDoublePrime( scndDeriv, fOfT, MAX);
   for  (i = 1;  i < MAX - 1;  ++i)
      cout << setw( 8 ) << scndDeriv[i];
   cout << endl;
   return 0;
}
```

FIGURE 10.11 *(Continued)*

```
//  Approximate the first derivative of function represented by the
//  first size elements of fOfX.  fOfX[0] represents f(0), fOfX[1] is
//  the observed value for f(1), and so on.
//     Pre: size >= 2
//
void fPrime( double firstDeriv[],  // output — first derivative values
             const double fOfX[],  // input  — array of f(0), f(1),...
             int size )            // input  — number of array elements
{
   int i;

   //  Forward difference
   firstDeriv[0] = fOfX[1] — fOfX[0];

   //  Central difference
   for  (i = 1;  i < size — 1;  ++i)
       firstDeriv[i] = (fOfX[i + 1] — fOfX[i — 1]) / 2.0;

   //  Backward difference
   firstDeriv[size — 1] = fOfX[size — 1] — fOfX[size — 2];
}


//
//  Approximate the second derivative of the function represented by
//  array fOfX.  Formula cannot be applied at endpoints, so
//  secondDeriv[0] and secondDeriv[size — 1] are left undefined.
//     Pre: size >= 2
//
void fDoublePrime( double secondDeriv[], // output — 2nd derivative array
                   const double fOfX[],  // input  — f(0), f(1), ...
                   int size )            // input  — number of array
                                         //          elements
{
   int i;

   for  (i = 1;  i < size — 1;  ++i)
       secondDeriv[i] = fOfX[i + 1] — 2 * fOfX[i] + fOfX[i — 1];
}
```

Sample Run

```
     Approximation of f' and f''
t(min)                 0     1     2     3     4     5     6
f(t) (km)           0.00  0.30  1.20  2.70  4.50  6.30  8.10
f'(t) (km/min)      0.30  0.60  1.20  1.65  1.80  1.80  1.80
f''(t) (km/min/min)       0.60  0.60  0.30  0.00  0.00
```

Section 10.3 Review Questions

1. Assume that the vehicle that is the subject of Table 10.5 accelerated from rest at a constant rate of 0.6 km/min² until it achieved a cruising speed of 1.8 km/min and then maintained this speed. Remembering that

$$distance = {}^1/_2 \times acceleration \times time^2$$
$$finalVelocity = acceleration \times time$$

   the function f would be defined as

$$f(t) = \begin{cases} \dfrac{0.6}{2}t^2 & 0 \le t \le 3 \\[2mm] 2.7 + 1.8(t-3) & t > 3 \end{cases}$$

   Compute the error (*exact – approximation*) in the approximated derivative values shown in Table 10.6.

2. Extend the program in Fig. 10.11 so it approximates f'' in two ways: once using the second derivative formula and once by calling **fPrime** twice to take the first derivative of the first derivative values.

10.4 Numerical Integration

The definite integral of a function $f(x)$ from $x = a$ to $x = b$ is the area under the curve of the function bounded by the lines $x = a$, $x = b$, and by the x axis (see shaded region of Fig. 10.12a). We write this integral as

$$\int_a^b f(x)\,dx$$

FIGURE 10.12 Definite Integral Represents Area "Under" a Curve

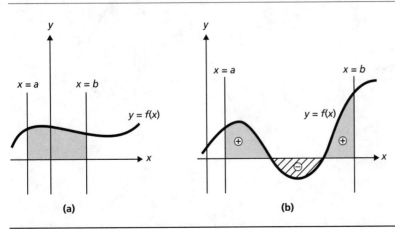

(a)   (b)

If the curve of the function dips below the x axis for x values between a and b, then the area "under" the curve in that region is the negative of the area between the curve and the x axis (see striped region of Fig. 10.12b).

Elementary calculus teaches a method for calculating a definite integral when an antiderivative of the function is known. However, many functions do not have easily calculated antiderivatives, and many others have anti-derivatives that produce results that ultimately require approximation. We can estimate the value of the definite integral of any continuous function by slicing the region under the curve into many equal-width subregions, ap-proximating the function by another curve on each subregion so we can compute the smaller area under this curve, and then adding up the areas of the subregions to calculate our approximation of the whole definite integral. Figure 10.13 illustrates this approach applied to approximating one definite integral.

In this case we are approximating our function f from $f(x_i)$ to $f(x_{i+1})$ as the line from $(x_i, f(x_i))$ to $(x_{i+1}, f(x_{i+1}))$. The subregions that we created in Fig. 10.13 are trapezoids (or triangles, which are simply trapezoids whose fourth side has length zero), figures whose area we know to be $\frac{h}{2}(f(x_i) + f(x_{i+1}))$ (half the base times the sum of the heights). This area will be negative if the curve is below the x axis in the region x_i to x_{i+1} because $f(x_i)$ and $f(x_{i+1})$ will be neg-ative. If we add up all of the subregion areas, we have

$$\tfrac{h}{2}[f(x_0) + f(x_1) + f(x_1) + f(x_2) + \ldots + f(x_{n-2}) + f(x_{n-1}) + f(x_{n-1}) + f(x_n)]$$

FIGURE 10.13 Approximating the Area Under a Curve with Trapezoids

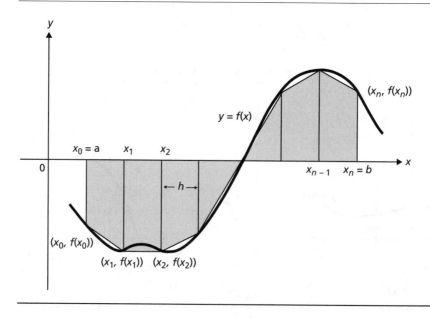

Noting that $f(x_0) = a$ and that $f(x_n) = b$, this simplifies to what is called the **trapezoidal rule**.

trapezoidal rule
method of approximating a definite integral by representing as a trapezoid each of many small slices of the area under the curve

> Trapezoidal Rule
>
> $$\int_a^b f(x)\,dx \approx \frac{h}{2}\left[f(a) + f(b) + 2\sum_{i=1}^{n-1} f(x_i) \right]$$
>
> where the interval $[a, b]$ is divided into n subintervals
>
> of length $h = \dfrac{b - a}{n}$

In theory, the smaller the value of h, the better our approximation of the definite integral will be, since the more trapezoids we use, the better they fit the curve. However, when h becomes very small, the error inherent in the numerical method becomes less important than the representational error present in a fixed-size memory cell and the cancellation error resulting from adding quantities of very different magnitudes. Figure 10.14 shows a function trapezoid that approximates the definite integral of function f from a to b using n subintervals.

FIGURE 10.14 Function That Applies the Trapezoidal Rule to Approximate a Definite Integral

```
//
//  Approximates the definite integral of f from a to b using the
//  trapezoidal rule with n subintervals.
//      Pre:  a < b,   n >= 1
double trapezoidal( double a,    // endpoints of interval of
                    double b,    //    integration
                    int    n )   // number of trapezoids
{
    double h;
    double sum;
    int    i;

    h = (b - a) / n;
    sum = f(a) + f(b);

    for  (i = 1;   i < n;   ++i)
        sum += 2 * f( a + i * h );

    return (h / 2.0 * sum);
}
```

We can apply an adaptation of the trapezoidal rule to approximate the definite integral of a function represented as a collection of observed data points, even if the subintervals are not of a uniform size. In this situation, we simply add the areas of the actual trapezoids. The area of each trapezoid is

$$\frac{1}{2}(x_{i+1} - x_i)(f(x_i) + f(x_{i+1}))$$

Simpson's Rule

Simpson's rule

method of approximating a definite integral of a function by using parabolas to model small segments of the function

If we desire a better approximation than the trapezoidal rule provides, we can use a curve that fits a slice of our function better than a line segment does. In the definite-integral approximation algorithm called **Simpson's rule**, we divide the integration interval into an even number of subintervals and fit parabolic curves (quadratic equations) to sets of three points: $(x_i, f(x_i))$, $(x_{i+1}, f(x_{i+1}))$, $(x_{i+2}, f(x_{i+2}))$. We calculate the area under the parabola between $x = x_i$ and $x = x_{i+2}$, under the parabola between $x = x_{i+2}$ and $x = x_{i+4}$, and so on. Simpson's Rule is often used by scientific calculators to approximate definite integrals.

Simpson's Rule

$$\int_a^b f(x)\,dx \approx \frac{h}{3}\Big(f(a) + f(b) + 4\big[f(x_1) + f(x_3) + \cdots + f(x_{n-1})\big] + 2\big[f(x_2) + f(x_4) + \cdots + f(x_{n-2})\big]\Big)$$

$$h = \frac{b-a}{n} \quad \text{and} \quad n \text{ must be even}$$

A Simpson's rule implementation will include a loop that evaluates f at x_1, x_3, x_5, ..., x_{n-1} (i.e., at all the x values with odd subscripts) and adds up these function values. Similarly, it must add up the values of f at x_2, x_4, x_6, ..., x_{n-2} [i.e., at all the x values with even subscripts except the interval endpoints $a(x_0)$ and $b(x_n)$].

Section 10.4 Review Questions

1. Define function `simpson` to implement Simpson's rule.
2. Write a program that uses both functions `trapezoid` and `simpson` to approximate

$$\int_{1.0}^{2.0} \frac{dx}{x}$$

for $n = 2$, 4, and 6. Your program should display the exact value of the definite integral (given that $\int_a^b \frac{dx}{x} = \ln b - \ln a$) and calculate the error in each approximation (*exact* – *approx*). Display your results in a table with these headings:

n	Exact	Trapezoidal Approx	Error	Simpson's Approx	Error

Before you run your program, predict its output for $n = 2$.

10.5 Solving First-Order Differential Equations

Mathematical modeling of the world around us frequently calls for the recovery of a function from knowledge of its rate of change—that is, the solution of a differential equation. Differential equations arise when we study concentration changes in chemical reactions, current flow in circuits, particle motion, population growth, environmental change, and heating and cooling of objects. Many differential equations can and should be solved analytically, using the techniques of calculus. However, for a first-order ordinary differential equation that resists analytical solution, there are numerical methods that we can apply to approximate a solution. In this section, we first study the Euler method and then investigate the Runge–Kutta method—an approach that is both more accurate and more complex than the Euler method.

A differential equation involves the derivative of a function y of x, a derivative that may be a function of x,

$$\frac{dy}{dx} = f(x)$$

or of x and y,

$$\frac{dy}{dx} = f(x, y)$$

or of y,

$$\frac{dy}{dx} = f(y)$$

Examples of first-order ordinary differential equations include

$$\frac{dy}{dx} = \sin x$$

$$\frac{dy}{dx} = 1 - \frac{y}{x}$$

$$\frac{dy}{dx} = x^2 + y^2$$

The first two of these equations can be solved analytically, but there is no closed-form algebraic solution to the third for all values of x and y.

To find a function y that solves a differential equation, we must know the function's value y_0 at some point x_0. Because of the need to know this initial value (x_0, y_0), differential equation problems are also called *initial value problems*.

Euler Method

Euler method

fairly simple method of solving a first-order differential equation; of recovering an approximation of a function f from its first derivative and an initial value

The **Euler method** approximates a solution to an initial value problem of the form

$$\frac{dy}{dx} = f(x, y), \qquad y(x_0) = y_0$$

by "growing" function y one step at a time beginning from the point (x_0, y_0) and using the rate of change computed by the known derivative f. Figure 10.15 illustrates how the Euler method begins from the initial value (x_0, y_0) and takes a step along the tangent to function y's curve, a tangent whose slope can be computed by evaluating $f(x_0, y_0)$. Thus the method approximates

FIGURE 10.15 Euler Approximation of Function y Given $dy/dx = f(x, y)$ and $y(x_0) = y_0$

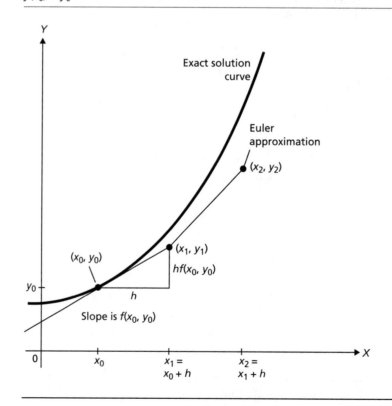

$$y(x_1) = y(x_0 + h) \quad \text{as} \quad y_0 + hf(x_0, y_0)$$

At the point (x_1, y_1), a new tangent is constructed whose slope is $f(x_1, y_1)$, and

$$y(x_2) = y(x_1 + h)$$

is approximated as

$$y_1 + hf(x_1, y_1)$$

In general, the Euler method computes each new approximation from the previous one as shown below.

Euler Method

$$x_{n+1} = x_n + h$$
$$y_{n+1} = y_n + hf(x_n, y_n)$$

If h is very small, the approximation may closely follow the actual $y(x)$ curve initially, but errors will accumulate as we take more steps.

EXAMPLE 10.2   Table 10.7 shows five iterations of the Euler method on the differential equation

$$\frac{dy}{dx} = x + y - 1, \qquad (x_0, y_0) = (0, 1)$$

with $h = 0.1$. Using

$$y(x) = e^x - x$$

as an analytical solution to the differential equation, the table also shows exact y values to five decimal places for each x and includes a column showing the error (*exact – approximation*) in the approximations.   ■

TABLE 10.7   Euler Approximation of Function y Given $dy/dx = x + y - 1$, $(x_0, y_0) = (0, 1)$, $h = 0.1$

n	x_n	Computation of y_n (approx)	y_n (approx)	y_n (exact)	Error
0	0.0	Given	1.00000		
1	0.1	$1.0 + 0.1(0.0 + 1.0 - 1)$	1.00000	1.00517	0.00517
2	0.2	$1.0 + 0.1(0.1 + 1.0 - 1)$	1.01000	1.02140	0.01140
3	0.3	$1.01 + 0.1(0.2 + 1.01 - 1)$	1.03100	1.04986	0.01886
4	0.4	$1.031 + 0.1(0.3 + 1.031 - 1)$	1.06410	1.09182	0.02772
5	0.5	$1.0641 + 0.1(0.4 + 1.0641 - 1)$	1.11051	1.14872	0.03821

Typically, it is not necessary to display all values computed by the Euler method. For example, if h is 0.01, we might display every hundredth value (output interval = 1).

Runge–Kutta Method

Runge–Kutta method
widely used method of solving a first-order differential equation; of recovering an approximation of a function f from its first derivative and an initial value

The **Runge–Kutta**[1] **method** is another numerical approach to recovering a function y from its first derivative

$$\frac{dy}{dx} = f(x, y)$$

and an initial value. Like the Euler method, the Runge–Kutta method computes each x_{n+1} by adding h to x_n, and it bases its computation of y_{n+1} on the values of x_n and y_n. However, the Runge–Kutta method uses a far more complex formula for y_{n+1}, namely

$$y_{n+1} = y_n + \frac{h}{6}(k_1 + 2k_2 + 2k_3 + k_4)$$

where

$$k_1 = f(x_n, y_n)$$

$$k_2 = f\left(x_n + \frac{h}{2}, y_n + k_1\left(\frac{h}{2}\right)\right)$$

$$k_3 = f\left(x_n + \frac{h}{2}, y_n + k_2\left(\frac{h}{2}\right)\right)$$

$$k_4 = f(x_{n+1}, y_n + k_3 h)$$

TABLE 10.8 Runge–Kutta Approximation of Function y Given $dy/dx = x + y - 1$, $(x_0, y_0) = (0,1)$, $h = 0.4$

Computing	Formula	Calculation	Result
k_1	$f(x_0, y_0)$	$0 + 1 - 1$	0.0
k_2	$f(x_0 + 0.2, y_0 + 0(0.2))$	$0.2 + 1 - 1$	0.2
k_3	$f(x_0 + 0.2, y_0 + 0.2(0.2))$	$0.2 + 1.04 - 1$	0.24
k_4	$f(x_1, y_0 + 0.24(0.4))$	$0.4 + 1.096 - 1$	0.496
y_1	$y_0 + \dfrac{0.4}{6}(0 + 2(0.2) + 2(0.24) + 0.496)$		1.09173

Exact $y_1 = e^{(0.4)} - 0.4 = 1.09182$ Error in $y_1 = 1.09182 - 1.09173 = 0.00009$

[1]There are actually several Runge–Kutta methods. Here we describe the classical fourth-order Runge–Kutta method.

Table 10.8 shows a Runge–Kutta approximation of y_4 for the initial value problem shown in Table 10.7, except that we use $h = 0.4$ instead of $h = 0.1$. Since the Runge–Kutta method requires four evaluations of the first derivative function for each step, whereas Euler requires only one, we must use a step size four times as large in order to make a fair comparison of the two methods.

Section 10.5 Review Question

1. Calculate approximations y_1, y_2, y_3, and y_4 by applying the Euler method with $h = 0.1$ to the initial value problem

$$\frac{dy}{dx} = x^2 + y^2, \qquad (x_0, y_0) = (0, 0)$$

Then apply one step of the Runge–Kutta method to the same problem, but this time use $h = 0.4$.

10.6 Software Designer Beware

Numerical methods programs rely on repeated computation to approximate a solution. When you design a loop to carry out this repetition, be sure that your loop will always exit. Analyze the iterative approximation formula to identify cases that will cause an attempt to divide by zero or will calculate a next approximation that is worse than the previous approximation. Design your loop so it will still exit gracefully in such cases.

When you test your implementation of a numerical method, always try first a test case that will require just a few iterations. Then apply the method to this same case by hand or using a spreadsheet. For example, if your method is to terminate when the difference between two successive approximations is less than some small number *epsilon*, use a fairly large value for *epsilon*, perhaps even 1 or 10. Then be sure your hand approximation matches your program's. If you test only cases for which you know the exact result, but which require many iterations, even a slightly incorrect implementation may generate an apparently correct approximation. For example, a Simpson's or trapezoidal rule implementation that neglected to add in one slice of the region under a curve would still yield a reasonable approximation when n (the number of subintervals) was quite large.

Chapter Review

1. Numerical analysis is the study of methods for approximating solutions to mathematical problems.

2. Newton's method is an iterative root-finding method that approximates the function whose root is sought by a tangent to the curve of the function in a region close to a root.

3. The secant method is an iterative approach to finding a root that approximates the function whose root is sought (f) by a line joining two points known to be on the curve $y = f(x)$.

4. Basic statistical methods studied in this chapter include algorithms for calculating the mean and standard deviation of a data set.

5. Linear regression analysis models as a straight line the relationship between a single dependent variable and a single independent variable.

6. The correlation coefficient is a statistic that indicates how well a line models the relationship between a dependent variable and an independent variable.

7. This chapter presents formulas for approximating the first and second derivatives of a function that is represented as a collection of data points.

8. The trapezoidal rule and Simpson's rule are methods of approximating a definite integral of a function that uses lines(trapezoidal) or parabolas (Simpson's) to model small segments of the function.

9. The Euler and Runge-Kutta methods are iterative approaches to solving a first-order differential equation.

We have only scratched the surface of this topic in our brief discussion of numerical methods. A small sample of the dozens of good references on the subject is listed below.

References on Numerical Methods

Akai, Terrence J. *Applied Numerical Methods for Engineers*, Wiley, 1993.

Gerald, Curtis, Patrick Wheatley. *Applied Numerical Analysis*, 6th Ed., Addison-Wesley, 1999.

Hamming, Richard. *Numerical Methods for Scientists and Engineers*, Dover, 1987.

Miller, Irwin, John E. Freund, Richard Arnold Johnson. *Probability and Statistics for Engineers*, Prentice Hall, 1999.

Press, William H., S.A. Teukolsky, W.T. Vetterling, B.P. Flannery. *Numerical Recipes in C: The Art of Scientific Computing*, 2nd Ed., Cambridge Univ. Press, 1993.

PROGRAMMING PROJECTS

1. Implement as a function the secant root-finding method described in Section 10.1. If function secant does not converge to a root (successive approximations differ by less than 0.0001) in 25 iterations, have it display an error message and return 0. Call function secant from a function you define named nthRoot that should approximate the nth root of any

constant c ($\sqrt[n]{c}$), given c and n. If $x^n = c$, then $x^n - c = 0$, and the nth root of c is a zero of the second equation. As your initial guesses, use $x_0 = c$ and $x_1 = c/n$.

2. You are designing a can shaped as a right circular cylinder with a capacity of 2 liters. You want to choose dimensions that minimize the surface area of the can. If r represents the cylinder radius in centimeters and h the cylinder height, the dimensions are related as

$$\pi r^2 h = 2000$$

Our cylinder's surface area can be expressed as

$$A = 2\pi r^2 + 2\pi rh$$

Expressing h in terms of r, we can rewrite the area formula as

$$A = 2\pi r^2 + \frac{4000}{r}$$

The graph of A is concave up throughout its domain. Thus a zero of dA/dr will give us a minimum value for A. Write a program that uses Newton's method to find this zero and then displays the desired cylinder dimensions. Be sure to define a function named `surfaceAreaPrime` to represent dA/dr.

3. Implement the class `Can` described in Section 6.1 Review Question 1. Include an additional constructor function that takes as its parameter the can's desired capacity in milliliters and chooses and sets the can's dimensions to accommodate the desired capacity while minimizing surface area (see Programming Project 2).

4. An engineer in a laboratory can perform fairly sophisticated tests and repairs on prototype products. In the field, particularly for consumer goods, tests and repairs must be simple or the cost of maintenance will be prohibitive. Machines that self-diagnose failures require especially simple tests.

    You are designing a simple algorithm to be implemented on a chip. The chip will be embedded in a complex machine to diagnose possible incipient failures. The chip will perform its diagnosis based on the knowledge that when all is going well, two measurable quantities x and y will vary as

$$y = 2x + 3$$

Write a program that estimates whether a given set of five user-input (x, y) pairs (representing data observed by the self-monitoring machine) fits the "ok" line closely enough. Generate 21 points on the line, using x between 0 and 20. Then combine the field data with these points and compute the correlation coefficient for the entire data set. If the correlation coefficient falls below 0.98, issue a `possible chip failure` message.

5. Design a class `SelfDiagChip` to represent the self-diagnosing chip described in Programming Project 4. This class should include as data components 26-element arrays in which to store the x and y values used in computing the data set correlation coefficient. The class should also include a constructor function with type `double` parameters m and b representing the line

$$y = mx + b$$

that describes how x and y vary when all is going well. This constructor should fill the first 21 elements of the x and y arrays included as data components. Also define a public member function `chipOK` that takes as parameters two 5-element arrays representing observed field data and returns the correlation coefficient of the combined data.

   Use class `SelfDiagChip` in a program that automates the selection of the correlation coefficient cutoff for the self-diagnosing chip problem. The new program should process several lists of five (x, y) pairs. Each list is labeled either "fail" or "ok," indicating whether or not the observed data set was accompanied by chip failure. Your program should combine each set of field data with the 21 points on the "all is going well" line and compute the correlation coefficient of the combined data. When all data sets have been processed, display the minimum correlation coefficient associated with an "ok" data set and the maximum correlation coefficient associated with a "fail" data set.

6. Design a class named `DataSet` whose private components are two type `double` arrays x and y whose maximum size is the constant `MaxSize` (20) and whose actual size is another private component. Define a constructor that initializes these three components. Include member functions that calculate the indicated values:

   a. `correl`—correlation coefficient
   b. `linearRegress`—linear regression coefficients (use output parameters)
   c. `mean`—arithmetic mean
   d. `stDev`—standard deviation

   Test your class using the data from Table 10.3.

7. Assume that you have designed a small, lightweight engine that performs perfectly on the floor of your lab. You then attach it to a boat and test it again. Once again the performance is flawless. However, when you take your supervisor for a demonstration ride in the boat, the engine makes a horrible noise and fails. Now you run many more tests, and sometimes the engine runs perfectly and sometimes it fails. One of your colleagues suggests that it fails when the water is cold. Another suggests that it fails when the air is hot. A third wonders aloud if the failure is related to the mass in the boat. You collect the following data, where N is the number of failures per hour, T(air) is the average air tem-

perature during the testing hour, and T(water) is the average water temperature:

N (fails/hr)	T(air) (°C)	T(water) (°C)	Mass in Boat (kg)
45	35	20	300
5	21	16	330
8	21	17	245
0	20	15	450
16	22	19	450

Write a program to determine which variables are linearly correlated with the number of failures per hour. Also check whether any of these variables are in turn linearly correlated with one another. Run your program once, looking for correlation coefficients satisfying

$$|r| \geq 0.95$$

In a second run, try a threshold of 0.7. You may wish to use the class DataSet described in Programming Project 6. What are the implications of your program's results?

8. Design a class ObservedFunction to represent a function composed of a list of observations collected at evenly spaced intervals, a function such as the distance function shown in Table 10.5. Assume that the initial observation is made at time 0, and that additional observations are recorded at times 1, 2, 3, and so on for some time unit. Include as private components of the class an array of observed values and the names of the time unit and the observation unit. For Table 10.5, these units would be "min" and "km." Either include a constructor function that initializes all components or overload the input extraction operator to initialize all components. Define a member function that approximates an ObservedFunction object's first derivative, storing this first derivative in an ObservedFunction object passed as a reference parameter. Use the central difference formula when possible. Define another member function to calculate the second derivative.

9. Write a program that approximates the force that a race car's brakes are exerting during a high-speed stop, given a table of the distances that the car has traveled down a test straightaway recorded at one-second intervals:

t(sec)	0	1	2	3	4	5	6	7	8
$f(t)$ (m)	0	44	82	115	143	166	181	186	190

You will apply the formula

$$force = mass \times acceleration$$

keeping in mind that acceleration is the second derivative of the distance function f. Of course, since the car is decelerating, the acceleration values will be negative. Ignore the fact that the car is burning fuel and has other forces acting on it. Display a table showing the input data, the acceleration values, and the force values. For the data shown, you will display no acceleration or force values for $t = 0$ and for $t = 8$. Make your program flexible enough to handle distance measurements taken over up to 30 seconds. You may wish to use the ObservedFunction class described in Programming Project 8.

10. The following table indicates the blood-sugar concentrations (mg/dL) of a research subject over an eight-hour period.

time	0	1	2	3	4	5	6	7	8
concentration	85	90	96	108	99	92	91	90	84

Approximate the rate of change of the concentration at times 0, 1, . . . , 8. Use the central difference formula when possible. Display a four-column table listing the time in the first column, the blood-sugar concentrations in the second, the rates of change in the third, and a one-word characterization of the concentration level in the fourth (either rising, falling, or stable). Characterize the concentration as stable if the magnitude of the first derivative is less than 3% of the concentration level at a given time. You may wish to use the ObservedFunction class described in Programming Project 8.

11. The voltage drop (V) across an inductance (L) is given by

$$V = L\frac{di}{dt}$$ where i is the current and t represents time.

Write a program that uses numerical differentiation to approximate V for $t = 0, 0.05, 0.1, 0.15, \ldots, 0.5$ given $L = 20$ and the following data:

t	0.00	0.05	0.10	0.15	0.20	0.25
i	4.95500	4.89936	4.73369	4.46172	4.08954	3.62552

t	0.30	0.35	0.40	0.45	0.50
i	3.08008	2.46546	1.79548	1.08518	0.35050

Use the central difference formula for interior points, and take forward and backward differences for endpoints.

Store the values for i in an array named current. Notice that

$$\text{current}[j] = f(t_0 + jh)$$

where t_0 is the initial value of t and h is the time difference between successive samples. Your program should display a table of this form:

t	i	di/dt	V
0.00	4.95500	?	?
0.05	4.89936	?	?
. . .			

12. Expand class ObservedFunction (see Programming Project 8) to include two member functions that approximate the definite integral of the function from time 0 to the time of the last observation. Use the trapezoidal rule for one member function; implement Simpson's rule for the other. The Simpson's rule function should display an error message and return 0 if the number of observations is even (and thus the number of intervals is odd).

13. Walden Water Wizards, Inc. wants a program that estimates the volume of a body of water based on its average depth, a list of n measurements of the width of the body of water taken at evenly spaced intervals (see Fig. 10.16), and the length between the measurements (h). Write a function called volApprox that takes as its parameters depth, list, n, and h and returns the approximate value. Use Simpson's rule to approximate the surface area of the body of water. Test your function thoroughly. You may wish to use the expanded ObservedFunction class of Programming Project 12.

14. Suppose that a battleship loses power when moving at a speed of 6 m/s. Of course, in reality, ship drag calculations are complex and typically involve drag forces proportional to both the square of the ship's velocity and to a geometrically dependent power of velocity (the so-called "wave drag component"). However, for this problem, let us assume that conditions are such that we can approximate the resistance to the ship's motion as proportional to the ship's velocity. Then the ship's distance from the point of power loss is governed by the differential equation

$$\frac{ds}{dt} = v_0 e^{-(k/m)t}.$$

FIGURE 10.16 Widths of Body of Water Measured at Evenly Spaced Intervals

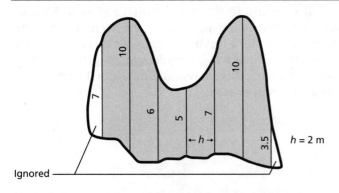

with the initial condition $s(0) = 0$. If $k = 44,000$ kg/s and $m = 25,500,000$ kg, what is the total distance that the ship has coasted at $t = 10$ seconds, $t = 20$ seconds, and so on for the first 60 seconds after the power loss? Use both the Euler and Runge–Kutta methods to approximate a solution, and compare your approximations to exact distances computed using

$$s(t) = \frac{v_0 m}{k}\left(1 - e^{-(k/m)t}\right)$$

After approximating a solution with $h = 10$ seconds, try $h = 5$ and $h = 1$.

15. You are assisting in a project to plan disposal of radioactive materials. Such materials decay according to the first-order differential equation

$$\frac{dy}{dx} = -cy$$

where y is the number of radioactive nuclei in a sample, x is time in years, and c is a constant related to the half-life of the radioactive material. The half-life is the time at which half of the original nuclei in the sample have decayed to other species. The constant c is related to the material's half-life as follows:

$$c = \frac{\ln(2)}{halfLife}$$

Here is a table of half-life values for some commercially used elements.

Cobalt 60	5.26 years
Plutonium 238	87 years
Strontium 90	28 years

Write a program that prompts the user for the half-life of a radioactive material, the number of years of decay to display in a table, and the time interval between lines of the table. Use the Runge–Kutta method with an initial value of $(0, 1)$, which means that at time 0, when the material is initially dumped, it contains 100% of its original radioactive nuclei. Then, in intervals prescribed by the user, display the fraction of the original radioactive nuclei left after a certain number of years of decay. Use a step size of 0.1, so 10 iterations will be required for each year of decay. Also display exact values using this analytical solution to the differential equation modeling radioactive decay:

$$y = e^{-cx}$$

Answers

Odd-Numbered Review Questions

Chapter 1

1. central processing unit
3. microprocessor
5. memory
7. word
9. Secondary storage
11. spiral
13. hardware; software
15. install
17. Software engineering
19. attributes, behavior, relationships

Chapter 2

Section 2.1

1. a. Line 14
   b. Lines 6 and 7
   c. Lines 9 and 11
   d. Lines 16 and 17
   e. Lines 10 and 12
   f. Lines 1 and 2
   g. Line 18

Section 2.2

1. `Difference of values = 4`

Section 2.3

1. `cout << "Distance = " << rate * time << " miles." << endl;`

   `Distance = 125 miles.`

Section 2.4

1. arithmetic overflow
3. representational error

Section 2.5

1.
```
x       y      n   m
14.5   11.0    9   5
```

```
z = x - n / m;
        ‾1‾
   ‾13.5‾
```
z = 13.5

```
b = x * y + m / n * 2;
   159.5
              ‾0‾
                ‾0‾
   ‾159.5‾
```
b = 159.5

```
i = int ( x + 0.5 );
        ‾15.0‾
    ‾15‾
```
i = 15

```
j = x * m - n % m;
   72.5
           ‾4‾
   ‾68.5‾
```
j = 68

```
k = m / -n;
       ‾-9‾    (Note: Sign of zero does not matter.)
   ‾0‾
```
k = 0

3.
```
p = p * q * r;
q = 6 * (1 - m);
```

Section 2.6

1.
```
t = -(L / R) * log(i / I);
    .166667
                   ‾.1‾
   ‾-0.166667‾
                ‾-2.302585‾
    ‾0.383764‾
```
t = 0.383764

Section 2.7

1. `using std::cout;`

Chapter 3

Section 3.1

1. 1 Selection
    2 Selection
    3 Repetition
    4 Sequential

Section 3.2

1. a. `heatRemoved / workDone >= MIN_PERFORMANCE && price <= MAX_PRICE`
   b. `double(heatRemoved) / workDone >= LOW_COEFF && double(heatRemoved)`
      `/ workDone <= HIGH_COEFF`
   c. `measDepth > MIN_DEPTH || degCelsius > MIN_TEMP`
   d. `!precip && !windy`
3. a. `!(x >= 0 && x <= 100)` or `x < 0 || x > 100`
   b. `!(age >= 18 && age <= 26 && eligible)`   or
      `age < 18 || age > 26 || !eligible`
   c. `!(height < 60 && weight < 2.9 * height ||`
      `veteran && weight < 3.1 * height)`   or
      `(height >= 60 || weight >= 2.9 * height) &&`
      `(!veteran || weight >= 3.1 * height)`
   d. `!(attractive || salary > 150000.00 || assets > 1000000.00)`
      or
      `!attractive && salary <= 150000.00 && assets <= 1000000.00`

Section 3.3

1. Repetition structure
3. Repetition structure

Section 3.4

```
1. if (windSpeed < 25)
      cout << "not a strong wind" << endl;
   else if (windSpeed <= 38)
      cout << "strong wind" << endl;
   else if (windSpeed <= 54)
      cout << "gale" << endl;
   else if (windSpeed <= 72)
      cout << "whole gale" << endl;
   else
      cout << "hurricane" << endl;
```

Section 3.5

```
1. brick
   concrete
   frame
```

```
3. if (watts == 15)
       lumens = 125;
   else if (watts == 25)
       lumens = 215;
   else if (watts == 40)
       lumens = 500;
   else if (watts == 60)
       lumens = 880;
   else if (watts == 75)
       lumens = 1000;
   else if (watts == 100)
       lumens = 1675;
   else
       lumens = -1;
```

Section 3.6

1. No. Variable depth is of type double, so it could not be used as the controlling expression in a switch statement.

Chapter 4

Section 4.1

1. a. Do not know in advance how many times the loop must repeat
   b. Loop control variable: work
   c. Loop repetition condition: (work != 0)
   d. cin >> work; use before the while statement to initialize and at the end of the while statement to update

3. a. Do not know in advance how many times the loop must repeat
   b. Loop control variable: diffApprox
   c. Loop repetition condition: (diffApprox >= maxError)
   d. diffApprox = fabs(newApprox - prevApprox); use before the while statement to initialize
      diffApprox = fabs(newApprox - prevApprox); use at the end of the while statement to update

Section 4.2

1. Statements containing << to display prompts for data *precede* statements containing >> for obtaining data.

   Statements containing << for echoing data *follow* statements containing >> for obtaining data.

   Prompts are used in interactive programs but not in batch programs. Batch programs should echo input; interactive programs may also echo input.

Section 4.3

1. a.
```
double  vol1, vol2, work, kTemp, n = 1.0;

cout << "Enter work in joules => ";
cin >> work;

while (work != 0) {
   cout << endl << "Enter initial volume in liters => ";
   cin >> vol1;
   cout << endl << "Enter absolute temperature => ";
   cin >> kTemp;

   vol2 = vol1 * exp((work/(n * R * kTemp)));
   cout << endl << "The final volume is " << vol2
      << " liters";

   cout << endl << "Enter work in joules => ";
   cin >> work;
}
```

   b.
```
double  vol1, vol2, work, kTemp, n = 1.0;

cout << "Enter work in joules => ";

for (cin >> work;  work != 0;  cin >> work)  {
   cout << endl << "Enter initial volume => ";
   cin >> vol1;
   cout << endl << "Enter absolute temperature => ";
   cin >> kTemp;
   vol2 = vol1 * exp((work/(n * R * kTemp)));
   cout << "The final volume is " << vol2 << " liters";

   cout << endl << "Enter work in joules => " << endl;
}
```

3. a.
```
double seriesSum = 1, newApprox, prevApprox, diffApprox,
         maxError;
int    ct = 2;

cout << "Enter the maximum error for approximation of pi=> ";
cin >> maxError;

prevApprox = sqrt( seriesSum * 6 );
seriesSum = seriesSum + (1.0 / (ct * ct));
newApprox = sqrt( seriesSum * 6 );
diffApprox = fabs( newApprox — prevApprox );

while (diffApprox >= maxError)  {
   ct = ct + 1;
```

```
        prevApprox = newApprox;
        seriesSum = seriesSum + (1.0 / (ct * ct));
        newApprox = sqrt( seriesSum * 6 );
        diffApprox = fabs( newApprox – prevApprox );
    }
    cout << "Approximation of pi is " << newApprox << endl;
```

```
b. double seriesSum = 1, newApprox, prevApprox, diffApprox,
        maxError;
   int    ct = 2;
   cout << "Enter the maximum error for approximation of pi=> ";
   cin >> maxError;

   prevApprox = sqrt( seriesSum * 6 );
   seriesSum = seriesSum + (1.0 / (ct * ct));
   newApprox = sqrt( seriesSum * 6 );
   cout << "diffApprox = " << diffApprox << endl;

   for (diffApprox = fabs ( newApprox – prevApprox );
       diffApprox >= maxError;
       diffApprox = fabs ( newApprox – prevApprox ))  {
      ct = ct + 1;
      prevApprox = newApprox;
      seriesSum = seriesSum + (1.0 / (ct * ct));
      newApprox = sqrt(seriesSum * 6);
   }

   cout << "Approximation of pi is " << newApprox << endl;
```

```
5. 1 1
   2 2
   2 1
   3 3
   3 2
   3 1
   4 4
   4 3
   4 2
   4 1
```

Section 4.4

1. Statement Executed	sum	odd	n	Effect
sum = 0;	0	?	8	Initialize sum to 0
for (odd = 1;		1		Initialize odd to 1
odd < n;				1 < 8 is true
sum += odd;	1			Adds 1 to the value of sum
odd += 2)		3		Adds 2 to the value of odd
odd < n;				3 < 8 is true
sum += odd;	4			Adds 3 to the value of sum
odd += 2)		5		Adds 2 to the value of odd
odd < n;				5 < 8 is true
sum += odd;	9			Adds 5 to the value of sum
odd += 2)		7		Adds 2 to the value of odd
odd < n;				7 < 8 is true
sum += odd;	16			Adds 7 to the value of sum
odd += 2)		9		Adds 2 to the value of odd
odd < n;				9 < 8 is false, so loop exits
cout << "Sum of positive odd numbers less than " << n << " is " << sum << "." << endl;				Displays: Sum of positive odd numbers less than 8 is 16.

3. i = 3;
   j = 9;

   i += 1;
   j -= 1;
   n = i * j;
   m = i + j;
   j -= 1;
   p = i + j;

5. ☐☐☐☐–28.75
   ☐☐☐☐–28.7490
   ☐☐☐☐☐☐☐–28.7

Section 4.5

```
1. a. double  vol1, vol2, work, kTemp, n = 1.0;
      char    badChar;

      cout << "Enter work in joules => ";
      cin >> work;

      while (work != 0 && !cin.fail())  {
          cout << endl << "Enter initial volume in liters => ";
          cin >> vol1;
          cout << endl << "Enter absolute temperature => ";
```

```
                    cin >> kTemp;

                    if (!cin.fail())  {
                        vol2 = vol1 * exp((work/(n * R * kTemp)));
                        cout << endl << "The final volume is " << vol2
                            << " liters" << endl;
                        cout << endl << "Enter work in joules =>";
                        cin >> work;
                    }
                }
                if (cin.fail()) {
                    cin.clear();
                    cin >> badChar;
                    cout << endl << "Error in data.  First invalid character > "
                        << badChar << endl;
                }

     b. double  vol1, vol2, work, kTemp, n = 1.0;
        char    badChar;

        cout << "Enter work in joules => ";

        for (cin >> work;  work != 0 && !cin.fail();  cin >> work)  {
            cout << endl << "Enter initial volume in liters => ";
            cin >> vol1;
            cout << endl << "Enter absolute temperature => ";
            cin >> kTemp;

            if (!cin.fail())  {
                vol2 = vol1 * exp((work/(n * R * kTemp)));
                cout << endl << "The final volume is " << vol2
                    << " liters" << endl;
                cout << endl << "Enter work in joules => ";
            }
        }
        if (cin.fail()) {
            cin.clear();
            cin >> badChar;
            cout << endl << "Error in data.  First invalid character > "
                << badChar << endl;
        }

  3. #include <iostream>
     #include <fstream>
     using namespace std;

     int MIN_COAL_REQUIRED = 10000;

     int main()
     {
```

```
        ifstream infile ("coaldata.txt", ios::in);
        ofstream outfile ("coal.out", ios::out);
        int     trainLoad, totalCoal = 0;
        char    badChar;

        outfile << "Trainloads Processed" << endl;
        infile >> trainLoad;

        while (!infile.fail())  {
            totalCoal = totalCoal + trainLoad;
            outfile << trainLoad << " tons" << endl;
            infile >> trainLoad;
        }
        if (infile.eof())  {
            outfile << "Scheduled coal arrival total of "
                    << totalCoal << " tons" << endl;
            if (totalCoal >= MIN_COAL_REQUIRED)
                outfile << "is sufficient for daily operation."
                    << endl;
            else
                outfile << "falls "
                    << MIN_COAL_REQUIRED - totalCoal
                    << " tons short of daily need." << endl;
        } else {
            infile.clear();
            infile >> badChar;
            outfile << "Error in input file at this character >> "
                << badChar << endl;
        }
        infile.close();
        outfile.close();
        return 0;
    }
```

Section 4.6

1. The sentinel loop is better implemented using the for statement because the
   for loop version tests the condition (num != Sentinel) only once per iteration
   of the loop.

Section 4.7

```
1. //
   //  Demonstrate conversion of digital data (taken from file
   //  "digital.txt") to analog audio tones.
   //      Pre:  file must contain at least one valid digit.

   #include <iostream>
   #include <fstream>
   using namespace std;
```

```cpp
const int LOW_TONE = 1070;
const int HIGH_TONE = 1270;

int main()
{
    int  timeUnits; // duration of one emitted audio tone
    int  tone;      // frequency of current tone (hertz)
    char digit;     // 0 or 1 scanned from file

    ifstream datafile( "digital.txt", ios::in );

    cout << "Demonstration of Digital to Analog Data Conversion
        << endl << endl;

    //  Determine initial tone based on initial valid digit
    datafile >> digit;
    while (digit != '0' && digit != '1') {
        cout << "Ignoring faulty digit: " << digit << endl;
        datafile >> digit;
    }
    cout << digit;
    if (digit == '0') {
        tone = LOW_TONE;
        timeUnits = 1;
    } else if (digit == '1') {
        tone = HIGH_TONE;
        timeUnits = 1;
    }

    // Convert digits remaining in file
    datafile >> digit;
    while (!datafile.fail()) {
        cout << digit;

        if (digit == '0') {
            if (tone == LOW_TONE) {  // tone continues
                ++timeUnits;
            } else {                 // tone changes
                cout << endl << "Emit " << tone
                    << "-hz tone for " <<
                    timeUnits << " time unit(s)." << endl;
                tone = LOW_TONE;
                timeUnits = 1;
            }
        } else if (digit == '1') {
            if (tone == HIGH_TONE)  { // tone continues
                ++timeUnits;
            } else {
```

```
                              cout << endl << "Emit " << tone
                                  << "-hz tone for " <<
                                  timeUnits << " time unit(s)." << endl;
                              tone = HIGH_TONE;
                              timeUnits = 1;
                      }
              } else {
                      cout << endl << "Ignoring faulty digit " << digit
                          << endl;
              }

              datafile >> digit;
      }

      // Emit tone that was under construction when data ran out
      cout << endl << "Emit " << tone << "-hz tone for "
          << timeUnits << " time unit(s)." << endl;

      datafile.close();
      return 0;
  }
```

Chapter 5

Section 5.1

1. 93
3.
```
  //  Rounds the value of num to designated number of decimal places
  //  Pre: num is defined and decimalPlaces >= 0
  //
  double round(double num, double decimalPlaces)
  {
          int    sign;        // -1 if num is negative, 1 otherwise
          double power,       // 10 raised to the decimalPlaces power
                 temp,        // copy of |num| with decimal point
                              // moved decimalPlaces to the right.
                 roundedNum;  // function result

          if (num >= 0)
              sign = 1;
          else
              sign = -1;

          power = pow(10.0, decimalPlaces);
          temp = fabs( num ) * power;
          roundedNum = int(temp + 0.5) / power * sign;

          return roundedNum;
  }
```

Section 5.2

1.
```
//
// Display instructions for the user
//
void instruct()
{
  cout << "This program determines whether or not new vehicles"
       << endl << "meet carbon monoxide emissions standards."
       << endl;
  cout << "If the vehicle's carbon monoxide emission exceeds "
       << maxCo << " grams per mile," << endl
       << "the vehicle does not meet the standard." << endl
       << endl;
  cout << "Respond to each prompt by typing the requested number"
       << endl << "and then pressing the Enter key." << endl;
}
```

Section 5.3

1.
```
//  Separates a number into three parts:  the sign, the whole
//  number part, and the fractional part.
//
void separate(char& sign, int& wholeNum,
              double& fraction, double number)
{
    if (number > 0)
       sign = '+';
    else if (number < 0)
       sign = '-';
    else
       sign = ' ';

    wholeNum = abs( (int)number );

    fraction = fabs( number ) - wholeNum;
}
```

3.

Data area for main	x	3.9
	y	12.7
Data area for swap	n1	~~3.9~~ 12.7
	n2	~~12.7~~ 3.9
	temp	3.9

Since swap takes value parameters, it has simply exchanged its own personal copies of x and y, not the originals. To correct, n1 and n2 must be reference parameters:

```
void swap( double& n1, double& n2)
{
    // no change in function body
}
```

Section 5.4

1.
```
const int INCHES_PER_YARD = 36;
const double CM_PER_INCH = 2.54;
//
//  Convert inches to whole centimeters (add .5 and truncate to round)
//
int toCm( int inches )
{
    return (int(inches * CM_PER_INCH + 0.5));
}

//
//  Convert yards to whole centimeters
//
int toCm( double yards )
{
    return (int(yards * INCHES_PER_YARD * CM_PER_INCH + 0.5));
}
```

Section 5.5

1.

Name	Visible in Function main	Visible in one (excluding for loop)	Visible in one's for Loop	Visible in Function two
one (function)	Yes	No	No	No
two (function)	Yes	Yes	No	Yes
LARGE (global constant)	Yes	Yes	Yes	Yes
var1 (variable in main)	Yes	No	No	No
var1 (one's parameter)	No	Yes	Yes	No
var2 (one's parameter)	No	Yes	Yes	No
alocal (local variable in one)	No	Yes	Yes	No
one (local variable in one)	No	Yes	Yes	No
two (local variable in one's loop)	No	No	Yes	No
one (two's parameter)	No	No	No	Yes
var1 (two's parameter)	No	No	No	Yes

Section 5.6

1.
```
bisect( 2.5, 6.5, 0.001 ) (original call)
bisect( 2.5, 4.5, 0.001 )
bisect( 2.5, 3.5, 0.001 )
```

3. ```
#include <cstdlib>

//
// Calculate x^n for integer n.
//
double power(double x, int n)
{
   double result;
   if (n == 0)
     result = 1;
   else
      result = result * power(x, n - 1);
   return result;
}
```

## Section 5.7

1. ```
//
//  Compute Btu's of heat lost by structure in coldest month
//
double computeHeatLoss(int heatingRequirement, double floorSpace,
                       int heatingDegreeDays)
{
     double heatLoss = heatingRequirement * floorSpace
                          * heatingDegreeDays;
     return heatLoss;
}


//
//  Calculate Btu's of heat obtained from one square foot of
//  collecting area in coldest month
//
double computeEnergyResource (int efficiency,
                              int solarInsolation,
                              int coldestMonth)
{
     double energyResource = efficiency * 0.01 * solarInsolation
                             * daysInMonth( coldestMonth );
     return energyResource;
}
```

Statements modified in main:

```
heatLoss = ComputeHeatLoss( heatingRequirement, floorSpace,
     heatingDegreeDays );
energyResource = computeEnergyResource( efficiency, solarInsolation,
     coldestMonth );
```

Chapter 6

Section 6.1

```
1. struct Point {
       double x, y;
   };
```

Section 6.2

```
1. double distance;
   distance = sqrt( pow( pt2.getX() - pt1.getX(), 2) +
                    pow(pt2.getY() - pt1.getY(), 2));
   cout << "The distance between (" << pt1.getX() <<
       ", " << pt1.getY() << ") and (" << pt2.getX() <<
       ", " << pt2.getY() << ") is " << distance << endl;
3. class Cylinder {
   public:
       Cylinder() {}
       Cylinder( double, double, string );

       double getBaseRadius() { return baseRadius; }
       double getHeight() { return height; }
       string getUnits() { return units; }

   private:
       double baseRadius, height;
       string units;
   };

   Cylinder :: Cylinder( double base, double ht, string u )
   {
       baseRadius = base;
       height = ht;
       units = u;
   }
```

Section 6.3

1. Object-Oriented Analysis of a Ratio
   Attributes
   - numerator
   - denominator

   Behavior
   - reduce fraction to lowest terms
   - constructor
   - constructor with initialization

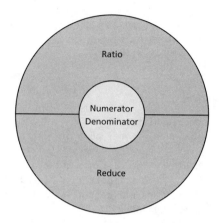

Attributes

Name	Description	Type/Class	Accessibility
numerator	Fraction numerator	int	private
denominator	Fraction denominator	int	private

Behaviors

Prototype	Description	Accessibility
void reduce (int, int)	Reduces fraction to lowest terms	public
Ratio ()	Constructor: Declares space for one Ratio object, leaving components representing attributes uninitialized	public
Ratio (int, int)	Constructor: Declares space for one Ratio object, initializing numerator to the value of the first parameter, and denominator to the value of the second parameter.	public

Additional Interfaces

Interface with	Description
Outside world	Defines operators >> and << for I/O of Ratio objects. Operator >> will take two type int values from the input source to initialize the attributes of a Ratio object. Operator << will display the values of the attributes in the form: numerator / denominator

Section 6.4

1. a. reference
   b. the type (class) of the right operand

3.
```cpp
#include <iostream>
using namespace std;

class Ratio   {

public:
    Ratio () {}          // Default constructor
    Ratio ( int, int ); // Constructor  2 - components initialized
    void reduce ();      // reduces fraction

private:
    int    num;   // numerator
    int    denom; // denomintor

friend  istream& operator>>  ( istream&, Ratio& ) ;
friend  ostream& operator<<  ( ostream&, const Ratio& );
};

//
//  Constructor that initializes components
//
Ratio  ::  Ratio ( int numerator, int denominator )
{
    num = numerator;
    denom = denominator;
}


//
//  Reduces fraction represented by a Ratio object by
//     dividing num and denom by greatest common divisor
//
void Ratio ::  reduce ()
{
    int n, m, r;
    n = num;
    m = denom;
    r = n % m;
    while (r != 0)  {
        n = m;
        m = r;
        r = n % m;
    }
    num  /=  m;
    denom  /= m;
}
```

```
//
//    Extract from input source the two components of a Ratio
//
istream& operator>> (istream& is,  Ratio& oneRatio )
{
    is  >> oneRatio.num  >> oneRatio.denom;
    return is;
}


//
//  Display a Ratio object as a common fraction
//
ostream& operator<< ( ostream& os, const Ratio& oneRatio )
{
    os  <<  oneRatio.num;
    if (oneRatio.denom != 1)
       os  <<  " / "  <<  oneRatio.denom;
    return os;
}


//
//  Driver to declare and manipulate a Ratio object
//
int main ()
{
    Ratio aRatio;
    cout  <<
        "Enter numerator and denominator of a common fraction"
        << endl  <<  "=> ";
    cin  >>  aRatio;
    cout  <<  endl  <<  "Fraction entered  = "  <<  aRatio
        <<  endl;
    aRatio.reduce();
    cout  <<  "Reduced fraction = "  <<  aRatio  <<  endl;
    return 0;
}
```

Section 6.5

1. a. An accessor
   b. *B,* type *A*

3.

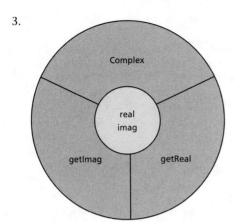

Section 6.6

1. reference, the function returns
3.
```cpp
class Complex {

public:
    Complex() {}                    // default constructor
    Complex( double, double );      // constructor initializes real, imag
    Complex( double );              // constructor permits conversion
                                    //    from real to Complex
    double getReal() const;         // accessor
    double getImag() const;         // accessor

private:
    double real;
    double imag;

friend istream& operator>> ( istream&, Complex& );
friend ostream& operator<< ( ostream&, const Complex& );
friend Complex operator+ ( const Complex&, const Complex& );
friend Complex& operator+= ( Complex&, const Complex& );

};


//
//  Adds two Complex numbers, returning the sum as a Complex object
//
Complex operator+ ( const Complex& c1, const Complex& c2 )
{
    Complex sum(c1);
    sum.real += c2.real;
    sum.imag += c2.imag;
```

```
        return sum;
    }


    //
    // Adds the right operand (a Complex number) to the left operand
    //
    Complex& operator+= ( Complex& c1, const Complex& c2 )
    {
        c1.real += c2.real;
        c1.imag += c2.imag;

        return c1;
    }
```

Section 6.7

1. a. Kind-of hierarchy
   b. Part-of hierarchy

3. ```
   #include <iostream>
   #include <cmath>
   using namespace std;

   const double PI = 3.14159265358979;

   class AngularDistance {  // Represents an angle measurement
                            // in degrees, minutes, and seconds

   public:
       AngularDistance() {}             // default constructor
       AngularDistance( int, int, int ); // constructor that initializes
       double InRadians() const;        // converts angle to radians

   protected:
       int degrees, minutes, seconds;
   friend ostream& operator<< ( ostream&, const AngularDistance& );
   friend istream& operator>> ( istream&, AngularDistance& );

   };

   class Triangle  {  // Represents a triangle as two angles and an
                      // included side.

   public:
       Triangle()  {}   // default constructor
       Triangle( const AngularDistance&,    // constructor that
                 const AngularDistance&, int& ); // initializes angle1,
                                               // angle2, and side
       Triangle( int, int, int,    // constructor that initializes
                 int, int, int,    // angle1, angle2, and the included
   ```
   ```

```
                 int );              // side, one attribute at a time
      void threeSides ( double&, double&, // returns the lengths of a
                        double& );       // triangle's three sides
private:
   AngularDistance angle1, angle2;
   int             side;
friend ostream& operator<< ( ostream&, const Triangle& );
friend istream& operator>> ( istream&, Triangle&);
};

// AngularDistance constructors and I/O operators omitted:  They are
// as shown in Fig. 6.16

//
// Converts an angle measurement from degrees, minutes, and seconds
// to radians.
//
double AngularDistance :: InRadians() const
{
   double radians;

   radians = (PI/180) * (degrees + (minutes/60.0) + (seconds/360.0));

   return radians;
}


//
//  Constructor that initializes a Triangle object with two angles
//  and the included side
//
Triangle :: Triangle( const AngularDistance& a1,
                      const AngularDistance& a2,
                      int& s )
{
   angle1 = a1;
   angle2 = a2;
   side = s;
}


//
//  Constructor that initializes the two angles of a Triangle object
//  one attribute at a time, and also initializes the included side
//
Triangle :: Triangle( int a1deg, int a1min, int a1sec,
                      int a2deg, int a2min, int a2sec,
                      int includedSide)
{
   angle1 = AngularDistance( a1deg, a1min, a1sec);
   angle2 = AngularDistance( a2deg, a2min, a2sec);
```

```
          side = includedSide;
   }

   //
   //  Returns the lengths of the triangle's three sides
   //
   void Triangle :: threeSides( double& a, double& b, double& c )
   {
      double   angleA, angleB, angleC;

      angleA = angle1.InRadians();
      angleB = angle2.InRadians();
      angleC = PI - (angleA + angleB);

      c = side;
      b = sin( angleB ) * ( c / sin( angleC ));
      a = sin( angleA ) * ( c / sin( angleC ));
   }

   ostream& operator<< ( ostream& os, const Triangle& tri )
   {
      os << "angle A measurement:  " << tri.angle1 << endl
         << "angle B measurement:  " << tri.angle2 << endl
         << "included side measurement: " << tri.side << " mm" << endl;
      return os;
   }

   istream& operator>> ( istream& is, Triangle& tri )
   {
         is >> tri.angle1 >> tri.angle2 >> tri.side;
         return is;
   }

   int main()
   {
      Triangle t;
      double   side1, side2, side3;

      cout << "Enter 2 angles in degrees, minutes, seconds" << endl
           << "and then enter the length of the included side" <<
           endl << "in mm => ";


      cin >> t;
      cout << t;

      t.threeSides(side1, side2, side3);

      cout << "The three side measurements are:" << endl
```

```
                       << "side1 = " << side1 << " mm" << endl
                       << "side2 = " << side2 << " mm" << endl
                       << "side3 = " << side3 << " mm" << endl;
        return 0;
   }
```

Member function `threeSides` is preferable because it prevents storage of inconsistent data.

Chapter 7

Section 7.1

1. `stress4` is a simple variable name, whereas `stress[4]` indicates the fifth element in an array named `stress`.

Section 7.2

1.
```
#include <iostream>
#include <cmath>
using namespace std;

const int SIZE = 10;

int main()
{
    int nCube[SIZE], i;

    for (i = 0; i < SIZE; ++i)
        nCube[i] = int(pow( i+1, 3 ));
    ...
}
```

3.
```
//
//  Converts a list of universal times to a list of local times
//

#include <iostream>
#include <fstream>
#include <iomanip>
#include <cmath>
using namespace std;

const int TSIZE = 20;

void timeChange ( int, int, int&, int& );

int main()
{
    int utc[TSIZE];      // list of Universal times
```

```
    int timeDiff;        // time difference in hours
    int local[TSIZE];    // list of local times
    int day[TSIZE];      // list of corresponding day numbers
    int i;

    ifstream infile("utc.txt", ios::in);

    // Code to fill utc, day, timeDiff with data
    cout << "Enter the time difference in hours." << endl;
    cin >> timeDiff;

    for (i = 0;  i < TSIZE;  ++i) {
       infile >> utc[i] >> day[i];
    }

    // Table header
    cout << " UTC Time   UTC Day   Local Time   Local Day"
                   << endl;

    // Conversion of Universal times to local times and table
    //       construction
    for (i = 0;  i < TSIZE;  ++i)  {
       cout << setw(7) << utc[i] << setw(10) << day[i];
       timeChange( utc[i], timeDiff, local[i], day[i] );
       cout << setw(12) << local[i] << setw(10) << day[i] << endl;
    }
    return 0;
}


//
// Converts a 24-hour-clock time in one time zone to an
// equivalent time in another zone where the time differs from
// the first zone by timeDiff hours.  The effect of the time
// change on the day is recorded in dayNum:  no change => same
// day, 1 added => next day, 1 subtracted => previous day
//
void timeChange ( int time, int timeDiff, int& newTime,
                   int& dayNum)
{

    newTime = time + (timeDiff * 100);
    if (newTime < 0) {
         newTime += 2400;
         --dayNum;
    }
    if (newTime > 2400)  {
         newTime -= 2400;
         ++dayNum;
    }

}
```

Section 7.3

1.
```cpp
#include <iostream>
using namespace std;

const int NOT_FOUND = -1;

//
//  Searches an array of integers to find the location of the
//  first occurrence of a specified value.  Returns the subscript
//  of the first occurrence of the specified value.
//
int search(const int list[], // input array to search
           int target,        // target value to search for
           int size)          // size of the array
{
   bool  found = false;
   int   counter = 0;

   while (counter < size && !found)
      if (target == list[counter])
         found = true;
      else
         ++counter;

   if (found)
      return counter;
   else
      return NOT_FOUND;
}
```

Section 7.4

1.
```cpp
if ( name1 == name 2 )
    cout << "The names match." << endl;
```
3.
```cpp
int size, i = 0;

if (s1.length() < s2.length())
   size = s1.length();
else
   size = s2.length();

while (i < size && s1[i] == s2[i])
   ++i;

string mtch = s1.substr(0, i);
```

Section 7.5

1. a. << for MonthRecord
   b. << for string
   c. << for int
   d. << for Cstring
   e. << for int
   f. << for string
   g. << for string
   h. << for int
   i. << for int
3. Add to class declaration (in public section):
   ```
   double sum() const;
   double average() const { return (sum() / size );
   ```
   After class declaration, add definition of sum:
   ```
   double Array :: sum() const
   {
      double total = 0;
      for (int i = 0; i < size; ++i)
         total += list[i];
      return total;
   }
   ```

Section 7.6

1. **Version 1**

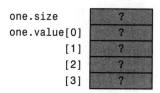

   Version 2

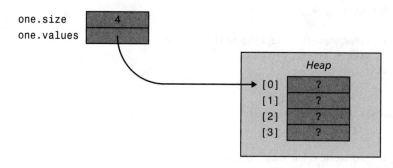

Chapter 8

Section 8.1

1.
```
//
// displays first column 2 and then row 1 of grid
//
void Grid :: col2Row1()
{
    int i;

    cout << "Column 2:" << endl;
    for (i = 0; i < gridRows; ++i)
        cout << powerGrid[i][1] << endl;

    cout << "Row 1:" << endl;
    for (i = 0; i < gridCols; ++i)
        cout << powerGrid[0][i] << "  ";
    cout << endl;
}
```

3. Changed portions:

```
class Grid {  // object type for monitoring power status

public:
    Grid() {}
    bool    powerOK() const;  // returns true if all sectors have power
    void    whereOff();       // displays subscripts of sectors
                              //   where power is off
    void    columnSums( int [] ) const;  // stores the column sums

private:
    int powerGrid[GRID_ROWS][GRID_COLS];
friend ostream& operator<< ( ostream&, const Grid& );
friend istream& operator>> ( istream&, Grid& );
};

int main()
{
    Grid pubServ;
    string inFileName;
    int    sums[GRID_COLS], i;

    cout << "Enter name of data file => ";
    cin  >> inFileName;
    ifstream infile( inFileName.c_str(), ios::in );

    infile >> pubServ;
    infile.close();
```

```
                cout << "Current grid" << endl;
                cout << pubServ << endl;
                if (pubServ.powerOK())
                   cout << "Power is on throughout grid." << endl;
                else
                   pubServ.whereOff();

                pubServ.columnSums( sums );

                cout << endl << "Column sums:" << endl;

                for (i = 0; i < GRID_COLS; ++i)
                   cout << sums[i] << "   ";

                cout << endl;
                return 0;
        }


        //
        //  Stores the sum of each column's values in array sums
        //
        void Grid :: columnSums( int sums[] ) const
        {
            int i, j, total;

            for (j = 0; j < GRID_COLS; ++j)  {
               total = 0;
               for (i = 0; i < GRID_ROWS; ++i)
                    total += powerGrid[i][j];
               sums[j] = total;
            }
        }
```

Section 8.2

```
1. //
   // Program that multiplies one matrix by another;
   // matrices' maximum sizes are MaxRows x MaxCols
   //

   ...

   //
   //  Repeatedly inputs two matrices from a file designated by the
   //  user.  Forms and displays their product.
   //
   int main()
   {
      Matrix m1;
```

```
        Matrix m2;
        string file1Name;

        cout << "Name of file containing the matrices => ";
        cin >> file1Name;
        ifstream infilOne( file1Name.cstr(), ios::in );
        infilOne >> m1;
        infilOne >> m2;

        while (!infilOne.fail())  {
            cout << endl << "Matrix 1" << endl << endl << m1 << endl
                << endl;
            cout << "Matrix 2" << endl << endl << m2 << endl << endl;
            m1 *= m2;;
            cout << "Matrix 1 x Matrix 2 = " << endl << endl << m1 <<
                endl << endl;
            infilOne >> m1;
            infilOne >> m2;
        }
        infilOne.close();
        return 0;
    }
    ...
```

3. Revised portions of Fig. 8.9

```
    class Matrix {  // Represents a varying-size matrix that
                    // can by input from a file
    public:
        Matrix() {}
        Matrix& operator*=( int );
        Matrix& operator*=( const Matrix& );
    private:
        int rows;
        int cols;
        int mat[MAX_ROWS][MAX_COLS];
    friend ostream& operator<<( ostream&, const Matrix& );
    friend istream& operator>>( istream&, Matrix& );
    };

    // Inputs a matrix from a file designated by the user and a
    // inputs a scalar.  Displays the matrix multiplied by the
    // scalar
    int main()
    {
        Matrix m1;
        string file1Name;
        int scalar;

        cout << "Name of file containing matrix => ";
        cin >> file1Name;
```

```
            ifstream infilOne( file1Name.c_str(), ios::in );
            infilOne >> m1;
            infilOne.close();

            cout << "Input integer to multiply matrix by => ";
            cin >> scalar;
            cout << "Matrix\n" << m1 << endl << " x " << scalar
                << " = \n";
            m1 *= scalar;
            cout << m1;

            return 0;
        }

        //
        //  Multiply a matrix by a scalar.
        //
        Matrix& Matrix :: operator*= ( int num ) // input
        {

            for (int i = 0;  i < rows;  ++i)
                for (int j = 0;  j < cols;  ++j)
                    mat[i][j] *= num;

            return *this;
        }
```

Section 8.3

1. Revised portions:
```
    #include <iostream>
    #include <fstream>
    #include <iomanip>
    #include <string>
    #include <cmath>
    using namespace std;

    . . .

    class Matrix {  //  Represents a matrix whose size can vary
                    //  up to MaxN x (MaxN + 1)
    public:
        Matrix() {}
        bool transformMatrix();  // finds solution to object's
                                 // system of linear equations
        void displaySolution( ostream& ) const;
        void outputLinear( ostream& ) const;
    private:
        int   rows;
```

```
    int   cols;
    double mat[MaxN][MaxN + 1];
  friend ostream& operator<< ( ostream&, const Matrix& );
  friend istream& operator>> ( istream&, Matrix& );
  };


  //
  //  Output an augmented matrix as a series of linear equations.
  //
  void Matrix :: outputLinear( ostream& os ) const
  {
    int i, j;
    for (i = 0; i < rows; ++i) {
      os << mat[i][0];
      os << "x_1 ";
      for (j = 1; j < cols - 1; ++j) {
        if (mat[i][j] < 0)
          os << "- ";
        else
          os << "+ ";
        os << fabs(mat[i][j]) << "x_" << (j + 1) << " ";
      }
      os << "= " << mat[i][j] << endl;
    }
  }
```
Call:
```
augMatrix.outputLinear( cout );
```

Section 8.4

1. There would be no constants MAX_ROWS, MAX_COLS, so the definition that uses them (operator>>) would change. The declaration of powerGrid in the private data members would become
   ```
   int **powerGrid;
   ```
   and a space-allocating constructor and a destructor would be needed. The definition of operator>> would be very similar to its definition in Fig. 8.13.

Chapter 9

Section 9.1

1. a. n   123
      x   3.145
      str   "xyz"
      ch   '3'

   b. n   123
      x   3.145
      str   "xyz"
      ch   '3'

c. x   123.0
   n   3
   ch   '.'
   str   "145"

d. str   "123 3.145 xyz"
   n   35
   ch   'z'

Section 9.2

1.
```
//
//  Repeatedly prompts for and inputs data until a numeric
//  value is entered. Returns the number as a type double.
//
double getnum()
{
   double num;
   char badChar;
   bool again;

   do {
      cout << "Enter a number=> ";
      cin >> num;

      if(cin.fail()) {
         again = true;
         cin.clear();
         cerr << "Invalid input: ";
         for  (cin.get(badChar);  !cin.fail() && badChar != '\n';
               cin.get(badChar))
            cerr << badChar;
         cerr << endl;
      } else {
         again = false;
      }

   } while (again);

   return num;
}
```

Section 9.3

1.
```
#include <iostream>
#include <fstream>
#include <iomanip>
#include <string>
using namespace std;
```

```
int main()
{
    string fuel[3];
    string unit[3];
    int  reserves[3];
    double production[3];
    int i;
    string restOfLine;

    ifstream in( "data.txt", ios::in );
    ofstream out("report.txt", ios::out );

    out << setiosflags( ios::left ) << setw( 15 ) << "FOSSIL FUEL"
        << setw( 20 ) << "     UNIT" <<
        "RESERVES(1988)   ANNUAL PRODUCTION" << endl;

    for  (i = 0;  i < 3;  ++i) {
        getline( in, fuel[i] );
        getline( in, unit[i] );
        in >> reserves[i] >> production[i];
        getline( in, restOfLine );
        out << setiosflags( ios::left ) << setw( 15 ) << fuel[i]
            << setw( 20 ) << unit[i] << resetiosflags( ios::left )
            << setw( 8 ) << reserves[i] << setiosflags( ios::fixed )
            << setprecision( 3 ) << setw( 18 ) << production[i]
            << endl;
    }

    return 0;
}
```

Section 9.4

1. All parameters that are not mentioned would be left as initialized.
   - Metals that can withstand pressures of 135 gigapascals:
     Low bound for tensile modulus (GPa) = 135
   - Characteristics of vanadium
     Low bound for name = "vanadium"
     High bound for name = "vanadium"
   - Metals with melting points of at least 1400°C and delivery within 15 days
     Low bound for melting point = 1400
     High bound for days to delivery = 15

3.
```
//  Initializes params to permit widest search.  Then prompts the
//  user to enter modifications to the search parameters.
//
void getParams(SearchParams& params)
{
```

```
        char response;

        initializeParams(params);

        for (response = menuChoose(params);
             response != 'q';
             response = menuChoose(params)) {
          switch (response) {
          case 'a':
            cout << "New low bound for name> ";
            cin >> params.lowName;
            break;

          case 'b':
            cout << "New high bound for name> ";
            cin >> params.highName;
            break;

          case 'c':
            cout << "New low bound for density> ";
            cin >> params.lowDensity;
            break;

          case 'd':
            cout << "New high bound for density> ";
            cin >> params.highDensity;
            break;

          case 'e':
            cout << "New low bound for melting point> ";
            cin >> params.lowMeltPt;
            break;

          case 'f':
            cout << "New high bound for melting point> ";
            cin >> params.highMeltPt;
            break;

          case 'g':
            cout << "New low bound for tensile modulus> ";
            cin >> params.lowTensMod;
            break;

          case 'h':
            cout << "New high bound for tensile modulus> ";
            cin >> params.highTensMod;
            break;

          case 'i':
```

```
                cout << "New low bound for days to delivery> ";
                cin >> params.lowDays;
                break;

            case 'j':
                cout << "New high bound for days to delivery> ";
                cin >> params.highDays;
                break;

            default:
                cout << "The letter " << response << " is not valid.\n";
                cout << "Please type a letter between a and j or q.\n";
            }
        }
    }

    //
    //  Displays each component of metal record. Leaves a blank line
    //   after metal display.
    //
    void show(const Metal& metal)
    {
        cout << "Metal " << metal.name << endl;
        cout << "  Density: " << metal.density << " g/cm^3\n";
        cout << "  Melting point: " << metal.meltPt << " degrees C\n";
        cout << "  Tensile modulus: " << metal.tensMod << " GPa\n";
        cout << "  Delivery within: " << metal.daysToDeliv <<
            " days \n\n";
    }
```

Chapter 10

Section 10.1

1. 1.50000
    −0.50000
    1.50000
    −0.50000

Section 10.2

```
1.  #include <iostream>
    #include <fstream>
    using namespace std;

    const int MAX_SIZE = 6;

    double arithmeticMean( const double [], int );
    void linRegress( double&, double&,
        const double [], const double [], int );
```

```
int main()
{
   int   i;
   double xlist[MAX_SIZE] = {50, 60, 75, 77, 86, 96}, // Data from
          ylist[MAX_SIZE] = {47, 41, 75, 65, 88, 89}, // Table 10.3
          slope, yIntercept;

   linRegress(slope, yIntercept, xlist, ylist, MAX_SIZE);

   cout << "The linear regression coefficients m and b are:"
      << endl;
   cout << "m = " << slope << endl;
   cout << "b = " << yIntercept << endl;

   return 0;
}

//
//  Computes the arithmetic mean (average) of the first
//  size (>= 1) elements of list
//
double arithmeticMean( const double list[], int size )
{
   int i;
   double sum = 0;

   for  (i = 0;  i < size;  ++i)
       sum += list[i];

   return (sum / size);
}

//
//  Uses the least-squares line fitting method to approximate
//  the slope (m) and the y-intercept (b) of a line fitted to
//  a data set defined by an array of y values, and an array
//  of corresponding x values.

void linRegress( double& m, double& b,
                 const double x[], const double y[], int size )
{
   int    i;
   double xMean, yMean, xyDiffSum = 0, xDiffSquaredSum = 0;

   xMean = arithmeticMean(x, size);
   yMean = arithmeticMean(y, size);

   for(i = 0;  i < size;  ++i)  {
```

```
                xyDiffSum += ((x[i] - xMean) * (y[i] - yMean));
                xDiffSquaredSum += ((x[i] - xMean) * (x[i] - xMean));
        }

    m = xyDiffSum / xDiffSquaredSum;

    b = yMean - (m * xMean);
}
```

Section 10.3

1.

t	0	1	2	3	4	5	6
$f'(t)$ exact	0.0	0.6	1.2	1.8	1.8	1.8	1.8
$f'(t)$ approx	0.3	0.6	1.2	1.65	1.8	1.8	1.8
error	−0.3	0.0	0.0	0.15	0.0	0.0	0.0

Section 10.4

1.
```
//
//  Approximates the definite integral of f from a to b using
//  Simpson's rule with n subintervals.
//

double simpson( double a, // endpoints of interval of
                double b, //     integration
                int    n )// number of subintervals
{
    double  h;
    double  evensum = 0, oddsum = 0;
    int    i;

    if ((n % 2) == 0) {
        h = (b - a) / n;
        for  (i = 2; i <= n;  i += 2)
            oddsum += f(a + (i - 1) * h);
        for  (i = 2; i <= n - 2;  i += 2)
            evensum += f(a + i * h);

        return (h / 3.0 * (f(a) + f(b) + (4.0 * oddsum)
                + (2.0 * evensum)));
    } else {
        cout << "Error: Number of subintervals must be even." << endl;
        return 0;
    }
}
```

Section 10.5

1. Euler method: $y_1 = 0$ $y_2 = 0.001000$ $y_3 = 0.005000$ $y_4 = 0.014003$
   $y_5 = 0.030022$

   Runge–Kutta method: $y_1 = 0.021359$

Appendix A
C, Parent Language of C++

The parent language of C++, C, is a high-level programming language developed in 1972 by Dennis Ritchie at AT&T Bell Laboratories. Because C was designed as a language in which to write the UNIX® operating system, it was originally used primarily for systems programming. Over the years, however, C has become a popular language in industry for a wide variety of applications.

C Data Types, Control Structures, Input/Output, and Functions

All of the simple data types we studied in C++ are available in C with the exception of bool. C uses the integers 0 and 1 to represent true and false. C includes all of the standard control structures we studied in C++: if, if–else, and switch statements for selection; while, for, and do–while statements for repetition. However, C standard input/output uses functions rather than operators such as >> and <<, and C programs often handle named constants by using the preprocessor directive #define for textual replacement rather than declaring and initializing named constants (for example, #define PI 3.1415926). This preprocessor directive is also available in C++. Figure A.1 shows side-by-side C++ and C versions of a program that calculates when it is safe to enter a room in which there has been a radiation leak. Notice that the programs are virtually identical except for the bolded regions. The C program uses a different style of comment: the character sequence /* marks the beginning of a comment and */ marks the end of a comment. This style of comment is also legal in C++ programs.

FIGURE A.1 Comparison of C++ and C Control Structures

```
//
//  Calculates and displays a table showing the safety level of a
//  room in which there has been a radiation leak
//

#include <iostream>  // library with I/O operators
#include <iomanip>   // library with output format manipulators
using namespace std;

const double SAFE_RAD = 0.466;    // safe level of radiation
const double SAFETY_FACT = 10.0;  // safety factor

int rad_table(double init_radiation, double min_radiation);

int main()
{
    int    day;          // day user can enter room
    double init_radiation,  // radiation level right after leak
           min_radiation;   // safe level divided by safety factor

    // Compute stopping level of radiation
    min_radiation = SAFE_RAD / SAFETY_FACT;

    // Prompts user to enter initial radiation level
    cout << "Enter the radiation level (in millirems)> ";
    cin >> init_radiation;

    // Displays table
    day = rad_table(init_radiation, min_radiation);

    // Display day the user can enter the room.
    cout << "\nYou can enter the room on day " << day << ".\n";

    return (0);
}


//
// Displays a table showing the radiation level and safety status
// every 3 days until the room is deemed safe to enter.  Returns
// the day number for the first safe day.
//
int rad_table(double init_radiation, double min_radiation)
{
    int    day;             // days elapsed since substance leak
    double radiation_lev;   // current radiation level

    day = 0;
    cout << "\n   Day   Radiation    Status\n         (millirems)\n";
    for (radiation_lev = init_radiation;
         radiation_lev > min_radiation;
         radiation_lev /= 2.0) {
        if (radiation_lev > SAFE_RAD)
            cout << "  " << setw(3) << day << setw(3) << ' ' <<
                setiosflags(ios::fixed) << setprecision(4) <<
                setw(9) << radiation_lev << "    Unsafe\n";
        else
            cout << "  " << setw(3) << day << setw(3) << ' ' <<
                setiosflags(ios::fixed) << setprecision(4) <<
                setw(9) << radiation_lev << "    Safe\n";
        day += 3;
    }

    return (day);
}
```

```
/*
 *  Calculates and displays a table showing the safety level of a
 *  room in which there has been a radiation leak
 */

#include <stdio.h>  /* library with printf and scanf */

#define SAFE_RAD 0.466     /* safe level of radiation               */
#define SAFETY_FACT 10.0   /* safety factor                         */

int rad_table(double init_radiation, double min_radiation);

int main(void)
{
    int     day;              /* day user can enter room              */
    double  init_radiation,   /* radiation level right after leak     */
            min_radiation;    /* safe level divided by safety factor  */

    /* Compute stopping level of radiation                            */
    min_radiation = SAFE_RAD / SAFETY_FACT;

    /* Prompts user to enter initial radiation level                  */
    printf("Enter the radiation level (in millirems)> ");
    scanf("%lf", &init_radiation);

    /* Displays table                                                 */
    day = rad_table(init_radiation, min_radiation);

    /* Display day the user can enter the room.                       */
    printf("\nYou can enter the room on day %d.\n", day);

    return (0);
}

/*
 * Displays a table showing the radiation level and safety status
 * every 3 days until the room is deemed safe to enter.  Returns the
 * day number for the first safe day.
 */
int rad_table(double init_radiation, double min_radiation)
{
    int     day;            /* days elapsed since substance leak      */
    double  radiation_lev;  /* current radiation level                */

    day = 0;
    printf("\n  Day   Radiation   Status\n        (millirems)\n");
    for  (radiation_lev = init_radiation;
          radiation_lev > min_radiation;
          radiation_lev /= 2.0) {
        if (radiation_lev > SAFE_RAD)
            printf("  %3d%3c%9.4f     Unsafe\n", day, ' ', radiation_lev);
        else
            printf("  %3d%3c%9.4f     Safe\n", day, ' ', radiation_lev);
        day += 3;
    }

    return (day);
}
```

TABLE A.1 Placeholders in Format Strings

Placeholder	Variable Type	Function Use
%c	char	printf/scanf
%d	int	printf/scanf
%f	double	printf
%lf	double	scanf
%s	char []	printf/scanf

C Standard Input/Output

C does not have classes, so the stream objects used for I/O in C++ are not available. Also, in C the programmer cannot overload function names or operator names. The C functions for standard input and output are part of the stdio library, which is included using

```
#include <stdio.h>
```

The standard output function, printf, takes a variable number of arguments. The first is always a format string that consists of characters to be displayed and placeholders for variables or expressions whose values are to be displayed. The remaining arguments are the variables or expressions to match up in order with the placeholders. Table A.1 lists commonly used placeholders for data types char, int, double, and Cstring (null-terminated array of char). One places numbers between the % and the next character of the placeholder to specify formatting information such as field width and precision.

Table A.2 compares the output formatting of comparable C++ and C statements.

TABLE A.2 Output Formatting in C and C++

C++	C	Meaning
cout << setw(3) << day;	printf("%3d", day);	Display the value of integer variable day right-justified in a field of 3 columns (%3d).
cout << setiosflags (ios::fixed) << setprecision(4) << setw(9) << radiation_lev;	printf("%9.4f", radiation_lev);	Display the value of floating-point variable radiation_lev with a decimal point and four digits to the right of the decimal point, and right-justify the value in a field of 9 columns (%9.4f).

Function `main` of the C sample program of Fig. A.1 demonstrates the C input function `scanf` in the statement

```
scanf("%lf", &init_radiation);
```

This function call skips over any blanks and newline characters before it takes the first group of nonblank characters encountered and tries to interpret this group as a real number for storage in `init_radiation`.

No Reference Parameters

Notice that `init_radiation` is preceded by the symbol &. This is C's address-of operator, which is necessary here because C has only one type of parameter passing—pass-by-value. Of course, it is important that `scanf` know the address of variable `init_radiation`, so the programmer must explicitly use an expression whose *value* is an address. Because of the unavailability of reference parameters, C programs use the address-of operator to pass a pointer to a variable used as an output argument and use the indirection operator * (which we met in *`this`) to follow such a pointer. To illustrate the declaration and use of pointers as output parameters, Figure A.2 presents side-by-side C++ and C versions of a function that separates a real number into its three components, sign, integer part, and fraction, and uses output parameters to send back its results. In the C version, statements declaring and using pointers are bolded.

In its C implementation (right side of Fig. A.2), function `separate` has one input parameter (`num`) and three output parameters (`signp`, `wholep`, and `fracp`) implemented as pointers. C uses the notation

```
char *signp
int *wholep
double *fracp
```

to indicate that `signp` is of type "pointer to `char`", `wholep` is of type "pointer to `int`", and `fracp` is of type "pointer to `double`". Since the addresses of corresponding actual arguments are passed when function `separate` is called, the value of `signp` is a pointer to the calling function's variable `sn`, `wholep`'s value is a pointer to the calling function's variable `whl`, and `fracp` is a pointer to `frac`. Notice that when the C version of `separate` needs to follow the pointers in its output parameters, it uses the indirection operator *:

```
*signp = '-';
*wholep = floor(magnitude);
*fracp = magnitude - *wholep;
```

FIGURE A.2 Implementing Output Parameters in C++ and C

```cpp
#include <cmath>

//
// Separates a number into three parts:  a sign (+, -,
// blank), a whole number magnitude, and a fractional part.
//
void
separate(double   num,      // input - value to be split
         char&    sign,     // output - sign of num
         int&     whole,    // output - whole number magnitude
                                            of num
         double& frac)      // output - fractional part of num
{
    double magnitude;       // magnitude of num

    // Determines sign of num
    if (num < 0)
        sign = '-';
    else if (num == 0)
        sign = ' ';
    else
        sign = '+';

    // Finds magnitude of num (its absolute value) and
    // separates it into whole and fractional parts
    magnitude = fabs(num);
    whole = floor(magnitude);
    frac = magnitude - whole;
{

// Fragment of calling function

double number = -58.3;
char sn;
int  whl;
double frac;

separate( number, sn, whl, frac);
```

```
#include <math.h>

/*
 * Separates a number into three parts:  a sign (+, −,
 * blank), a whole number magnitude, and a fractional part.
 */
void
separate(double  num,     /* input − value to be split        */
         char    *signp,  /* output − sign of num             */
         int     *wholep, /* output − whole number magnitude
                                      of num                  */
         double *fracp)   /* output − fractional part of num  */
{
     double magnitude;     /* magnitude of num                 */

     /* Determines sign of num */
     if (num < 0)
          *signp = '−';
     else if (num == 0)
          *signp = ' ';
     else
          *signp = '+';

     /* Finds magnitude of num (its absolute value) and
        separates it into whole and fractional parts      */
     magnitude = fabs(num);
     *wholep = floor(magnitude);
     *fracp = magnitude − *wholep;
}

/* Fragment of calling function */

double number = −58.3;
char sn;
int  whl;
double frac;

separate( number, &sn, &whl, &frac);
```

Libraries

Since C has no classes, there are no libraries equivalent to the stream and string object libraries iostream, fstream, iomanip, and string. However, many of C++'s other libraries are derived from comparable C libraries, and Table A.3 shows three corresponding header files. You can see that in general, if a C++ library was derived from a comparable C library, you can reconstruct the header file name used in C by simply removing the leading "c" from the name used in C++ and adding ".h".

Data Structures and Files

The arrays and structure types that we have studied in C++ are also available in C. Since C does not have classes, it uses a pointer to a predefined structure type called FILE to access a data file. Table A.4 compares C++ and C statements for declaring, opening, accessing, and closing both input and output files.

TABLE A.3 Comparable C++ and C Standard Libraries

C++ Name	C Name
<cmath>	<math.h>
<cstdlib>	<stdlib.h>
<cctype>	<ctype.h>

TABLE A.4 File I/O in C++ and C

C++	C	Meaning

ifstream in("data.txt",
    ios::in);
	FILE *in;
	in = fopen("data.txt",
	    "r");
		Declares in as a variable to access open input file data.txt.

in >> num >> x;	fscanf(in, "%d%lf", &num, &x);	Fills variables num and x with data from file accessed by in.

ofstream out("res.txt",
    ios::out);
	FILE *out;
	out = fopen("res.txt",
	    "w");
		Declares out as a variable to access open output file res.txt.

out << "Num = " << num
    << endl << "x = " <<
    << x << endl;
	fprintf(out,
	    "Num = %d\nx = %.2f\n",
	    num, x);
		Writes values of num and x (with labels) to output file accessed by out.

in.close(); out.close();	fclose(in); fclose(out);	Closes files accessed by in and out.

Appendix B
Selected C++ Standard
Functions/Macros

Syntax	Header File	Purpose
`void abort(void);`	`cstdlib`	Abnormally terminates a program.
`int abs(int x);`	`cstdlib`	Returns the absolute value of an integer.
`double acos(double x);`	`cmath`	Returns the arc cosine of the input value (argument must be in the range –1 to 1).
`double asin(double x);`	`cmath`	Returns the arc sine of the input value (argument must be in the range –1 to 1).
`void assert(int test);`	`cassert`	If test evaluates to zero, assert prints an error message and aborts the program.
`double atan(double x);`	`cmath`	Calculates the arc tangent of the input value.
`double atan2(double y,` `    double x);`	`cmath`	Calculates the arc tangent of y/x.
`int atexit(void (*func) (void));`	`cstdlib`	Registers a user-defined function to be called by exit at normal program termination.
`double atof(const char *s);`	`cmath`	Converts a Cstring pointed to by s to double.
`int atoi(const char *s);`	`cstdlib`	Converts a Cstring pointed to by s to int.
`long atol(const char *s);`	`cstdlib`	Converts a Cstring pointed to by s to long.

`void *bsearch(const void *key,`
`    const void *base,`
`    size_t nelem, size_t`[1]` width,`
`    int (*fcmp) (const void *,`
`            const void *));`
	`cstdlib`	Binary search of the sorted array base: returns the address of the first entry in the array that matches the search key using the user-defined comparison routine fcmp; if no match is found, returns 0.

[1]`size_t` is a type used for memory object sizes and repeat counts.

Syntax	Header File	Purpose
`void *calloc(size_t nitems, size_t size);`	cstdlib	Allocates a memory block of size nitems × size, clears the block to zeros, and returns a pointer to the newly allocated block.
`double ceil(double x);`	cmath	Returns the smallest integer not less than x.
`clock_t`[2] `clock(void);`	ctime	Returns processor time elapsed since the beginning of program invocation.
`double cos(double x);`	cmath	Calculates the cosine of a value (angle in radians).
`double cosh(double x);`	cmath	Calculates the hyperbolic cosine of a value.
`char *ctime (const time_t`[3] `*time);`	ctime	Converts date and time value pointed to by time (the value returned by function time) into a 26-character Cstring representing local time.
`double difftime (time_t time2, time_t time1);`	ctime	Calculates the difference between two times in seconds.
`div_t div(int numer, int denom);`	cstdlib	Divides two integers, returning quotient and remainder in a structure whose elements are quot and rem.
`void exit(int status);`	cstdlib	Terminates program. Before termination, all files are closed, buffered output (waiting to be output) is written, and any registered "exit functions" (posted with atexit) are called; status of 0 indicates normal exit; a nonzero status indicates some error.
`double exp(double x);`	cmath	Calculates the exponential function e^x.
`double fabs(double x);`	cmath	Calculates the absolute value of a floating-point number.
`double floor(double x);`	cmath	Returns the largest integer not greater than x.
`double fmod(double x, double y);`	cmath	Calculates x modulo y, the remainder of x divided by y.
`void free(void *block);`	cstdlib	Deallocates a memory block allocated by a previous call to calloc, malloc, or realloc.

[2]`clock_t` is a type used to represent processor time.
[3]`time_t` is a type used to represent a calendar time.

Syntax	Header File	Purpose
`double frexp(double x,` `  int *exponent);`	cmath	Splits a double number into mantissa and exponent.
`char *getenv(const char *name);`	cstdlib	Returns the value of a specified variable.
`struct tm *gmtime` `  (const time_t *timer);`	ctime	Converts date and time to Greenwich mean time (GMT).
`int isalnum(int c);`	cctype	Predicate returning nonzero if c is a letter or a decimal digit.
`int isalpha(int c);`	cctype	Predicate returning nonzero if c is a letter.
`int iscntrl(int c);`	cctype	Predicate returning nonzero if c is a delete character or an ordinary control character.
`int isdigit(int c);`	cctype	Predicate returning nonzero if c is a decimal digit
`int isgraph(int c);`	cctype	Predicate returning nonzero if c is a printing character other than a space.
`int islower(int c);`	cctype	Predicate returning nonzero if c is a lowercase letter.
`int isprint(int c);`	cctype	Predicate returning nonzero if c is a printing character.
`int ispunct(int c);`	cctype	Predicate returning nonzero if c is a punctuation character.
`int isspace(int c);`	cctype	Predicate returning nonzero if c is a space, tab, carriage return, new line, vertical tab, or formfeed.
`int isupper(int c);`	cctype	Predicate returning nonzero if c is an uppercase letter.
`int isxdigit(int c);`	cctype	Predicate returning nonzero if c is a hexadecimal digit (0 to 9, A to F, a to f).
`long labs(long int x);`	cmath	Computes the absolute value of the parameter x.
`double ldexp(double x,` `  int exp);`	cmath	Calculates $x \times 2^{exp}$.
`ldiv_t ldiv(long int numer,` `  long int denom);`	cstdlib	Divides two `long int`s, returning quotient and remainder in a structure whose components are quot and rem.

Syntax	Header File	Purpose
`struct tm * localtime` `  (const time_t *timer);`	`ctime`	Accepts the address of a value returned by `time` and returns a pointer to a structure of type `tm` in which the time is corrected for the time zone and possible daylight savings time.
`double log(double x);`	`cmath`	Calculates the natural logarithm of x.
`double log10(double x);`	`cmath`	Calculates $\log_{10}(x)$.
`void *malloc(size_t size);`	`cstdlib`	Allocates a block of `size` bytes from the memory heap and returns a pointer to the newly allocated block.
`int mblen` `  (const char *s, size_t n);`	`cstdlib`	Returns the size in bytes of the multibyte character pointed to by s (n is the maximum size of the character.)
`size_t mbstowcs(wchar_t *pwcs,` `  const char *s, size_t n);`	`cstdlib`	Converts up to n multibyte characters from string s to wide characters stored in array `pwcs`.
`int mbtowc(wchar_t *pwc,` `  const char *s, size_t n);`	`cstdlib`	Converts the multibyte character accessed by s to a wide character of type `wchar_t`.
`time_t mktime(struct tm *t);`	`ctime`	Converts the time in the structure pointed to by t into a calendar time.
`double modf(double x,` `  double *ipart);`	`cmath`	Splits a double into integer and fractional parts, both with the same sign as x.
`double pow(double x, double y);`	`cmath`	Calculates x^y.

`void qsort(void *base, size_t`
`  nelem, size_t width,`
`  int (*fcmp) (const void *,`
`  const void *));`
	`cstdlib`	Sorts array base using the quicksort algorithm based on the user-defined comparison function pointed to by `fcmp`.

`int rand(void);`	`cstdlib`	Returns successive pseudorandom numbers in the range from 0 to `RAND_MAX` (constant defined in `cstdlib`).
`void *realloc(void *block,` `  size_t size);`	`cstdlib`	Attempts to shrink or to expand the previously allocated block to `size` bytes, copying the contents to a new location if necessary.
`double sin(double x);`	`cmath`	Calculates the sine of the input value (angles in radians).
`double sinh(double x);`	`cmath`	Calculates hyperbolic sine.
`double sqrt(double x);`	`cmath`	Calculates the positive square root of a nonnegative input value.

Syntax	Header File	Purpose
`void srand(unsigned seed);`	`cstdlib`	Initializes random number generator.

`size_t strftime(char *s,`
`  size_t maxsize, const char`
`  *fmt, const struct tm *t);`
	`ctime`	Formats time for output according to the `fmt` specifications; returns the number of characters placed into s.

`double strtod(const char *s,` `  char **endptr);`	`cstdlib`	Converts string s to a `double` value; if endptr is not null, it sets *endptr to point to the character that stopped the scan.
`long strtol(const char *s,` `  char **endptr, int radix);`	`cstdlib`	Converts a string s to a `long` value in the given radix; if endptr is not null, it sets *endptr to point to the character that stopped the scan.

`unsigned long strtoul`
`  (const char *s,`
`  char **endptr, int radix);`
	`cstdlib`	Converts a string s to an `unsigned long` value in the given radix; if endptr is not null, it sets *endptr to point to the character that stopped the scan.

`int system` `  (const char *command);`	`cstdlib`	Executes an operating system command.
`double tan(double x);`	`cmath`	Calculates the tangent of an angle specified in radians.
`double tanh(double x);`	`cmath`	Calculates the hyperbolic tangent.
`time_t time(time_t *timer);`	`ctime`	Gives the current time, in seconds, elapsed since 00:00:00 GMT, January 1, 1970, and stores that value in the location pointed to by `timer`.
`int tolower(int ch);`	`cctype`	Converts an integer `ch` to its lowercase value. Non-uppercase letter values are returned unchanged.
`int toupper(int ch);`	`cctype`	Converts an integer `ch` to its uppercase value. Non-lowercase letter values are returned unchanged.
`size_t wcstombs(char *s, const` `  wchar_t *pwcs, size_t n);`	`cstdlib`	Converts a string of wide characters to a string of multibyte characters (changes no more than n bytes of s).
`int wctomb(char *s,` `  wchar_t wchar);`	`cstdlib`	Stores in s the multibyte representation of wide character `wchar`.

Appendix C
Selected C++ Input/
Output Facilities

Input/Output Operators

Operator	Header File	Left Operand	Right Operand	Expression Value
>>	iostream	Reference to an input stream	Variable into which >> stores data from input stream	Reference to the input stream
<<	iostream	Reference to an output stream	Expression whose value is output to the output stream	Reference to the output stream
<<	iostream	Reference to an output stream	Output stream manipulator that changes format of subsequent output sent to the output stream	Reference to the output stream

Output Stream Manipulators

Manipulator	Header File	Action	Argument	Action that Argument Specifies
setiosflags	iomanip	Turns on behavior specified by argument	ios::left	Left-justify output in the prescribed field
			ios::right	Right-justify output in the prescribed field
			ios::dec	Use base 10
			ios::oct	Use base 8
			ios::hex	Use base 16
			ios::showpoint	Display decimal point

Manipulator	Header File	Action	Argument	Action that Argument Specifies
setiosflags (*cont.*)			`ios::scientific`	Use scientific notation for floating-point numbers
			`ios::fixed`	Show floating-point numbers with decimal point and as many digits to the right as specified by current precision
resetiosflags	iomanip	Turns off behavior specified by argument	See `setiosflags`	
setw	iomanip	Sets field width for next output to stream	Integer field width	
setprecision	iomanip	Sets precision for floating-point output	Integer precision (number of digits displayed to the right of decimal point)	
endl	iostream	Ends current output line	None	

I/O Stream Member Functions

Function	Argument(s)	Result
clear	None	Changes stream state, clearing failure flags.
setstate	ios::failbit	Signals a failure on the stream.
eof	None	Returns true if an input from the stream has detected end of file.
fail	None	Returns true if a stream operation has failed.
open*	File name (a Cstring)	Opens file, if possible, and associates stream with open file.
close*	None	Closes file. If file is an output file, writes final buffer to file before closing.

*Member of ifstream, ofstream objects; requires fstream header file.

Appendix D
Selected Facilities
Provided by Class string

The preprocessor directive

```
#include <string>
```

provides access to class string and all its facilities. Table D.1 presents some of the most commonly used string functions and operators.

TABLE D.1 Selected Operations and Functions Defined for Class string

Facility	Example	Purpose

Construction	`string s1, s2("Hello");`
	`string s3(s2);`
	`string s4(", there");`
		Declares string variables s1 (initialized to the empty string by default), s2 (initialized using Cstring "Hello"), s3 (initialized as a copy of string s2), and s4 (initialized to ", there").

Whitespace-delimited input	`cin >> s1;`	Skips over whitespace, if any. Then stores in s1 the next group of characters input up to the first whitespace character.
Whole-line input	`getline(infile, s1);`	Skips nothing in infile. Stores all characters up to (not including) the next '\n' or up to end-of-file in s1 and removes newline from the input line.

TABLE D.1 *(Continued)*

Facility	Example	Purpose
Specific-character-delimited input	`getline(infile, s1, ',');`	Skips nothing in `infile`. Stores all characters up to (not including) the next comma (the third parameter is the delimiter character) or up to the end-of-file in `s1` and removes the delimiter character from the input line.
Concatenation without modifying operands	`cout << s2 + s4 << endl;`	Forms string `"Hello, there"` by concatenating s2 and s4. Strings s2 and s4 are unchanged.
Concatenation, changing left operand	`s2 += s4;`	New value of s2 is `"Hello, there"`.
Access (read/write) a single character at a specified position.	`cout << s4[3] << s4.at(4)` `   << endl;`	If s4 is `", there"`, displays he `[]` does no range checking; at aborts on an attempt to access an out-of-range character.

Access a copy of a substring starting at a specified position and taking a certain number of characters (or the rest of the string).	`cout << s2.substr(7, 3) <<`
	`   endl << s2.substr(8) <<`
	`   endl;`
		If s2 is `"Hello, there"`, displays
		    the
		    here

Find a string, Cstring or character in the current string and return the position of its leftmost occurrence or return –1 if not found.	`cout << s2.find(s4) <<`
	`   endl << s2.find("el") <<`
	`   endl << s2.find('t')`
	`   << endl;`
		If s2 is `"Hello, there"` and s4 is `", there"`, displays 5, then 1, then 7.

Return position of first occurrence of one of the characters of the string, Cstring, or character argument in the current string (or –1 if not found), starting at position 0 unless another starting position is specified.	`cout <<`
	`   s2.find_first_of("!.,&?")`
	`   << endl;`
	`if (s2.find_first_of('o', 6)`
	`      == -1)`
	`   cout << "Can't find o\n";`
		If s2 is `"Hello, there"`, displays 5, the position of the comma, and then `"Can't find o"`, because the letter 'o' is not found searching from position 6 to the end.

TABLE D.1 *(Continued)*

Facility	Example	Purpose
In the current string find first occurrence of a character *not* found in the string, Cstring or character argument (or –1 if all are found), starting at position 0 unless another starting position is specified.	```cout << s2.find_first_not_of("!.,&?") << endl;```	If s2 is "Hello, there", displays 0 since the first character of s2 is not one of the designated punctuation marks.
Current string length	```cout << s2.length() << endl;```	Displays length of "Hello, there", which is 12.
Case-sensitive lexicographical comparisons <, <=, >, >=, ==, !=	```string wd1("dog"), wd2("cat"); if (wd1 < wd2) cout << wd1; else cout << wd2; cout << " comes first " << "alphabetically.\n";```	As long as both strings contain all upper- or all lower-case letters, comparisons are alphabetical, where < means "comes first alphabetically." Example displays "cat comes first alphabetically."
Check for empty string	```if (s2.empty()) cout << "s2 = the empty string\n"; else cout << "s2 isn't empty\n";```	Function empty returns true if current string is "". If s2 is "Hello, there", code fragment displays "s2 isn't empty".
Reset string variable to the empty string.	```s2.clear();```	Function clear sets the current string to be the empty string.
Exchange the values of two string variables.	```wd1.swap(wd2);```	If wd1 is "dog" initially, and wd2 is "cat", after the call to swap, wd1 is "cat" and wd2 is "dog".
Convert a string to a Cstring.	```s2.c_str()```	Returns a null-terminated array of characters representing the value of s2.

Appendix E
C++ Operators

Table D.1 shows the precedence and associativity of C++ operators. The precedence table is followed by a table that lists the operators described in this textbook along with the number of operands required by each and the section of the text that explains the operator.

TABLE E.1 Precedence and Associativity of Operations

Precedence	Operation	Associativity
Highest (evaluated first)	(*expression*)　　: :	
	array[..]　　*f*(..)　　.　　->　　postfix ++　　postfix --	left
	prefix ++　　prefix --　　unary *　　unary & unary +　　unary -　　!　　~　　new　　delete　　sizeof	right
	.*　　->*	left
	binary *　　/　　%	left
	binary +　　　　binary -	left
	<<　　>>	left
	<　　>　　<=　　>=	left
	==　　!=	left
	binary &	left
	^	left
	|	left
	&&	left
	||	left
	? :	right
	=　　*=　　/=　　%=　　+=　　-= >>=　　<<=　　&=　　^=　　|=	right
Lowest (evaluated last)	,	left

TABLE E.2 Where to Find Operators in Text

Operator	Name	Number of Operands	Section Where Found
(*expression*)	parentheses	1	2.5
::	scope resolution	2	6.3
array[..]	subscript	2	7.1
f(..)	function call	varies	2.6
f(..)	function call notation for explicit type conversion	2	2.5
.	direct member access	2	6.1
++	increment	1	4.4
− −	decrement	1	4.4
unary *	indirection	1	6.5
unary −	arithmetic negation	1	2.5
!	logical negation (not)	1	3.2
new	dynamic memory allocation	1	7.6
delete	memory deallocation	1	7.6
*	multiplication	2	2.5
/	division	2	2.5
%	remainder	2	2.5
+	addition	2	2.5
−	subtraction	2	2.5
<<	output insertion	2	2.3
>>	input extraction	2	2.3
<	less than	2	3.2
>	greater than	2	3.2
<=	less than or equal	2	3.2
>=	greater than or equal	2	3.2
==	equality	2	3.2
!=	inequality	2	3.2
&&	logical (boolean) and	2	3.2
||	logical (boolean) or	2	3.2
=	assignment	2	2.5
*= /= %= += −=	arithmetic compound assignment	2	4.4

Appendix F
C++ Keywords

asm	do	inline	short	typeid
auto	double	int	signed	typename
bool	dynamic_cast	long	sizeof	union
break	else	mutable	static	unsigned
case	enum	namespace	static_cast	using
catch	explicit	new	struct	virtual
char	extern	operator	switch	void
class	false	private	template	volatile
const	float	protected	this	wchar_t
const_cast	for	public	throw	while
continue	friend	register	true	
default	goto	reinterpret_cast	try	
delete	if	return	typedef	

Appendix G
Microsoft Visual C++ Integrated Development Environment, An Introduction

Preface

This appendix is structured as a laboratory to give students a hands-on introduction to the features of the Microsoft Visual C++ integrated development environment that are most important for beginning programmers. The text of this appendix is available at the Addison Wesley Longman site that provides access to all the code figures from this text—www.aw.com/cssupport. Instructors may prefer to download the appendix document (appendixG.doc) and customize it with pathnames reflecting their local installation. Before using this appendix, verify that your version of Visual C++ is 6.0 or higher. If you are using Visual C++ 6.0, you must have installed Service Pack 3 or higher in order for `friend` functions and operators to compile properly. Service Packs are available from the Downloads section of www.microsoft.com.

Preliminaries

Before beginning this lab, ask your instructor how to enter the Visual C++ environment on your laboratory's computers. Write down the access method using one of these notations:

1. <u>Start</u> / <u>Programs</u> / <u>Microsoft Visual C++</u> / <u>Microsoft Visual C++</u>
   This notation means
   - Click on <u>Start</u>
   - In the menu that appears, move the mouse pointer to <u>Programs</u>
   - In the menu that appears from <u>Programs</u>, move the mouse pointer to <u>Microsoft Visual C++</u>
   - In the final menu, click on <u>Microsoft Visual C++</u>

2. Double click on the Visual C++ icon.

Microsoft
Visual C++

Enter Visual C++ _____

When the lab instructions say, "Enter Visual C++ environment," you will execute the access method you have written above.

Now identify the directory on your computer's hard drive where you plan to store your source code files and data files. Write the pathname of this directory below

sourceNdata _____

In this appendix, when we refer to *sourceNdata*, you will use the pathname you have identified above.

For ready access to the code figures used in this lab, go to the Addison Wesley Longman site www.aw.com/cssupport and copy to *sourceNdata* this file: fig02_13.cpp

Open, Compile, and Run an Existing C++ Program

1.0   Enter the Visual C++ environment. If Visual C++ displays a "tip," click the <u>Close</u> button.

2.0   Open the C++ source file fig02_13.cpp that you copied to *sourceNdata*. Select <u>File</u> / <u>Open</u> or the open folder icon, find directory *sourceNdata*, click on fig02_13.cpp, and click <u>Open</u>. Delete any lines of the file that are not part of the program (e.g., the figure title, output from the program).

3.0   Compile and run fig02_13.cpp.

   3.1 To COMPILE: Select <u>Build</u> / <u>Compile fig02_13.cpp</u>
      If you are not currently using a workspace, you will need to create one in order to run your program. Here are two ways to create a new project workspace. We will use a) now and b) in a later example.
      a) When you first compile a source file, a prompt will ask, "Would you like to create a default project workspace?" Click on <u>Yes</u> to use this method now.
      b) You can create a workspace manually by choosing <u>File</u> / <u>New</u> / <u>Win 32 Console Application</u> (on the Projects tab).

   3.2 To RUN: Select <u>Build</u> / <u>Build fig02_13.exe</u>, then <u>Build</u> / <u>Execute fig02_13.exe</u>.

   3.3 Enter as input data a population of 130000.

   3.4 After observing the results, type any key to remove the execution window. Then close your workspace (<u>File</u> / <u>Close workspace</u>), but answer <u>No</u> to the question "Close all document windows?"

Modify, Save, and Rerun an Existing C++ Program

1.0   If fig02_13.cpp is not open, open it. Then save it under another name: Select <u>File</u> / <u>Save as</u> and type in fig02_13mod.cpp as the file name.

2.0   Make two changes to the source code.

■ Insert an additional comment at the beginning of the program that includes **your name**:

```
// Modified by Jane Q. Student
```

■ Insert an additional output statement after the declaration of variable `flowEst` (substitute **your own name**):

```
cout << "Output from Fig 2.13 as modified by Jane Q. Student\n";
```

Then save your modified version (<u>File</u> / <u>Save</u>).

3.0   Create a new workspace using <u>File</u> / <u>New</u> / <u>Win 32 Console Application</u> (on the Projects tab). Type in *sourceNdata* as the location and fig02_13mod as the project name. Be sure <u>Create</u> new workspace is selected. Click <u>OK</u>. Select <u>An empty project</u> and click <u>Finish</u>. Then click <u>OK</u> to accept the defaults. View fig02_13mod.cpp again: <u>File</u> / <u>Recent Files</u> / <u>fig02_13mod.cpp</u>. Compile and run the revised program using the data 130000 as before. (Answer <u>Yes</u> to the question regarding adding the file to the project.) Before closing the execution window and the workspace, print out your program and its output as described in the next section. You may also wish to skip to the section "C++ Syntax Error Messages" before closing your workspace.

Print Out a Program and Its Output

The directions that follow assume that you have just executed a C++ program and that the execution window containing the program output is still on your screen.

1.0   To get a printout of the contents of the execution window:

a) Position the mouse pointer in the upper left corner of the execution window. There is a small DOS icon there.

b) Click once to open a menu.

c) Choose <u>Edit</u> / <u>Mark</u>.

d) Highlight the contents of the execution window.

e) Open the menu in the upper left corner again.

f) Choose <u>Edit</u> / <u>Copy</u>, which will copy the contents of the execution window to the Clipboard.

g) Enter Microsoft Word: <u>Start</u> / <u>Programs</u> / <u>Microsoft Word</u>.

h) Change the font to Courier New.

i) Use the command <u>Edit</u> / <u>Paste</u> to paste the contents of the Clipboard to the document.

     j) Use the command <u>File</u> / <u>Print</u> or click on the printer icon to send the document to the printer.

     k) Exit Word.

     l) Click on the execution window and press any key to close it.

2.0 To get a printout of your source code:

     a) Make sure that the window containing the source code is the active window.

     b) Select <u>File</u> / <u>Print</u> or click on the printer icon to send the source file to the printer.

Enter, Compile, and Run a New C++ Program

1.0 Enter the Visual C++ environment. If Visual C++ displays a "tip," click the <u>Close</u> button.

2.0 Create a new workspace using <u>File</u> / <u>New</u> / <u>Win 32 Console Application</u> (on the Projects tab). Type in *sourceNdata* as the location and choose a project name (we'll assume you choose projname). Be sure <u>Create</u> <u>new</u> <u>workspace</u> is selected. Click <u>OK</u>. Select <u>An empty project</u> and click <u>Finish</u>. Then click <u>OK</u> to accept the defaults.

3.0 Open a new file by selecting <u>File</u> / <u>New</u> / <u>C++ Source File</u>. Be sure <u>Add</u> <u>to Project</u> is checked, name the file projname.cpp, and choose *sourceNdata* as the location. Type in the source code of the new program and save it.

4.0 Compile and run projname.cpp.

     4.1 To COMPILE: Select <u>Build</u> / <u>Compile projname.cpp</u>

     4.2 To RUN: Select <u>Build</u> / <u>Build projname.exe</u>, then <u>Build</u> / <u>Execute</u> <u>projname.exe</u>.

     4.3 Enter data as required.

5.0 After observing the results (and printing them if desired), type any key to remove the execution window. Then close your workspace (<u>File</u> / <u>Close workspace</u>), answering <u>Yes</u> to the question "Close all document windows?"

C++ Syntax Error Messages

Take out a sheet of paper on which to jot down your answers to the questions in this section. Then compare your answers to those at the end of Appendix G. If fig02_13mod.cpp is not open, open it.

1.0 Edit your revised program in fig02_13mod.cpp by deleting the semicolon in the declaration of popThou. Recompile the program. What error message appears? You will likely need to scroll up in the window at the bottom of your screen to see error messages. Highlight the error message and press <u>Enter</u>. An arrow now indicates in your source file the point where this error was detected. Can you explain the message?

2.0 Now replace the ; you deleted, and comment out the declaration of popThou.

```
// double popThou;
```

Recompile the program. Then highlight the first error message and determine the line it refers to. Explain the message.

3.0 Restore the declaration of popThou and comment out the first #include line. Recompile the program and explain the messages produced.

4.0 Restore the commented-out #include and save the file. Select <u>File</u> / <u>Close Workspace</u>, answering <u>Yes</u> to the question about closing all document files.

Using the Debugger To Single-Step Through a Program

When you have a program that is aborting or producing incorrect results, it is very helpful to execute it one statement at a time so you can determine which statement is not behaving as you had anticipated it would.

1.0 Open fig02_13mod.cpp, compile it (<u>Build</u> / <u>Compile fig02_13mod.cpp</u>) and build the executable file (<u>Build</u> / <u>Build fig02_13mod.exe</u>).

2.0 Execute the program one statement at a time: instead of <u>Build</u> / <u>Execute</u>, use <u>Build</u> / <u>Start Debug</u> / <u>Step Into</u>. Then repeatedly type the <u>F10</u> key and watch the results of executing each statement.

3.0 After each insertion of output in stream cout, click on the DOS icon that appears in the task bar at the bottom of the screen so you can observe the output. Then click in the source code window and continue typing <u>F10</u>. Respond to the prompting message with 130000.

4.0 To exit the debugger, use <u>Debug</u> / <u>Stop Debugging</u>.

Answers to Syntax Error Questions

1. The error message is "missing ';' before type int." The arrow points to the line after the line with the omitted semicolon because the compiler can't know the semicolon is missing until it sees the next symbol—int in this case.
2. The error message is "'popThou' : undeclared identifier." The arrow points to the first statement that uses variable popThou.
3. Multiple error messages complain about the names std, cout, and cin, and about the operands of operators << and >>. These names and operators are defined in standard library <iostream>, which we have neglected to include.

Appendix H
Borland C++ Builder Integrated Development Environment, An Introduction

Preface

This appendix is structured as a laboratory to give students a hands-on introduction to the features of the Borland C++ Builder integrated development environment that are most important for beginning programmers. The text of this appendix is available at the Addison Wesley Longman site that provides access to all the code figures from this text—www.aw.com/cssupport. Instructors may prefer to download the appendix document (appendixH .doc) and customize it with pathnames reflecting their local installation.

Preliminaries

Before beginning this lab, ask your instructor how to enter the Borland C++ Builder environment on your laboratory's computers. Write down the access method using one of these notations:

1. <u>Start</u> / <u>Programs</u> / <u>Borland C++ Builder</u> / <u>C++ Builder</u>
   This notation means
   - Click on <u>Start</u>
   - In the menu that appears, move the mouse pointer to <u>Programs</u>
   - In the menu that appears from <u>Programs</u>, move the mouse pointer to <u>Borland C++ Builder</u>
   - In the final menu, click on <u>C++ Builder</u>
2. Double click on the <u>Borland C++ Builder</u> icon.

C++Builder

Enter C++ Builder _____

When the lab instructions say, "Enter C++ Builder environment," you will execute the access method you have written above.

Now identify the directory on your computer's hard drive where you plan to store your source code files and data files. Write the pathname of this directory below

sourceNdata _____

In this appendix, when we refer to *sourceNdata*, you will use the pathname you have identified above.

For ready access to the code figures used in this lab, go to the Addison Wesley Longman site www.aw.com/cssupport and copy to *sourceNdata* this file: fig02_13.cpp

Open, Compile, and Run an Existing C++ Program

1.0   Enter the C++ Builder environment.

2.0   Open the C++ source file fig02_13.cpp that you copied to *sourceNdata*. Select <u>File</u> / <u>Open</u> or the open folder icon, find directory *sourceNdata*, click on fig02_13.cpp, and click <u>Open</u>. Delete any lines of the file that are not part of the program (e.g., the figure title, output from the program). Then highlight the entire program (<u>Edit</u> / <u>Select All</u>) and copy it to the Clipboard: <u>Edit</u> / <u>Copy</u>. Close the source file: <u>File</u> / <u>Close</u>.

3.0   Create a Console Application: Select <u>File</u> / <u>New</u> and double click on the <u>Console Wizard</u> icon. Verify that <u>Console</u> and <u>EXE</u> are selected, and then click the <u>Finish</u> button.

4.0   Highlight all the code in the source file window that appears (<u>Edit</u> / <u>Select All</u>) and replace it with the clipboard contents: <u>Edit</u> / <u>Paste</u>. Modify the source file so the interactive console window will not disappear before you have a chance to view the results:

    4.1 At the beginning of the file, add the preprocessor directive
    `#include <conio>`

    4.2 Just before the return statement, add the statement `getch();` This statement causes the program to wait for input of a character, so the interactive console window will remain on your screen until you type a character.

5.0   Save the revised source file and associated project: <u>File</u> / <u>Save Project As</u>. Type fig02_13 as the project name and click the <u>Save</u> button. Answer <u>Yes</u> to the question.

6.0   Compile and run fig02_13.cpp.

    6.1 Select <u>Run</u> / <u>Run</u>.

    6.2 Enter as input data a population of 130000.

    6.3 After observing the results, type any key to remove the execution window.

Modify, Save, and Rerun an Existing C++ Program

1.0 If fig02_13.cpp is not open, open it. Copy its contents to the clipboard (Edit / Select All, Edit / Copy) and then close it and any open project files: File / Close All.

2.0 Create a Console Application: Select File / New and double click on the Console Wizard icon. Verify that Console and EXE are selected, and then click the Finish button.

3.0 Highlight all the code in the source file window that appears (Edit / Select All) and replace it with the clipboard contents: Edit / Paste.

4.0 Make two changes to the source code.

■ Insert an additional comment at the beginning of the program that includes **your name**:

```
// Modified by Jane Q. Student
```

■ Insert an additional output statement after the declaration of variable `flowEst` (substitute **your own name**):

```
cout << "Output from Fig 2.13 as modified by Jane Q. Student\n";
```

Save the revised source file and associated project: File / Save Project As. Type fig02_13mod as the project name and click the Save button.

5.0 Compile and run the revised program using the data 130000 as before. Before closing the console window and the project, print out your program and its output as described in the next section.

Print Out a Program and Its Output

The directions that follow assume that you have just executed a C++ program and that the console window containing the program output is still on your screen.

1.0 To get a printout of the contents of the console window:

a) Position the mouse pointer in the upper left corner of the console window. There is a small DOS icon there.

b) Click once to open a menu.

c) Choose Edit / Mark.

d) Highlight the contents of the console window.

e) Open the menu in the upper left corner again.

f) Choose Edit / Copy, which will copy the contents of the console window to the Clipboard.

g) Enter Microsoft Word: Start / Programs / Microsoft Word.

h) Change the font to Courier New.

i) Use the command Edit / Paste to paste the contents of the Clipboard to the document.

        j)   Use the command <u>File</u> / <u>Print</u> or click on the printer icon to send the document to the printer.

        k)   Exit Word.

        l)   Click on the console window and press any key to close it.

2.0   To get a printout of your source code:

        a)   Make sure that the window containing the source code is the active window.

        b)   Select <u>File</u> / <u>Print</u> to send the source file to the printer. If your C++ Builder is not set up to communicate with your printer, you can print the source code from Microsoft Word, as you did the program output.

Create, Compile, and Run a New C++ Program

1.0   Enter the C++ Builder environment.

2.0   Create a Console Application: Select <u>File</u> / <u>New</u> and double click on the <u>Console Wizard</u> icon. Verify that <u>Console</u> and <u>EXE</u> are selected, and then click the <u>Finish</u> button.

3.0   Highlight all the code in the source file window that appears (<u>Edit</u> / <u>Select All</u>) and delete it. Type in your source code. Be sure to design the source file so the interactive console window will not disappear before you have a chance to view the results:

    3.1 At the beginning of the file, use the preprocessor directive
         `#include <conio>`

    3.2 Just before the `return` statement, include the statement
         `getch();` This statement causes the program to wait for input of a character, so the interactive console window will remain on your screen until you type a character.

4.0   Save the new source file and associated project: <u>File</u> / <u>Save Project As</u>. Type a project name and click the <u>Save</u> button. Answer <u>Yes</u> to the question.

5.0   Compile and run the new project.

    5.1 Select <u>Run</u> / <u>Run</u>. Check error messages, revise and rerun until program prompts for data.

    5.2 Enter input data as needed.

    5.3 After observing the results, type any key to remove the console window.

C++ Syntax Error Messages

Take out a sheet of paper on which to jot down your answers to the questions in this section. Then compare your answers to those at the end of Appendix H. Open your project fig02_13mod (<u>File</u> / <u>Open Project</u>, select <u>fig02_13mod</u> project icon, and click on <u>Open</u> button).

1.0   Revise the source file by deleting the semicolon in the declaration of popThou. Recompile the program. What error messages appear? Initially, there will be an arrow in front of the first message, and the cursor in the source code window will indicate where this first error was detected. Can you explain the first message? Then double-click on the second error message. An arrow now indicates in your source file the point where this error was detected. All errors after the first are fall-out from the first error.

2.0   Now replace the ; you deleted, and comment out the declaration of popThou.

```
// double popThou;
```

Recompile the program. Then read the error message and determine the line it refers to. Explain the message.

3.0   Restore the declaration of popThou and comment out the #include of <iostream>. Recompile the program and explain the messages produced.

4.0   Restore the #include. Then select File / Close All and answer Yes to the question.

Using the Debugger To Single-Step Through a Program

When you have a program that is aborting or producing incorrect results, it is very helpful to execute it one statement at a time so you can determine which statement is not behaving as you had anticipated it would.

1.0   Open project fig02_13mod (File / Open Project, select fig02_13mod project icon, and click on Open button).

2.0   Prepare to execute the program one statement at a time, watching the values of the variables change: Instead of Run / Run, use Run / Step Over, then Run / Trace Into. Then set up the watch window to track the program's variables. For each variable, select Run / Add Watch, type in the variable name in the box labeled Expression, and click OK. Move the Watch List window to a part of your screen where it doesn't overlap the source code window (Click and hold on Watch List and drag the window to where you want it, then release.) You may need to move the source code window as well. Then click on the source code window, repeatedly type the F8 key, and watch the results of executing each statement.

3.0   After each insertion of output in stream cout, click on the DOS icon that appears in the task bar at the bottom of the screen so you can observe the output. Then click in the source code window and continue typing F8. Respond to the prompting message with 130000.

4.0   To exit the debugger, complete execution of the program or use Run / Program Reset.

Answers to Syntax Error Questions

1. The first error message is "Declaration syntax error." The cursor is within the line after the line with the omitted semicolon because the compiler can't know the semicolon is missing until it sees the next symbol—int in this case.

2. The error message is "Undefined symbol 'popThou'." The cursor is within the first statement that uses variable popThou.

3. Two error messages complain about the names cout and cin . These names are defined in standard library <iostream>, which we have neglected to include. The other two messages are fall-out from the fact that the compiler cannot translate the statements that use cout and cin.

Appendix I

Character Sets

This appendix shows two character sets: the American Standard Code for Information Interchange (ASCII) and the Extended Binary Coded Decimal Interchange Code (EBCDIC). Unprintable characters are represented by their usual names, and within these names, the characters' common abbreviations are shown in boldface type. For example, the null character is represented by the abbreviation NUL, and the start-of-heading character by the abbreviation SOH. The table shows the numeric character codes in base 10.

Character	ASCII Code	EBCDIC Code
NULl	0	0
Start **O**f **H**eading	1	1
Start of **T**e**X**t	2	2
End of **T**e**X**t	3	3
End **O**f **T**ransmission	4	55
ENQuiry	5	45
ACKnowledge	6	46
BELl	7	47
Back**S**pace	8	22
Horizontal **T**ab	9	5
Line **F**eed	10	37
Vertical **T**ab	11	11
Form **F**eed	12	12

Character	ASCII Code	EBCDIC Code
Carriage **R**eturn	13	13
Shift **O**ut	14	14
Shift **I**n	15	15
Data **L**ink **E**scape	16	16
Device **C**ontrol **1**	17	17
Device **C**ontrol **2**	18	18
Device **C**ontrol **3**	19	19
Device **C**ontrol **4**	20	60
Negative **A**c**K**nowledge	21	61
SYNchronous	22	50
EO**T** Block	23	38
CANcel	24	24
End **O**f **M**edium	25	25

Character	ASCII Code	EBCDIC Code
SUBstitute	26	63
ESCape	27	39
File Separator	28	34
Group Separator	29	
Record Separator	30	53
Unit Separator	31	
SPace	32	64
!	33	90
"	34	127
#	35	123
$	36	91
%	37	108
&	38	80
' (single quote)	39	125
(	40	77
)	41	93
*	42	92
+	43	78
, (comma)	44	107
- (hyphen)	45	96
. (period)	46	75
/	47	97
0	48	240
1	49	241
2	50	242
3	51	243
4	52	244
5	53	245
6	54	246
7	55	247
8	56	248
9	57	249
:	58	122
;	59	94

Character	ASCII Code	EBCDIC Code
<	60	76
=	61	126
>	62	110
?	63	111
@	64	124
A	65	193
B	66	194
C	67	195
D	68	196
E	69	197
F	70	198
G	71	199
H	72	200
I	73	201
J	74	209
K	75	210
L	76	211
M	77	212
N	78	213
O	79	214
P	80	215
Q	81	216
R	82	217
S	83	226
T	84	227
U	85	228
V	86	229
W	87	230
X	88	231
Y	89	232
Z	90	233
[	91	180
\	92	177
]	93	181

Character	ASCII Code	EBCDIC Code
^	94	106
_ (underscore)	95	109
`	96	121
a	97	129
b	98	130
c	99	131
d	100	132
e	101	133
f	102	134
g	103	135
h	104	136
i	105	137
j	106	145
k	107	146
l	108	147
m	109	148
n	110	149
o	111	150
p	112	151
q	113	152
r	114	153
s	115	162
t	116	163
u	117	164
v	118	165
w	119	166
x	120	167
y	121	168

Character	ASCII Code	EBCDIC Code
z	122	169
{	123	178
		124	79
}	125	179
~	126	161
DELete	127	7
Punch oFf		4
Lower Case		6
SMM (repeat)		10
REStore		20
New Line		21
IdLe		23
CC (backspace)		26
Interchange File Separator		28
Interchange Group Separator		29
Interchange Record Separator		30
Interchange Unit Separator		31
Digit Select		32
Start Of Significance		33
BYPass		36
Start Message		42
Punch oN		52
Upper Case		54
¢		74

Index

abort, 487
abs, 59, 487–489
absolute value, 56, 59, 487–489
abstract data type, 227
access,
   sequential array, 279, 281
   specifier, 232
     class, 223, 233
     component, 221, 266
     private, 228, 232, 360, 501
     protected, 255, 501
     public, 228, 232, 501
   two-dimensional array, 332
accessor, class member, 223, 225
accumulator, 7
acidity of liquid, 108
acos, 487
addition, 50–51
   member operator, 247
address, memory, 5–6, 23, 174
adjacency matrix, 374
ADT, 227
airborne locations, relative, 269
aircraft,
   database, 401
   labeling, 92
airline reservation system, 403
allocation,
   heap-dynamic memory, 313–319, 323,
     359–365
   memory, 313–319, 323, 359–365, 488, 490
ALU, 4, 7
analysis, 19

object-oriented, 228–229, 254, 304
and operator (&&), 76–77
answers, review question, 441–478
antibiotic effectiveness, 106
apostrophe, 47–48
application, 13
approximation, 405, 433
   π, 115–116, 152
arc
   cosine, 487
   sine, 487
   tangent, 487
argument, 57
   array element, 285
   conversion for overloaded functions, 183
   correspondence, 208
     reference, 176
   list correspondence, 164
   output, 175–178
arithmetic/logic unit, 4
ARPAnet, 11
array, 276–322
   as local variable, 322
   character, 297
   class, heap-dynamic,
     data member, 367
     destructor, 323
     stack-based data member, 367
   dynamically allocated, 313–319, 359–365
     two-dimensional, 359–365
   element, 276
     argument, 285
     final, 276

Reference Guide to C++ Constructs

Construct	Section	Example of Use
library header inclusion	2.1	`#include <iostream>`
for format manipulators	4.4	`#include <iomanip>`
for file use	4.2	`#include <fstream>`
for math library functions	2.6	`#include <cmath>`
for string use	2.4	`#include <string>`
namespace use	2.1	`using namespace std;`
comment	2.1	`//  C++ construct examples`
definition of named constant	2.1	`const int NAME_LEN = 15;` `const double MAX_RATE = .095;`
class definition	6.2	`class PartOrder {`
access specifier	6.4	`public:`
constructor	6.2	`    PartOrder() {}` `    PartOrder( const string&, int, double );`
member function prototype	6.2	`    double totalCost() const;` `private:`

data members	6.2	`    string    name;`
		`    int       quantity;`
		`    double    eachPrice;`
		`};`

constructor definition	6.2	`//`
		`//  Constructor that initializes components`
		`//`
		`PartOrder :: PartOrder (const string& partName,`
		`    int howMany, double price)`
		`{`
		`    name = partName;`
		`    quantity = howMany;`
		`    eachPrice = price;`
		`}`

function interface comment	5.1	`//`
		`// Calculate total cost of order`
		`//`

member function definition	6.2	`double PartOrder :: totalCost() const`
		`{`
		`    return (eachPrice * quantity);`
		`}`

function prototype	5.1	`void factor( int, int&, int& );`
main function heading	2.1	`int main()`
variable declaration		`int num, size;`
simple	2.1	`double x, y;` `char ch;`
array	7.1	`int nlist[MAX_SIZE];`
object	6.2	`PartOrder oneOrder;`
pointer	7.6	`int* list;`
input file	4.2	`ifstream infil( "mydata.txt", ios::in );`
output file	4.2	`ofstream outfil( "myout.txt", ios::out );`
with initialization	2.1	`double sum = 0.0;` `int ct = 0;`

Construct	Section	Example of Use
with initialization (*cont.*)	7.1	`int monthTotals[12] = {0, 0, 0, 0, 0, 0, 0,` `                       0, 0, 0, 0, 0};`
	6.2	`PartOrder order( "clamp", 5, 1.20 );`

function definition	5.1	`//`
		`// Factor number into its smallest factor`
		`// greater than 1 and the corresponding`
		`// other factor`
		`//`

function heading	5.1	`void factor( int num,`
reference parameters	5.3	`              int& smallGtOne, int& other )`
local variable	5.1	`{` `    int trialDiv;`

if statement	3.3	`    if (num % 2 == 0) {`
		`        smallGtOne = 2;`
		`    } else {`
		`        smallGtOne = 0;`
		`        trialDiv = 3;`
		`    }`

while statement	4.1	`    while (smallGtOne == 0`
logical operator and	3.2	`           && trialDiv < sqrt( num ))`

math library function call	2.6	`        if (num % trialDiv == 0)`
		`            smallGtOne = trialDiv;`
		`        else`

operator with side effect	4.4	`            trialDiv += 2;`
		`    if (smallGtOne == 0) {`
		`        smallGtOne = num;`
		`        other = 1;`
		`    } else {`
		`        other = num / smallGtOne;`
		`    }`
		`}`

for loop	4.3	`for (infil >> num;`
input-failure checking	4.2	`     !infil.fail();`
input extraction operator	2.3	`     infil >> num)`
output insertion operator	2.3	`    outfil << "Number (" <<`
increment operator	4.4	`        ct++ << ") " <<`
output formatting	4.4	`        setw( 4 ) << num << endl;`

switch statement	3.5	`switch (ch) {`
		`case 'S':  cout << "Satisfactory";`
		`           break;`
		`case 'U':  cout << "Unsatisfactory";`
		`           break;`
		`case 'I':  cout << "Incomplete";`
		`           break;`
		`default:   cout << ch;`
		`}`

do-while statement	4.6	`do {`
		`    cout << "Enter a command." << endl <<`
		`        "A(dd), D(elete), or Q(uit)>>> ";`
		`    cin >> ch;`
		`} while (ch != 'A' && ch != 'D' && ch != 'Q');`

dynamic array allocation	7.6	`list = new int[num];`
deallocation	7.6	`delete[] list;`